RICHARD ALDINGTON

To Kate

with warmest good wishes

from Viv

February 2014

RICHARD ALDINGTON
Poet, Soldier and Lover
1911-1929

VIVIEN WHELPTON

The Lutterworth Press

The Lutterworth Press
P.O. Box 60
Cambridge
CB1 2NT
United Kingdom

www.lutterworth.com
publishing@lutterworth.com

ISBN: 978 0 7188 9318 7

British Library Cataloguing in Publication Data
A record is available from the British Library

First Published, 2014

Contents

Part One

Poet and Lover

Part Two

Soldier

PART THREE

EXILE

List of Illustrations

Preface

'Do we need another biography of Richard Aldington?' the current writer was asked in 2008. The answer she gave was a strong affirmative. It is now nearly twenty-five years since Charles Doyle's biography, years in which Aldington has become no more familiar to the reading public, even to those who are keenly interested in the literature of the First World War. True, his admirers have done him proud: the 'New Canterbury Literary Society', an association of Aldington enthusiasts, produces a quarterly online newsletter; the late Professor Norman Gates followed his critical evaluation of the poetry and his checklist of the Aldington correspondence with *Richard Aldington: An Autobiography in Letters* in 1992; and Caroline Zilboorg's edition of the Hilda Doolittle–Aldington correspondence, *Richard Aldington and H.D.: Their Lives in Letters 1918-1961* (2003), is the most thorough and sympathetic study ever attempted of the relationship between the two poets. But the wider public still remains ignorant of this extraordinary man and writer. This in a period marked by a revival of interest in the literature of the Great War (to which, in both verse and prose, he made a vital contribution), along with the publication of compelling recent biographies of several of its writers, Wilfred Owen, Isaac Rosenberg, Siegfried Sassoon and Edward Thomas.

Warmth, passion and vitality characterised the life and work of Richard Aldington. However, he was also that Renaissance figure, a man of letters. (The fact that such personalities are uncommon today is indicated by the fact that there is no gender-neutral term.) For the first half of his life he was a poet, critic and translator; he then became a novelist. In his later years – and controversially – he was a biographer. Men of letters are often neglected precisely because of the breadth of their achievement. Aldington the young Imagist is familiar to poets and academics and has recently appeared in a fine group biography of those colourful characters, *Les Imagistes* (Helen Carr's *The Verse Revolutionaries*, 2009); but Aldington the poet and chronicler of the First World War and its impact on his generation has been much neglected in recent years, despite Michael Copp's 1992 edition of his war poetry, *An Imagist at War*. Aldington, almost uniquely among the war poets, addresses the plight of the survivor in the aftermath of war.[1] Fortunately, Penguin have now re-issued (in the Penguin Classics imprint) the 1929 edition of Aldington's war novel, *Death of a Hero*, a best-seller at the time of its publication and described by George Orwell as 'much the best of the English war books'.[2] Aldington's short stories of the war (collected as *Roads to Glory*) are also available, and were published by the Imperial War Museum in a new edition by David Wilkinson in 1992.

It is with the earlier years of Aldington's adult life that this volume is concerned. These were the years in which he figured as one of the Imagist poets and in which he fell in love with, and married, another of them; the war years, in which his personal and literary life fell apart; the post-war years, in which he painfully tried to put his life together again, and to re-establish his literary career; and, finally, the weeks at the end of the twenties in which he wrote *Death of a Hero*, his blistering attack on all that had made that terrible war possible, and his own 'goodbye to all that'. He would never again be domiciled in England.

Acknowledgements

I wish to express my gratitude to the estate of Richard Aldington and its agents, Rosica Colin Ltd., for the encouragement I have received since starting this project; in particular from Joanna Marston at Rosica Colin and from the late Catherine Aldington.

Excerpts from the writings of Richard Aldington, as specified in the Bibliography, are reproduced by kind permission of the Estate of Richard Aldington c/o Rosica Colin Limited, London.

Richard Aldington's memoirs, *Life for Life's Sake* (© Richard Aldington 1941, 1969); his novels, *The Colonel's Daughter* (© Catherine Guillaume 1931, 1958, 1986), *All Men are Enemies* (© Richard Aldington 1933, 1960, 1988) and *Very Heaven* (© Richard Aldington 1937, 1987), the short story 'Farewell to Memories'; *Voltaire, D.H. Lawrence: An Appreciation, Portrait of a Genius, But . . .* and *Pinorman*; Prefaces to *Some Imagist Poets 1915* and *A Fool i' the Forest* and the Foreword to *War and Love*; *Literary Studies and Reviews*; articles originally published in: *The New Age*, *The Sphere*, *The Egoist*, *The New Freewoman*, *Times Literary Supplement*, *The English Review*, *The Monthly Chapbook*, *Poetry* and *The Little Review*; letters published and unpublished; and poems: from *The Complete Poems of Richard Aldington* (© Richard Aldingtom 1948), *The Love Of Myrrhine and Konallis and Other Prose Poems* and *Images of War*; and poems unpublished by Aldington: 'Angelico's Coronation', 'Beauty Unpraised', 'To D.H. Lawrence', 'Blizzard', 'It is bitter . . .' and 'The Walk'.

Extracts from *Death of a Hero* by Richard Aldington (© 1929 Richard Aldington, © 1956 by the Estate of Richard Aldington) are reproduced by kind permission of Penguin, a division of Penguin Group (USA) LLC.

Excerpts from *Bid Me To Live* (© 1960 Norman Holmes Pearson), *Palimpsest* (©1968 Southern Illinois University Press), *Asphodel* (© 1992 Duke University Press), *Paint it Today* (© 1992 Perdita Schaffner), *Tribute to Freud* (© 1956, 1974 Norman Holmes Pearson), *End to Torment* (© 1979 New Directions and the Trustees of the Ezra Pound Literary Property Trust) and from the poems and letters of H.D., published and unpublished, are reproduced by permission of Pollinger Limited and New Directions Publishing Corporation. My especial thanks to Katy Loffman at Pollinger for her kind interest.

Quotations from the letters and works of Ezra Pound (© 1950 by Ezra Pound. © 1984, 1991, 1993 by the Trustees of the Ezra Pound Literary Property Trust, © 2010, 2013 by Mary de Rachewiltz and the Estate of Omar S. Pound) are used by permission of New Directions Publishing Corporation, agents.

Quotations from the letters and works of Bryher (© 2013 by The Schaffner Family Foundation) are also used by permission from New Directions Publishing Corporation.

My thanks go to Linda Flint for permission to quote from the letters of F.S. Flint, from an article in *The Egoist* and the poem, *Soldiers*, and to David Higham Associates for permission to quote from the writings of Herbert Read.

I am indebted to the following libraries and institutions for permission to quote from or cite unpublished manuscripts in their collections:

Beinecke Rare Book and Manuscript Library, Yale University: Bryher Papers, General Collection (GEN MSS 97); George Plank Papers, Yale Collection of American Literature (YCAL MSS 28); Ezra Pound Papers, Yale Collection of American Literature (YCAL MSS 43); Richard Aldington Papers, General Collection (GEN MSS 321); and H.D. Papers, Yale Collection of American Literature (YCAL MSS 24)

Houghton Library, Harvard University: Amy Lowell Collection (MS Lowell 19- letters from H.D. (8), Richard Aldington (9), John Gould Fletcher (431), F.S. Flint (432), D.H. Lawrence (709) and Ezra Pound (982); and MS Lowell 19.1 – letters from Lowell to Richard Aldington (16) and H.D. (15)); the John Cournos Collection (I bMS Eng 998 and IIb MS Eng 998.1); and the T.S. Eliot editorial correspondence 1904-1930 (bMS Am 1432 (4-15)

Special Collections Research Center, the Morris Library, Southern Illinois University, Carbondale: Richard Aldington Collection (1/1/MSS 068)

Harry Ransom Humanities Research Center at the University of Texas at Austin: Richard Aldington Collection, Ezra Pound Collection, Glenn Hughes Collection, Frank Stuart Flint Collection

Special Collections, Charles E. Young Research Library, University of California, Los Angeles: letters from Richard Aldington to Harold Monro and from Richard Aldington to Charles Bubb, in the Harold Monro Papers (Collection 745).

Special Collections Department at the University of Victoria: letters from Richard Aldington to Herbert Read and letters from Richard Aldington to Harold Monro (Sir Herbert Edward Read Fonds (SC100))

The Huntington Library, San Marino, California: letters from Richard Aldington to Alec Randall (HM 40701 – 40708)

Special Collections at the Brotherton Library, University of Leeds: Clement Shorter Collection (BC MS 20c Shorter); Bonamy Dobrée Collection (BC MS 20c Dobrée)

Senate House Library, University of London: letters from Richard Aldington to Thomas Sturge Moore in the Thomas Sturge Moore Papers (MS978/1/2/1)

Special Collections at the University of Exeter: Jan Mills Whitham Literary Papers (EUL MS 38)

Poetry Collection, State University of New York at Buffalo: letters from Richard Aldington to Harold Monro

Special Collections Research Center at the University of Chicago Library: records of *Poetry: A Magazine of Verse* (Box 30, Folders 8-11)

My thanks go to the staff of these institutions for all the assistance I have received, in particular to James Bantin of the Morris Library and Emily Roehl of the Harry Ransom Center, whose patience and helpfulness have been unstinting and invaluable.

While every effort has been made to obtain permission from holders of copyright material produced herein, the publishers would like to apologise for any omissions and will be pleased to incorporate missing acknowledgements in any further editions.

I have personal thanks to express to two institutions and a number of individuals who have helped me enormously on the way. I thank the Arvon Foundation for giving me the opportunity to learn from two fine biographers, Sally Cline and Carole Angier; and I am very grateful for Sally's continued support and encouragement.

Stephen May has also encouraged me from the moment I set off on the path of literary biography.

I am also grateful to the Biographers' Club for selecting the project for the shortlist for the 2011 Tony Lothian Prize, a spur that I needed so much at the time.

However, it is The New Canterbury Literary Society, the community of Aldington scholars and enthusiasts, that has been my principal support line. In the U.S.A. I was delighted to meet up with Shelley Cox, Aldington's bibliographer, who has made all her research available to me. Caroline Zilboorg's edition of the letters of Richard Aldington and H.D. and Michael Copp's edition of the letters of Aldington and F.S. Flint have been at my side throughout my work and both Mike and Caroline have responded to all my queries with promptness and patience, as has David Wilkinson, who generously made available to me all his research findings on Aldington's life at Padworth in the 1920s. Mike has also translated several of Aldington's letters for me. Andrew Frayn, the NCLS editor, has offered me constant guidance. Without the encouragement and support of these five people, and also of Simon Hewett, who made his private Aldington archive available to me, the task would have been considerably more difficult. I wish also to thank Adrian Barlow for his insights into Aldington's writings and Helen Carr, whose biography of the Imagists, *The Verse Revolutionaries*, has been an inspiration to me.

My grateful thanks go also to Peter Simkins, who kindly checked the accuracy of the military information in the book, and to Mike Lawson for his help with maps of the Western Front.

Throughout the project I have received kindness and encouragement from Jennifer Aldington-Emous and Tim Aldington, whose enthusiasm at the prospect of a new biography of their uncle was inspired by their memories of his kindness to them in their youth.

I have also been extremely fortunate in my publishers and have benefitted enormously from the constructive support and advice of Adrian Brink, Director at The Lutterworth Press, Emily Reacher, my editor, and Bethany Churchard.

I conclude with gratitude to my husband, Barrie Whelpton, who has been my most rigorous critic but also my most constant supporter, and without whom I could not have completed this work.

Introduction

Aldington published his memoirs in 1941, calling the book *Life for Life's Sake*: hedonism was his credo. Interviewed in 1930 at the age of thirty-eight and at the height of his success as the author of the bestselling *Death of a Hero*, he told the journalist Louise Morgan, 'I like travelling, conversation, gluttony and wine-bibbing, swimming, the movies. I like, too, architecture, painting and sculpture as "objects of contemplation". I like walking. And, above all, I like making love.'[1] With the exception of the movies, the 19-year-old poet would have said much the same, although the gluttony and wine-bibbing were perhaps later additions to the repertoire. The writer added, 'I've read extensively in the literature of the past – French, Italian, Greek and Latin as well as English'. At nineteen, Aldington had already embarked on that programme of reading. Its importance for him, then and always, was its capacity to inform and illuminate 'the life of the here and now – the life of the senses'. 'If we do not live in these we scarcely live at all'.[2]

Aldington's life-story in the period covered by this volume is dominated by three beautiful, remarkable and tenacious women: his first lover, Brigit Patmore, to whom he returned at the end of the 1920s; Hilda Doolittle, or H.D. (*passim*), with whom he lived for less than five years but whom he was to love for the rest of his life; and Dorothy Yorke, the *femme fatale* for whom he left H.D. Yorke became his companion throughout the ten painful years of his recovery from the effects of the war and the failure of his marriage to H.D., only to be discarded as he emerged, chrysalis-like, in 1929.

In the dedication of *Life for Life's Sake* Aldington wrote: 'Yeats used to say of George Moore: "Other men kiss and don't tell; George Moore tells and doesn't kiss." I would give a great deal to write as well as George Moore, but in this respect I prefer to be like other men.' This reticence with regard to his long-term relationships (four in all) and to his numerous other sexual liaisons was partly due to his respect for the women involved; it was also, of course, self-preserving, particularly after his attempt to be 'modern', open and honest about his affair with Dorothy Yorke effectively destroyed his marriage in 1918. He was a very private man throughout his life; surprisingly, given his gregariousness. His daughter told the current writer that her father failed to tell her in 1950 that her mother had left the two of them permanently, and never spoke with her about the reasons for that abandonment.[3] This despite the fact that the relationship between the 12-year-old Catherine and her father was a very close one. Nor did 'Catha' know of the existence of H.D. until she met her as an adult; and even then she learned nothing of the intimate relationship her father had shared with the elderly poet. She remarked in 2000, 'For cultivated and analysed people, they were much given to silence! They had words for writers, but few for their children.'[4]

Much earlier in his adult life, Aldington had lost a child: H.D.'s baby was still-born in 1915, when she was twenty-eight and her husband twenty-two. The couple's suppression of their feelings in the aftermath of this trauma was a significant contributing factor in their subsequent estrangement. Julia Ashton, H.D.'s alter-ego in her autobiographical novel, *Bid Me To Live*, thinks, 'She had lost the child a short time before. But she never thought of that. A door had shuttered it in, shuttering her in, something had died that was going to die. Or because something had died, something would die.'[5]

Aldington's reticence poses a problem for the biographer. For some relationships at some periods there is extant correspondence; that between himself and H.D. from 1918 until her death in 1961 is the most important; but after their separation he destroyed all their pre-1918 correspondence and her letters to him until 1920. After 1920 their correspondence ceased for nearly a decade.

The literary biographer who believes that the life illuminates the work hopes to find that the converse is also true. Aldington's novels, particularly *Death of a Hero* and *All Men Are Enemies*, are indeed strongly autobiographical. Both books demonstrate powerfully the impact of the war on him, at the time and in the aftermath. Nevertheless, the scrupulousness which prevented him from 'kissing and telling' extends to his fictional work: those who have attempted to see H.D. and Dorothy Yorke (also known as Arabella) in Elizabeth and Fanny, the two leading female characters in *Death of a Hero*, have found that the fictional women are not accurate reflections of the real. Aldington insisted to H.D. that his models were actually those celebrities of the Paris bohemian scene, Nancy Cunard and Valentine Dobrée (with both of whom Aldington conducted liaisons), but that Elizabeth and Fanny are replicas of these two women is also unconvincing. It is in Aldington's poetry that we find an authentic treatment of each of his significant love affairs at its most intense: in *Reverie* (1917), *Images of Desire* (1919), *The Eaten Heart* (1929), *A Dream in the Luxembourg* (1930) and *The Crystal World* (1937).

However, Aldington and his lovers figure prominently in the writings of others; in the writings of the lovers themselves, and of 'third parties', both groups often having resentments to off-load. These works are either memoirs or *romans à clé*, and many of them are very revealing. Of course, such works can be traps for the unwary. The novels are far more illuminating than most of the memoirs (his own included), which suffer either from inaccuracies of memory or from being exercises in self-promotion. The novels, partly because they were written so soon after the events they narrate, often burn with pain or bitterness and lack the creative detachment that turns life into literature. Such are John Cournos's *Miranda Masters* (1926),

Brigit Patmore's *This Impassioned Onlooker* (1926) and *No Tomorrow* (1929), and Jennifer Courtenay's *Several Faces* (1930). While equally revealing, D.H. Lawrence's *Aaron's Rod* (1922) and Louis Wilkinson's *The Buffoon* (1916) display more cold malice than white heat.

H.D.'s novels stand apart from the rest. They are remarkable for being both vividly close to the events and polished works of art. No biographer can ignore their invitation to stand in the wings and watch the action unfold. She was a meticulous observer of the world immediately around her. Of course the perspective is partial, but its absence of bitterness (though not pain) helps us to trust the story. She worked consistently through the decade following the war to make sense for herself of the troubled events of her recent past, in *Palimpsest* (1926), *Paint it Today* (composed 1921), *Asphodel* (composed 1921-1922), *HER* (composed 1926-1927) and *Bid Me To Live*, which, although not published until 1960, was begun in 1918.

While Aldington did not betray his lovers in his fiction, he was less generous towards certain of his fellow-writers and towards his parents. The former are savagely satirised in *Soft Answers* and *Death of a Hero*, the latter in several of the novels but principally *Death of a Hero*. This leads us to a second problem for the biographer: Aldington's public reticence extended to his family. The reader of *Life for Life's Sake* is led to assume, through omission, that he was an only child; in fact he had three siblings, admittedly much younger than himself, Margery, born when he was six years old, Patricia, born when he was sixteen, and Tony, born two years later. There is very little extant correspondence between him and the rest of his family; mostly postcards sent on his first visits to Paris and Italy. However, we have the damning portraits of his parents in the novels – and the passages of his conversation about them that appear in H.D.'s *Asphodel*.

Equally damning of his parents and of his early life in general is the bleak poem 'Childhood'. The social and emotional circumstances of his upbringing were clearly an important influence on his personal development and on his later social attitudes, but we must piece them together from some very partial evidence. This volume begins with an examination of Aldington's life from the moment in 1911 when he embarked on his literary career and a life of his own choosing; but we shall 'roll back' to the problem of his childhood in the second chapter.

The biographer must also piece together the true picture of Aldington's war experience to fully reveal his character. In the past his military experiences have been neglected by biographers, despite the evidence in his poetry and the fiction of the great impact they had on him – and the post-traumatic state in which he was left for several years after the war. Barbara Guest, H.D.'s biographer, comments that, 'His army career had not been all that disagreeable. It is only necessary to compare his book [*Death of a Hero*] with Robert Graves's *Goodbye to All That* to realise that Aldington's experiences are not so desperate or tragic as he would have us believe. . . . The truth seems to be that he never fired a shot. He had managed to be sent from camp to camp in England, rising in rank, until he had finally applied for a commission. . . . his regret seems mainly to have been for the waste of time and the needless postponement of his real career.'[6] Despite the fact that Charles Doyle calls this account 'not entirely unfair', it is nonetheless a complete distortion of the facts of Aldington's military record and its impact on him, as we shall show in due course.[7]

Love, childhood and war: they can help us to understand this man, so apparently contradictory in his life and his work. A romantic idealist but also a sensualist; an aesthete and a sceptic; a feminist who loved and respected women but who ended more than one relationship with excessive ruthlessness; a poetic innovator who resisted modernism; a rebel who was also a traditionalist. A poet, soldier and lover.

PART ONE
Poet and Lover

Richard Aldington, 1916

1. Bohemia: London, 1911-1912

A beginning is an artifice, and what recommends one over another is how much sense it makes of what follows.   (Ian McEwan, *Enduring Love*, 1998)[1]

In the spring of 1911, Richard Aldington's undergraduate career at University College, London came to an end after less than two terms. He would later describe this episode of his life as marking 'the departure from buttressed respectability towards the freer if frowstier fields of Bohemianism'.[2]

His departure from the university was forced upon him, the result of his solicitor father's failed financial speculations, and he would always resent it: both because it denied him academic standing, and because he hated not to be in control of his life. It also confirmed him in his contempt for his father's ineptitude in managing his affairs, a contempt to which he would give expression in several fictional portrayals. Such was the pain of this youthful experience that he attempted in later years to rewrite the scenario, by representing the university course as unsatisfying (probably true), and implying that he had been asked to leave the college because of his rebelliousness (untrue).[3]

At the opening of Aldington's fifth novel, *Very Heaven* (1937), Chris Heylin's tutor reflects: 'What does one say to an undergraduate whose parents have lost their money? . . . Oughtn't I to help this boy? Bright lad. Pity to be a clerk or something. How, in point of fact, does one 'help'? . . . Whatever happens, life will turn sour in his mouth at forty.' Chris's own sense of loss and his anger towards his tutor and his parents are palpable: 'What am I to say to the old codger? He won't understand in the least. . . . How can he know what it is to have life crash around you? . . . But what am I to do, my god what *am* I to do? Chauffeur, barman, bank-clerk, airman, dole-man, door-man, butter-slapper, thief? They take it pretty calmly at home. *Nearly everything has been lost, darling, and we fear you must come home at once, not another penny can we spare for you.* That means: Get a job. Help the rich to keep rich. I'd a life's work planned. . . . I'm merely young, healthy, strong, reasonably intelligent and not bad-looking, so nobody does anything or cares.'[4]

Aldington started to take control of his own story when he rejected the most obvious route open to a literate young man without money or qualifications: a post as a clerk in the City. Fortunately, his own sociability had gained him another opening. The sports editor on one of the London dailies, whom he had met amongst a group of friends with whom he went rowing on the Thames, offered him a free lodging in his flat in Bloomsbury and the opportunity to report on sporting events two or three afternoons a week.[5] This offered him freedom, time to write poetry, a slender income – and did not, he felt, constitute selling his soul.

However, as *Very Heaven* intimates, the 18-year-old who walked south down Gower Street on that spring morning of 1911 may not have been as convinced of his good fortune as he later led himself to believe. Certainly, his few months at University College had disappointed his academic expectations. Perhaps it was predictable that a widely-read young man with a passion for the classics and literature and an enormous aptitude for languages would find the first year of a London undergraduate degree unsatisfying. He says of his English lecturer, Gerald Gould (then 'a white hope of English poetry'), that although he was a good lecturer, 'as far as I was concerned he had to expound authors already familiar'.[6] Aldington had no contact with the most eminent of the university's lecturers, A.E. Housman, the poet and Professor of Latin, who was merely 'seen occasionally cruising gloomily about the corridors';[7] W. P. Ker, Quain Professor of English Language and Literature and a fine medieval scholar, was also unknown to him.

However, student life had made Aldington the centre of a lively-minded group of young men, including Alec Randall, later a diplomat (and a life-long friend), Arthur Chapman, another aspiring poet, tragically drowned during the 1911 summer vacation, and Vivian Gaster, son of the Chief Rabbi.[8] Randall later commented on what a romantic figure Aldington had seemed to them all, 'with his handsome features, his sparkling merry eyes, his reddish beard and velvet jacket and flowing bow tie'.[9]

For a time after leaving university his chosen path would be a more isolated one, and he would need a steady nerve to manage it. He had the advantage of knowing to what he aspired: 'the way of life of the good European . . . to know and to enjoy the best that had been thought and felt and known through the ages'.[10]

The London literary scene in this period was vibrant and open to new ideas. Helen Carr tells us that, 'London's intellectual and creative life was based on a series of interconnecting, loosely constituted groups which gathered around certain publishers, editors, writers, literary hostesses and actresses as well as in societies and informal discussion groups.'[11] The literary giants were still the few remaining Victorians, Thomas Hardy, Henry James and the critic Edmund Gosse. The established writers of the new century were all now in their mid forties to early fifties, men such as Joseph Conrad, John Galsworthy, Arnold Bennett, George Bernard Shaw and H.G. Wells, and women like May Sinclair, Ethel Colburn Mayne and Violet Hunt. These were writers strongly alive to the political and social issues of the day, if not, for the most part, stylistic innovators. Many of them were regular reviewers in the newspapers and journals, so that standards of taste were not solely determined by the more conservative critics

Ezra Pound, 1913

such as Gosse or Arthur Waugh and E.B. Osborn (literary critics for the *Daily Telegraph* and *The Morning Post*, respectively), Arthur St John Adcock (editor of *The Bookman*) and the poets Hilaire Belloc and Henry Newbolt, influential though these writers were.

The poetry scene was perhaps the most diverse. Although the 'Aesthetic' or 'Decadent' poets of the 1890s were long gone, their influence was still felt. (Both Ezra Pound and Aldington were admirers of Swinburne.) Of the 'Rhymers' Club' poets who succeeded them, only W.B. Yeats, Ernest Rhys and Arthur Symons were still on the scene.[12] Yeats was a towering presence in the literary world, although much of his time in recent years had been spent in Ireland, establishing the Abbey Theatre. Rhys was a generous supporter of new poets and their ideas. Symons was the chief apologist in England for the French Symbolist movement; partly as a result of his work as a literary critic, a range of French poets from Baudelaire to Laforgue was read and discussed amongst aspiring writers and in the literary journals of the day.

The older, more established poets centred on The Poets' Club, founded in 1908, which met at the United Arts Club in Mayfair for a monthly dinner followed by speeches or readings. Newbolt and the banker, Henry Simpson, were its presidents and the young T.E. Hulme its secretary.[13] In response to a very disparaging review of the Club's 1908 Christmas anthology in the *The New Age* by F.S. Flint, Flint and Hulme met up in March 1909 and started the more informal weekly meetings of less conventionally-minded poets at the Tour Eiffel Restaurant in Percy Street off the Tottenham Court Road. The group included Edward Storer, the Irish poets Desmond FitzGerald and Joseph Campbell, Florence Farr, the actress and friend of Yeats, and the American, Ezra Pound.

Young writers also clustered round the editorial teams of the two progressive journals of the day, *The New Age* and *The English Review*. The latter was the brainchild of Ford Madox Hueffer, later Ford Madox Ford, the novelist and critic. He had founded the monthly journal at the end of 1908, in response, according to his account, to the refusal of all existing newspapers and journals to print Thomas Hardy's 'A Sunday Morning Tragedy' (his ballad about a young woman who dies from an abortion). From Hueffer's offices above a butcher's shop at 84 Holland Park Road, *The English Review* printed work by both established and 'new' writers. By the end of 1909, Hueffer had been forced to sell the journal after only twelve issues, but under the editorship of Austin Harrison it continued to publish the work of a wide range of contemporary writers until well after the First World War.

The full title of *The New Age* was *The New Age: a Weekly Review of Politics, Literature and the Arts* and its editor, Alfred Orage, purchased it in 1907 to provide a cultural platform for Fabian socialism. The range of views expressed in its pages, however, was broad, and it covered most of the controversial issues of the day. Like *The English Review* it published new young writers and reviewed their work, if not always favourably.

During 1910, as Hulme became more interested in philosophy than in poetry, the Tour Eiffel meetings fell away; but in their place he instituted weekly gatherings of artists and intellectuals at 67, Frith Street, the home of his friend Dolly Kibblewhite. It was here one autumn evening in 1912 that Ezra Pound would meet the senior civil servant and sponsor of the arts Edward Marsh and his friend, the Cambridge poet Rupert Brooke: they were planning an anthology of recently published poetry.[14] They invited Pound to contribute, but the three could not agree on what to select from his *oeuvre*. In consequence, he would not appear in the 1912 *Georgian Poetry* amongst other young poets like Lascelles Abercrombie, John Drinkwater and Wilfred Gibson who had gathered round Brooke and Marsh and would come to be known as the Georgians.

Aldington was soon to be introduced to the world of Flint, Hulme and Pound; but first he was to meet one of the three women who would dominate his life for the next twenty years and more. His introduction to her came through mutual friends, the Hilberys: 'She [Maude Hilbery] . . . asked me one day, 'Will you see a clever boy we know who is alone in London because he won't go into his father's law business? All he wants to do is write. He's got some job reporting for a paper – mostly football matches I believe!'[15]

In 1911 Brigit Patmore was twenty-nine years old and the mother of two small sons.[16] Her charm and beauty, her minor talent as a pianist, her husband's successful career in insurance and the fact that he was the grandson of the Victorian poet Coventry Patmore all gave her the status, means and aptitude for the role of literary hostess, which she would acquire by the end of 1911. It was a role she desired not because she was an aspiring writer but because of her fascination with literary people and her dissatisfaction with her marriage to the philandering

Deighton Patmore. Her older son Derek wrote in 1968: 'My earliest memories of my mother are of a lovely young woman with red-gold hair. She had a pale creamy complexion which emphasised the gleaming colour of her hair, and her eyes, which were grey, though sometimes tinged with green, had a melancholy expression. . . . She craved love and affection.'[17]

D.H. Lawrence's fictional portrayal of Patmore echoes this description. Lawrence's 'Clariss' is 'a frail, elegant woman – fashionable rather than Bohemian . . . cream and auburn, Irish, with a slightly-lifted upper lip that gave her a pathetic look.'[18] The novelist Violet Hunt wrote later: 'She was very beautiful with a queer, large, tortured mouth that said the wittiest things, eyes that tore your soul out of your body for pity and yet danced.'[19]

Patmore was instantly smitten by Aldington, a 'lively, humorous boy . . . tall and broad-shouldered, with a fine forehead, thick longish hair of the indefinite colour blond hair turns to in adolescence, very bright blue eyes, too small a nose and a determined mouth'.[20] There was mutual enchantment and before long they were lovers.

In early 1911, shortly after the Patmores' move from Fulham to 52, St Helen's Gardens in Kensington, Brigit had received a visit from Violet Hunt, a client of her husband. The two women became friendly and Patmore started to attend Hunt's weekly literary *salon* at South Lodge, on Campden Hill Road. She occasionally accompanied Hunt on some of her excursions to campaign for women's suffrage, although the two women's recall of this aspect of the relationship differs. Hunt remarks rather acidly in her memoirs: 'She was no real suffragette, though she had collected with me and rattled her box at stations. Nothing but her eye protested. Delicately cynical, she accepted things as they were.'[21]

In September 1911 Hunt's lover, Ford Madox Hueffer, novelist and founder of *The English Review*, had been residing in Germany for a year in an unsuccessful attempt to obtain a divorce from his wife. Hunt and Hueffer (allegedly) underwent a marriage ceremony in France, returning to London in November as Mr and Mrs Ford Madox Hueffer. (The resultant scandal would lead to a libel case being brought by Hueffer's real wife). With the couple's return to South Lodge in November 1911, Hunt's tea parties resumed, and in her drawing room one Tuesday afternoon Patmore observed a long slim, young man with a shock of curly reddish hair, leaning back in a low arm chair, 'as self-possessed as Violet's superb grey Persian cat sitting on the window-sill.'[22] This was the 26-year-old American, Ezra Pound, who had spent most of August in Germany, working as Hueffer's secretary. Now he was bursting onto the London literary scene in earnest – for the second time. His idols were the medieval and Renaissance poets of Southern Europe, his more recent models Browning, Rossetti and Yeats.[23] It was his desire to meet Yeats which had first drawn him to London in 1908 and he had thrived there socially and creatively. Yet, despite publishing four volumes of poetry and one book of literary criticism, he had been unable to make a living and had been forced to return to the U.S. in 1910. He had lasted only eight months back home, achieving neither literary nor financial advancement; Europe – and specifically London at this stage of his life – was his cultural milieu and it was here, he knew, that he would make his name as a poet.

Patmore was keen to introduce her young lover to him. She invited both men to tea: 'They seemed to enjoy it all very much and went away together, Ezra enchanted to have a young mind to indoctrinate and Richard overjoyed to find someone who was interested in him and who knew what it meant to write poetry.'[24] This relationship would deteriorate in later years, but it would remain an important one for the younger poet. He wrote to Amy Lowell in 1917, at a time when the two men were not on speaking terms, 'We were great friends, very great friends, and I cannot forget how much his knowledge and sympathy meant to me, after many years of spiritual isolation. . . . '[25] Nearly three decades later he would write: 'Ezra was a citizen of the world, both mentally and in fact. . . . Instead of pap, he fed me meat.'[26]

Patmore, Pound and Aldington became inseparable but the stage was now set for the entry of the fourth member of the group and Pound was the impresario who would engineer it. He was tied into a web of sexual relationships that must by now, as the young women concerned began to occupy the same geographical space, have exercised his ingenuity to manage.

At the age of sixteen he had met and fallen in love with Hilda Doolittle, a year younger than himself and the daughter of the professor of astronomy at the University of Pennsylvania, where Pound was an undergraduate. Four years later they had become unofficially engaged. When he first left for Europe in 1908, the status of the engagement was unclear; and during his two-years absence a young woman, Frances Gregg, came into H.D.'s life 'like a blue flame'[27] and filled the vacuum left by Pound.[28] Whereas H.D.'s relationship with Pound had been intellectual and romantic, in Gregg she found a passionate lover. Their relationship was disrupted on Pound's return (and much to H.D.'s distress) when he and Gregg were mutually attracted.

When Pound returned to Europe in February 1911, the status of his engagement to H.D. was still unclear. In July Gregg and her mother embarked on a European tour, and H.D. went with them; by the end of September they were in London, where Pound proceeded to organise their social calendar.

There was a further complication. On his first visit to London Pound had fallen in love with Dorothy Shakespear, the daughter of Olivia Shakespear, novelist, literary hostess and the friend and former lover of Yeats. Dorothy, although the same age as H.D., was closely supervised by her parents. While they approved of Pound as a poet, they did not (and in this respect they resembled Hilda's parents) view him as a suitable son-in-law; his access to her had been severely restricted. Back in London in 1911, he felt more confident of his prospects, financially and matrimonially, and on 11 October – less than two weeks after the arrival of Frances and Hilda – he formally asked Henry Hope Shakespear for Dorothy's hand. Pending Hope's investigations of Pound's financial affairs, the engagement remained unofficial. No-one in Pound's circle knew of his attachment.

At the end of October the American women were due to sail home, but H.D. was eager to remain in London and her parents agreed that she should stay until their retirement trip to Europe the following year. She accompanied Frances and

Brigit Patmore, 1913

Mrs Gregg to Liverpool for their embarkation before returning to London alone, excited but apprehensive, desperately missing Frances, for whom her passion was unabated, and uncertain about the status of her relationship with Pound. He took on the role of her 'nearest male relation', organising her enrolment as a reader at the British Museum and requesting Brigit Patmore to ask her to tea.[29]

Patmore tells us: 'The tall girl I went to meet at the entrance [to Patmore's club near Piccadilly] seemed too fragile for her height and build. Had her head been held high and her shoulders straight, she would have looked, as Richard might have said, "like a goddess". But no goddess ever showed such extreme vulnerability in her face, nor so wild and wincing a look in her deep-set eyes. She had soft brownish hair, a pallid complexion and a pouting sensitive mouth, but a magnificent line of jaw and chin gave a reassuring strength.'[30]

At Patmore's house H.D. met Richard Aldington. She was charmed by both of them; they were equally fascinated by her. There has been speculation that Patmore, like H.D., was bisexual. In 1919, in response to being sent the manuscript of her lesbian friend Bryher's autobiographical novel, H.D. would write that she wanted Patmore to see it, 'because she is sensitive and feels (knows in another way) and because she is so intensely and vitally interested in women who are more than women, or different from what is ordinarily accepted as such.'[31]

Patmore certainly seems to have felt safer in her relationships with women than in those she had with men. However, she craved – and courted – male admiration and desire (as both H.D. and Violet Hunt would discover to their cost), perhaps to compensate for her unfulfilling marriage, perhaps behaviour she had learned from her mother. She wrote in her memoir, 'The love of sorrow I learned from my mother, who passionately believed a man could be faithful and kind, and, finding this not so, grieved her wild heart to death'.[32]

In H.D.'s autobiographical novel *Bid Me To Live*, 'Julia' says of Morgan, the Patmore character: 'If she wanted women, let her have women, not use women, as Julia felt she did, as a sort of added touch of exoticism, something to stir and excite. . . . She had seen it often enough, Morgan with her arms around him, and her "Oh, darling, it's really women I love."'[33] This more malicious representation of Patmore's sexual proclivities seems to hit the mark, but it was an insight that would come later; for now, the two women became close friends.

It is not easy to understand why, over the ensuing months, Patmore became willing to surrender her young lover to H.D. Caroline Zilboorg suggests that 'Patmore found her [H.D.] charming and sexually attractive, and probably encouraged her own lover in his attentions to H.D. out of a genuine willingness to foster romantic relationships but also impulsively as a way of loving H.D. vicariously through him.'[34]

It may simply have been a case of giving in to the inevitable, as the young couple's shared love of literature and of all things Greek, as well as their shared aspiration to be poets, brought them together. It is also unlikely that Patmore's relationship with Aldington was rooted in much more than friendship and physical attraction – and, on her part the fillip of having a handsome and virile lover ten years her junior, on his the excitement of having as his first sexual partner an older, beautiful, sexually experienced woman of higher social class. For Patmore, this affair could not, of course, have progressed much further without risk to her social position. Meanwhile, their friendship brought the three of them great pleasure. Patmore recalled years later, 'We three were bound together, but lightly, gaily. We liked being together. We laughed and read, walked about London, looked at pictures, had meals in tea-rooms.'[35]

H.D., 1913

Pound appears to have been oblivious of the complexities of his friends' feelings for one another, flinging himself into the role of poetic mentor of H.D. and Aldington, studiously ignoring H.D.'s requests for clarification of the status of her relationship with him, but giving her the job of acting as his hostess. He managed to keep his real matrimonial intentions hidden until the spring of 1912.

Pound also (if we are to trust H.D.'s autobiographical novel, *Asphodel*) criticised her grey chiffon dresses as 'all right for Philadelphia' but 'too nun-ish' for London, and persuaded her to move from her lodging house in Great Ormond Street to Portman Square, as somewhere he could more easily send his friends. As for her poetry, it was 'not modern enough' and yet 'too modern' for him to recommend to journals (as he had Frances Gregg's verse).[36]

Why did H.D. stand for this patronage? She had a deep lack of self-confidence. The provincial gentility of her background and the strict, though kindly, religious discipline to which she had been accustomed, seem to have led to a continuing anxiety about the opinions of others on her part. The only girl in a family of six children, she had been expected by her father, of whom she was very fond, to achieve great things. Hence the choice for her of Bryn Mawr, the prestigious women's college. Like Aldington, however, she had dropped out of university (during her second year), but in her case because of academic failure. Like Aldington again, she subsequently chose a partial account of the facts, explaining that she had had to give up her course because she was ill. She does seem to have gone through some kind of nervous breakdown at this time, but whether this was cause or consequence of her withdrawal from college is unclear.

She had lived at home while attending college, commuting daily; and at home she remained afterwards, quietly studying on her own. Her novel *Paint It Today* gives us a glimpse of H.D.'s feelings at this stage of her life: 'She felt instinctively that she was a failure by all the conventional and scholarly standards. She had failed in her college career, she had failed as a social asset with her family and the indiscriminate mob of relatives and relays of communal friends that surrounded it. She had burned her candle of rebellion at both ends and she was left unequipped for the simplest dealings with the world.'[37]

The chance to travel with the Greggs must have seemed a liberation. She had been romantically involved with Pound since she was fifteen, her parents' disapproval of him only adding further excitement to the romance. (The same was true of her relationship with Gregg.) From the start he had played the role of her mentor and teacher. An intelligent girl with a love of nature and of literature, and creatively gifted, she may have lacked belief in herself as a woman and as a scholar: but she did believe in herself as a poet. Pound did not discourage her; but what he most needed from a woman was a belief in *his* creative powers. In London, however, in a social world alien from her own, H.D. needed him, to guide her through the traps of middle-class society and protect her reputation; this may have been a world of artists, but the standards of moral conduct were still strict – as poor Violet Hunt would soon discover. Whether Pound was the man to provide her with this protection we might question; but he was all she had.

We might also wonder why Professor and Mrs Doolittle were willing to allow their only daughter to live in London for several months, alone except for a young man whom they had thought unsuitable as a husband for her. They clearly trusted her good sense and respected her desire to study. They may also have had the

wisdom to recognise that, back home again, with no new prospects, she would
languish. In any case, young American women of the period had greater social
freedom and independence than their British counterparts; Dorothy Shakespear
was rarely out of her mother's sight.[38]

Aldington was a breath of fresh air to H.D., and he clearly admired both her
beauty and her intellect; this was a relationship of equals, or, if there were any
inequalities, she was the superior. Throughout his life he would believe her to
be the greater poet.[39] They shared a love of classical Greece, its mythology and
its literature, and set about learning the language and translating texts together,
chiefly the poets of the *Greek Anthology*. At nineteen, Aldington was not yet old
enough to be eligible for a reader's ticket; he depended on her to copy materials
from the British Museum Reading Room for him. They met daily.

Pound, H.D. and Patmore became the centre of Aldington's social and creative
life, but through them he met other artists and writers. Perhaps the two most
important were Frank Flint and Harold Monro. Flint was the same age as Pound,
but a Londoner from an extremely poor background who had educated himself
and mastered ten languages. His paid employment was as a post office clerk but he
was appointed poetry reviewer on *The New Age* in 1908 when only twenty-three
(although by 1911 he had ceased to hold this post). His first poetry collection, *In
the Net of the Stars*, was published in 1910. It was Flint who, with T.E. Hulme, had
started the Tour Eiffel poets' meetings and both Pound and Aldington were to learn
a great deal from his knowledge of contemporary French poetry. Aldington and
Flint became close friends; their frank, lively and mutually influential relationship
would last for more than a decade, although in the mid 1920s, as Aldington
struggled to put his life back together after the war and as the two men's lifestyles
became increasingly incompatible, their friendship would come to an abrupt end.

It was Harold Monro's new journal which would carry, in August 1912, Flint's
influential survey of contemporary French poetry. Monro, a melancholic 32-year-
old poet, had embarked on a mission to disseminate new English poetry more
widely: through a literary journal, the *Poetry Review*, which began publication
in January 1912, and through a poetry bookshop, which opened in Devonshire
Street at the end of that year.[40] Dominic Hibberd, Monro's biographer, describes
his 1911 collection of verse, *Before Dawn*, as 'perhaps the first collection
of genuinely modern English poetry'.[41] Monro came to be associated chiefly
with Edward Marsh's Georgian poets, whose anthologies his bookshop would
publish. However, he was a good friend to the young Aldington, who wrote
short reviews and notices for the *Poetry Review*, and he would publish Aldington's
first collection of poetry in 1915 as well as the first of the Imagist anthologies in
April 1914.[42]

A letter from Aldington to Monro, undated but clearly from the spring of 1912,
gives an indication of Monro's interest in the younger poet, but also of Aldington's
good humour, shrewd judgement and confidence in his own creative powers:

My dear fellow,

Your rebuke was perfectly just and justifiable, and argues an interest flattering to me.

The real answer is this: If I am so feeble-minded as to remain permanently under Pound's influence, God help me, I'm not worth bothering about. If I am so dull and stertorous-minded as not to be influenced by a man of Pound's intellect – then also God help me. I know I am extremely susceptible to other people's influences, especially when they are congenial folk, but I think they always simmer down and become absorbed in the Kosmic RA![43]

In the spring of 1912 Aldington was still working for his sports editor and spending a great deal of time with H.D. and with Pound. April, however, brought a storm to this serene social landscape. H.D. received a letter from Gregg with the news that on 10 April she was to marry an English lecturer, Louis Wilkinson, and that they would embark immediately for London on their way to the continent, where he was due to lecture. Both the news of the marriage and the imminence of Gregg's arrival were a terrible shock for H.D.

Predictably, the reunion was a traumatic one. Gregg seems to have persuaded H.D. that it was for her sake that she had entered into this marriage and that she wanted H.D. to travel with her and Wilkinson, so that the two women could be together again.[44] The truth seems to have been even more complicated: a mutual attraction existed between Gregg and Wilkinson's friend, the Welsh writer and lecturer John Cowper Powys, who, married himself, had brought Wilkinson and Gregg together to facilitate his access to the latter. Powys had travelled to London with them.

H.D. was torn between her passion for Gregg and the satisfactions of the life that she had been living for the last six months. Whether feelings for Aldington were also involved is hard for us to tell. What both her fictionalised accounts of the incident intimate is that H.D. took Aldington along to meet Gregg and that the latter, alert to the presence of a rival for H.D.'s affections, adopted a shrewd tactic to undermine him: she suggested that he lacked *class*. 'He has the manners of an innkeeper's son.[45] . . . I hated him to open the door for you and brush your shoulder. . . . I think him under the surface, unclean.'[46] 'Fayne Rabb', remarks the narrator of *Asphodel*, 'made people seem common.'

The response of H.D.'s two male friends, Aldington and Pound, to her proposed travels with Gregg is more surprising. Pound had the measure of Gregg of course, and the fact that he took charge was in character; what was less characteristic was his immediate grasp of the sexual complexities of the situation and the good sense with which he acted. He was concerned that H.D. would find herself compromised emotionally as well as morally if she followed the couple to Europe; he also suggested that she owed it to Gregg to give the marriage a chance of success.

He, too, seems to have played the class and reputation card: ' "Did you ever hear

Frank Flint

of your mother going to Bruges or Ghent or Little Rock or Athens, Ohio, with
anyone on their honeymoon?" "Well, no – not exactly on their – " "Exactly."'[47]
When remonstrating failed, he picked her up in a cab on the morning of the
trio's intended departure, took her to Victoria Station, informed Wilkinson and
Gregg that she would not be accompanying them, retrieved the cheque for her
travel ticket from Wilkinson and whisked her and her luggage away in another
cab.

   H.D. may have been a little relieved that the decision had been made for her,
but she was in a state of shock. She was, therefore, appreciative of the tact and
understanding of her other male friend. Aldington recognised how important
Gregg was to her and that the break was devastating; he also knew that she needed
sympathy. The narrator of *Paint It Today* writes: 'He was English and of another
world and it was much pleasanter reviewing the irreparable past with him than

with Raymond [Pound].' She continues: 'I had never met anyone in my life before who understood the other half or the explanatory quarter of the part of the sentences I left unsaid.'[48] Trust, so vital a quality for H.D., was being established between them.

However, the tranquillity of her London life had been disturbed, and she felt that she must get away, at least for a while, to restore her equilibrium. Paris, the city she had seen in Gregg's company less than eight months earlier, seemed a good choice. It was familiar, within easy reach, and offered cultural delights to transport her out of her recent misery. Pound would be there briefly, in transit for his projected summer walking tour of troubadour country. There would also be Walter Rummel, of whom we shall hear more shortly. Aldington suggested that he might come; he had never been to Paris. However, to do so, he would have to give up his sports-reporting post and the income it gave him. At the beginning of May H.D. left London, leaving her young admirer with a dilemma to resolve.

2. Family Secrets

The child is father of the man. . . .
(William Wordsworth, 'My Heart Leaps Up. . . . ', 1802)

It is impossible to understand George unless you know his parents.
(Richard Aldington, *Death of a Hero*, 1929)[1]

Somebody found my chrysalis
And shut it in a match-box.
My shrivelled wings were beaten,
Shed their colours in dusty scales
Before the box was opened
For the moth to fly.   (Richard Aldington, 'Childhood', 1915)

In both *Asphodel* and *Paint It Today* the Frances Gregg character attempts to alienate her lover from the young English poet to whom she is attracted, by mocking his masculine physicality and his lack of social refinement. In *Paint It Today* 'Josepha' refers to 'Basil' as 'that fat, sleek, beautiful youth type'; and in *Asphodel*, after talking with 'Fayne Rabb at their reunion, 'Hermione' realises that: 'Darrington looked rather like a head-waiter in his evening dress. His face was too heavy, too Flemish for the collar'. She wonders 'Was that the country girl his governor had copped or who had (was it?) copped his governor?'[2] In both respects, Aldington could be contrasted unfavourably with Pound. Pound was equally tall but much slighter in build, almost elfin in appearance, less threateningly masculine, and certainly bourgeois in origins – particularly on his mother's side.

If we are to trust the two novels, the young poet was not only conscious of his lack of refinement but did not attempt to hide it. 'I'm a bit florid at times. True British roast beef', Darrington tells Hermione, '. . . My governor you know married a country wench. Damn clever of her. She copped the old fellow down hunting. I was born six months after.'[3] What we do know – and what Frances Gregg knew – is that these deficiencies could be made to weigh with H.D. She wrote to Pound's mother while she was engaged in playing the role of Pound's hostess in 1912, '[Ezra] always has some under-dog at hand. One Thursday it was a derelict

Jessie May and Margery Aldington c. 1901

poet called Flint who made the fatal mistake of marrying his landlady's daughter, a hopeless little cockney!'[4] H.D. was playing to her audience, as she was wont to do in her letters, but her comments make it hard to realise that Frank Flint shortly became a close friend.

Class and male sexuality, problematic areas for H.D., are the keys to understanding Aldington and to unlocking his childhood. His own account of his background in the 1941 memoir, *Life for Life's Sake* contains many factual errors and omissions. We are prompted to speculate whether these were unconscious or not and what motivation lay behind them. Part of the explanation is that this is not autobiography but memoir – an urbane account of the life experiences of a successful and cosmopolitan writer provided for the entertainment of a literary American readership. It was also intended to be a portrait of a British way of life written at a time when Britain was under siege. Perhaps it is no surprise that we have to pick our way very carefully through it to discover the 'real' Aldington.

Fortunately, we also have fictional representations, *romans à clé* which really do seem to reveal some of the secrets of Aldington's childhood. If we are reluctant to trust the savagely satirical versions in his *Death of a Hero* (1929) and *Very Heaven* (1937), then the unpublished manuscript (*circa* 1935) of another autobiographical novel, *Pavane to an Unborn Child* by Aldington's sister, Margery Lyon Gilbert, should embolden us, since it echoes so many of Aldington's own fictionalised revelations of their shared childhood.

The marriage of 26-year-old Albert Edward Aldington to the 19-year-old Jessie May Godfree on 2 November 1891 was a 'shot-gun' wedding. Edward Godfree Aldington was born eight months later. (While still a young boy, he chose the name Richard for himself in preference to Edward.) It was the first of many demonstrations that Albert, although an educated man and an avid reader, was an incompetent in everyday matters. Both *Death of a Hero* and *Very Heaven* suggest that he was trapped into marriage by a young woman determined to move out of working-class poverty.

Nell Bywater in *Very Heaven*, clearly based on May Aldington:

> was conditioned in one of those sprawling households. . . . To spite them she wallowed in *A Lady of Quality, Lorna Doone, John Halifax Gentleman, In the Golden Days*, Tennyson and Rossetti, all the sinister compensatory sentimentalities of a predatory epoch. Even more she disliked the scrimping and subterfuges, the meagre larder, the cutting down and re-making of older sisters' dresses, the recurrent bailiff by the kitchen hearth. From childhood she listened to dreams and plots of 'good marriages'. And as that was – or seemed – the only way of escape she became almost a monomaniac on the subject.[5]

The satirical portrait is not without sympathy but what puzzles the narrator – as it must have puzzled the author – was how Nell reconciled her 'ideology of mooning sentiment' with her 'startling eye to the main chance'.

May's father was a sergeant major in the Royal Army Hospital Corps and her family life bore a close resemblance to that of the Hartlys in *Death of a Hero*. Eliza Burden, her mother, a shoe-maker's daughter from Kent, had given birth to a daughter and two sons before her marriage at the age of twenty to Charles Godfree, a Devonian who had been posted to the School of Musketry at Hythe. Six more children had followed by the time Eliza was forty, of whom May, born in 1872, was the oldest. She had experienced the typically itinerant life of the military family, moving between Hythe, Dover and Portsmouth and even to Bermuda, where her brother Henry was born. On leaving school, she went to work for her mother's two youngest sisters, who ran the Bell and Anchor Inn at Sandwich, and when her father retired from the army and went to live in London with his wife and the youngest four children, she stayed on in Kent with her aunts.

It was to the Bell and Anchor that Albert Aldington came in the early autumn of 1891, seeking a rural holiday. He had grown up in Edgbaston in Birmingham in a typically Victorian nonconformist household, very different from May's. His father was a baker and Albert's oldest brother had joined his father in the family business while the next one had become a Wesleyan minister. There were high hopes for Albert, who was a clever boy, born a decade or so later than his older brothers. He trained to become a solicitor but by 1891 he had failed in his attempt to establish a practice and was working in Portsmouth at a high street bookseller's and stationer's.

It seems that May was sufficiently misled by Albert's intelligence, manners and apparent prosperity to believe him to be the escape route for which she had been looking, while Albert had never encountered such unbridled feminine charm. How soon each became disillusioned it is hard to tell. The 15-year-old Tom [Richard] in *Pavane to an Unborn Child* tells his young sister, as he tries to console her during a major parental row, 'I don't think they ever did care for each other very much. He married her because he really is rather a silly old ass. And she married him to get away from home.'[6] *Death of a Hero* is kinder, its target the social system that had produced these two individuals: 'George Augustus did not know how to make a living; he did not know in the very least how to treat a woman. . . . As for Isabel – what she didn't know includes almost the whole range of human knowledge. The puzzle is to find out what she *did* know. . . . On the other hand, both George Augustus and Isabel knew how to read and write, pray, eat, drink, wash themselves, and dress up on Sundays. They were both pretty well acquainted with the Bible and Hymns A. and M.'[7]

When their son was born on 8 July 1892, May and Albert were still living in Portsmouth, but when Richard was a toddler they moved back to Kent – to Dover, where Albert started a legal practice. (*Death of a Hero* suggests that his father's death in 1893 brought him the funds to make this move.)[8] He also attempted to make his fortune as a writer, producing in 1896 a rather laboured, if historically authentic, novel set in the Elizabethan period, entitled *The Queen's Preferment*. It seems to have made few ripples on the publishing scene and he never tried again to write another book. ('Curious, that though literate, he wrote so badly', Aldington would remark to his younger brother, sixty years later.)[9]

He does seem to have managed, however, to build up his legal practice. By September 1898, when Richard's sister Margery was born, the family were living in 'a highly respectable house in the residential quarter of the town',[10] a moderately large town house resembling, as Aldington says in *Life for Life's Sake*, the old brownstone houses in New York, though built of yellow brick. In the front was 'a fine avenue of old trees' and in the rear 'a longish but narrow garden.'[11] Number 5, Godwyne Road is no longer standing, but several similar houses in the street remain, solid and unostentatious. May had a cook and a nursemaid to help her run the household.

Aldington's portrait of Dover in the early years of his childhood is a bleak one. In both *Life for Life's Sake* and the poem 'Childhood' the town is sordid, provincial and grey, and it is almost always raining. 'We lived in a world made almost wholly by men, and very dull men too, cut off from earthy verities by bricks and decorum. Nature we touched only at its tamest and most banal, in public parks rich in suburban flora and that odd plant "Keep off the Grass", or in little walled gardens.'[12] 'Childhood' clearly references Wordsworth's 'Ode on Intimations of Immortality'; this infant is born trailing its clouds of glory, but the physical and social environment into which it is thrust stunt its emotional and imaginative development:

> . . . the beauty a child has
> And the beautiful things it learns before its birth,
> Were shed, like moth scales, from me.[13]

Sometime around 1902 to 1903, the family moved to a larger and more modern house in Deal, more in keeping with May's social aspirations, but nine miles to the north-east of Dover, so that Albert Aldington had to take the train to reach his office in Castle Street. Now the silences, gaps and misinformation begin, but we must assume that his son made the same daily journey: Aldington tells us that he spent 'the larger part of several years' at school in Dover, 'being manufactured into the sort of human product a not too intelligent provincial society thought [he] should be'.[14] He seems to have attended a small prep school before moving on in September 1904, when only just twelve years old, to Dover College. The college had been founded thirty years earlier and was sited in the grounds of Dover's twelfth century Benedictine Priory in the heart of the town, looking up towards the equally old castle on the cliffs above. Several of the medieval buildings remained and the surroundings were – and still are – pleasant, but Aldington's memories of that period were grim. He described his days at the college as 'a perpetual struggle against a conditioning which was repulsive to [him].' The curriculum was taught without enthusiasm, while stress was laid upon 'mere games' and upon 'a narrow-minded bourgeois outlook.' He maintained in *Life for Life's Sake* that: 'Backed by a quasi-military discipline this inculcation of prejudices was most harmful. Under the guise of turning out gentlemen it produced a pack of stupids.' He admitted that the price he paid for successful resistance to this regime was considerable, 'both in nervous tension and in ignorance, which had to be made good by desperate hard work later.'[15]

This was a minor public school, for the sons of the middle classes, aiming to turn out not intellectuals and thinkers, but 'gentlemen', who would enter the professions and the military or civil service, the bourgeois world to which his parents had worked hard to gain entry but whose values the young Aldington

School House, Dover College

already despised. It was also, like most public schools, a boarding school; 'day boys' constituted less than a quarter of the school's population and were grouped in a separate 'house', Crescent House. Being a day boy may have helped Aldington to resist the institutional ethos, but it would also have made him conscious of being an 'outsider'. However, college records show that despite his youth he was already successfully playing rugby (an indication of his sturdy build even then), and he admitted in a 'potted autobiography' requested by Amy Lowell in 1917 that rugby was the only thing he enjoyed at school.[16]

Life for Life's Sake leads us to understand that he attended Dover College until the family left Kent for London, shortly before he went to university in 1910. Even Margery Lyon Gilbert's unpublished 'Early Memories of Richard Aldington' dates her brother's attendance at Dover College as *starting* in the autumn of 1906.[17] However, the records at Dover College reveal that he had left the school by June that year, shortly before his fourteenth birthday.[18] We are left to speculate not only about the reasons for his departure but also about why he chose not to make it clear that he spent less than two years at the college.

From his account of the school in his memoir, we may conclude that his parents withdrew him because he was unhappy; he may even have refused to return for a third year. It is possible that Albert could not afford the fees any longer. Although he appears to have been quite prosperous by this time, May's desire to maintain a high standard of living must have been a drain on his resources. In the summer of 1906 the family moved to a house called Rothiemay in the village of St-Margaret's-at-

Cliffe, set on the cliffs above St Margaret's Bay, only four miles north-east of Dover and separated from the town by the South Foreland, an uninhabited area of chalk downs. Travelling into Dover – for Albert and his son – would have become easier rather than more difficult.

Maybe her son's education was simply not a priority for May. Significantly, the activities on which Isabel in *Death of a Hero* lavishes her time include 'malforming her children's minds' and 'capriciously interfering with their education'.[19] Ursula Bloom's memoir, *Holiday Mood*, to which we shall return shortly, tells us of this St Margaret's period: '[Aldington's] people were well off, and had a comfortable house in which they entertained quite a lot'.[20] In *Life for Life's Sake* Aldington makes several references to having to undergo an operation as a teenager, but this would seem to have been a couple of years later.[21] At one point he writes that, 'owing to an operation and other reasons I had practically a whole year to myself.'[22] The 'other reasons' are a puzzle, yet it is unlikely that an operation alone (probably for a hernia) would have necessitated a year's absence from school.

What we do know is that the move to St Margaret's Bay and the – albeit temporary – freedom from schooling were a liberation, imaginatively and intellectually, for the young Aldington. This was the point at which his reading, particularly of poetry, became all-consuming, fed by his father's extensive library: 'George went at George Augustus's books with the energy of a fierce physical hunger.'[23] In *Life for Life's Sake* Aldington tells us that his passion for poetry was fired up by his discovery of Keats's *Endymion* and its 'world of enchantment': 'what poem was fitter to charm an immature mind . . . ?'[24] (The appeal of this work to the adolescent boy tells us much about his sensibilities.)

Whether he underwent any further formal schooling is not clear. His University College matriculation records in 1910 inform us that he had attended Dover College and then had a 'private tutor', and that his formal qualifications consisted of Oxford Local Examinations in English, Maths, Latin, French and Greek in 1908 (around the time of his sixteenth birthday). He told Lowell in his 1917 letter that he had attended a 'Seminary for Young Gentlemen' at St Margaret's Bay 'at the age of seven'. It seems improbable that he was taken daily to St Margaret's from Dover as a young child and much more likely that – prep school or not – he attended this institution as a teenager, when the family were living in the village. His sister recalls his attending 'Mr Sweatman's Academy' in the summer of 1906, but since she then recalls his going on to Dover College that autumn, we need to be wary. The 1901 census shows that Sydney Edward Sweatman was still an assistant master at a school in Clapham in that year (when Aldington was nine years old); his school at 'Sunnydene' in St Margaret's at Cliffe was established around 1906 and the 1911 census shows that he took in pupils up to the age of at least fifteen. Perhaps Sweatman was the 'private tutor' who prepared the young Aldington for his examinations. Is all this just an instance of poor memory on Aldington's part? More probably, the subject of his schooling was an embarrassment and he learned to adapt the facts to make a convincing, and more conventional, narrative.

St Margaret's Bay

Both *Life for Life's Sake* and *Death of a Hero* devote considerable space to other educative influences, chiefly that of Dudley Grey (*Death of a Hero*'s Dudley Pollack), a middle-aged man living in the village with his wife, 'an accomplished man of the world, well bred with charmingly easy manners, dressed with a careless elegance, a good shot, a good horseman'.[25] Initially, Aldington tells us, he visited the couple's house to play chess with Mr Grey, but he was soon learning more from his mentor than he had ever learned at school: 'He talked of the theatre and grand opera, of symphonic and chamber music. . . . The classics, which had been a dreary school task, he brought alive. He made me see that Homer and Horace were as much living poetry as Keats and Shakespeare. Under his urging I made a strenuous effort and taught myself to read French. He introduced me to French poetry, and it was charming to see his enthusiasm for Ronsard and André Chénier. He started me off on Italian. He made me learn to ride a horse. . . . ' Grey's 'deepest enthusiasm', however, was for Italy, for Italian art and literature, and he inspired the boy with a longing to visit that country.

The move to St Margaret's developed not only Aldington's appetite for reading but also his love of nature. Another formative influence mentioned in *Life for Life's Sake* was a local field naturalist and lepidopterist, the Reverend Francis Austin, and the boy became a keen butterfly-collector. Then there was the Hilbery family, Londoners who took regular breaks at St Margaret's. Maude Hilbery and her two youngest brothers, Malcolm and William, men in their early twenties, befriended the 15-year-old and the brothers introduced him to walking, not a leisure activity favoured by the provincial bourgeoisie, who preferred golf and bridge.[26] Both *Life for Life's Sake* and *Death of a Hero*, in which the brothers appear as 'the Coningtons', devote several pages to the pleasures of these early hikes, not just those in Kent but also a longer trip with William to Dorset and the West Country. It was not only the walking and the countryside that made such an impression on the teenager: 'For the first time he felt and understood companionship between men – the frank, unsuspicious exchange of goodwill and talk, the spontaneous collaboration of two natures.'[27]

Then there were the pleasures of the seashore, the swimming, the prawning, the exploring of the rock pools along the shore-line at low tide, with 'the dazzling white cliffs' behind, the light blue sea 'surging gently' at the tide-edge and the gulls and kittiwakes 'soaring or perching in crevices, filling the air with sharp plaintive calls'.[28] *Death of a Hero* lists the sensuous delights of 'George's' adolescent existence as: 'listening to the sound of the wind as you fell asleep; watching the blue butterflies and the Small Coppers hovering and settling on the great lavender bush; taking off your clothes and letting your body slide into a cool, deep, clear rock-pool while the great kittiwakes clamoured round the sun-white cliffs and the scent of sea-weeds and salt water filled you; watching the sun go down and trying to write something of what it made you feel, like Keats; getting up very early in the morning and riding out along the white empty lanes on your bicycle; wanting to be alone and think about things and feeling strange and happy and ecstatic. . . . '[29]

It sounds a sensuous but solitary adolescence. Yet Ursula Bloom was a companion one year, staying with the family in the summer when she and Aldington became teenagers: 'We were both standing on the threshold of life, and seeing it lying there before us, and wondering what we should do with it.'[30] Bloom was a family friend and would become a prolific and popular novelist in later life. In her memoir, *Holiday Mood*, she alludes to meeting 'delightful friends' of Aldington's (named Cork and Bags). Aldington does not make any reference in his memoir to his sister Margery, six years his junior; but her record of their childhood shows her to have been an eager and admiring companion: 'That summer [1906] he was in roaring form, and I basked and blossomed in the glow of his good spirits. Natural history and archaeology were our main interests. In the former, I was allowed to carry the 'killing bottle' and in the latter he let me use a little hammer pick with which we hunted for fossils in the chalk cliffs.'[31] 'Pita', the protagonist of the unpublished novel Gilbert wrote in later years, recalls:

Days like this at the Bay. The rough handle of my wooden spade in my hot palms as we made the most of the tiny patch of sand when the tide raced in little ringlets towards us. Bathing and someone huge and strong holding one's trembling limbs above the terror of the deep water – Excelsior: The Excelsior Café, the dry cakes, the acid drops, how lovely, blended with warm milk and the salt to one's lips . . . The long climb up the resin-scented Zig-Zag for lunch, the comfortable roll of Tom's [Aldington's] shoulders as one went pick-a-back along the last stretch, because he took pity on one's bedraggled sticky exhaustion.[32]

There were also adolescent flirtations. Gilbert recalls: 'My governess, Gladys . . . had a sister called Daisy who wore a big black bow at the back of her head. I soon discovered that Richard was delighted whenever we met Daisy, especially bathing, when, like a happy young porpoise, he would dive around us. We both thought Daisy was very, very pretty. I believe if he could get away, he would go and talk to her when I'd gone to bed.' In *Death of a Hero* 'Maisie' is 'a slightly coarse, dark type, a little older than George and much more developed' and the affair progresses rather further than 'talking'.[33] Shockingly, in the 1915 poem 'Daisy', Aldington encounters this childhood sweetheart years later as a prostitute on Oxford Street.[34]

Unlike his fictional counterpart, George Winterbourne, the young Aldington does not seem to have been sexually precocious. Later letters to various lovers recall two particular erotic boyhood experiences, both of which were also converted into fictional material. In *All Men Are Enemies*, Tony's young nurse, washing and dressing in front of her young charge, 'quite unknowingly showed Tony that a healthy woman's body is lovely and desirable', so that in adolescence 'his visual memory suddenly brought before him the vision of Annie, as he had so often seen her, naked to the waist, with her breasts moist and silvery with water or downy with sunlight as she sat before her wooden-framed mirror.' The visit of an older cousin further initiates the young teenager, as she allows him to visit her in her bedroom early every morning, where 'he lay in her arms in the new-found rapture of touch'.[35]

For the young boy, these early erotic experiences, thrilling but innocent, were both at odds with, but also mysteriously connected to, the 'goings on' (as Ursula Bloom puts it) of the adult members of the middle-class community of St Margaret's. *Death of a Hero* lyrically evokes the 'sheep-and-wind-nipped turf of the downs', the inland hamlets, farms and Norman churches, but contrasts them with the 'pretentious surbanity' of Martin's Point [St-Margaret's-at-Cliffe] with 'its golf and its idleness and tea-party scandals'.[36] Bloom called it 'a simple little village on the face of things, and a most sophisticated village underneath it all.' 'Everyone,' she continues, 'knew everyone else, and in a lot of cases a good deal better than they should have done.'[37] Bloom was an Anglican clergyman's daughter and she was astonished – and entertained – by the 'very modern' behaviour of the adults at St Margaret's: 'It was my first introduction to Bohemian life and I was surprised and interested in the flagrant love-making that went on. I had always thought that when you were married you couldn't, which all goes to show what a nice mind I had. . . . Never have I been in such a place for what the servants call "goings-on".'[38] To the young Aldington, of course, such behaviour was merely suburban.

Both Aldington's and his sister's novels suggest that their mother was an active practitioner of this dubious sexual code; she also attained some local notoriety by publishing a titillating and sentimental novel entitled *Love Letters that Caused a Divorce*. She went on to publish five more similar novels and two selections of bad verse over the next decade; it is not clear whether they were principally part of her campaign to keep the family – and herself – financially afloat, a bid to show her

husband that she was more talented than he, or an aspiration to become another
Elinor Glyn. She certainly cultivated the friendship of the literary agent, Hughes
Massie, who was another summer visitor to St Margaret's in 1905; Gilbert tells us
that her mother's first novel was written at his suggestion.

One newcomer who set tongues wagging was the prolific popular novelist Guy
Thorne, who also published under his real name, C. Ranger Gull.[39] In 1906 he
and his wife came to live at Wanstone Court, an old farmhouse on the outskirts
of the village, and *Death of a Hero* suggests that May Aldington, ever-impressed by
celebrity and an aspiring novelist herself, was quick to acquire his friendship. Gull
only stayed for a year, as he lost all his money in a mining investment and had to sell
up and move away: but Aldington's short-lived acquaintance with him (and with
his friend, the aging wit, 'writer of drawing room ballads' and 'prototype of the
literary lounger', Charles Cotsford Dick) led to his discovery that the literary
world might be less narrow-minded, but was home to as much complacency and
sham as provincial society. 'My awe at this eminent personage was tempered by the
fact that his conversation was very worldly, not to say mundane, and apt to run on
the theme of his superiority to all other living authors.'[40] *Death of a Hero* is kinder.
Gull is (appropriately) 'Mr Slush', but 'he did occasionally look around him; he
was not wholly blinkered with prejudice and unheeding blankness like most of the
middle-class inhabitants of Martin's Point.'[41]

Aldington's life in this period was not confined to St Margaret's, nor was it
only the friendships of Dudley Grey and the Hilbery brothers that opened up new
horizons for him. Albert Aldington, although working long hours to support his
wife's chosen lifestyle, found the time to take his son on day-trips to Calais and on
longer trips to Paris, Antwerp and Brussels. Yet, and despite the fact that his father
was a man of culture and learning, with none of his wife's vulgarity, materialism or
temper, Aldington seems to have had little respect for him, and there is no suggestion
in *Life for Life's Sake* of any closeness between them. Of course, the bitterness of the
portraits in *Death of a Hero* and *Very Heaven* arises from the devastating impact on
Aldington of Albert's later mismanagement of his financial affairs: 'He had a genius
for messing up other people's lives. The amount of irreparable harm which can be
done by a really good man is astounding.'[42]

It does seem that the young Aldington shared his mother's contempt for the
mild Albert. Faced as role models with a weak and incompetent father and a
manipulative and domineering mother, the child must have felt it safer to identify
with the mother. He portrays her viciously in *Death of a Hero*:

> She was a woman who constantly dramatised herself and her life. She was
> as avid of public consideration as an Italian lieutenant, no matter what the
> quality of the praise. . . . She was a mistress of would-be revolutionary
> platitudes about marriage and property but, in fact, was as sordid, avaricious,
> conventional and spiteful a middle-class woman as you could dread to meet.
> Like all her class, she toadied to her betters and bullied her inferiors. But with
> her conventionality, she was, of course, a hypocrite. In her kittenish moods,

which she cultivated with a strange lack of a sense of congruity, she liked
to throw out hints about 'kicking over the traces'. But, as a matter of fact,
she never soared much above tippling, financial dishonesty, squabbling, lying,
betting and affairs with bounderish young men. . . . [43]

Nevertheless, he understood from early on that she had an instinct for survival.
Death of a Hero again: 'I have far more sympathy for Isabel than for George Augustus.
She was at least the wreck of a human being. He was a thumb-twiddler, a harmless
praying-Mantis, a zero of no value except in combination with her integer.'[44] May
Aldington may have been (as her daughter wrote) 'strong-willed and emotionally
turbulent' and, more despicably as far as her son was concerned, materialistic and
hypocritical, but there was also a sensuality which, although tainted in her with
sentimentality, he seems from early on to have recognised in himself. The adult
Aldington would feel guilt for the child's and adolescent's instinctive choice of the
mother; Dorothy Yorke, a later lover, said of him after his death: 'I think Richard
spent his life trying to get away from the mother in him and to attain the father in
him.'[45]

Meanwhile, the insecurity of both children was intensified by the rows between
their parents. 'In later years', wrote Gilbert, 'I have thought she flourished and
thrived on a first class "row" at least once a week, but it shattered the rest of us.'
In *Pavane to an Unborn Child* the young Pita is frightened by a violent night-time
argument in which her mother repels her husband's sexual advances and he
reproaches her with the latest of her affairs.

Worse was to come. In 1908 Albert suffered financial ruin through having made
some ill-advised investments. *Life for Life's Sake* is, understandably, silent on this
event in Aldington's life. May was outraged. As *Very Heaven* puts it:

> [I]t was altogether unspeakably rotten and unfair that after twenty-five years
> of 'a good match' its one compensation was lost, and Nelly Heylin once
> more found herself in the unpleasant world of foreclosed mortgages, County
> Court writs, and cheques returned R/D. Not that Frank was extravagant.
> But he fiddle-faddled money away. And he had the senseless habit of believing
> in the Stock Exchange tips he heard about at Clubs, a habit which proved
> more expensive than a multitude of ordinary vices. His latest feat, and the
> proximate cause of the present crisis, was investing heavily in some idiot
> 'invention' floated by a bucket shop. Frank's tardy discovery that the thing
> was bogus was euphemistically known in the family as The Shock.[46]

In *Very Heaven*, Frank 'transposed his moral inability to deal with the situation
into a physical disability; and went to bed, clamouring for peace and quiet, and
leaving Nell to face the music.' *Pavane* and *Death of a Hero* suggest that Albert
Aldington did worse than this; he ran away:

> George Augustus had gone to London on his usual weekly trip, and as
> usual George had met the six o'clock train. No George Augustus. He met
> the seven-ten, the eight-fifty and the eleven-five, the last train: and still no

George Augustus. No telegram, no message. A feeling of impending calamity hung over the house that night, and there was not much sleep for Isabel and George. Next morning a long rambling letter, emotional and vague, arrived from George Augustus. The gist was that he was ruined and in flight from his creditors.

Death of a Hero continues: 'Later investigations showed that his affairs were not so compromised as he had imagined; but the sudden mad flight ruined everything. In a day the Winterbournes dropped from comparative affluence to comparative poverty.'[47]

Both novels focus on the enormity of the loss for the teenage boy. Here is *Pavane*:

What a pitiful, beautiful figure was Tom in those days. The sun still shone, the cross-channel boats went like little clockwork toys across the glassy water. But gone were his hopes of cricket colours, the promised week at Canterbury, staying at the 'Rose and Crown' with them all. . . . All this was gone for ever.

Now every morning, with his young face puckered into a thousand strange wrinkles of worry, carrying a little black bag, and followed by volleys of mingled hysteria and sound commonsense from the distracted Jessie, he set off to catch the old bus for another interview with the solicitors who were trying to rescue something from the wreck. Or so they said.[48]

The narrator of *Death of a Hero* writes:

The effect on George was really rather disastrous. After the almost sordid distress of his early adolescence, he had succeeded in saving the spark, had built up a life for himself, had created a positive happiness. But all that rested, in fact, on the family money. The distrust of himself and others which had gradually disappeared, the sense of suspicion and frustration, came flooding back with renewed bitterness. . . . Other incidents confirmed this mood. Both Isabel and George Augustus rather pushed George forward to take the brunt of the calamity. . . . It was George who had to interview insolent tradesmen and creditors, and plead for further credit and 'time'. It was George who recovered £90 in gold which had been stolen by the office boy, and was refunded. It was George who was sent to persuade his father to come back and face out the storm. It was George who was made to go and collect rents from suspicious and uneasy tenants. It was George who had to see the solicitors and try to get a grasp of the situation. They even accepted his offer of the few pounds (birthday gifts saved up) which he had in the Post Office savings bank. Rather a shock for a boy not seventeen, who had been living an *exalteé* inner life, and who had been led to believe that his material future was assured. It is not wholly surprising that he was very unhappy, a bit resentful, and that his mistrust became permanent, his modesty diffidence.[49]

The most painful aspect of it all, worse than all the humiliations, must have been the realisation that the '*exalteé* inner life' and the 'positive happiness' had rested upon the money and bourgeois lifestyle that the young man himself so despised.

May Aldington was pregnant for the third time; presumably some kind of truce had latterly taken place in the marriage. 'Rothiemay' had to be sold and she and her two children moved to Sandwich. Albert's financial schemes had included the buying and letting of properties and while most had now to be sold, a 'small meagre house in a row of villas', 1 Poplar Avenue, became the family home, 'which after the space and comfort of what they had always accepted as their due, irked each in their way.'[50] Margery Aldington's sympathies are not hard to guess; the narrator of *Pavane* writes: 'Mummie set no good example; she was loud in her laments and furiously denounced the man who had landed them there. The fact was that poor daddy was one of those who might, if left to himself, have provided them with a humble but fairly reasonable existence, but hounded and urged by Mummie's fiery energies and ambitions, he had got up a pace that was quite beyond his limited capacity. He stumbled; and who was quicker to see that he was a "goner" than Mummie, and hasten the coup de grace? Now he was gone from them, slinking in disgrace in the slums of some far away northern town.'

How often Albert was with them is hard to tell; he was now trying to establish himself in Malcolm Hilbery's firm in Holborn. He was certainly absent on 7 February 1909 when his daughter, Joan Patricia Le Gros Aldington, was born. A few months later the family followed him to London, renting a house in Harrow ('which was even then becoming a mediocre suburb'). Only now does *Life for Life's Sake* touch on the woeful story; the whole episode is summarised in an understatement that, 'If there was ever a danger of my falling a victim to respectability, it was averted by a sudden change in the family fortunes which took me to London.' Aldington tells us that this period was for him 'three or four lifeless months' in which he dropped into 'moods of melancholy' and found 'the present distasteful and the future unattractive'.[51] There would certainly have been pressure on him from May to find paid employment, however menial. Albert seems to have been more understanding; there is extant a letter from him to the editor of *The Spectator*, asking if a position could be found for his son on that journal. He lists his qualifications: 'As an old lover of the classics I can vouch for the boy's ability in this direction. His knowledge of French is good, of art excellent, of English Literature, for his age quite remarkable. His productions, particularly in poetry, are equally distinctive, and withal, he is tall, muscular and can do a twenty mile walk any day of the week.'[52] Whether Aldington would have been happy on the staff of such a conservative journal is another matter, but no offer was ever made.[53]

Towards the end of 1909 Albert's financial affairs began to look up. The family moved on to a reasonably substantial modern house in Cromwell Road, Teddington. It might not have been the countryside, but it was near to Bushey Park, through which one could walk to Hampton Court: 'In the early morning, when the dew was still on the grass, there was a wonderful freshness under that majestic avenue of elms and chestnuts, four deep on either side.'[54] Aldington seems also to have acquired new friends through rowing on the Thames, among them the journalist who would offer him work when he was forced to leave University College. And to University College he went in the autumn of 1910.

The Mermaid Inn at Rye

Albert, however, was not done with financial failure. *Life for Life's Sake* tells us that in early 1911, 'By means of a complicated series of speculations my father contrived to lose his money, and was practising his profession in London not very successfully.'[55] Whether this constituted a new 'Shock' or simply means that Albert's attempts to make good the disaster of 1908 were not succeeding, we do not know, but the upshot was his son's premature departure from the university. May had obviously not prepared herself for a further fall in the family's fortunes, as she had become pregnant again; her fourth child, Paul Anthony Glynne Aldington, was born on 10 May 1911. She may have been a temperamental woman, but she was always resourceful. Her son, more quick to sympathise than his sister, tells us that: 'With characteristic energy and good sense my mother eventually solved that problem [the lack of money] by buying and running a famous old Sussex inn.'[56] As soon as she had recovered her physical strength, May departed with the two younger children to the picturesquely medieval Mermaid Inn at Rye, which she would run for the next thirteen years. She knew how to run a public house, of course, but she tried to make this one a cut above, calling it 'The Mermaid Club' and trying to attract a middle-class clientele.

A curious footnote to the story of May at The Mermaid is a handful of letters from Rupert Brooke to his lover Ka Cox, written while he was staying there for a few days in March 1912 with his friend James Strachey. Brooke mocks the conversation of 'Colonel Aldington, May, Anabel and Dick' as he listens to them in the 'Smoking Room' of the inn. He tells Cox,

They're all in evening dress! And they talk – there are these people in the world – about Bridge, Golf and Motoring. They're playing Bridge –

But then the *most* extraordinary thing is about "Colonel" Aldington, May, Anabel and Dick. Because – it turns out – *they* keep the Inn. ('Very *Old* Place – you see these beams?') She's written a book of poems and *several* novels.

Brooke's 'hurried glance' through the Club's Visitors' Book disclosed '95 Colonels, Sir E. Ray Lankester [the evolutionary biologist] and Horace A. Vachell [the novelist]'.[57] Clearly May was succeeding in attracting the kinds of guest she wanted. However, Mike Read, Brooke's biographer almost certainly misidentifies May's three fellow bridge players. It is unlikely that 'Colonel Aldington' is Albert; more probably May already had one of those ninety-five military gentlemen 'in tow'. 'Dick' is almost certainly not Aldington himself, since, although he did visit his mother, he would not have stooped to playing bridge and talking about golf and motoring; and Read identifies 'Anabel' as Dorothy Yorke, whom Aldington did not meet until 1917.[58] Nevertheless, Brooke's *vignette* of May and her life at The Mermaid, although cruel, is convincing.

All this helps us to understand a little more the complex adult Aldington became. While he despised the late-Victorian values of the middle-class, their materialism, their rigid codes of behaviour (and the resultant hypocrisy) and their philistinism, Aldington had grown up in a family which clung with difficulty to its place in middle-class society, because of its less-than-middle-class roots, his mother's vulgarity and dubious moral conduct and his father's financial incompetence. They were outsiders. He perceived the moral and cultural hollowness of the class, but the anger with which he would articulate this view in his fiction was motivated by rejection. The insecurity of the parents communicated itself to the child and was compounded by the volatility of his parents' marriage, leaving him a prey to self-pity for the rest of his life. Most of all, as Dorothy Yorke discerned, his early identification with his mother left him with a legacy of sensuality, of moral irresponsibility – and ultimately of self-loathing.

3. The Perfect Year: France and Italy, 1912-1913

Youth, spring in a Mediterranean island, Greek poetry, idleness — these were the simple factors of an enchantment whose memory will only end with life.
(Richard Aldington: 'Theocritus in Capri', 1924)[1]

France is a polished gem, a priceless intaglio, England is a great wide rose spread just before its falling, Italy is a live ember burning the hearts of men.
(H.D., *Asphodel*, 1921-1922, pub.1992)[2]

In Paris in the spring of 1912 H.D. was in mourning for her relationship with Gregg. Her surroundings reminded her of their time there together; she even lodged in the pension in the Rue Jacob where they had stayed in the autumn. She was not entirely alone, but the friendships she made or resumed increased her confusion and misery. Walter Rummel, a fine pianist and composer, was two years younger than Pound and the two men had been close friends since 1908. The child of a German father and an American mother, he had settled in Paris and become a leading interpreter of Debussy. H.D. had already met him on several occasions, the first in 1910 when Rummel had been touring the U.S. and stayed with Pound and his family at Swarthmore. She and the Greggs had visited him in Paris in 1911 and Rummel had been in London twice since, even taking H.D. to concerts on two occasions. She was a lover of music and was attracted to this charming and talented man. In *Asphodel* Hermione remarks: 'Walter, suavity, fragrance (can a man be fragrant?). O Walter you are like great dogwood trees, men are trees sometimes. . . . Your face is alabaster. You are more beautiful than anything one could ever have imagined.'[3]

Through Rummel she met another close friend of Pound's, the 30-year-old expatriate pianist from Indiana, Margaret Cravens. It was Rummel who had introduced Pound and Cravens in 1910, and she had since been paying Pound an annuity of two hundred dollars, which constituted the major part of his regular income. H.D. was puzzled by Cravens and by the exact status of her relationship with Pound. There was even a portrait of him on the wall of the living room in Cravens's Right Bank apartment.'[4] *Asphodel* suggests that it was Cravens who gave H.D. the first piece of disconcerting news she was to receive on this visit to Paris: of Pound's secret engagement to Dorothy Shakespear. Certainly Cravens knew of it and had even invited Shakespear to visit her. (Dorothy had refused on the grounds that her engagement to Pound was not a formal one.) According to *End to Torment*, however, it was Rummel who told H.D. of the 'understanding' between Pound and Shakespear, possibly even before she made the journey to Paris.

Whatever the truth of the matter, we can guess that this news would not have been a complete surprise; in *Asphodel* Hermione even wonders, 'Had he told her? He mumbled, murmured, had a way of hurling sonnets at her and asking her opinion. Was that his way of telling? Had he told her?'[5] Pound arrived in Paris on the same day as H.D., 1 May. 'I shall be here 3 weeks inspecting the state of Art', he told his parents.[6] He was staying in Rummel's apartment in the Rue Raynouard while they worked together on settings for troubador songs, but he was also finding time to see Cravens, and H.D. also met with him on a couple of occasions in that first fortnight.

It was certainly Cravens who gave H.D. the next piece of unwelcome news: Walter Rummel was also secretly engaged – to the pianist Therese Chaigneau, whom H.D. had recently met:[7] 'Was she a spectator then? Was she to be always looking, watching, seeing other people's lives work out right? Hermione seemed to herself suddenly forgotten. As old maids must feel turning out lavender letters, letters gone dim and smelling of sweet lavender.'[8] First Frances, then Ezra, now Walter: the first two of these relationships had been deeply problematic and the last merely a fantasy, but H.D. must have felt more bereft than ever.

This made her relationship with Aldington take on an especial importance. He had been writing to her. *Asphodel* again: ' . . . there was one thing to hang on to. Those letters that she had swept up from the hall table, the letters that she had picked up from the floor, the letters slipped under the door, the letters that she was taking so for granted, as much now of her routine of life as her early morning chocolate or her toothbrush, became by some turn of events, something super-natural, sub-normal, something that must spell escape, regeneration, beatitude. . . . Letters in the light of Shirley [Cravens] just turned thirty might mean something. Must mean something.'[9] They were certainly a measure of his determination to come in person and he did so on 15 May, giving up his part-time journalism and determining to manage for now on a small allowance that his parents agreed to give him (and which explains the fact that he made the effort to send postcards from Paris to each member of the family apart from the baby). The lodgings he took in the Rue de la Grande Chaumière in Montparnasse were recommended by his former mentor, Dudley Grey. It was his first visit to Paris and he was delighted by the city and its wealth of art treasures.

H.D. was also delighted; the diary she kept at the time records: 'As if after great turmoil – confusion – weariness . . . Richard has come! Last night all the city was a new thing – revisited as one falls first upon one's first old city – and to me for the first time.'[10] In *Asphodel*, 'Paris suddenly became (with the coming of Darrington) Paris.'[11] They visited galleries together and sat in the Jardin du Luxembourg, writing poems in their notebooks and (H.D.) sketching. Aldington would write in *Life for Life's Sake*: 'I have never known anybody, not even Lawrence, with so vivid an aesthetic apprehension. . . . To look at beautiful things with H.D. is a remarkable

Frances and Oliver Gregg, 1915

experience. She has a genius for appreciation, a severe but wholly positive taste. She lives in the heights, and never wastes time on what is inferior or in finding fault with masterpieces. She responds so swiftly, understands so perfectly, re-lives the artist's mood so intensely, that the work of art seems transformed. You too respond, understand, and relive it in a degree which would be impossible without her inspiration.'[12] A revealing insight into their appreciation of visual art and the strength of their shared commitment to Hellenism is a sonnet he wrote in H.D.'s notebook on 4 July in response to Fra Angelico's 'The Coronation of the Virgin' in the Louvre:

Angelico's Coronation
To H.D.

> Almost indeed thou drawest me to thy feet
> Frail gentle Christ, almost thy sway
> Might take me from the pride of my straight way,
> Almost I were content in my defeat;
> I am most glad to know thee, where the sweet
> Saints hymn thee and the cherubim essay
> Their music like the tremor of the day,
> Still echoes which the golden hills repeat;
>
> But if I loved thee, and thy fragile hands
> Tenderly touched me as thou crownest her
> I would grow weary for the wild blithe earth,
> Scurry of satyr-hooves in dewy lands,
> Pan-Pipes at noon, the lust, the shaggy fur,
> White bosoms and swift Dionysiac mirth.

They also read poetry together, particularly the French symbolist Henri de Régnier, and Helen Carr suggests that Régnier may have influenced the way in which both young writers moved away from formal metre over the coming months, although Aldington would always maintain that the impetus came from Greek choruses.[13] They saw Pound, who was sceptical of their mutual enchantment – or perhaps jealous, writing to his parents: 'Hilda's last Englishman is also very charming . . . he has crossed the channel and taken to drawing and velvet jacket, and they seem to share a talent for leisure. But they are probably too much alike for a "life-interest." '[14] He left on his planned tour of troubadour country on 26 May, calling on Margaret Cravens before he left.

What happened next would have a traumatic impact on all of the group, but most lastingly on H.D.. She went to call on Cravens on the Sunday afternoon of 2 June, having been invited to tea. Aldington was hard on her heels. A maid opened the door and told H.D. that Cravens had killed herself. On the previous morning she had written farewell notes to Pound and to Rummel, had attended a tea-party at Therese Chaigneau's house in Passy in the afternoon, and on her return to her apartment at around eight o'clock in the evening had shot herself through the heart with a small pistol.

She had been subject to depression. She had lost all her siblings, her mother and two grandparents when growing up, and her father had committed suicide a year earlier. Alone in Paris and losing confidence in her musical talent, she must have felt even more isolated when the two men whose companionship and encouragement she depended upon both became engaged. Her thirty-first birthday fell just days before her suicide. The content of her notes (since destroyed) apparently suggested that it was Rummel rather than Pound with whom she had been in love, but both men were stunned by what had happened.[15] Rummel wrote to Pound, who came straight back to Paris, arriving on 10 June. He resumed his travels at the end of the month, but his feelings can be gauged by his response to a sympathetic letter from Dorothy Shakespear: 'I won't say, "don't write me trivial things", but write to [me] gravely for a little.'[16] (What he could not tell her was that, with the loss of the major part of his income, their marriage prospects now looked bleak.)

H.D. not only observed Pound's suffering and wondered how far his conduct had contributed to Cravens' suicide; she also took on responsibility herself. She identified with Cravens, an expatriate woman pursuing her artistic ambitions far from home and family, and wished that she had shared her own fears and anxieties with her and encouraged Cravens to talk. Hermione says: 'I know she was alone too much. . . . She had got away from home. Shirley had escaped and this had happened. Would this happen to them all, to all of them?' and she concludes, 'Darrington might help her to work and she could have something, claim something out of all this.'[17] Pound had not saved Cravens and could not save her, but Aldington, who admired her and her work, she could trust. She had moved her lodgings once, at Cravens' suggestion;[18] now she moved again: into the Rue de la Grande Chaumière.

All three young poets were back in London by late July 1912. Aldington and H.D. both moved to (separate) rooms at 6, Church Walk, Kensington, presumably at the suggestion of their 'mentor', who had long been established at number 10; and Aldington took a part-time job at the newly formed Garton Peace Foundation.[19] (In his memoir he would comment, of course with hindsight, that 'we were in the position of a group of very little mice planning to put bells on an extremely large and intractable cat.')[20] Pound must at some point have felt obliged to inform the Shakespear parents that his financial circumstances had deteriorated (although it is unlikely that he ever told them the whole story) and they kept their daughter out of town for much of the next year. Olivia wrote to him on 13 September making it clear that, since he had no future with Dorothy, she expected him to stay away, adding, 'I've seen too much of girls wasting their lives on men who can't marry them, they generally end up by being more or less compromised demivierges.'[21] So Pound was free to spend time with Aldington, H.D. and Patmore: his letters to Dorothy are spattered with remarks such as 'R. and H. routed me out this A.M. and we have spent the idlest of days', 'I have conversed and had meals with Richard and Bridgit [sic] and the Dryad', 'We've all dined with the Hamadryad's she-poet [Gregg, who had returned to London with Wilkinson]' and 'I play tennis with Ford in the afternoons and dine with Richard and the Dryad.'[22] (Whereas for Aldington, H.D. was 'Astraea', the celestial virgin, to Pound she had always been a tree nymph: this probably says more about the two men – and their personal perceptions of H.D. – than about H.D. herself.)

Patmore writes in her memoir of an occasion that summer when she, the novelist Rachel Annand Taylor, H.D. and Aldington spent a few days together in Rye. Aldington stayed at The Mermaid while the others took rooms nearby. Taylor

10 Church Walk

was a semi-invalid and insisted that the others took walks without her, so one day they walked to Winchelsea. In the church Aldington picked up a bible, opened it randomly and started to read aloud the story of the calculated rape of Tamar by her half-brother, Amnon;[23] H.D. was shocked by the brutality of the story, particularly at the description of the hatred Amnon felt towards Tamar after he had raped her. Patmore characteristically remarks: 'She and Richard . . . seemed to see an appalling truth, perhaps a horrible fascination in this phrase, which to my simple and savage knowledge of love – that imperial greatness – was just an expression of the barbarous inhabitants of a strange land.'[24]

However, the focus of Aldington's and H.D.'s lives was their writing, under the supervision of Pound; 'Richard has just brought me a bad poem and departed with dampened spirits', writes Pound to Shakespear in early September.[25] And so the Imagist movement was born – out of the poetic experiments of Aldington and H.D. and Pound's twofold ambition: to promote himself and, more laudably, to bring about a renewal of British poetic form. The immediate impetus was also twofold: an invitation from Harriet Monroe, the editor of the new Chicago journal, *Poetry: a magazine of verse*; and the enigmatic conclusion Pound provided to the preface to *Ripostes*, his new collection of poems.

Born in 1860 in Chicago, Monroe was a freelance journalist and poet who had been introduced to Pound and his work (by May Sinclair) when she came to London in 1910 on her way to visit her sister in China. On her return home, she determined (like Harold Monro in England) to found a monthly journal dedicated to publishing and promoting the best new verse, and she set about finding a hundred subscribers willing to donate fifty dollars a year for five years. The first issue of *Poetry* appeared in October 1912. Pound accepted with alacrity Monroe's invitation to become the journal's (unpaid) 'foreign correspondent', although awkwardly aware that the time he had spent in recent months on his account of his troubadour travels – a book that was shortly to be abandoned – and on his new volume of verse, *Ripostes* (itself 'scarcely more than a notice that my translations and experiments have not entirely interrupted my compositions'),[26] meant that he had very little of his own writing to give her. However he sent two contributions for the first issue, telling her that one of them, the poem 'Middle-Age', was 'an over-elaborate post Browning "Imagiste" affair'. This is his first known use of the term and it seems strange to us to find 'over-elaborate' and 'Imagiste' occurring in the same sentence. At this stage he seems to have taken up the term without any precise idea of what he meant by it.

His first *published* use of it was in *Ripostes* in October 1912. Appended to this volume of his poems were 'The Complete Poetical Works of T.E. Hulme' (five short poems) along with a 'Prefatory Note' which grudgingly acknowledged the groundwork for change in poetic form laid down by Hulme's Tour Eiffel group ('certain evenings and meetings of two years gone, dull enough at the time, but rather pleasant to look back upon') but questioned whether they could be said to have constituted a 'School of Images'. In any case, the preface continues, even if such a school did exist, 'its principles were not so interesting as those of the "inherent dynamists" or of *Les Unanimistes*.'[27] Pound appears to have been fairly ignorant of these tendencies in contemporary French poetry until reading Flint's comprehensive survey of them in the August 1912 issue of *Poetry Review*, so his conversion had been a rapid one. (By 18 August he was telling Monroe, 'you must keep an eye on Paris'.)[28] He saw that the French 'schools' offered him a way forward and his preface concludes mysteriously: 'As for the future, *Les Imagistes*, the descendants of the forgotten school of 1909, have that in their keeping.' By this stage Imagism is clearly a 'movement' but who were the 'Imagistes'?

Aldington supplies the answer: himself and H.D.: 'My own belief is that the name took Ezra's fancy, and that he kept it *in petto* for the right occasion. If there were no Imagists, obviously they would have to be invented. Whenever Ezra has launched a new movement . . . he has never had any difficulty about finding members. He has just called on his friends.'[29] Pound sent Monroe three of Aldington's poems ('Choricos', 'To a Greek Marble' and 'Au Vieux Jardin' – what Aldington refers to in his memoir as his 'first free verse poems'), which appeared in the second issue of *Poetry* in November with the following note: 'Mr Richard Aldington is a young English poet, one of the "Imagistes", a group of ardent Hellenists who are pursuing interesting experiments in *vers libre*; trying to attain in English certain subtleties and cadences of the kind that Mallarmé and his followers have studied in France'. The journal's 'foreign correspondent' was furious: Aldington and H.D. might be 'ardent Hellenists' but neither Hellenism nor even *vers libre* were the central planks of his new 'mouvemong' (as Aldington, in affectionate mockery of Pound's pretentiousness, would call it). 'Imagisme is concerned solely with language and presentation. Hellenism & vers libre have nothing to do with it', Pound insisted.[30]

Aldington and H.D. first discovered that they were 'Imagistes' in late September when they met up with a Pound energised by the drafts of some poems that H.D. had given him.[31] As so often with this group of friends, the historic meeting took place in a teashop. H.D. recalled it as having been at the British Museum, Aldington in Kensington; since both were regular venues, the confusion is understandable.[32] However, the vividness of H.D.'s account of what happened that day seems all the more remarkable when we realise that it was written forty-six years later: ' "But Dryad, . . . this is poetry." He slashed with a pencil. "Cut this out, shorten this line. 'Hermes of the Ways' is a good title. I'll send this to Harriet Monroe of *Poetry*. Have you a copy? Yes? Then we can send this, or I'll type it when I get back. Will this do?" And he scrawled "H.D. Imagiste" at the bottom of the page.'[33] The ambivalence of H.D.'s feelings towards Pound is apparent here: the 'slashing' and 'scrawling' project his power and her vulnerability, but we can also sense her reliance on him and her pleasure at his praise.

Her mentor wrote enthusiastically to Monroe: 'I've had luck again, and am sending you some *modern* stuff by an American. I say modern, for it is in the laconic speech of the Imagistes, even if the subject is classic. . . . This is the sort of American stuff that I can show here and in Paris without its being ridiculed. Objective – no slither; direct – no excessive use of adjectives, no metaphors that won't permit examination.'[34] Clearly, Imagism – or *Imagisme* – was starting to reach a definitive state in Pound's thinking. H.D's 'Verses, Translations and Reflections from "The [Greek] Anthology"' appeared in the January 1913 issue of *Poetry*, and Monroe's note (presumably vetted this time by Pound) read: ' "H.D. Imagiste" is an American lady resident abroad whose identity is unknown to the editor. Her sketches from the Greek are not offered as exact translations, or in any sense as finalities, but as experiments in delicate and elusive cadences, which attain sometimes a haunting beauty'.[35] In the same issue, Pound's 'Status Rerum' from London declared that: 'The youngest school here that has the nerve to call itself a school is that of the *Imagistes*. . . . One of their watchwords is Precision'.[36]

1913 would be an important year for the development of the Imagist movement and the refinement of its principles, but we shall return to these subjects in the next chapter. Meanwhile, another ripple troubled the surface of the developing relationship of Aldington and H.D. Professor and Mrs Doolittle were about to undertake their projected retirement tour of Europe, expected their daughter to join them and intended, on its completion, to take her home with them. Pound wrote to Shakespear in late September 1912: 'The Dryad is much depressed at the prospect of returning to its parental bosom.'[37]

H.D. met up with her parents in Genoa on 14 October 1912, along with her girlhood friend and neighbour Margaret Snively and Snively's father. The Reverend Snively was on his way to take up a permanent post at the Episcopalian church in Nice and he and his daughter would spend several weeks with the Doolittles in Florence before departing in early December. According to Aldington's memoir, it was only when he received a postcard from H.D. showing a hillside of blossoming almond trees and bearing the words, 'These will be full out in a few weeks', that he decided to join her. Monroe's payment of forty dollars for the poems printed in *Poetry* fortuitously arrived in the same postal delivery. He was still in receipt of his allowance from his parents and he managed to persuade Orage to commission from him a series of paid articles on Italy for *The New Age*.[38]

The Doolittles had moved on to Rome by early December and, giving up yet another part-time job and his room in Church Walk, Aldington arrived there on the nineteenth to spend eight weeks in lodgings in the Via Sestina near the Spanish Steps. He would spend the majority of his time escorting H.D., sometimes with her mother, around the cultural attractions of the capital. To judge by his *New Age* articles, he found Rome a mixed experience, with 'columns in the Greek manner, fragments of Imperial palaces, mediaeval campanili, early, middle and late Renaissance architecture mixed up with the sordid little toy houses produced by our Great Commercial Civilisation.' He was repelled by the 'gaudy marbles of San Pietro and all the baroque ornaments of the late Renaissance', and not unaware of a mood of militarism and of heart-rending poverty, but he wrote lyrically of his visits to the Alban Hills, clearly more moved by natural beauty than by urban settings.[39]

The tone of his *New Age* articles, which ran weekly from 13 February to 10 July, is that of a 20-year-old aspiring to be cosmopolitan, witty and knowing. The writing has some of the arrogance of Pound's journalism (Helen Carr compares it to contemporary 'ego-journalism') but without the latter's comprehensive lack of self-doubt.[40] The depth of Aldington's learning is apparent but his eagerness to demonstrate it hints at his awareness of its limits. He is honest enough to admit this: 'I have only my taste to guide me; I am neither a sculptor not a painter. I know hardly anything of the technique of these arts – scarcely more than Pater, and certainly less than Hazlitt . . . and for the first time in my life I feel almost diffident about dogmatising.'[41] Nevertheless he *does* 'dogmatise': 'And in spite of Mr Shaw, who thinks that because he is virtuous there shall be no more cakes and ale, we still dream of the city walled with jasper, where folk, like the ancient Greeks, are more concerned with beauty and the beautiful appearance of things, than any system or work of ethics and conduct.'[42] It is a curious mixture of the opinionated and the innocent; but it is this search for the Hellenic ideal, along with a love of natural beauty, that informs the writing whenever he finds the confidence to be serious: 'But if I write more upon the arts in Naples, I will tell of the exquisite Greek bronzes and marble reliefs and statues, which are worth travelling any distance, and enduring an eternity of Tramontane [north wind],' and this at Pompeii: 'You sit down on a broken mossy wall; the lizards jerk through the sparse herbs or bask motionless on the grey stones, and for a few moments, in the silence, you know something of the peace that passes all understanding.[43] Across the bay the wonderful blue hills rise and fall towards Sorrento, the sea hardly ripples in the still air, and a faint cloud of steam drifts from the cone of Vesuvius. What a city!' Yet he can't refrain from the misanthropic conclusion: 'Thank God it is uninhabited!'[44]

The Doolittles left Rome for Naples on 12 February and Aldington followed two days later, but when the Doolittle parents moved on to Venice on 6 March, the diary reveals that Aldington and H.D. travelled together on a later train. Clearly their wish to be together was being accommodated. At the very start of their acquaintance, he seems to have endeared himself to Hilda's mother by escorting her to an American embassy tea-party when her rebellious daughter refused to accompany her.[45] Mrs Doolittle kept a diary of their tour and, although it is chiefly devoted to details of places visited and activities undertaken, its language, as Caroline Zilboorg point out, is often a clue to the dynamics of the relationships.[46] Her first mention of Aldington is on 20 December when: 'Hilda [is] out with R.A.' but by 24 December he has become 'Richard', while her observation on 18 December that 'Hilda was feeling particularly well' shows a mother's intuitiveness. Represented by H.D. on his arrival in Rome as merely a journalist friend of Ezra and herself who was in Italy on an assignment, he gradually won over the Doolittle parents with his adaptability and cheerfulness – and his ability to make their daughter happy. Steeped in reading about Italy from the days of Dudley Grey's teaching onwards and possessing a deep appreciation of beauty, he must also have been a helpful guide.

However, the novelist Phyllis Bottome, an acquaintance of Pound's who met the group in Rome, presents a different view, referring in her memoir to the young couple's 'unkind treatment of H.D.'s simple and kindly parents'.[47] Perhaps, like most young lovers, they were inclined to give parents the slip on occasion and even to mock their simplicity. Aldington constantly satirised the American tourist in his New Age articles. From Naples he wrote: 'Those sordid transpontines litter up the place, until it resembles (I am told) a cross between Atlantic City and Brighton', while of Pompeii he observed: 'There is no particular gain in rushing through like an American.' By the end of his visit he had become vitriolic towards 'Pittsburg and Middle West', whether 'ignorant and noisy, or ignorant, gauche and silent', and demanded why they 'pollute Italy with their commercial corpses'.[48]

In the Aldington archive of the Morris Library at Southern Illinois University lies the typescript of a poem Aldington never published. The bleakness of Naples in March is conveyed through what would soon be recognisably 'Imagist' methods, but the attempt to describe the scene at Pompeii lacks precision, despite the somewhat desperate use of colour epithets, and has none of the confidence and poise of the prose account quoted above. Already, reconciling Imagist principles with the need to convey emotion was proving difficult:

Today the wind is cold in Naples;
The rattling streets are gusty;
Beggars moan at every half-sunned corner;
The Mergellina chokes with driving dust —
And the alleys reek.

I wish we could lie here for days and days,
It is so good to lie on the short grass
And lean against the old house wall,
To watch the green-flanked lizards,
To hear a bee or two
Humming around the tiny stunted flowers.

It would be so good
To lie here under the blue sky,
Below the red-scented cone
With its whisp of white smoke
To remind us of death and the gods
For days and days and days
In the warmth and the silence.

It was the 'austere beauty' of the three Greek temples of Paestum (where Aldington spotted 'the American tourist bolting his lunch on the temple stairs'), their 'quiet superiority and augustness', along with the arrival of spring, which began to make the tour magical for both Aldington and H.D. The more serious tone and lyrical quality of his *New Age* articles from this point on are very marked, although he can't pass up the opportunity for a jibe at modernity: 'What part have we in this loveliness? We have built Balham and Manchester and the new law courts as our memorials — and here stand these perfect creations, abandoned and silent, with all the life that created them lost, but still such a delicate rebuke to our vulgarity.'[49] This part of the coast south of Naples had been settled by Greek colonists in the sixth century B.C. and from here, along the 'Amalfi Drive' from Vietri to Sorrento, Nature became 'Theocritus and Homer in form and colour.'[50] The Hellenists had come into their inheritance. Indeed, Capri, once they arrived there on 14 March, was for them the land of the Sirens, 'the country where Odysseus came' and, even more importantly, Theocritus's country, 'a miniature Sicily'.[51] They were working together on translations of Theocritus. 'To love the beauty of Italy', the *New Age* correspondent insisted, 'one must have known the deep passionate love for Greece.'[52] Even the flowers and trees, so evocatively described in the articles, were appreciated not simply for their natural beauty but for their symbolic associations: 'The white violet . . . gained a new mysterious beauty because it was the flower of Meleager . . . and a plane tree was not a botanical object, but the platanos, the broad, rustling foliage in whose shade Plato talked with Phaedrus of divine love.'[53] Of course, Aldington and H.D. were not the first to appreciate

the Hellenic inheritance of Italy; Aldington was steeped in the writings of John
Addington Symonds, Hellenist and historian of the Renaissance, even if he felt
it incumbent upon him to mock Symonds's 'somewhat Asiatic rhetoric' in his
New Age articles.[54]

The lacuna in Aldington's prose writing about his six months in Italy, whether
the *New Age* pieces and the twenty-one postcards he sent to his family or the
account years later in *Life for Life's Sake,* is his blossoming love affair with H.D.;
even the fact of her presence is elided. Only a handful of poems, the fictional
account in *All Men are Enemies* of Anthony Clarendon's stay on 'Aeaea' in 1914
with his lover, Katha, and Aldington's assertion, forty years later, that the spring
of 1913 was the happiest of his life, hint at their time together in Italy. The time
they spent on their own on Capri (what, according to H.D., Pound referred to as
their 'unofficial honeymoon'), was an idyll.[55] Only ten days after they all arrived
on the island the Professor and Mrs Doolittle left for Sicily; the young couple
were to have five weeks alone together in the peaceful village of Anacapri. H.D.'s
Autobiographical Notes record: 'C.L.D. [Professor Doolittle] leaves, mother joins
him in Sicily, I am alone, move from Paradiso to little room in top of house, in
garden, R.A. and work on Greek and walks. . . . ' We can assume that the 'little
room' to which she moved from the Hotel Paradiso was in the Pensione del
Lauro where Aldington was staying. Her parents could not have failed to be aware
of the nature of the relationship; their leaving the two of them alone together
suggests a remarkably liberal outlook. Perhaps they were pleased to see their
daughter so happy; and, after Gregg and Pound, this young Englishman must
have seemed pleasingly straightforward and trustworthy. Clearly his youth and
lack of income did not concern them. They must also have been very conscious
that the only future currently 'on the table' for their 26-year-old daughter was
to return home with them to a small-town life that had already made her listless
and unhappy.

We can guess at Aldington's own happiness by reading between the lines
of the *New Age* articles, of his 1924 essay, 'Theocritus in Capri', and even
of *Life for Life's Sake,* where he comments: 'It was wonderful, it was even – as
Rochefoucauld would have denied – *delicieux* to be young and alive in Italy in the
spring then'. 'In Anacapri time stood still between Monte Solaro and the blue
waves far below.'[56] As ever, H.D.'s fiction fills the gap: 'It was you who taught
me to love those things, Capri Nero, Capri Bianco, cigarettes, the pear trees
against Solaro were a mass of blossom and there were prickly pear and cactus.
The small goats scampered before us and there was that singular goat-herd (for
a long time we thought we'd dreamed it) piping under that one clump of cool
willows. Cool willows and below, so far below that one could for a breath have
flung oneself down, the sea.' Hermione continues with intimate recollections
of the playfulness of young lovers: 'So I turned to the sea. Do you remember? I
went first. You were heavier. You were surprised and I loved plaguing you. You
had only seen me in London and in Paris and you had no idea what I was like
really.'[57]

The Temple of Neptune at Paestum

While H.D. would use her fiction to replay both the joys and the agonies of her private life, Aldington would always be reticent. In the face of his mother's emotionalism and prurience, secrecy and evasion had become habits from his early years. As for his *New Age* articles, they were a serious professional commission for the young writer. However, there is one passing reference to his travelling companions – as 'two somnolent elders and a great artist'; the Doolittle parents would not have been flattered, unlike their daughter, who was probably shown the *New Age* pieces.[58]

Much more revealingly, in the archives of the Morris Library, amongst Aldington's notebooks of the period, is a folded slip of paper on which is a record of food bills paid at Anacapri (vino, spaghetti, coffee, butter, cheese, sardines . . .); on the reverse is a love letter:

> . . . You pretend to be modest, at another time voluptuously give me all delights. . . . Modesty remains at the edge of the bed (I think that's rather good). A girl should put off modesty with her clothes (another sound doctrine!); chaste with others, she should be wanton with me. . . . Have no kind of shame; often put your arms around my neck, Make my mouth tremble with your moist little lips, give me many kisses, give me many. Let them be quickened suddenly without any reason, or let them be kisses long held. . . . Then give me all the exquisite delights, all these happy caresses; I will give them to you. Let our bodies be joined with intertwined limbs: half-reclining, let side touch side. Touch lips; and cheeks; let naked breast beat on breast, and foot touch foot.

Monte Solaro

It is not a letter that was written to be *sent*; like much of the material in their notebooks at that time, it was written to be read and enjoyed together – along with the vino and the spaghetti and the sardines. Small wonder that when the time came, they were reluctant to leave Capri.

Meanwhile, both Pound and Dorothy Shakespear had arrived in Italy but there was to be no unofficial honeymoon for them. Dorothy and her mother, along with Dorothy's friend and cousin Georgie Hyde-Lees, had set off for Tivoli, via Paris and a dinner with Walter Rummel, at the end of March.[59] Pound had followed the same route a week later, deciding that he must get to Paris and meet some of the contemporary French poets whose work he was now lauding: Vildrac, Duhamel, Romains and Arcos. He also met two young American poets there, John Gould Fletcher and Skipwith Cannell, of whom we shall hear more. From Paris he travelled to his favourite Italian haunt, the little (and cheap) village of Sirmione on Lake Garda. 'I have been about a bit & I guess I know heaven when I arrive', he had written to his parents in 1910, the year he had discovered Sirmione.[60] In 1913 it must have been a bitter-sweet return: it was during his first sojourn there that Olivia and Dorothy had visited him and he and Dorothy had fallen in love. Subsequently, he had been forbidden to see or contact her and had returned to America to find work (without success), but had been back in Sirmione for June and July of 1911, en route for his second assault on London and the Shakespears. Now he was once more considered ineligible. Letters passed between Tivoli and Sirmione but a meeting was not permitted.

Pound's thoughts turned to H.D. and Aldington, with whom he planned to meet up in Venice. He told Dorothy: 'The pair of 'em, wholly Hellenized at Capri, are going to be very much [out] of place in bella Venezia.'[61] A week later he sent her an extraordinary poem:

Soul of a dog, un-hound, capriped,
I have seen you sniffing and snoozling about among my flowers,
So, ho! And at last they have tamed you.

Ut flosculus hyacinthus. . . .
What do you know of these things?
What *do* you know of horticulture?
But take it, I leave you the garden.

Come Auster, Come Apeliota,
And see the faun in our garden.
And if you but move or speak,
this thing will run at you
and scare itself to spasms.[62]

Feigning to be baffled, he asked Dorothy: 'Can you make head or tail of this damned thing. I *thought* I'd done a pome and *now* I'm hanged whether I can tell whether anything gets over the footlights.'[63] Dorothy's objective and mainly positive response shows her either failing to appreciate the autobiographical nature of the poem or (more likely) deciding that it was safer not to touch on it. She knew that 'Faun' was Pound's nickname for Aldington and would have been aware of the erotic aspects of the classical faun, particularly as Pound had taken the Shakespear ladies only weeks previously to see Nijinsky's sensual performance of *L'Après-Midi d'un Faune* in London. Nor could she have failed to understand who had now 'tamed' the faun and to whom Pound was referring as *his* 'flowers'. The poem bristles with sexual resentment, and 'But take it, I leave you the garden' suggests a gift (if H.D. *was* his to give) grudgingly bestowed. Maybe he had surprised himself by his animosity, because on 3 May he told Dorothy, 'Go ahead and see if you can diagnose it.'[64]

Clearly Pound was curious and could not keep away. He was in Venice by 2 May, writing to Dorothy the following day: 'R. and H. seem to be falling in love with each other somewhere en route from Napoli. I suppose I'll have to be ready with a pontifical sanction & then try to soothe their respective progenitors.' He had to wait to perform this role: leaving Capri at the end of April, H.D. and Aldington had spent a night in Naples and then gone on to Florence, rather than coming directly to Venice where H.D.'s parents were awaiting their arrival. Pound therefore found the Doolittles alone – and lonely. They had been in Venice since 17 April, having left Sicily on 25 March and travelled via Rome and Bologna. 'I found the dryad's family disconsolate on the piazza yesterday afternoon & spent the evening consoling them for the absence of their offspring', Pound wrote to Dorothy on 5 May.[65] He spent the next evening with them too. The free dinners were probably welcome, but they must have seemed a bizarre little group: the quiet and dignified elderly couple and the flamboyant young man whom they had rejected as a suitor for their daughter. (It was while they were in Venice that Mrs Doolittle would tell H.D. that during her absence from home, her father had burnt all her letters from Pound.)

Walter Rummel

The errant couple may have made Aldington's need to visit Florence for his work their excuse: he had only seen the city briefly on his journey to Rome in December, and his final two articles for *The New Age* were indeed devoted to Florence and its art treasures. However, they must also have wanted to extend their 'unofficial honeymoon'. H.D. certainly recalled their late arrival in Venice as an act of defiance: 'Early spring in Capri; mother goes to Sicily. I meet them in Venice, after trip up with R.; we stayed longer than they expected. Ezra is here; general feeling of disapproval', and: 'Rebellion, stay on in Florence, go Venice, cheap third class.'[66]

Pound was able to satisfy his curiosity on 7 May: 'The Dryad has arrived with its faun. She doesn't seem much more in love with it than when she left London, but her family distresses her & seems to drive her more fawn-wards.'[67] Given the acceptance that the Doolittles had so far shown of Aldington's relationship with their daughter, it seems an odd conclusion and perhaps the result of wishful thinking; he was certainly amending his position two days later: 'H and R are submerged in a Hellenism so polubendius and so stupid that I drop in the street about once in every 15 minutes to laugh at them . . . I don't know – Hellenism? True, they have attained a dullness almost equal to the expression *(facial)* of gk. statuary – but I wonder – I think they *must* be in love.'[68] On the evening of 8 May he held a gondola party for them all. Professor Doolittle did not participate; perhaps an evening on the water was not good for his health. His wife recorded the occasion in her diary: ' . . . in and out the various canals – light wonderful! Hilda and Richard in one, Ezra and I in the other. Back 11.30.'[69] Aldington wrote a love poem:

> Like a gondola of green scented fruits
> Drifting along the dark canals of Venice,
> You, O exquisite one,
> Have entered into my desolate city.

Professor Doolittle left for the U.S.A. on 15 May and Pound set off for home; he was back in London by the end of the month, as were the Shakespears. In early June Aldington, H.D. and her mother left Venice and moved on to Verona, and then to Sirmione, where they stayed for two-and-a-half weeks (in Pound's own, aptly named, Hotel Eden), Aldington frequently taking Mrs Doolittle rowing on the lake. On 22 June they left Sirmione, H.D and her mother to meet up once more with Professor Doolittle in Verona, Aldington on his way to Paris. Two weeks later, H.D. left her parents in the Alps, on their way to Switzerland, Austria and Germany, and joined him in Paris – in time for his twenty-first birthday on 8 July.

They remained in Paris until the end of the month. It was a replay of their spring 1912 trip. They also enjoyed the company of Henry Slonimsky, a young Polish-American philosopher, who had been at Pennsylvania University with Pound and who had just completed his doctorate on Heraclitus and Parmenides at the University of Marburg in Germany. Aldington had met him at one of Hulme's Tuesday evenings at Frith Street and both he and H.D. found him inspiring, particularly for the clarity and enthusiasm with which he expounded on Hellenic philosophy. Slonimsky would remain a friend for the rest of Aldington's life and he would write to the philosopher in 1939: 'Things base and petty wither when you are near. The strange thing is that you are quite unaware of your own grandeur.'[70] We might here remark the contrast with Pound's personality, and in *Life for Life's Sake* Aldington tells us that, 'Ezra never appreciated Slonimski [*sic*], because Ezra never listened to him.' He continues: 'But H.D., with her swift and unerring response to whatever is beautiful and lofty, at once comprehended his greatness and his charm.' Clearly Slonimsky's presence was one of the delights of this trip: 'What evenings we spent listening to him in Paris! *Noctes Atticae*. On a bench under the trees in the Petit Luxembourg, away from the noise and glare of the cafés, we would sit for hours while he talked to us of Hellas and Hellenism, of Pythagoras and Plato – "a kingly man" – of Empedocles and Heraclitus, of Homer and Thucydides, of Aeschylus and Theocritus. We knew just enough to understand, to be moved by the beauty and grandeur of what he set before us.'[71]

By the beginning of August 1913 the two young poets were back in London, in lodgings in Church Walk (this time at number 8) with their mentor, and the work of the 'mouvemong' proceeded apace. It was interrupted on 4 September by the arrival in London of Professor and Mrs Doolittle, in time for yet another celebration, H.D.'s twenty-seventh birthday on the tenth. Professor Doolittle had become ill, however, and once he started to recover a doctor advised recuperation on the south coast. The couple went to Bournemouth where they were visited on 19 September by their daughter and her lover: 'Eventful day. Richard and Hilda came today to talk about the future. – Such a lovely time & I am happy for them both!' wrote Mrs Doolittle in her diary. By the end of the month she was back in London, 'to get Hilda's things together' – presumably her trousseau.

The couple were married on 18 October at the Kensington Registry Office. Pound and H.D.'s parents were the only others present. When Aldington's own family were informed of the marriage we do not know. An obvious absentee was Patmore; she was ill in hospital. Mystery surrounds this 'illness'. Violet Hunt speaks of visiting Patmore in a nursing home after 'she had had a terrible operation'.[72] H.D. and Aldington always believed this to have been an abortion. Pound, in characteristic fashion, wrote to his mother: 'Brigit Patmore is very ill but they have decided to let her live, which is a mercy as there are none too many charming people on the planet.'[73]

4. 'Les Jeunes': Creativity and Carnival, 1913-1914

The spring of 1914 was the most beautiful and brilliant spring London was ever to know — the last miraculous moment before a great rose drops.
(Phyllis Bottome, *The Challenge*, 1952)[1]

Shortly after the wedding and her parents' departure for the United States, H.D. wrote cheerfully to Isabel Pound: 'We want to live in Paris but we will stay here for a few months.'[2] She could not know that events would overtake their excited plans for their future. Meanwhile, they moved into a small flat not far from Church Walk, at 8 Holland Place Chambers.

During their eight-month absence the founder of Imagism had been busy, no doubt Olivia Shakespear's ploy of keeping her daughter out of town as much as possible continuing to allow him time for his projects. Not that his social calendar was empty. In letters to his parents that summer he speaks of playing tennis with Hueffer 'more or less every day', attending 'a terribly litterary [*sic*] dinner', watching cricket at Lords, attending a concert of Walter Rummel's and the Russian ballet, staying with Frederic Manning at the Brasted cottage of the American literary hostess, Eva Fowler, and attending a garden party at South Lodge.[3] 'The Hueffers have had a garden party with everyone one has ever met,' he wrote in early July.[4] In fact the guest list on 1 July was part of an attempt on Hunt's part to enlist support for her liaison with Hueffer. Drummed out of the country in the spring after his wife had fought a successful libel case against the pair, they had decided to return to London and face down public disapproval. (Sadly for Hunt, Hueffer spent most of that summer falling in love with Patmore, who was their guest — and acting as Hueffer's secretary — at their country retreat, Knap Cottage at Selsey in Sussex.)

Nevertheless Pound had been busy. 'The rest of my activities you can follow fairly well in print', he told his mother.[5] His first project had been to set out his Imagist manifesto, which appeared in the March 1913 issue of *Poetry* in the form of an article by Flint and Pound's 'A Few Don'ts by an Imagiste', a 'few' amounting to around twenty, if we include the 'dos' as well as the 'don'ts'.[6] The most emphatic are those which relate to language: 'Go in fear of abstractions. Use no superfluous word, no adjective, which does not reveal something.'[7] But there are also strictures on prosody: 'Don't chop your stuff up into separate *iambs*. Don't make each line stop dead at the end, and then begin every next line with a heave. . . . A rhyme must have in it some element of surprise . . . it must be well used if used at all.'[8] Flint's article contained the three Imagist 'rules':

1. Direct treatment of the 'thing' whether subjective or objective.
2. To use absolutely no word that did not contribute to the presentation
3. As regarding rhythm: to compose in sequence of the musical phrase, not in sequence of a metronome.[9]

Surprisingly, there is no specific reference here to the image; in fact, Pound tells his readers that, while the Imagists also held 'a certain "Doctrine of the Image"', this 'did not concern the public.' Presumably, he had not yet thought through this aspect of the project. However, he does state that:

An 'Image' is that which presents an intellectual and emotional complex in an instant of time. I use the term 'complex' rather in the technical sense employed by the newer psychologists, such as Hart, though we might not agree absolutely in our application.

It is the presentation of such a 'complex' instantaneously which gives that sense of sudden liberation; that sense of freedom from time limits and space limits; that sense of sudden growth, which we experience in the presence of the greatest works of art.[10]

His main objective now was the compiling of an Imagist anthology to rival the Georgian one. *Georgian Poetry 1911-1912* was published by Harold Monro at the Poetry Bookshop in December 1912 and edited by Edward Marsh, patron of the arts, Private Secretary to Winston Churchill and friend of Rupert Brooke. It was by the summer of 1913 already in its sixth edition. He realised that four poets (himself, Aldington, H.D. and Flint)[11] do not an anthology make; the Georgian one had seventeen. He set about finding other eligible contributors. There were three more Americans to hand: one was his friend William Carlos Williams, whose poetic development he had been overseeing at a distance since he first came to London;[12] then there were Fletcher and Cannell, whom he had met in Paris earlier in the year and who were now in London.[13]

Amongst the English poets the choice of Allen Upward, 50-year-old lawyer, novelist and amateur anthropologist, reflected Pound's new interest in oriental poetry; Upward's 'Scented Leaves – from a Chinese Jar' appeared in the September issue of *Poetry* and nine of these prose poems would go into the anthology. Pound could, of course, call on his tennis partner for a poem; Hueffer contributed the only long (and rhymed) poem in the collection. Meanwhile, Yeats had brought to Pound's notice a needy young expatriate Irish writer; he showed the would-be impresario James Joyce's 1907 collection, *Chamber Music*, and Pound decided to make use of one poem.[14]

The remaining two contributors, both Americans, would become close friends of Aldington and H.D. and exert an enormous influence over their lives for the next few years. John Cournos they had probably met before going to Italy, either when

Holland Place Chambers

he had come to interview Pound for his newspaper or through Slonimsky, a mutual friend.[15] Like H.D., Cournos was a Philadelphian, but his social background was very different. A Russian Jew, he had fled from the Ukraine to the U.S.A. with his mother, step-father and five siblings when he was ten years old; he had endured a life of grinding poverty and left school at fourteen in order to support the family. Working in a newspaper office, he had gradually managed to climb up the ranks and by 1912, when he came to Europe, was the art critic on the *Philadelphian Record*.

In contrast, Amy Lowell was a member of an extremely distinguished and wealthy Boston family; one of her brothers was an astronomer, and founder of the

Lowell Observatory, the other the President of Harvard. Much the youngest of five children, she had grown up lonely and self-conscious about her overweight frame, but she had recently formed a fulfilling relationship with the actress Ada Russell, a partnership which would last for the rest of her life. Lowell's first collection of verse, *A Dome of Many Coloured Glass*, was published in Boston in October 1912. It is what Helen Carr refers to as 'cautiously conventional' verse.[16]

In January 1913 Lowell read H.D.'s poems in *Poetry*, followed in March by the Flint/Pound Imagism articles. She was determined to meet these poets, and set sail for London, with a letter of introduction from Monroe. She arrived in late July when Aldington and H.D. were still in Paris; they would not make her acquaintance until the summer of 1914. Pound went to meet her in her luxurious suite at the Berkeley Hotel, writing to Dorothy (in Yorkshire), 'I've had fat dinners with Miss Lowell and launched her on Ford and the Eagle [Yeats].'[17] He told his mother, 'Miss Lowell gives me hopes for the future of America. She says her brother is as intelligent [*sic*] as she is so there may even be some hope for Harvard.'[18] Clearly – for now – these two eccentric and forceful individuals were getting on well. Pound is unlikely to have been impressed with Lowell's published verse, or even with the two poems that would appear (along with Flint's 'Four Poems in Unrhymed Cadence') in *Poetry* in July, but he did accept for the anthology the sensuous love poem, 'In a Garden'.

And so the battle-lines were drawn up for 'les jeunes' to mount their attack on the verse tradition. Well, almost. At the last minute, Fletcher, who had been introduced to Lowell during her visit and had also got on with her very well, decided that he did not want to be an Imagist. Moreover, he tried to make trouble. He wrote to Lowell, now back in America, advising her to stay away from the Imagist anthology, telling her that the 'real' editor was Aldington, which is why he was to have so many poems in it (ten, as opposed to H.D.'s and Pound's six each and Flint's five) and would use everyone else's weakest work, so that his own would 'shine by comparison.' 'If Aldington were really any good as a poet, he added, 'I would not care. But I hate to see a rigged-up game being played on the public to boom a silly cub who deserves nothing but a licking.'[19]

The lengthy letter contains more than a whiff of paranoia. The son of a wealthy Arkansas businessman, Fletcher had had a sheltered childhood and was reclusive and prone to depression; in 1950 he would take his own life. His relationships tended to be volatile, those with Pound and Lowell in particular. He would soon change his mind about Aldington and develop cordial relations with him and H.D., but for now he refused to be included in the anthology. His memoir includes a vivid portrait of the Aldingtons at this time: 'They were, it seemed to me, an oddly assorted couple, providing a complete contrast. While H.D. was tall, slim, lithe, with a pale oval face framed in masses of dark hair, and a nervous shyness of manner that only emphasised her fragility, Aldington was bluff, heavy and robust, with the square shoulders of an athlete, the bullet head of a guardsman, and a general tendency to beefiness which proclaimed his British quality. He was, I judged, extremely young, possibly a few years younger than H.D., and I had read nothing of his except a few poems, which, in their somewhat playful and faunlike imagism, were obviously derivable from hers.'[20] Frances (Gregg) Wilkinson, now back in the U.S.A., would undoubtedly have concurred with these descriptions.

There was one other young writer whom Pound might have chosen for his anthology, but who would join the Imagist ranks a year later and have an even more significant impact on the lives of the Aldingtons. For now, Pound had his reservations about his work. Pound had met D.H. Lawrence in 1909 through Hunt and Hueffer (who had just printed some Lawrence poems in *The English Review*). Since then *The White Peacock*, *The Trespasser* and *Sons and Lovers* had been published, but Lawrence had been living on the continent since May 1912 after eloping with Frieda Weekley. Pound sent Monroe some of Lawrence's poems in September, telling her: 'Lawrence, as you know, gives

John Cournos, 1924

me no particular pleasure. Nevertheless we are lucky to get him. Hueffer, as you know, thinks highly of him. I *recognise* certain qualities of his work. . . . As a prose writer I grant him first place among the younger men.'[21] But he was anxious that Monroe would not give preference to the Lawrence poems over Fletcher's, which he had sent her in August. (She did not: Fletcher's poems appeared in December and Lawrence's in January 1914.)

In August Pound told Monroe: 'I'm sending you our left-wing *The Freewoman*. I've taken charge of the literature dept.'[22] His most driving ambition had been to find a journal in England to do for him and for Imagism what *Poetry* was doing in America. He was always on the look-out for a wealthy sponsor to enable him to set up his own journal, but this was the next best thing. Its full title was *The New Freewoman*. Dora Marsden, a former school-teacher and militant feminist, had left the Women's Social and Political Union (and subsequently the Women's Freedom League) in order to found a weekly journal, *The Freewoman*.[23] The periodical was committed to more than women's suffrage, dealing with the wider issues of their economic, sexual and reproductive rights, and it had adopted a progressive stance on marriage, sexuality and sexual orientation. Attracting much controversy, it had been forced to close in October 1912, after an eleven-month run, because of the bankruptcy of its publisher and because W.H. Smith refused to distribute it any longer.

However, another determined and remarkable woman had provided the bulk of the funds, and raised the rest, to enable the journal to be revived. Where Marsden was a fiery individualist, Harriet Shaw Weaver was a quiet but committed socialist and humanitarian; but she admired and believed in Marsden, and Weaver's organisational ability became crucial to the realisation of Marsden's vision.[24] *The New Freewoman* began fortnightly publication on 15 June 1913. Marsden's agenda had become philosophical and individualist rather than political and feminist and was influenced by her reading of *The Ego and Its Own* by the nineteenth-century German philosopher, Max Stirner.[25] She wrote in the first issue: 'Having no Cause, we have no sacred ground, and no individual interpretations of life will be debarred beforehand. In the clash of opinions we shall expect to find our values.' It was this variety of opinions that her assistant editor, the 20-year-old Rebecca West, was keen to see the new journal encourage, in particular through literary and artistic contributions.[26] West was a friend of Hueffer and Hunt and through them had met Pound that summer. On her advice, Marsden approached him to see if he was interested in becoming a literary editor for the journal. Pound leapt at the opportunity, persuading Fletcher to provide the funds which would enable him to pay his contributors – although he and Fletcher would soon fall out and the funding would be withdrawn; contributors to the journal (and to its successor, *The Egoist*) never would be paid.

Pound launched his pages in the fifth issue in August with an article on Imagism. Though signed by West, it was actually a summary of the key points from Flint's and Pound's essays in the March issue of *Poetry* and was followed by seven Pound poems. Arriving back in England, H.D. and Aldington were delighted to hear that her 'Sitalkis' and his 'To Atthis' would appear in the next issue, along with poems by Flint, Lowell, Cannell and Williams, and that six more Aldington poems would appear in the subsequent issue. But Pound had bigger plans for Aldington. In October West resigned, partly because she was losing sympathy with Marsden's idealistic individualism, finding herself more in tune with the practical socialism of *The Clarion*, for which she was also writing. Pound persuaded Marsden to appoint Aldington as West's successor. By January 1914 the logic of Marsden's philosophy brought about another name-change and *The New Freewoman* became *The Egoist*; six months later Marsden herself surrendered the role of editor to Weaver, and became simply a 'contributing editor', allowing her to retire from London and concentrate on the long, dense philosophical articles with which the journal almost invariably opened. Meanwhile, Pound 'turned the N.F. over to Richard', although he would continue to write for it (under a range of *noms de plume* as well as in his own name), and directed his energies elsewhere.[27]

Aldington's first journalistic contributions were two satirical pieces ('Un dialogue dirisoire' and 'Un monologue dirisoire') in the two October issues, displaying the same contempt for the British middle class and its values that he had expressed towards its American counterpart in his *New Age* articles earlier in the year. More disturbingly, there is a marked strain of misogyny: he remarks that 'the English write from the desire for imaginary women, their own being too repellent', and that 'the most unpleasant, discourteous and ignorant animal in the world is a middle-aged, middle, middle-class English woman.'[28] We know enough of Aldington's family background to understand the origin of these attitudes, but regular readers of *The New Freewoman* must have been, at the least, disconcerted by their virulence. He was more perceptive – and more relaxed and tolerant – when he turned his hand to reviewing, which he would do regularly.

The most important roles *The Egoist* played on the pre-war and wartime literary scene, apart from promoting Imagism and the poets connected with it, were in serialising key modernist novels (first *Portrait of the Artist as a Young Man*, then Wyndham Lewis's *Tarr* and, finally, *Ulysses*); in promulgating contemporary French writing; and in flying the flag for classical literature. Pound was responsible for the first of these functions. (In the case of Joyce, Weaver would carry on Pound's work by giving Joyce financial support for the next twenty-five years and by publishing both of the novels through The Egoist Press.) It was Aldington, however, who was chiefly responsible for the journal's focus on contemporary French poetry and on classical writers. Where the former was concerned, Pound still had the enthusiasm of the late convert and ran a series of articles on the French poetic scene in *The New Age* from early September until mid-October (one of the reasons for Fletcher's fury with him, since he drew on books that Fletcher had lent him, but without acknowledging the debt); but it was the appearance of French poetry and of reviews by Aldington and others in *The Egoist* that maintained the momentum of critical attention. More modest than Pound, Aldington also publicly acknowledged his indebtedness to Fletcher and to Flint.

In particular, he became an enthusiast for the work of Remy de Gourmont, whose *Horses of Diomedes* Pound had started to serialise in *The New Freewoman* in August.[29] Gourmont's appeal for Aldington, who would continue to translate his work over the next twenty years, is summed up by comments he wrote after the war (and three and a half years after Gourmont's death): 'Remy de Gourmont meant to us the type of the artist – the man who lives purely to create the work of art and to whom nothing else is of essential importance. . . . He came to care chiefly for truth, sought always to express precisely what things, events, experience, imaginations meant to him.' Two qualities that Aldington particularly prized in Gourmont were his hatred of 'cant' and his tireless search for 'what the Greeks meant by the word "sophrosyne".'[30]

For Aldington's prime passion remained the Hellenic world view – or, rather, what he perceived that view to be. In an article entitled 'Anti-Hellenism' in the second issue of *The Egoist* he wrote: 'Now it is very good to be fond of Egyptian things, and fond of Indian things, and intrigued with Buddhism, and amorous of China – Chinese art is delightful – but I do not see why new fashions in artistic creeds should compel us to say that simple and happy and healthy works of art are entirely bad.' That this is partly a riposte to Pound, who had moved on from his 1912 admiration for the Indian poet Rabindrinath Tagore to an absorption in Chinese poetry and an enthusiasm for contemporary art, is clear from what follows: ' . . . though I admit, as I have admitted before, the great value of, say, the sculpture of Mr Epstein and the painting of M. Picasso and the latest poems of Mr Pound and even the works of Signor Severini, M. Barzun and so on, I find that there is still a strange allure about the ordinary uninteresting things which the Greeks loved – health and beauty and youth in the midst of friends.'[31]

As if to prove the point, nine short Aldington parodies of Pound, entitled 'Xenophilometropolitania' followed this article. Pound took it in good humour, writing to his father, who had expressed some concern about this betrayal: 'Do not bark, scratch or bite. . . . No-one whom I hadn't had under my own jurisdiction could have done the job so well. They attest a definite manner and do not in the least affect one's enjoyment of the originals. I was delighted with them.'[32]

Aldington may not have been an iconoclast, but under his assistant editorship the literary pages of *The Egoist* championed the kind of poetry which was both original in style and subject matter and not universally popular. Harold Monro did likewise; as a result, the Poetry Society had claimed back the *Poetry Review* at the close of 1912 and placed it under the conservative editorship of the poet Stephen Phillips. Monro had launched the quarterly *Poetry and Drama* as its successor, while his Poetry Bookshop, a publisher as well as promoter and retailer of new poetry, was formally opened at 35 Devonshire Street in January 1913. Across the Atlantic, Harriet Monroe's choices of poet frequently exasperated the irascible Pound, but in March 1914 the 21-year-old Chicago journalist Margaret Anderson launched *The Little Review* dedicated to publishing experimental writing and publicising international art.

Generally, however, poetry remained, as J.B. Harmer reminds us, 'seriously dislocated from living speech': 'The strenuous modernism of the continent was not easily acclimatised in Britain and America. . . . Too often the form was mechanical; diction archaic; content varied between clichés and the journalistic immediacy of such writers as William Watson and Henry Newbolt.'[33] The circulation of the 'little' journals was small, even in these years before the war pushed artistic battles into the background.[34] Pound might rail against poetry which was 'merely a spreading of Keatsian decoration over different but similar surfaces' but popular taste did not change.[35] In such a market-place the 'mouvemong' had to make a clamour to be heard.

In the first half of 1914 the Imagists staged three events that set out the battle lines of the movement. The importance which they attached to the first of these, a rather minor affair, is a clue to their strategy, or, more accurately, to *Pound*'s strategy. He formed a committee onto which he was careful to draft not only Aldington and Flint, but also Yeats and his friends Victor Plarr and Thomas Sturge Moore, members and associates of the former Rhymers Club, as well as his own friend, Frederic Manning, and, perhaps surprisingly, John Masefield, 'Georgian' poet and author of the 1911 popular success, *The Everlasting Mercy*.[36] In fact, Pound would tell readers of *Poetry*, there were more poets whom he would have invited had they been available: Lawrence (in Italy), Padraic Colum (in Ireland), Joyce (in Austria) and Brooke ('somewhere in the Pacific').[37] The purpose of this committee was to plan how to honour a controversial figure, the 73-year-old poet Wilfrid Scawen Blunt.

Pound spent the whole winter of 1913/14 out of town – at Stone Cottage in Coleman's Hatch, Sussex, only thirty miles from Blunt's home, Newbuildings Place, near Horsham. He was staying with Yeats, acting as his secretary and companion. Yeats knew Blunt from the latter's involvement in Irish nationalist politics (for which he had served a term in prison) and because he had written a play for the Abbey Theatre. Blunt was an aristocrat and a former diplomat, who had travelled extensively in the Middle East and supported Egyptian nationalism. He had written no poetry for a decade but was notorious for his anti-imperialist views and for his various love affairs. (He was separated from his wife, the grand-daughter of Lord Byron.) The plan to pay tribute to him seems to have been something that Yeats and Pound hatched together. Pound's own poem for the occasion says it all:

> Because you have gone your individual gait,
> Written fine verses, made mock of the world,
> Swung the grand style, not made a trade of art,
> Upheld Mazzini and detested institutions;
> We, who are little given to respect,
> Respect you. . . . [38]

Pound could hardly hold Blunt up as a stylistic innovator, but commented that he was 'about the last man who has been able to use the old-fashioned Elizabethan "grand style" effectively.'[39] Yeats's inspiration for the idea must have been his own visit (with Henry Newbolt) to Dorchester on 2 June 1912 to present the 72-year-old Thomas Hardy with the gold medal of the Royal Society of Literature. Hardy, too, had been a rebel against the conventions of Victorian society (and was still an active – and far superior – poet), but now occupied the position of a 'grand old man' of literature, and had even been offered a knighthood (which he had refused).

Informed of the committee's intentions, Blunt declined to travel to London, so on Sunday 18 January 1914, Pound, Aldington and Flint, along with Yeats, Plarr and Sturge Moore arrived at Newbuildings Place to attend a formal lunch, later referred to as the Peacock Dinner, because peacock – still feathered – was served. Pound presented Blunt with a small marble casket created for the occasion by the young French sculptor Gaudier-Brzeska.[40] This box was carved on one side with a recumbent, naked female figure and contained copies of poems written by each member of the committee, including Manning and Masefield (who did not attend).

Blunt seems to have been a little baffled by the whole occasion, but to have enjoyed it, afterwards referring in his diary to these 'queer looking young men with shock heads of hair but capital fellows as it turned out, intelligent, and with a great knowledge of literature ancient and modern also some wit and as far as I could judge good hearts.'[41] He was even more baffled by their poetry, commenting, 'I waited for a rhyme that did not seem to come.'[42] For Yeats, the contrast between this occasion and the extremely awkward lunch that he and Newbolt had eaten at Max Gate with the warring Thomas and Emma Hardy in 1912 must have been striking.

The committee (presumably under the orders of their convenor) made the most of the event: it was announced beforehand through a letter in *The Times*; Yeats subsequently wrote a report for that paper; and, in addition to Pound's report in *Poetry*, one by Aldington appeared in *The Egoist*.[43] The importance they all attached to the occasion and the absence from it of the poet whom the group themselves considered to be the finest of the Imagists are both clues to its symbolic function. It was certainly an attempt to show that contemporary poetry was anti-establishment, but it was also a statement of its virility. Pound, says Helen Carr, 'wanted to create an alternative masculinity for the artist, and Blunt was an ideal model.'[44]

Blunt was the perfect choice not only because of his anti-imperialism but because of his reputation as a philanderer. The sexual nature of the Gaudier-Brzeska box and the serving-up of the peacock reflected the flamboyance and heterosexual 'maleness' of the event, in which both sides were compliant. Blunt later confessed to being disconcerted by the female image on the box and turning it towards the wall, but at the lunch his own choice of reading was a poem about Don Juan.[45] The occasion was an exercise in male bonding; H.D's presence would have compromised this fundamental aspect and was clearly never envisaged.

The heterosexual masculinity of the avant-garde agenda in art and literature would emerge more clearly when Vorticism arrived that summer. 'Pound, Hulme and [Wyndham] Lewis,' Carr argues, 'were all intent on reinventing themselves as representatives of a new kind of masculinity – brash, authoritarian, contemptuous.'[46] For poets like Pound and Aldington, who owed much to the decadent tradition – including its rejection of Victorian morality – an assertion of heterosexual masculinity was perhaps necessary. Aldington's own choice of poem ('In the Via Sistina', about a prostitute seen in Rome) for what Pound referred to as the 'reliquary' was clearly prompted by the group's shared understanding of the meanings of the occasion.

In February 1914 came a more important event: the publication of their anthology, *Des Imagistes*.[47] Thanks to help from Cournos, it appeared first as a complete issue of the New York journal, *The Glebe*, edited by his friend, the American poet Alfred Kreymborg, and then in book form from the *Glebe*'s publishers, Alfred and Charles Boni.[48] In England the Poetry Bookshop published it in April.

Meanwhile the Shakespears had given in to pressure from Pound and Dorothy, and the couple were married (at St Mary Abbot's Kensington, at Hope Shakespear's insistence) on 20 April. Pound was at Stone Cottage on his honeymoon when the English edition of the anthology appeared. Aldington wrote to tell him of the (few) reviews, which included some 'malignant squelch' in *The New Age* but an encouraging response from Edward Thomas in *The New Weekly* and – surprisingly – praise from *The Morning Post*.

Aldington was a little diffident about reviewing the anthology himself, but used his *Egoist* review as an opportunity to reiterate the 'rules' of Imagism: 'direct treatment of the subject'; as few adjectives as possible'; 'a hardness as of cut stone' ('no slop, no sentimentality'); 'individuality of rhythm'; and 'the exact word'. He spoke appreciatively of H.D. (for him the finest of the Imagists, whose verse was 'like nicely carved marble') and of Pound and Flint (calling the latter an 'Impressionist'), but remarked that the work of five of the poets (Joyce, Hueffer, Upward, Cannell and Cournos) was not, in his view, Imagist at all.[49] In the same article he reviewed

The Peacock Dinner, Newbuildings Place, 18 January 1914.

From left to right: Victor Plarr, Thomas Sturge Moore, W.B. Yeats, Wilfrid Blunt, Ezra Pound, Richard Aldington and Frank Flint

a collection by Horace Holley, another expatriate American friend of Fletcher's; Aldington was scathing about Holley's *Post-Impressionist Poems*, describing the rhythms as 'curiously derivative', the language as pompous, inflated, rhetorical and unnatural, the poems as unemotional and uninteresting. As a result, he must have felt obliged to accept Holley's verse review of *Des Imagistes* in the next issue:

> *The Mice*
>
> In the world's cupboard
> The scamper of little feet,
> A new sound.
>
> O busy sharp-teethed mice
> Nibbling your anxious bellies full,
> Fear not:
> The Cat was belled long since
> By mice of a bolder generation!
>
> Nay rather beware the tightness of your own tummies
> Little mice,
> Since already you have eaten the Greek Anthology
> And now your glistening white teeth
> Gnaw the fat tomes of Chinese Wisdom.
>
> What would you do with the Lute of Jade,
> O little mice?
> This is indeed a dainty luncheon,
> O little mice,
> O Imagists!

Holley's satire not only accuses the group of derivativeness but suggests the limited impact that they were making on the literary scene. Pound, now attracted by avant-garde sculpture and painting, perhaps partly because it seemed to have greater shock value, was now writing more about those media in *The New Age* and *The Egoist* than he was about poetry. He was moving towards the third and final 'event', the launch of a new 'mouvemong', which he had conceived in company with Lewis, whom he now saw as 'the most articulate voice' of an age 'which has not yet come into its own.'[50] 'Vorticism' was to include Imagism – indeed to elucidate its doctrine of the image. The term would encompass art as well as poetry; but its inception would eventually bring about a split in the Imagist group.

A number of other events in London in the spring and early summer served to give contemporary art a high profile and to pave the way for the arrival of Vorticism. The Italian Futurist Marinetti had visited London frequently since 1910; Aldington had reviewed a performance of his poetry in *The New Freewoman* on 1 December 1913 – with a mixture of bemusement, admiration and his usual good-humoured tolerance.[51] Futurism aimed to capture, in art, poetry and music, the dynamic energy and speed of the modern technological world; it rejected the representational in art, realism in fiction and Romanticism in poetry, and expressed itself through a discourse of violence. Aldington admired Marinetti's vivid 'Impressionism', his fearless experimentation and his contempt for the bourgeoisie, but disliked the abstraction and rhetoric of his poetry.

Pound's artist friends were initially in sympathy with Futurism, although most of them saw Cubism as their main influence. Pound had allied himself with Lewis and Gaudier-Brzeska, and with T.E. Hulme, who was now writing art criticism regularly in *The New Age*. In March 1914 Lewis founded the Rebel Arts Centre at 38 Great Ormond Street; it would only last four months, as a rift with his former lover and sponsor, Kate Lechmere, resulted in her withdrawal of support, but it brought together a number of contemporary artists with a similar vision.[52] Amongst those who lectured there was Marinetti himself.

Meanwhile Monro had also given Marinetti cautious support, printing his work in *Poetry and Drama* in September 1913. When the Futurist returned to London in 1914 Monro gave a dinner for him on 4 May, which was attended by Aldington and Flint as well as by Victor Plarr, Sturge Moore and the poet J.C. Squire.[53] Walter de la Mare and Gerald Gould dropped in after the meal, but Pound was still at Stone Cottage with Dorothy. Monro had also invited some more 'establishment' figures, who had declined to attend, such as Newbolt, Marsh, Chesterton and even Hueffer. However, there was one senior poet who would not escape Marinetti's company; after the dinner several of the party took him to visit Yeats at his flat in Woburn Buildings. Aldington later recalled that after Yeats had read some of his poems, 'which Marinetti would have thought disgustingly *passéistes* if he had understood them', the visitor was invited to perform some of his, which he did – so loudly that 'neighbours were knocking in protest on the floor, ceiling and party walls' and Yeats had to ask him to stop.[54]

By now Aldington saw Marinetti chiefly as an object of derision, and he and Pound (now back in London) hatched a scheme to ridicule him publicly. On 28 May Marinetti gave a lecture on (male) Futurist clothing; such clothing, said the manifesto, was to be simple, loose-fitting and colourful. With the help of Dorothy and H.D. (who were not invited to accompany them) the two designed and wore to the lecture green trousers, orange shirts and blue jackets.

This episode was nothing compared to that which the rebel artists were planning. While Richard Nevinson had wholeheartedly identified with Futurism, Lewis could no longer stand being in its shadow. When Nevinson unwisely published an English Futurist Manifesto ('The Vital English Art') in *The Observer* on 7 June 1913, affixing to it not only his own name and that of Marinetti but those of his fellows at the Rebel Art Centre (along with Epstein and Bomberg), Lewis and his associates were incandescent with rage, publishing statements of their dissociation from the manifesto in the following Sunday's *Observer*, in *The New Weekly* and in *The Egoist*.[55] They also turned up on the evening of 12 June at the Doré Gallery where Nevinson and Marinetti were to share a platform to launch English Futurism and, led by Gaudier-Brzeska, Lewis and Hulme, heckled the pair loudly, Gaudier keeping up a chant of 'Vorticism!'

On 2 July Vorticism itself arrived – through the publication of the journal *Blast: A Review of the Great English Vortex*, its bright pink cover and bold typography as radical and aggressive as its contents. The movement's manifesto took the form of two lists, of the 'blasted' in society and of the 'blessed', along with several pages of aphorisms, and was signed by Pound and Aldington, along with Lewis, Gaudier-Brzeska, Malcolm Arbuthnot, Lawrence Atkinson, Jessica Dismorr, Cuthbert Hamilton, William Roberts, Helen Saunders and Edward Wadsworth. There were further lengthy statements on Vorticism by Lewis, Pound and Gaudier-Brzeska and the magazine featured illustrations by several of the artists and literary contributions from Pound, Hueffer (the first instalment of what would become *The Good Soldier*), Lewis and Rebecca West.[56]

That Pound considered Imagism as central to Vorticism and had not lost interest in the earlier movement was evident in a more reflective essay he wrote for *The Fortnightly Review*.[57] Although the article is entitled 'Vorticism', he devotes more space to discussing 'Imagisme' and after reiterating the 'three rules', goes on to develop in detail the concept of the image, which he associates with 'intensity'. The image is 'the equivalent of the painter's pigment' and is never simply ornamental or 'an idea', but 'the word beyond spoken language', 'a radiant node or cluster'. In fact, he concludes, 'it is what I can, and must perforce, call a VORTEX, from which, and through which, and into which, ideas are constantly rushing.' Intensity is seen as the most important characteristic of both Imagist poetry and Vorticist art and he is as keen to dissociate the former from Symbolism, which deals in association and where symbols have a 'fixed value', as he is to distinguish the latter from Futurism, which is a 'spreading, or surface art'. Imagism is, then, the poetic expression of Vorticism.[58]

Aldington, a signatory to the Vorticist manifesto, was initially enthusiastic, writing on 1 July 1914 that *Blast* was 'the most amazing, energised, stimulating production [he] had ever seen.'[59] By the next issue of *The Egoist*, when he had time to reflect on its contents, he was still supportive, but slightly concerned about what he saw as the movement's 'religious overtones' and very critical of the satires Pound had contributed to *Blast*. With an irony he must have enjoyed employing, he wrote: 'Mr Pound is one of the most modest, bashful, kind creatures who ever walked this earth; so I cannot help thinking that all this enormous arrogance and petulance and fierceness are a pose. And it is a wearisome pose.'[60] Pound, however, was relishing the pugnacious language espoused by Lewis (and Marinetti); writing about 'The New Sculpture' in *The Egoist* in February, he had declared that, 'The artist has been aroused to the fact that the war between him and the world is a war without truce. That his only remedy is slaughter.' In not too many months such language would come to seem in poor taste.

Aldington and H.D. continued to be on good terms with Pound, although H.D. later confessed to having been 'rather taken aback' when she discovered that Pound (in preparation for his marriage, although that was still a secret) had taken the flat

immediately opposite theirs, number 5 Holland Place Chambers.[61] He moved in
on 2 March and was married seven weeks later; their friend Cournos took over
his room in Church Walk. In late March Aldington and Pound went together for a
long weekend's visit to Newbuildings Place. According to *Life for Life's Sake*, Blunt
astonished them by appearing at dinner 'in the full dress of an Arab sheik' and asking
them to share in a toast of 'damnation to the British government'.[62] Aldington –
still only twenty-two years old – relished the high jinks and combativeness of the
Pound camp, but he also took pride in his editorial responsibilities and shared
H.D.'s essential seriousness, her passion for classical literature and love of nature.
She had never been an enthusiast for the 'mouvemong', preferring to walk her
own path.

They began to inhabit other worlds than Pound's. In particular, they were
introduced by Cournos to three expatriate Americans who arrived from
Philadelphia in April 1914. George Plank was an illustrator and wood-engraver
who was already making his name as the designer of the art-deco covers of *Vogue*.[63]
His friends were James Whitall and his wife, Mildred. Whitall was a wealthy and
well-connected young Quaker who had left his father's business to seek a career
as a writer and translator in England. At the Whitalls' home in Chelsea and, from
the spring of 1915, at their summertime residence (Vale End, near Guilford), the
Aldingtons entered a world that was elegant and civilised.

Whitall was entranced with the Aldingtons and, like Fletcher's, his memoir
contains vivid portraits of them both in this period. He recalls H.D. as 'tall, slender,
strangely beautiful, sensitive, possessed of a gift for making one feel important
and for the moment absorbingly interesting to her', but what fascinated him was
his sense that, 'a great literature had laid its spell upon her, flooding her mind
with images of a hard clear beauty.' He tells us that 'she often sat with us, chatting
of everyday things, when I am sure that her spirit was somewhere near the shores
of the Aegean.' However, he is quick to assure us that 'these absences were never
embarrassing and they made her returns to our world the more delightful', as she
entered into their talk with 'disarming enthusiasm' and 'delivered herself with such
amazing speed and clarity on any subject that might be uppermost.' This sounds like
an unconscious and disarming trait, but we might take note that H.D.'s heroine,
Raymonde, in 'Murex' 'had trained herself (or Ray Bart the poet [Pound] had so
trained her) to carry on her apparently eager and ecstatic conversation and to stand
posed, apart, sustained in some other region.'[64]

Aldington, on the other hand, 'may have been a voyager into other worlds, but
he never gave evidence of it and always seemed to be treading with unmistakeable
firmness the ground upon which he actually stood.' 'His energy of brain and body',
we are told, 'was like a fresh strong wind which envigorated without whipping
skirts about or blowing off hats.' For Whitall, Aldington's good looks and high
spirits 'made his intolerance of the existing order more than endurable.' For Whitall
was never under any illusion that his own view of the world order was the same as
Aldington's – or Cournos's: '[My] living and writing were not a rebellion against
convention. I was, in the matter of living, anxious to occupy an unobtrusive niche

that would not cut me off from any particular sort of person or influence; and as to writing, I was deeply conscious of my need to work at fundamentals. I had neither the equipment nor the desire to go in for experiment.'[65] Eventually, these political and artistic differences would drive Aldington and Whitall apart, but for now the friendship was rewarding for them both.[66] That, even at this stage, Aldington had his reservations about Whitall is evident from a comment that he made in a letter to Flint: 'I met a little American with £1000+ per annum, [illegible word] to £10,000 per ditto. Knows nothing; has translated Judith Gautier's poems, (Judith Gautier's!!) & got it ACCEPTED AT ONCE BY CONSTABLE'S. I lectured him for an hour on you; hope it did some good.'[67] George Plank, always predominantly an artist, would remain on good terms with both Aldingtons, and particularly H.D., for much longer.

Meanwhile they were seeing more of Flint, who was containing his irritation with Pound's high-handedness with difficulty; there had nearly been a rift over the 'Blunt affair', when Flint was convinced that Pound had only invited him to join the illustrious committee because of his short-hand skills, which would prove useful in recording the speeches made at the dinner.[68] A year earlier he had shown good-humoured tolerance and some loyalty in his response to the fury of Robert Frost, yet another expatriate American poet, at Pound's cavalier approach to his work, telling Frost: 'You know his bark is much worse than his bite and that much that seems offensive to us externally is merely external and a kind of outer defence – a mask.'[69] Now his patience was wearing thin. However, we must not read too much into the absence of his name from the list of signatories to the *Blast* manifesto, since it seems that Lewis had intended to ask Flint's permission to add his name, but had neglected to do so.

Unlike Aldington and Pound, Flint had to juggle the demands of a full-time and poorly-paid clerical job and a young family – his wife was now expecting their second child – with reading, translating and writing. He could not know that H.D. had described him to Isabel Pound two years previously as 'a derelict poet' who had married 'a hopeless little Cockney' (and H.D. would probably have been horrified to be reminded of the fact), but his disadvantaged upbringing had made him sensitive to personal slights. Aldington's correspondence with him in this period shows the former as appreciative and encouraging towards his friend's writing and sensitive to his personal circumstances – and to his pride.

The other friend who was becoming increasingly important in the Aldingtons' lives was Cournos. It seems hardly coincidental that Aldington in this period was drawn to two individuals – Flint and Cournos – who had struggled against appalling poverty and misery to become writers. 'I had fought in the trenches of life since I was ten', Cournos tells us in his autobiography.[70] It was the seriousness with which these two men pursued their calling that won them the trust and respect of both H.D. and Aldington; the increasingly carnavalesque behaviour of Pound and Lewis – both products of more comfortable upbringings – formed a striking contrast.

In the spring of 1914 H.D. and Aldington spent a couple of quiet weeks at

Hindhead in Surrey (thus missing Pound's wedding) and, shortly afterwards, H.D. took over from Patmore as Hueffer's amanuensis in his writing of the novel that was to become *The Good Soldier*. It was exhausting work, as both Pound (in 1911) and Patmore had discovered, and Aldington became anxious about her health, writing to Flint in early July that she was suffering from 'mental strain'.[71] Hueffer wrote later: 'When I was dictating the most tragic portion of my most tragic book to an American poetess she fainted several times. One morning she fainted three times. So I had to call in her husband to finish the last pages of the book. He did not faint. But he has never forgiven me.'[72] In May, when H.D. and Aldington were visiting The Mermaid Inn at Rye, Hueffer was invited to dinner, and Aldington tells the story of how delighted the impressionable Albert Edward was with Hueffer's personal anecdotes about literary celebrities – until Hueffer mentioned having met Byron. However, Aldington comments: 'I have known many men in my time, but few so fundamentally innocent of real harm as Ford.'[73]

The next major event in the history of Imagism would not be engineered by Pound. It was the arrival in England on 3 July of Amy Lowell, complete with car, chauffeur and maid, and accompanied by Ada Russell. This time she met Aldington and H.D., and Flint too, and was delighted with them, and they with her. Her relationship with Pound, however, while it began amicably enough, would deteriorate beyond repair by the time she departed for home two months later.

For some months he had been trying to persuade her to put her money behind a journal. His first proposal had been *The Egoist*, which was stumbling financially. However, an 'anonymous' gift of £250 (from Harriet Weaver, who responded quickly when Dora Marsden expressed some alarm at what Pound was planning) had rescued the journal from their joint clutches.[74] Now he was suggesting that she launch a new quarterly or purchase the *Mercure de France*. Lowell resented his assumption that she had a fortune to spend on establishing a journal for Pound and his friends; in any case she had ideas of her own. The poems printed in the February *Egoist* and in the April *Poetry* had established her credentials as an Imagist and she had a new collection due out from Macmillan in both America and England; meeting her publisher was one of the purposes of her visit.[75] Now she wanted to see a new Imagist anthology and to secure for it a mainstream publisher.

Pound was organising a dinner at the expensive Dieudonné Restaurant in Ryder Street to launch *Blast*, and Lowell and Russell were invited. It took place on 15 July and seems to have been a suitably rowdy occasion. It was followed, only two nights later, by another dinner at the same venue, this time hosted by Lowell, to celebrate the publication of *Des Imagistes*. Lowell's guests, apart from Russell, were Pound, Dorothy, Aldington, H.D., Flint, Fletcher, Upward, Cournos, Hueffer, Hunt and Gaudier-Brzeska.[76] That Lowell was the host hints at her intentions and Pound clearly felt his position threatened. Fletcher recalled that the atmosphere from the start was 'one of embarrassed expectancy'.[77]

At the end of the meal, Lowell called upon Hueffer to make a speech, an opportunity he used to pour scorn on the whole notion of Imagism and certainly on the right of either Lowell or Pound to call themselves imagists. Pound now called on Upward, who proceeded in the same vein. Lowell then asked Aldington to speak, an opportunity he used to pursue his own agenda – that the essence of Imagism resided in the restoration of the Hellenic view of life; when he challenged Gaudier to explain why he hated Greek sculpture, an argument broke out between the two of them, with Lowell attempting to intervene, pointing out that this had little to do with either Imagism or poetry. Pound meanwhile, according to Fletcher, slipped quietly out through the staff entrance, came back (followed by several curious waiters) wearing 'a large tin bathtub' on his head and announced that from now on the 'Imagistes' would be called the 'Nageistes', declaiming the final line of Lowell's 'In the Garden': 'Night, and the water, and you in your whiteness bathing'. Despite the general hilarity (clearly occasioned by the vision he had prompted of the ample figure of Lowell 'in her whiteness bathing'), the object of his joke responded with what Fletcher describes as 'unruffled dignity', so victory was denied to Pound – for now.[78]

Whether that evening's experience made Lowell more determined to have a hand in the future of imagism or not, by the end of the month she had formulated a plan which she put in writing to Pound. At the same time she and Russell held another dinner – a more intimate affair in her hotel suite at the Berkeley, with only Aldington, H.D and D.H. Lawrence as guests. This was the first time either Lowell or the Aldingtons had met Lawrence, who was back in England for what he expected to be a short visit: for his wedding (which took place on 13 July, at Kensington Registry Office, where Aldington and H.D. had been married); for Freda to attempt to see her children; and for him to arrange publication of some short stories and his next novel. Amy put forward her plans: she would put up the money to enable them to find a mainstream publisher for five annual anthologies. Each poet would have equal representation and would choose his or her own contributions; there would be no single editor. They liked her proposal; so did Fletcher, Hueffer and Flint, who were also approached. Pound did not.

He wrote to Lowell on 1 August: 'You offer to find a publisher, that is, a better publisher, if I abrogate my privileges, if I give way to, or saddle myself with, a dam'd contentious, probably incompetent committee. If I tacitly, tacitly to say the least of it, accept a certain number of people as my critical and creative equals . . . I don't see the use. Moreover, I should like the name "Imagisme" to retain some sort of a meaning. It stands, or I should like it to stand for hard light, clear edges. I cannot trust any democratized committee to maintain that standard. Some will be splay-footed and some sentimental.'[79] There could be no meeting of the ways and Pound refused to contribute to the new anthologies.

While H.D. was concerned about upsetting Pound, she and the others welcomed Lowell's scheme. Lowell's disagreement with Pound would now be over the issue of the 'brand'. Was *Imagisme* (or even its Anglicised version) a name to which he held exclusive rights? Since he was in the process of refining his conception of it within the framework of Vorticism (as his September article in *The Fortnightly Review* would

Amy Lowell

reveal, along with another in *The New Age* in January 1915),[80] he must have felt that this was the case, and he wrote to Lowell quite amicably on 12 August, telling her that her scheme was 'excellent' but that she should call her annual anthology *Vers Libre* or even, if she wanted 'to drag in the word Imagisme', employ a subtitle, such

Ford Madox Hueffer, 1914

as 'an anthology devoted to Imagisme, vers libre and modern movements in verse'. He remarked pointedly that her anthology would obviously consist in great part of 'the work of people who have not taken the trouble to find out' what he meant by 'Imagisme'.[81]

He did not make it clear to whom he was alluding, but a letter to Monroe in January 1915 spelled it out: '[Lowell] wants in Lawrence, Fletcher, her own looser work. And the very discrimination, the whole core of significance I've taken twelve years of discipline to get at, she expects me to accord to people who have taken fifteen minutes' survey of my results.'[82] Lowell, a shrewd businesswoman, knew that she needed the brand-name if the anthologies were to make an impact, particularly in America, where *Poetry* (through Pound's efforts) had quite effectively publicised the movement. She would write to Aldington in January 1915, when he and H.D. were still attempting to find an amicable solution: 'Imagiste' has come to have a certain meaning among lovers of poetry, and, although Ezra is known to have invented it, it has swung far beyond him and really become a word to designate a certain kind of poetry. For that reason it has a commercial value, as people interested in our sort of poetry know that they are getting it when they see the word 'Imagiste' on the cover.'[83] Flint, when she approached him for an opinion, would support her, writing: 'Never mind about Ezra. He no more invented imagism than he invented the moon. I have all the documents in proof.'[84] From now on the gloves would be off as far as Flint's dealings with Pound were concerned.

Harriet Monroe

Pound's worst fears were realised in October when Macmillan's American arm
produced an advert for Lowell's new collection, *Sword Blades and Poppy Seed*, that
proclaimed her to be 'the foremost member of the "Imagists" – a group of poets
that includes William Butler Yeats, Ezra Pound, Ford Madox Hueffer. . . . '[85]
His response was withering – and so vitriolic that he frightened Macmillan off
publishing the new Imagist anthology; Lowell had to search elsewhere for a
publisher.

However, another, and more-or-less unexpected, conflict now burst upon them
all. Arriving at the Berkeley on the night of 30 July,1914, Lawrence, who had come
from a meeting with Edward Marsh, had told Lowell and her other guests that
Marsh now viewed British involvement in the war as inevitable. In *Life for Life's Sake*
Aldington writes that before Lawrence arrived, he himself had been sitting at the
open window in Lowell's room from where he could see a news stand on Piccadilly,
'with a flaring poster: "Germany and Russia at War: Official"', and that he saw
the newsman unfold another poster that read: 'British Army Mobilised'.[86] Since
neither event took place until two days later, we can take this as poetic licence, but
it makes the point: for three of the five people in that room life as they knew and
loved it was coming to an end. For Lawrence, H.D. and Aldington the war would
be a grim nightmare.

5. The Imagist Poet: 1912-1916

Aldington has his occasional concentrations, and for that reason it is also possible that he will do a fine thing. There is a superficial cleverness in him, then a great and lamentable gap, then the hard point, the true centre, out of which a fine thing may come at any time. (Ezra Pound, January 1915)[1]

Richard Aldington brings his sad modernity into the heart of his Greek world. His joy in beauty which was pure joy to the ancient Greek who had to do with beauty unadulterated and unstained, his joy has in it a deep, incurable dissatisfaction. Beauty hurts him as it did not and could not hurt the Greek; because he sees that its position in the modern world is dangerous and impermanent. (May Sinclair, May 1921)[2]

We shall close this account of the pre-war years with a consideration of Aldington's published poetic output by the time he went to war in 1916.[3] In 1918, when he was soldiering on the Western Front, Harriet Monroe would send him a copy of her review of his *Reverie: A Little Book of Poems for H.D.*[4] In it she harked back to the first poem of his that she had ever read, 'Choricos', and quoted from a letter she had recently received from an American subscriber also serving on the Western Front:

> Certain poems like the *Choricos* of Aldington have shuddered with me along night roads, and through their bold beauty have saved me from terror when one of the great shocks — the explosion of an enemy shell, the sudden presence of pain or awful agony, the nearness of death — fell without preface upon me.
>
> I remember once particularly, in the drab of light of a cloudy dawning, when I saw near the edge of a road a poilu quietly lying. I should have fainted, I think, from the sheer tragedy of the incident, had I not heard singing in my head, Aldington's invocation to death.

Aldington, though clearly pleased, remarked in a letter to H.D., 'I don't really believe that he thought of anything *but* shells when shells were falling.'[5] However, the publication of this review must have prompted a rush of 'Choricos moments' from soldier-subscribers, because in her 1937 autobiography, Monroe recalled yet another soldier's letter:

A pretty heavy bombardment was going on above and most of us were not
without fear. We jerked out an occasional sentence and smoked heavily, and
altogether wished we might be some miles back; when some fellow from
the west, quite simply – naturally, it seemed then – began Aldington's
'Choricos'. We listened, fell upon it eagerly; were thankful. As he came
to the invocation to death he stood up full length, his head at the *abri*, and
recited those splendid lines with an aristocracy of accent which gave them
sympathy and understanding. I tell you those lines are immortal; more than
that they offered us immortality to share in.[6]

'Choricos', first printed in the second issue of *Poetry* in November 1912, and
thus one of the first Imagist poems to be published, has excited both admiration
and censure from commentators. Monroe admired its 'Greek-marble-like beauty'
and Norman Gates 'its long swinging cadences'.[7] Charles Doyle believes that, 'as
a vehicle of elegiac expression it is highly successful.'[8] However, for W. J. Harmer,
'the language is faded or trite, the rhythms are borrowed'[9] and Thomas MacGreevy
found 'plenty of Swinburnism in it'.[10] All these judgements are valid. The poem (its
rhythms prompted by Aldington's reading of the hero's invocation to Artemis at
the opening of Euripides's *Hippolytus*)[11] is an elegy of seventy-six unrhymed lines,
organised into seven sections of varying lengths. Its subject is stated in the opening
lines:

> The ancient songs
> Pass deathward mournfully.

The poem follows this journey, 'from the green land' and 'the waters' towards
the 'quiet level lands' that Proserpine 'keeps for us all'. Norman Gates suggests
that the ancient songs represent 'all things Greek'.[12] The songs become a band
of singers, joined by the poet himself. Abandoning love, art and nature, as Death
comes upon them, they arrive at the 'swallow blue halls / By the dark streams
of Persephone'. There follows 'one last song', a hymn to death:

> Death,
> Thou art an healing wind
> That blowest over white flowers
> A-tremble with dew;
> Thou art a wind flowing
> Over dark leagues of lonely sea;
> Thou art the dusk and the fragrance;
> Thou art the lips of love mournfully smiling;
> Thou art the pale peace of one
> Satiate with old desires;
> Thou art the silence of beauty,
> And we look no more for the morning·
> We yearn no more for the sun,
> Since with thy white hands,

> Death,
> Thou crownest us with the pallid chaplets,
> The slim colourless poppies
> Which in thy garden alone
> Softly thou gatherest.

In the final twelve lines of the poem the speakers kneel before Death, as she lays flowers upon them with her 'thin cold hands':

> And the illimitable quietude
> Comes gently upon us.

For all the musicality of the rhythm, the restrained but sensuous beauty of the language and the elegiac mood that these achieve, there is some over-reliance on archaisms and emotive epithets and on repetition (although it might be argued that this is a characteristic device in a hymn). The poem recalls Swinburne's 'Hymn to Proserpine', itself written in Grecian hexameters:

> Where the poppies are sweet as the rose in our world, and the red
>   rose is white,
> And the wind falls faint as it blows with the fume of the flowers of
>   the night,
> And the murmur of spirits that sleep in the shadow of Gods from
>   afar
> Grows dim in thine ears and deep as the deep dim soul of a star,
> In the sweet low light of thy face, under heavens untrod by the sun,
> Let my soul with their souls find place, and forget what is done
>   and undone.

Lines from 'Choricos', like those describing the arrival of Death, do, as MacGreevy points out, possess a Pre-Raphaelite quality, but generally the poem avoids the dramatic visual effects and heavy sensuousness of the Swinburne poem, as well as its strong authorial voice:

> Brushing the fields with red-shod feet,
> With purple robe
> Searing the flowers as with a sudden flame

The other 'death-wish' poem of which the reader might be reminded is 'Ode to a Nightingale'. At the end of *his* poem, Keats is forced back into the real world; the young Aldington, on the other hand, struggles to reconcile the real and the ideal. The exquisite beauty and sense of longing in his 'Grecian' poems can seem escapist:

> I am not of these about thy feet,
> These garments and decorum;
> I am thy brother,
> The lover of aforetime crying to thee,
> And thou hearest me not.   ('To A Greek Marble')

> O Artemis,
> Girdle the gold about you,
> Set the silver upon your hair
> And remember us —
> We, who have grown weary even of music,
> We who would scream behind the wild dogs of Scythia.
>
> ('At Mitylene')

It is not only the Greek poems that are tinged with melancholy:

> Where wert thou born
> O that woe
> That consumes my life?
>
> ('Beauty Thou Hast Hurt Me Overmuch')

> That which sets me nighest to weeping,
> Is the rose and white colour of the smooth flag-stones
> And the pale yellow grasses
> Among them.   ('In An Old Garden')

However, the handful of poems inspired by the months in Italy and by Aldington's early love for H.D. often achieve that narrow perfection of which strict Imagism is capable, the 'clean and sure technique' which John Gould Fletcher praised:[13]

> We will come down to you,
> O very deep sea
> And drift upon your pale green waves
> Like scattered petals.
>
> We will come down to you from the hills,
> From the scented lemon groves,
> From the hot sun.
> We will come down,
> O Thalassa,
> And drift upon
> Your pale green waves
> Like petals.   ('Amalfi')

> A rose-yellow moon in a pale sky
> When the sunset is faint vermillion
> On the mist among the tree boughs
> Are you to me.   ('Images III')

> She has new leaves
> After her dead flowers,
> Like the little almond-tree
> Which the frost hurt.   ('New Love')

Generally, the least satisfying poems are those which take the contemporary world as their subject matter. 'In the Tube', 'Cinema Exit' and 'Church Walk, Kensington' display revulsion from modernity – and from humanity:

> A row of eyes,
> Eyes of greed, of pitiful blankness, of plethoric complacency
> Immobile,
> Gaze, stare at one point,
> At my eyes.   ('In the Tube')

> Millions of human vermin
> Swarm sweating
> Along the night-arched cavernous roads.   ('Cinema Exit')

> The cripples are going to church.
> Their crutches beat upon the stones,
> And they have clumsy iron boots.

> Their clothes are black, their faces pitched and mean;
> Their legs are withered
> Like dried bean pods

> Their eyes are as stupid as frogs'.   (Church Walk, Kensington)

In 'Church Walk, Kensington', Aldington goes on to contrast the ugliness of the cripples with the beauty of the natural and Grecian worlds:

> And the god, September,
> Has paused for a moment here
> Garlanded with crimson leaves.
> He held a branch of fruited oak.
> He smiled like Hermes the beautiful
> Cut in marble.

John Gould Fletcher wrote of this poem: 'There we have it all: a sense of the sordidness of existence, of the wayward and casual beauty with which nature decks that sordidness; irony and pity, concealed yet poignant; and I know not what feeling of nostalgia and transience that arises somehow from all these.'[14] Fletcher may have been right about the irony, but the pity is indeed concealed; and the two worlds remain unreconciled.

Yet Aldington occasionally achieves that reconciliation. The clearest example is 'Interlude', here (like 'Church Walk, Kensington' above) quoted in its entirety:

> Blow your tin squeals
> On your reedy whistle.
> Here they come
>   dancing

> White girls,
>   lithe girls,
> In linked dance
> From Attica.
>
> Gay girls dancing
>   in the frozen street,
> Hair streaming and white rainment
> Flying,
> Red lips that first were
> Red in Ephesus.
>
> Gone!
> You? Red-nose, playing by the Red Lion,
> You!
> Did you bring them!
>
> Here, take my pennies,
> *Mon semblable, mon frère.*

The playful typography is perhaps an affectation, but the use of colour, repetition, assonance and alliteration to link the real and fantasy worlds conveys beauty, humour, energy and a love of life, even of the wintry war-time life of London.

However, it is wartime London that is the clue to the misanthropy of poems like 'In the Tube' and 'Cinema Exit'. By mid 1915 when these two poems were written, not only had Aldington's vibrant pre-war social world started to break down (along with his relationships with Pound and Ford)[15] and the physical environment of London itself become bleak, but his own situation as a young civilian had begun to trouble him. The 'brasslike eyes' in the tube accuse him: '*What right have you to live?*' Like Lawrence, he hated the war but could not bring himself to be a pacifist; and, like Lawrence too, he seems at first to have attempted to resolve this mounting internal conflict by projecting his feelings outwards, against the mass of humanity.

However, the poetry also begins to betray other struggles, creative and personal. There are hints in the 1915 and 1916 anthologies that Imagism was becoming a strait-jacket out of which he could not yet successfully break, with the result that some of his work neither satisfies Imagist principles nor makes good poetry. A clear example is 'Daisy' from the 1915 anthology, another poem quoted here in its entirety:

> You were my playmate by the sea
> We swam together:
> Your girl's body had no breasts.
>
> We found prawns among the rocks;
> We liked to feel the sun and to do nothing;
> In the evening we played games with the others.
> It made me glad to be by you.

Sometimes I kissed you,
And you were always glad to kiss me;
But I was afraid – I was only fourteen.

And I had quite forgotten you,
You and your name.

Today I pass through the streets.
She who touches my arm and talks with me
Is – who knows? – Helen of Sparta,
Dryope, Laodamia . . .

And there are you
A whore in Oxford Street.

In an article in *The New Republic* entitled 'Egoism in Poetry', Padraic Colum was highly critical of the way in which the ostensible subject of this poem, the childhood sweetheart who became a prostitute, is made merely an occasion for 'the writer's own moment'.[16] Indeed, as in 'Church Street, Kensington', there is a disturbing absence of compassion. But while the Imagist dénouement lacks moral sense, the earlier part of the poem is *aesthetically* weak. There is no evidence here of Aldington's ear for the rhythmic potential of *vers libre*; even as prose this is clumsy – and emotionally mawkish. The confused emotions of the adolescent boy must have been difficult for the adult poet to convey imaginatively, but we find ourselves thinking that it might have been better not to have attempted the task.[17]

In 'Whitechapel' and 'Eros and Psyche', from the 1916 anthology, emotion and idea struggle for dominance and the consequence is a failure of poetic imagination. Perhaps by now their themes, the contrasts between urban modernity and the ideal worlds of either Nature or classical Greece, were too well worn. Here are the closing lines of 'Whitechapel':

Soot; mud;
A nation maddened with labour;
Interminable collision of energies –
Iron beating upon iron;
Smoke whirling upwards, speechless, impotent.

In vain the shrill far cry
Of kittiwakes that fly
Where the sea waves leap green.
The meadows Aprilene –

Noise, iron, smoke;
Iron, iron, iron.

The devices used to convey the contrast are laboured and mechanical, the images contrived. In 'Eros and Psyche' the contrast between the Hellenic and contemporary worlds is imaginatively realised in the sight, from the top of a bus, of a statue of the two figures abandoned in 'an old dull yard' in north London:

> What are they doing here in Camden Town
> In the midst of all this clamour and filth?
> They who should stand in a sunlit room
> Hung with deep purple, painted with gods,
> Paved with dark porphyry . . .
> Or in a garden leaning above Corinth,
> Under the ilexes and the cypresses,
> Very white against a very blue sky . . .

The ending is 'imagistic':

> And I glimpse them, huddled against the wall,
> Half-hidden under a freight-train's smoke,
> And I see the limbs that a Greek slave cut
> In some Italian town,
> I see them growing older
> And sadder
> And greyer.

But much of the poem, comparable in length to 'Choricos', is discursive in manner. Contrasting the situation of the Greek statue with that of Richard Cobden in a nearby square, Aldington writes:

> And though no-one ever pauses to see
> What hero it is that faces the Tube,
> I can understand very well indeed
> That England must honour its national heroes,
> Must honour the hero of Free Trade –
> Or was it the Corn Laws? –
> That I can understand.

There is no evidence here of key Imagist principles such as cadence, compression or concreteness. In 1924 Aldington would write to Herbert Read: 'I abandon, cast off, utterly deny the virtue of 'extreme compression and essential significance of every word'. I say this is the narrow path that leadeth to sterility. It makes a desert and you call it art. . . . I say, pox on your intensities and essences; know what you know, feel what you feel, think what you think, and put it down, write, write, write!'[18] By then he was on the path to becoming a novelist, but was still confronting the challenge of how to produce narrative and reflective texts in free verse that satisfied the ear and the imagination of the reader.

The poem that most displays this problem is 'Childhood', which appeared in the 1915 anthology. Even Amy Lowell wrote in *The Little Review*: 'Somehow, the poem is not as good as it ought to be. I suspect that Mr Aldington has not yet quite mastered the technique of the long poem. Feeling is there, and we get the dullness of the little town perfectly, and the stale, salt smell of the harbour; and there are excellent descriptions – the public park, and the wonderful box in the attic – but the poem as a whole does not 'get over.' Necessarily more discursive than the shorter poems, it has not enough command of the dramatic to succeed. Having taught himself for years to say things in the fewest possible words, the length of this poem has weakened the poet's method. He must study the requirements of the longer poem a little more before he will be quite at home in it.'[19]

This account is extremely perceptive about the poem's technical shortcomings. The problem, however, was as much personal as creative. Aldington's antipathies towards his parents had not yet been confronted; in 1929 the devastating satire of *Death of a Hero* would attempt the task. Meanwhile, of what could he accuse them? Of providing him with a comfortable (and literate) but isolated middle-class upbringing in a dull town? The opening line, which recalls 'the bitterness, the misery, the wretchedness of childhood', is not supported by the subsequent description of the dull town, the dull schooling, the lack of anything to see, to do or 'to play with'. Norman Gates provided one of the most insightful criticisms when he wrote: 'What we have in the poem is the author's looking back and giving unnecessary sympathy to the child he once was. . . . In a sense the poem has two voices. The man speaks bitterly of his childhood, but as he does the child's voice breaks through to deny him. The memory 'of a white dog staring into a gramophone' does not seem 'dull and greasy and sordid' but rather like something that would have appealed to a little boy. Surely 'the little harbour' connoted more things to the boy than 'a salt dirty smell'? . . . The poem might have been a better poem if the man had remained silent and permitted the boy to speak. We might have heard much more clearly the pathos of his boyhood, if indeed it existed.'[20] Only in the poem's key image, which appears at the beginning, middle and end, is the poet's bitterness given imaginative expression:

> Somebody found my chrysalis
> And shut it in a match-box.
> My shrivelled wings were beaten,
> Shed their colours in dusty scales
> Before the box was opened
> For the moth to fly.

It was an image that would resurface in the novel *Rejected Guest* almost twenty-five years later.

A poem that shows some of the same shortcomings is 'At Nights', which appeared in *Images (1910-1915)*. The poem is a tribute to H.D., a celebration of their love, clearly inspired by Browning's 'By the Fireside'. Like the latter, it opens and closes with the poet sitting and watching his wife as she reads or muses, and expresses thankfulness:

> And now at nights,
> Now that everything has gone right somehow
> And I have friends and books

And no more bitterness,
I sit here, shading my eyes,
Peeping at you, watching you,
Thinking.

but the central section of the poem returns to the childhood:

I think of when I first saw the beauty of things –
God knows that I was poor enough and sad enough
And humiliated enough –
But not all the slights and the poorness and the worry
Could hide away the green of the poplar leaves . . .

The poem deals with an aspect of Aldington's early life which is entirely absent from 'Childhood': his delight in nature. He even says of the external world, 'I saw that it was good.' What it shares with the latter poem, however, is the strain of self-pity – a strain which hinders poetic detachment and results in such weak lines as 'all the slights and the poorness and the worry' and even: 'Now that everything has gone right somehow'. The latter line shows us a man who sees himself as the passive recipient of good fortune, just as he was formerly the victim of his childhood circumstances. Where 'By the Fireside' celebrates the *achievement* of love, 'At Nights' tells us how (undeservedly?) *lucky* the writer feels. Time would show that he was optimistic to suggest that there was 'no more bitterness' or even that this was a settled relationship. Nevertheless, we can see the poet starting to use his writing to engage with his deepest feelings. Imagism would not afford him the tools for the task; but it would be a while before his attempts to move away from it would produce art.

It was the war that produced some of his finest imagist poems of the period. In these we see, powerfully visualised, his sense of the holocaust, of the destruction of nature and culture, that the war threatened:

A pear tree, a broken white pyramid
In a dingy garden, troubles me with ecstasy. . . .

And I am tormented,
Obsessed,
Among all this beauty,
With a vision of ruins,
Of walls crumbling into clay.   ('London: May 1915')

Dark clouds, torn into gaps of livid sky,
Pierced through
By a swift searchlight, long and white like a dagger.
The black murmuring crowd flows, eddies, stops, flows on
Between the lights
And the banks of noisy booths.
                    ('Hampstead Heath: Easter Monday 1915')

The white body of the evening
Is torn into scarlet,
Slashed and gouged and seared
Into crimson,
And hung ironically
With garlands of mist.

And the wind
Blowing over London from Flanders
Has a bitter taste.   ('Sunsets')

The most understated of these, yet the most poignant, is 'Fantasy' (1915):

The limbs of gods,
Still, veined marble,
Rest heavily in sleep
Under a saffron twilight.

Not for them battle,
Severed limbs, death, and a cry of victory;
Not for them strife
And a torment of storm.

A vast breast moves slowly,
The great thighs shift,
The stone eyelids rise;
The slow tongue speaks:

'Only a rain of bright dust
In the outer air;
A little whisper of wind;
Sleep; rest; forget.'

Bright dust of battle!
A little whisper of dead souls!

PART TWO
Soldier

6. War: 1914-1916

Things fall apart; the centre cannot hold;
Mere anarchy is loosed upon the world,
The blood-dimmed tide is loosed, and everywhere
The ceremony of innocence is drowned;
The best lack all conviction, while the worst
Are full of passionate intensity.

(W.B. Yeats, 'The Second Coming', 1919)

A cloud. Five years. This was the present. A flame about a city. Small city railings
splintered and city parks infested with a black trail of livid wretched creatures who
shivered against each other as the crash came nearer. Who woke as from a dream when
distant rumblings died away, and scurried like black rats, fleeing the sinking wreck,
washing up on the pavements, as if from the city about to sink, fleeing, black lines to
subterranean safety. (H.D., *Paint It Today*, composed 1921)[1]

At eleven o'clock on the evening of Tuesday 4 August 1914 H.D., Aldington and
Cournos stood together in the vast crowd outside Buckingham Palace to hear King
George V's proclamation that Britain and Germany were at war. Like most of those
around them they had not foreseen this war, although they are unlikely to have
shared in the general mood of excitement that ensued.

All that summer conflict had been threatening. Cournos tells us that 'there was
a dynamism in the air fraught with the sense of dire things to come. A strident
note, as of hysteria, crept into life.'[2] The conflict anticipated was not, however,
with another nation, although it was on several fronts. Buckingham Palace, where
the trio witnessed the proclamation of war, had been its focus only recently. On
21 May 1914 Emmeline Pankhurst had been arrested at the gates of the palace as
she tried to present a petition to the King. She had been in and out of prison ever
since, under the notorious 'Cat and Mouse' legislation.[3] The suffragette campaign
had become increasingly violent and lawless and had included Mary Richardson's
slashing of Velázquez's 'Rokeby' Venus at the National Gallery in March and similar
acts of vandalism since, a trend that must have given lovers of art like H.D. and
Aldington cause for concern.[4]

The palace had also been the location, only two weeks before, of the King's
(unsuccessful) attempt to resolve another conflict: that between the Irish

Nationalists and the Ulster Unionists. This dispute had similarly been escalating, with the 'Curragh Mutiny' in March, the gun-running of the Ulster Volunteer Force in April and the killing of three civilians by British troops on 26 July, when the Irish Volunteers also attempted to bring in arms.[5] With the issue of partition unresolved, civil war seemed inevitable.

Class conflict had been intensifying too. Over the last four years there had been constant, massive and often unofficial strikes by dockers, miners and railway workers, some of which had involved acts of sabotage or violent clashes with the police and the military. A general strike would almost certainly have occurred had war with Germany not been declared in August 1914. For Asquith and his Liberal government the war must have appeared to be a salvation. On 10 September all imprisoned suffragettes were released and Emmeline Pankhurst announced that The Women's Social and Political Union would end all its militant activities and support the war effort. The Home Rule Bill was enacted on 18 September, but suspended for the duration of the war, the issue of partition still unresolved; and the majority of Irish Nationalists committed themselves to support the war. The workers, meanwhile, succumbing to the wave of patriotism that hit the country, not to mention the strident views of the popular press, ceased their subversive activities – for the present.

We might wonder why Aldington and H.D. had shown little interest in the political scene over the last three years. Their friends Sinclair and Hunt – and even Patmore to a limited extent – were actively involved in the suffragist movement; their friendship with Flint might have inclined them to Socialist sympathies; and Aldington was frequently in the company of Yeats (although the latter kept himself at a distance from everyday politics) and was familiar with the poetry of younger committed Nationalists like Padraic Colum, Joseph Campbell and Desmond FitzGerald, the last two of whom had been members of the Tour Eiffel group.[6]

H.D. was, of course, like Pound, Fletcher, Cournos and their new friends George Plank and the Whitalls, an outsider, but we might have expected her to be sympathetic towards the suffragist cause. The problem lay both within the movement and within H.D. herself. By 1914 a large number of women – Weaver and Marsden amongst them – had begun to see the right to vote as too limited a platform on which to fight for women's liberty, given the overwhelming social, educational and moral constraints under which women were labouring. However, as Gillian Hanscombe and Virginia Smyers have observed, there is a curious contrast between the feminism implicit in the absolute commitment of many modernist women writers to their art and its demands and their non-involvement in the suffragist cause. Hanscombe and Myers argue that these writers, H.D. amongst them, saw the liberation of women as a *cultural* rather than a *civil* matter, 'to be pursued first in the battle zones mapped out in every woman's inner life, next in the social arenas of every woman's personal life, and finally in every painting, poem or piece of prose taking shape under a woman's hand.'[7] We shall have cause to return to H.D. and her brand of feminism later in this chapter.

What of Aldington? His upbringing had made him implacably opposed to both the conventional (and hypocritical) morality of the English middle class — what he refers to in *Death of a Hero* as 'cant' — and to its materialism. In recent years his acquaintance with men like Cournos and Flint had made him aware, like Anthony Clarendon, the protagonist in his 1933 novel, *All Men are Enemies*, of 'how grossly ignorant he had been kept of the baser realities of society'. The circumstances of the character Stephen Crang, in whose 'sharp pale face' Clarendon sees 'the bitter years of undeserved suffering' may well have been based on Frank Flint's early life. Yet characters like Crang and Robin Fletcher, who seek political solutions to social ills, are not portrayed as attractive personalities. For Aldington, 'Communism [was] only Capitalism upside down.' Like Clarendon, he retained his faith in 'the life of the senses', as opposed to Crang's 'life of abstractions and systems and catch words.'[8] Despite his increasing impatience with the dense deliberations of Dora Marsden, he was, like her, an 'egoist'; all institutions were suspect.

So how did he react to the arrival of war? In 'Notes on the Present Situation' in *The Egoist* of 1 September his chief concern was what would happen in the arts. He saw clearly that patriotism would not produce art: 'The impulse is too vague, too general; the impulse of art is always clear and particular.' He ended by echoing a campaign already running in the press: 'While France sends poets, painters and probably philosophers to fight, England cannot even call up her cricket and football teams. I'm damned if I'll be killed while there are five hundred professional football teams, with their attendant ministers, unslain', an opinion that managed to be both populist and elitist.[9] He would write to Lowell (now back in Boston) on 21 October: 'I think perhaps we over-civilised ones are apt to think too highly of mere life; and I feel sometimes that perhaps after all a long peace becomes a disease which only war can remedy.'[10] We may find this view shockingly arrogant and insensitive, but it was one widely held during the first few months of the war — though probably not by those who had already suffered bereavement.

In the light of these attitudes, it comes as a surprise to read in *Life for Life's Sake* that in August 1914, 'following a suggestion of T.E. Hulme's', Aldington went down to the headquarters of the H.A.C. to enlist.[11] Hulme enlisted on 10 August; whether or not they went together, Aldington certainly went at an early date as we find him writing to Monroe on 16 August: 'I gave in my name to the Honourable Artillery Company but they regarded my exotic appearance with so much suspicion that I positively felt that I must be a German spy. So far they haven't called on me, but I guess I'll have to go, if we lose the big battle now pending.'[12] However, according to *Life for Life's Sake*, Aldington was told at Armoury House that 'there wasn't the slightest chance of [his] ever getting into the army' because of his medical history, that is, the (hernia?) operation he had had as a teenager. The medical examination was certainly more stringent in 1914 than it became later when the need for fighting men became more pressing. Yet it is worth our noting that this rejection on medical grounds is a late addition to the story — and a detail that would have given his 1941 American audience a belief in his good faith at the start of the war. His operation is dated in this account as having taken place in 1910 (the year he came to London and turned eighteen), whereas we know that it took place at least two years – possibly even four years – earlier. By 1941 the 'German spy' aspect of the anecdote as told to Monroe has also been elaborated; we are told that after his abortive attempt to enlist, he wandered by mistake into the armoury and was promptly arrested by a corporal on suspicion (because of his 'small beard and French jacket') of being a German spy.

Everything about Aldington's circumstances and opinions in 1914 makes us mistrust this version of the story: he valued his position as assistant editor of *The Egoist*; with Lowell's anthology plans, he had just become involved in a long-term literary project; he had concerns about H.D.'s health and welfare; and he had no moral or political convictions that would prompt him to enlist. We can add to this the fact that Hulme, always more of a friend of Pound's (until his recent fight with Lewis), was not a character whom Aldington respected or admired, as he indicates in his memoir.[13] Furthermore, as a married man, Aldington was not in the group being targeted for recruitment. However, the notion of registering an interest with the most prestigious unit in the Territorial Army might have had its attractions and perhaps that was all that 'giving in his name' amounted to. (The H.A.C. was overwhelmed with applications.) On the other hand, we do know that there was a widespread assumption that this war was going to be a short-term affair; perhaps Aldington felt that the experience was worth signing up for and would not last long enough to impede his literary career.[14]

In fact, he was already considering a move to America: he told Monroe in that August letter that he was discussing this option with Lowell. It would seem that Lowell was happy to do for Aldington what she had been reluctant to do for Pound: set him up as the editor of a literary journal. This scheme was one they would both return to periodically over the next sixteen months, although, given the need for fighting men, his chances of obtaining permission to emigrate receded as the months went by. H.D. was also hesitant about returning to America, and Lowell herself blew hot and cold over the scheme.

In the opening weeks, Lowell was the only Imagist actually involved in the war: she made a large donation to Herbert Hoover's organisation for repatriating Americans trapped on the continent and became one of the five hundred volunteers meeting trains at Charing Cross to offer food, shelter and finance to some of the hundred thousand of her fellow citizens who were eventually shipped back home. Lawrence was trapped too – he and Frieda could not return to their home in Italy. Furthermore, Methuen had rejected the manuscript of *The Rainbow*. Unable to afford accommodation in London, he found a cheap terraced cottage to rent in Chesham in Buckinghamshire. On 27 August Lowell took Aldington and H.D. with her to visit him. A few days later she left for the States, the selections for the new anthology almost complete.

Gradually, other Americans made their exit. Pound's parents, who had been visiting over the summer to meet their new daughter-in-law, departed, Homer at the end of August to return to work, Isabel not until two months later. Fletcher left in mid-November. He was now in a relationship with Daisy, the not-yet-divorced wife of Malcolm Arbuthnot the photographer, but seems to have decided that he needed to escape her, although he justified the decision to Lowell as brought on by 'the war and the resulting utter confusion of intellect and intelligence that it has brought about over here', and his hope that this would be America's opportunity 'to prove herself fit to carry on the great traditions of literature and the arts.'[15]

The war brought others back from the continent. Two young men studying in Germany and forced to leave prematurely were Aldington's university friend Alec Randall, who had been working towards a doctorate in German literature at the University of Tübingen, and an American, the 26-year-old Thomas Stearns Eliot, who was on a summer course at Marburg when war broke out. He was bound for a year's scholarship at Merton College, Oxford, but would spend more time in London, where a former Harvard colleague, Conrad Aiken, introduced him to Pound.[16] Startled to find a 'modern' poet whom he had not himself trained, Pound remedied matters by taking Eliot under his wing, and persuading the reluctant Monroe to print 'The Love Song of J. Alfred Prufrock'. (The poem finally appeared in *Poetry* in June 1915.) He also introduced Eliot to Yeats and to his Vorticist friends, but not, it seems, to Aldington and H.D., who would not meet him for another three years. Given that they lived across the landing from Pound, the omission suggests the beginnings of an estrangement, but other factors may have been responsible.

H.D. discovered in early September 1914, that she was pregnant. Her health had given Aldington concern even earlier in the year but her pregnancy made her particularly weak and tired, and Hunt took her off to Selsey. She remained there until mid-November, while Aldington visited at weekends. Hueffer was busily engaged in writing government propaganda, and Aldington, who had been acting as his secretary during the completion of *The Good Soldier* in July, was now employed to do research for him. Hueffer's friend, the politician Charles Masterman, had been given the task of running a war propaganda bureau, which he inaugurated on 2 September 1914 by inviting twenty-five prominent British writers to Wellington House at Buckingham Gate on the Strand to discuss ways in which they could contribute to Britain's interests.[17] Hueffer was not present, but Masterman prevailed on him to undertake the work.

Hueffer would produce two publications, *When Blood is their Argument: an Analysis of Prussian Culture*, which attempted to demonstrate the arid intellectualism and militaristic ideology of the culture now dominating the recently united Germany; and *Between St Dennis and St George: a Sketch of Three Civilisations*, a comparison of the German, British and French cultures to the detriment of the first, which is represented as 'infinitely more bellicose than any other people and any other State of occidental Europe', while the French led 'a life of dignity and common sense'. 'From English life, as I have experienced it', Hueffer claimed, 'the idea of physical violence has almost vanished except from among the lower classes.'[18] (Perhaps he had not been observing the recent language and behaviour of the suffragettes – or the Vorticists.) War, he went on to argue, was, paradoxically, the only means available for the defeat of militarism.

For a time, Aldington seems to have been influenced by these arguments, writing to Lowell in early December that the war was one of 'democracy against autocracy, of the individual against the state, of the Anglo-Latin civilisation against the Prussian.'[19] He continued: 'It is to decide whether a state whose fundamental principle is that war is its primary duty can overcome by intrigue and by force states which are devoted to the principle that the primary duty of the state is the happiness of the individual.' Gradually, he became more critical of the effects of militant nationalism; he would write in *Life for Life's Sake*: 'All sorts of things were wrong in that pre-1914 world; they must have been, to end up in so lamentable a bankruptcy. But it had two advantages which were lost in the struggle. There was a rough and ready European order, even a world order, in which the great majority unconsciously believed. And though foreigners might be despised and laughed at, they were not hated merely because they came from the other side of a frontier and spoke another language.'[20] For the time being, however, he would participate in the government-sponsored war against *Kultur* and we may feel that we can excuse him for this short-sightedness more than we can Hueffer, who, as Samuel Hynes points out, was 'the son of a German scholar, the good European [and] last year's Germanophile.'[21] Perhaps this was exactly the problem, although Hueffer would retain his German surname throughout the war, not abandoning it until 1919, when he became Ford Madox Ford.

His period of working closely with Hueffer left Aldington disenchanted with the older man. He wrote to Lowell: 'My constantly being with him has dispelled the last of my illusions regarding him . . . he is incurably vain and self-satisfied.'[22] However, at a time when literary magazines were under threat, with costs rising and audiences shrinking (Monro's *Poetry and Drama* ceased publication in December 1914, while *The Egoist* moved from fortnightly to monthly publication in January 1915), the income was welcome. As would so often be his habit, he attempted to help his friends too: Flint was hired to translate a propaganda article of Hueffer's into French; and Alec Randall was taken on for German translation work.[23] That Aldington also commissioned from Randall a series of articles on contemporary German poetry, which ran in *The Egoist* from June 1915 until August 1916, is an indication that he was no diehard chauvinist – or perhaps just that he wished to be provocative. Of course, contributions to the journal were unpaid, and even Aldington's guinea a week editorial salary was cut in November 1914 as part of an effort to keep the journal viable.

Another artist whom he tried to help was Gourmont, ill and suffering severe financial hardship in war-torn France. Aldington wrote to Lowell, who sent him a gift of money and placed six Gourmont articles, which Aldington translated, in *The New Republic*. While American commercialism had angered Pound in the affair of the Macmillan advert and its complete misrepresentation of Imagism, American Puritanism now made Aldington furious, as the journal demanded cuts in the text and eventually turned the articles down. Fortunately, Lowell persuaded the *Boston Evening Transcript* to accept them. A similar problem had meanwhile affected the progress toward publication of the new Imagist anthology. When Macmillan declined to publish it, Lowell had persuaded her friend Ferris Greenslet, literary adviser at Houghton Mifflin, to take it on. He was happy to do so provided that Hueffer's 'On Heaven', which was considered blasphemous, was excluded. Flint and Aldington expressed their annoyance and Hueffer declined the invitation to submit an alternative piece. The new anthology went ahead without him.

Pound's comment in a letter to his mother in December, 'Hilda back from the country – looking more robust', shows that relations between the two couples were still cordial, but, with Aldington's work for Hueffer completed, he and H.D. now moved to Hampstead – to a larger flat (with 'a real bathroom and a kitchen') at 7, Christchurch Place. They were near the Heath and 'away from Kensington squabbles'.[24] Some months later they would be joined by the newly-married Alec and Amy Randall, who moved in to number 3. Life appeared for a time more encouraging and H.D.'s health improved in the fresher air. For a while Aldington even made joint plans with George Plank for launching their own journal, but the financial realities of the project soon daunted them.

As the publication date for *Some Imagist Poets* drew closer, Aldington prepared a special 'Imagist' issue of *The Egoist* for May.[25] Flint was to write a 'history' of the movement, and the Imagists and others would contribute reviews of the individual poets: Flint on H.D., Fletcher on Lowell, Aldington on Flint, Olivia Shakespear on Lawrence and Ferris Greenslet on Fletcher. Aldington also contributed a (rather patronising) piece on Pound but declined to include one on himself, and invited Monro to review the anthology. The issue included a new poem from each of the six, as well as one by Sinclair and one by Marianne Moore.[26]

The outcome was far from what had been hoped for; in fact it constituted a series of disasters. First, Fletcher's essay on Lowell was so adulatory – and out-of-tune with the even-handedness of the other essays – that Aldington was forced to edit it, bringing about fury from Fletcher and a conflict with Lowell, who started to think that the English 'faction' were out to sideline their two trans-Atlantic partners. Worse still, Monro's review, the 'centrepiece' of the issue, was highly critical – in parts even reminiscent of Horace Holley's satire of the previous year. He pointed out (mindful, perhaps, that he would soon be publishing the second Georgian anthology) that the Imagists were 'only one of the latest groups in the forward movement of English poetry' and commented that they seemed 'more concerned effectively to describe their rapid impressions than faithfully to record their abiding sentiments'. In his opinion, their 'most conspicuous defect' was a 'labour to appear skilful'.[27] Lowell was so shocked by this negative review that she refused to circulate the hundred and fifty copies of the issue that she had been sent for distribution to Boston bookshops. She had other reasons too: Lawrence's poem was the disturbing 'Eloi, Eloi, Lama Sabachthani', a sexualised account of a soldier's experience of bayoneting an enemy; and she considered that Dora Marsden's lengthy opening article would daunt any prospective purchaser.

Fortunately, the issue sold well in England. Furthermore, the Aldingtons' ever-supportive friend Sinclair came to the rescue in the June issue with a riposte to Monro in the form of an essay on H.D. (whose poetry, she said, proved 'the power of the clean, naked, sensuous image to carry the emotion') and a defence of Imagism which defined the Image with a precision of which Pound would surely have approved, had he read it.[28] He certainly read the May issue and reacted immediately – perhaps as Flint had intended he should – to the 'History of Imagism'. Flint had attributed the origins of Imagism to the Tour Eiffel group and, in particular, to Hulme and Storer, mentioning also his own early advocacy of *vers libre*. He had pointed out that Pound was a latecomer to that group and had not shown any interest in its ideas until 1912. He had concluded his essay with the pronouncement that 'there is no difference, except that which springs from differences of temperament and talent, between an imagist poem of today and those written by Edward Storer and T.E. Hulme.' The fall-out continued for months and chiefly took the form of an extremely abusive correspondence between Flint and Pound. Always mindful of their friendship with the latter, Aldington and H.D. kept out of the line of fire. 'We are both so angry – though we wouldn't have E.P. know we are annoyed for the world – silence is the best, for us, I think, and surely the simplest policy!' H.D. wrote to Flint.[29] Her letters to him were always diplomatic.

The anthology was selling particularly well in America, partly because Lowell worked hard to promote it and partly because it stimulated a great deal of controversy.[30] Aldington's preface added to the amount of paper now devoted to manifestos of Imagism. In it he set forth six principles which were, he said, 'the essentials of all great poetry'. Three of them were familiar, echoing both his own essay in *The Egoist* of 1 June 1914 and Pound's original pronouncements in *Poetry*: the use of 'the *exact* word', 'new rhythms' and the production of poetry which was 'hard and clear, never blurred or indefinite'. The fourth principle was the requirement to 'present an image'. Since this is amplified by the statement that 'poetry should render particulars exactly and not deal in vague generalities', it seems to be simply a reworking of Pound's original prohibition of 'abstractions' or a restatement of the notion of 'direct treatment', rather than a consideration of the whole doctrine of the image such as Pound had recently been attempting. There were two new principles, one being 'absolute freedom in the choice of the subject', a particular preoccupation of Aldington's, used as he was to criticism for employing classical subjects rather than contemporary ones. The last was the declaration that 'Most of us believe that concentration is of the very essence of poetry.' The concept is not elaborated and the particular wording of the statement is surprising: is there a suggestion that some of the poets in the anthology were falling short of Imagist best practice?

Meanwhile, the war was intruding on their lives. One of the first of their friends to be involved was Sinclair, who had spent three weeks as a volunteer with a field ambulance unit in Belgium early in the war and was still dealing with the trauma of that experience. Earlier still, in August 1914, Aldington had gone with his friends to Charing Cross to see Gaudier-Brzeska off to join the French army; in June 1915 they learned that he was dead. He was twenty-three years old. Hulme had been back in England, wounded, since mid-April, and Gaudier's death led to an estrangement between himself and Pound as they both attempted to deal with the problems of the dead man's estate. The next member of their circle to enlist was the most surprising of all: the 41 year-old Hueffer, desperate to escape from his troubled relationship with Hunt, enlisted in the Welch Regiment at the end of July.

It was, however, a private grief that came to Aldington and H.D. that year. On 20 May 1914 H.D. went into labour. At two o'clock the following morning a still-born baby girl was delivered. Aldington wrote in a distressed state to Lowell only hours later, telling her: 'She (Hilda) was in a good nursing home and had an obstetrical specialist. I haven't seen the doctor but the nurse said it was a beautiful child & they can't think why it didn't live. It was very strong but wouldn't breathe. Poor Hilda is very distressed, but is recovering physically. I don't think there is any danger.'[31]

In both *Tribute to Freud* and in her fiction, H.D. explores the circumstances of her loss of this child. In the memoir she tells us that the still-birth was caused by 'shock and repercussions of war news broken to me in a rather brutal fashion.'[32] From the unpublished 1950s fictionalised memoir, *Magic Mirror*, we are led to understand that it was Aldington who broke the news of the sinking of the *Lusitania* to her in this 'brutal fashion': 'Rafe Ashton destroyed the un-born, the child Amor, when a few days before it was due, he burst in upon the Julia of that story [*Bid Me To Live*], with "don't you realise what this means? Don't you feel anything? *The Lusitania has gone down*"'. However, we need to note that alongside this statement H.D. wrote neatly in pencil on the typed manuscript: 'But this never happened. Surely this was fantasy.'[33] The *Lusitania* was sunk off the Irish coast by a German U-boat on the afternoon of 7 May, and the resultant loss of twelve hundred lives (128 of them American) would have appalled a sensitive person like H.D., whose imagination would instantly have called up the terrible scenes. It is also perfectly possible that Aldington's immediate reaction to the news was excitement, in the expectation that the outcome would be America's entry into the war. (Indeed the complicity of the British government in the disaster is still a matter of debate.)

If this experience was traumatic for H.D., we might have expected a miscarriage, not that she would deliver a still-born child at full term two weeks later, a child which had not died *in utero* but was 'strong' and 'wouldn't breathe'. What is important is not whether this explanation of the loss of the child is credible but the fact that H.D. recalled it in these terms. It tells us of her need to find a cause – and to attribute blame. (Perhaps the pencilled note on the manuscript is her own recognition of this fact.) Similar processes are at work in her much earlier reworking of the experience in *Asphodel*.[34] 'Hermione' recalls the nurses' disapproval of her husband's not having enlisted and their telling her that other women in the nursing home have husbands who are wounded or missing: 'Their cheeks went pink with almost consumptive joy and fervour while they drove and drove and drove one towards madness. Why isn't Mr Darrington in Khaki?' Hermione continues: 'Khaki killed it. They killed it. . . . Good old ecstatic baby-killers like the Huns up there.'

In *Asphodel* the 'Huns' play an active role in the still-birth as the baby is delivered in an air-raid, although the first air-raid on London did not take place until ten days after H.D.'s confinement. That she remained in the unsympathetic atmosphere of the 'real' nursing home for a further three weeks, presumably on medical advice, can only have exacerbated her distress.

Barbara Guest argues a more extreme interpretation of H.D.'s explanation for the still-birth, maintaining that H.D. had not wanted the child and 'placed her guilt . . . on an international episode.'[35] *Asphodel* certainly suggests that H.D. found pregnancy terrifying:

> . . . almost a year and her mind glued down, broken, and held back like a wild bird caught in bird-lime. The state she had been in was a deadly crucifixion. Not one torture (though God that had been enough) but months and months when her flaming mind beat up and she found she was caught, her mind not taking her as usual like a wild bird but her mind wings beating, beating and her feet caught, her feet caught, glued like a wild bird in bird-lime. Darrington hadn't known this. No one had known this. No one would ever know it for there were no words to tell it in. How tell it? How tell it? You can't say this, this . . .but men will say O she was a coward, a woman who refused her womanhood. No, she hadn't. But take a man with a flaming mind and ask him to do this. Ask him to sit in a dark cellar and no books . . . but you mustn't. You can't. Women can't speak and clever women don't have children. So if a clever woman does speak, she must be mad. She wouldn't have had a baby if she hadn't been.[36]

This passage is worth examining closely. Its anger is that of the feminist and the woman artist. Are pregnancy and motherhood compatible with artistic creation? 'Clever women don't have children'; Sinclair, Hunt, Lowell, Moore, H.D.'s fellow women artists, were childless. To have attempted to have a baby *and* to continue to be an artist must mean that one is mad. This is not, however, the speaker's view; it is the view, she asserts, of the patriarchal society she inhabits. She hadn't 'refused her womanhood', but she was being expected to accept it without speaking out about her fears and her sense of entrapment; were she to defy this taboo she would be branded as 'mad'. H.D.'s pregnancy was probably unplanned; the couple may well have been daunted by the prospect of parenthood, particularly given the war and their restricted income; but there is no evidence that the child was unwanted. Guilt may have been a factor in the grief and depression that H.D. experienced after the loss of her child, but it is a common response in cases of stillbirth, as is the insistent need for explanation.

In a letter to his mother on 23 May, Pound wrote: 'Hilda's infant died so don't send it a christening spoon, or embarrass Mrs Doolittle with enquiries. Hilda is, I believe, recovering quite nicely.'[37] What is interesting about this comment is not Pound's characteristic awkwardness with emotion but the assumption of Isabel's prior knowledge of the pregnancy, which has not otherwise been mentioned in Pound's correspondence with her. Isabel had been in London until the end of October 1914 and we can infer from this letter that H.D., thousands of miles away from her own mother, had shared the news of her pregnancy with her. Pound's 'Hilda back from the country – looking more robust' back in December thus takes on a new significance.

Sea Garden, the collection of twenty-seven poems which H.D. would publish in September 1916, covers a period of four years, so it is hard to tell whether she suffered a creative block during her pregnancy – or indeed in the months following the loss of her child. As a body, these poems, lyrical but also dramatic, work through moods of loneliness, suffering and longing but also defiance, hope and ecstasy. A few we can certainly date to the period of her pregnancy: five appeared in *Poetry* in March 1915 – they would win her the third prize in the journal's annual poetry awards at the end of the year – and another, 'Mid-Day' appeared in the May 1915 issue of *The Egoist*.[38] Helen Carr points out that this last poem is (paradoxically) a powerful exploration of the loss of creativity:[39]

> I am anguished – defeated.
>   . . . A slight wind shakes the seed-pods –
> my thoughts are spent
> as the black seeds.
> My thoughts tear me,
> I dread their fever.
> I am scattered in its whirl
> I am scattered like
> the hot shrivelled seeds. . . .
> the poplar is bright on the hill,
> the poplar spreads out, deep-rooted among trees.
>
> O poplar, you are great
> among the hill-stones,
> while I perish on the path
> among the crevices of the rocks.

Whatever had been the effect of her pregnancy, the loss of the child would have a devastating long-term impact on H.D. and on her marriage. James Whitall had observed the way in which H.D. managed to function effectively in a social context while at the same time standing apart, 'sustained in some other region', but the months ahead would place increasing strain on such coping strategies. For the artist the partition walls between art and life are necessarily porous, but H.D.'s writing, particularly her prose work, reveals how barely for her they existed at all.

When she left the nursing home on 11 June, Aldington took her straight to Eva Fowler's country cottage at Daisy Meadow in Brasted, where they stayed for a couple of weeks, on their own for much of the time. He wrote to Flint: 'We are on a hillside looking out across half a county; there are deep-scented white carnations, red large poppies, blue and yellow lupins, gladiolus, irises, pansies and roses, in the garden; we get our water from a well & use a dainty earth closet. Et ego in

Arcadia. There is a quarry full of wild red fox-gloves within half a league. I shall abandon poetry and become a market gardener.'[40] Since it would probably have been Pound (or Dorothy) who arranged for them to have the use of Eva Fowler's cottage, we can guess that he was still involved in their lives, even while in the midst of his verbal battle with Flint. H.D.'s welfare would always be of concern to him, even if he had, at times, strange ways of demonstrating it. She and Aldington moved on from Kent to the country home of the Whitalls in Surrey, relaxing in the beautifully-tended garden and walking in the peaceful wooded Tillingbourne Valley and up on the North Downs.

Here Aldington discussed with Whitall his latest scheme: a 'Poets' Translation Series' which was advertised in the August *Egoist*. Six translations, by Aldington, H.D., Flint, Whitall and Storer, appeared in the journal between September and February 1916 and were also printed to be sold as individual pamphlets or by subscription.[41] An advertisement claimed that the scheme arose from the wish to create both 'a higher standard of poetry' and 'an appreciation of the writers of antiquity', but only H.D.'s choruses would receive any critical acclaim. Nevertheless, the series sold well, particularly as Lowell canvassed all her friends and acquaintances in the U.S. to take out subscriptions. Aldington would turn increasingly to translation as the war progressed: when anxiety numbed his creative impulse, translation made him feel that he was still being productive; but the Greek world also offered escape. He told Lowell: 'The Greeks are so far away from a modern romantic restlessness; with them every emotion is hidden and calmed into an exquisite art convention.'[42]

Whether hiding emotion was the best route for Aldington at this period is questionable; he seems not to have been able to face sharing with H.D. the sense of bereavement they must both have felt, displacing his pain into a concern for her physical health. A childhood which had left him both wary of female emotion and guarded with his own feelings had equipped him poorly to cope with the first grief of his adult life. *Bid Me To Live* suggests that H.D. also suppressed her feelings: 'She had lost the child only a short time before. But she never thought of that. A door had shuttered her in, something had died that was going to die. . . . If the wound had been nearer the surface, she could have grappled with it. It was annihilation itself that gaped at her.'[43] The couple returned to London on 7 July and Aldington wrote to Lowell: 'Hilda is very much better – is, in fact, so well that I have to keep her from doing too much.'[44] Even *The Egoist* looked temporarily more secure, with an increase in subscriptions, and more encouraging reviews of the anthology were starting to appear: 'Opinion is beginning slightly to turn our way', Lowell was told.[45]

The positive mood did not last: 'Time had them by the throat.'[46] London in the autumn was grim, with an increase in bombing raids and an enforced black-out. Aldington's ambivalence towards the war faced him with a moral dilemma that he felt increasingly unable to resolve. He wrote in *Life for Life's Sake*: 'I lost the serenity and harmony which forms a large part of real success in life. I thought it was a plain duty to be in the army. . . . On the other hand I thought war an insanity.'[47] Furthermore, the couple's physical relationship was adversely affected by H.D.'s fear of a further pregnancy, something her doctor had advised her against as long as the war and her nervous condition persisted. In *Bid Me To Live* Julia speaks of: 'Three weeks in that ghastly nursing-home and then coming back to the same Rafe. Herself different. How could she blithely face what he called love, with that prospect looming ahead and the matron, in her harsh voice, laying a curse on whatever might then have been, "You know you must not have another baby until after the war is over." Meaning in her language, you must keep away from your husband, keep him away from you. When he was all she had, was country, family, friends.'[48] There is a sub-text here ('what he called love') and, given the alternatives available to abstinence, the reader is prompted to suspect that the speaker (along with her creator?) is denying her own aversion to physical contact.

She told Lowell at the end of November, 'I feel rather useless for the atmosphere created by the war has half-paralysed my creative powers.'[49] As usual, only part of the full story was made available for Lowell's consumption, but she would write again in January, when the non-appearance of her allowance from her parents caused her to turn to Lowell for money (readily and sympathetically given): 'I haven't been very well otherwise I could manage. My nerves were so shattered last spring that I couldn't find any reserve of strength.'[50]

In August 1915, Lawrence and Frieda returned to London, to the ground-floor flat of a semi-detached house in the Vale of Health, only five minutes' walk from the Aldingtons' home off Hampstead Square. He was awaiting the appearance of *The Rainbow*, a revised draft of which Methuen had finally agreed to publish, and spent some time in H.D.'s company while Aldington was at the *Egoist* offices in Bloomsbury and Frieda off on her own pursuits. The two writers' grim portrayals of war-time London – in H.D.'s *Bid Me To Live* and *Paint It Today* and in Lawrence's *Kangaroo* – show us how similarly they responded to the bleakness of the world around them. Lawrence's sensibility was finely attuned to suffering and in *Bid Me To Live* Julia tells Rafe, who is concerned about her correspondence with 'Rico': 'He was the only one who seemed remotely to understand what I felt when I was so ill.' When Rafe responds with, 'We all understood that,' Julia thinks, 'Let him have it his own way. They didn't. No-one had understood but Rico.'[51] Aldington himself confided to a correspondent years later that Lawrence was the only person who had understood what was wrong between himself and H.D. at the time, 'though,' he added, 'I couldn't talk of it to him – it was too painful.'[52]

At the time he was more critical of his fellow-artist, writing to Lowell: 'He has a vast red beard and is very cantankerous and anti-war. . . . He is dying of consumption, of course.'[53] With this letter to Lowell, Aldington enclosed his contributions for the 1916 anthology, referring inappropriately to them as his 'seven poor little children, a little consumptive some of them.' He had more reason for sympathy with Lawrence when the publication of *The Rainbow* on 30 September was greeted with such condemnation by the popular press that in early November the Methuen offices were raided and all copies destroyed under the Obscene Prints Act of 1857. Lawrence was plunged once more into poverty, and at the end of the year moved to a cottage in Cornwall loaned by a friend.

When news of this event reached Lowell in Boston, she wondered whether the inclusion of Lawrence in the 1916 Imagist Anthology might prove risky. (Her verdict on the controversy typifies the elitism which at times appalled her young English friends: 'I think perhaps the peasant type of mind is not at its happiest in speaking of erotic subjects.')[54] Aldington was indignant, both on the grounds of the injustice of the ban on *The Rainbow* and because he felt that Lawrence was an asset to the anthology. He pointed out that the second Georgian anthology, containing several Lawrence poems, had just sold out on the first day of its publication. There was no further talk of excluding Lawrence, although it was probably Ferris Greenslet's reassurance that convinced Lowell, rather than Aldington's outburst. She had realised how hasty he could be. Having found him an American publisher for his first poetry collection, Edmund Brown's Four Seas Company, she had to endure his frustration – often misdirected at her – at the publisher's tardiness, first in bringing the book out and then in promoting it and paying the royalties. Meanwhile the English edition, entitled *Images (1910-1915)*, appeared under the Poetry Bookshop imprint at the beginning of December, along with Flint's *Cadences*. To the two poets' delight, and Monro's surprise, the books sold well, if in the hundreds, as compared to the thousands of *Georgian Poetry 1913-1915*.

Lowell's proposal to help Aldington establish a new journal in Boston ('an American *Mercure*') was still 'on the table'. The introduction of conscription, although initially only for unmarried men, was now a certainty and H.D. had begun to see a return to America as a way out of her personal nightmare, writing to Lowell of her excitement at the prospect. However, once they got down to practicalities, Lowell took fright. Aldington's insistence that her offer of $5,000 to start the journal would be inadequate, unless they could also obtain five thousand subscribers and some advertising was perhaps less worrying than his demand for complete editorial control. His strategies for evading conscription were also alarming. While his initial plan was for his father, now working as a civil servant in the Ministry of Munitions, to use what little influence he could command, and while he expressed some small faith in his adolescent hernia operation to exempt him from service, his major proposal (a suggestion of his father's) was that if Lowell would write a letter to indicate that the proposed journal would be supportive of the Allied cause, he could take this to the Foreign Office. Such was Lowell's horror that her lengthy letter of retraction and excuse was preceded by a cable.

On 27 January 1916 the Military Service Act was passed. From 1 March that year all *unmarried* men between the ages of nineteen and forty-one and without dependent children would be deemed to have enlisted. There was little doubt that the act would soon be extended to include married men. With the American option closed to them, Aldington and H.D. needed to leave London, both for her health's sake and because they could not afford to remain where they were. It was Cournos, whom Aldington had been helping for the last few months with his translation of *The Little*

Demon by the Russian novelist, Feodor Sologub, who came up with a scheme for their move to the country. He, too, was in straitened circumstances and needed to move out of London. He had friends living very cheaply on Exmoor. The plan was that the Aldingtons would find a cottage to rent in the same locality, with a room for him to occupy as soon as the authorities would allow him (as an alien) to leave London. On 25 February they moved all their possessions to 44 Mecklenburgh Square, where Cournos was already renting a small room and where the landlady had agreed to store their furniture and effects. That evening there was a farewell dinner at their favourite restaurant, the Isola Bella in Bloomsbury, with Cournos, Flint and Plank, and the next morning they left for North Devon.

In 1913, the year before he had taken over Pound's old room in Kensington, Cournos had shared lodgings in Hampstead with Carl Fallas, a young journalist from Manchester. Like Cournos, Fallas had gone to work on a newspaper (*The Manchester Evening Chronicle*) as a young teenager, but in 1906, aged twenty-one, he had set off on four years of travel, working on newspapers in Ceylon and Japan before returning home via San Francisco and a voyage round Cape Horn as a crewman on a clipper. In 1912 he had married and come to London with his wife and baby to try his hand as a short-story writer for periodicals. Aldington, who remained in touch with him (if intermittently) until Fallas's death in 1962, recalled in *Life for Life's Sake* Fallas's 'gift of alert curiosity about human beings and their ways . . . his lively knack for telling yarns of his varied experience . . . his streak of poetic sensibility,' while Cournos comments in his autobiography on Fallas's 'earthy sense of humor, which saved us from many a dismal situation.'[55] Cournos describes Florence Fallas ('Flo'), who was the same age as Aldington, as 'very good-looking, fully a head taller than Carl; charmingly simple, a country-girl in spirit.'[56] In 1914 the Fallases, with their small daughter, Leonora, and another friend, John Mills Whitham, had moved to North Devon where they could live much more cheaply than in London.

In his memoir, Aldington suggests that Fallas and Whitham were models of 'The Realist and the Idealist', and resembled Sancho Panza and Don Quixote: where Fallas was a cheerful sceptic, Whitham was 'the prisoner of a cast-iron non-conformist conscience . . . a man of inflexible character and *idées fixes*, yet warm-hearted, unselfish and an eloquent talker.'[57] In 1915 Whitham had just published the second of two deeply pessimistic novels.[58] He was a conscientious objector, and would briefly be imprisoned for his beliefs, while Fallas, not yet forced to a decision, was, like Aldington, undecided.

Living in very straitened circumstances on Exmoor since the beginning of the war, Whitham and the Fallases had grown very close. The Fallases had taken two rooms in a cowman's cottage in Mannacott Lane near Martinhoe; Whitham had a room in Trentishoe, two miles away. He would write to Fallas twenty years later: 'Do you ever realise the fools the three of us were in those Mannacott days; and what magnificent folk we were too! What truly authentic artists and philosophers we were as we struggled to keep alive in a rural remoteness, whilst one half of the civilised world tried to scatter the brains and bowels of t'other half!'[59]

A tragedy had befallen the Fallases at Martinhoe. Carl tells the poignant story in his memoir of the stillbirth of a son, of how the cowman made them a small coffin and of how Carl and the rector buried the child. The baby had been in a breach position and the cowman had gone to fetch the doctor. By the time he arrived – on horseback through the snow – the baby had died.[60] From a letter written by Florence nearly fifty years later, we can infer that she and H.D. told each other of their sad experiences, but it was not enough to help H.D. come to terms with what had happened to her.[61] Of Florence, her husband wrote: 'But she was no more prone than I to repine in protracted grief, at that time, for what befell. Doubtless, if she had been less vital in spirit, and in body, this infant, her second, would not have chosen that unprepared hour to make its dashing, impetuous entry into the world – one small foot, one small leg, leading the way.'

The countryside was under six inches of snow when the Aldingtons arrived at their temporary lodgings in Martinhoe but the landscape was starkly beautiful. In less than two weeks they had found a cottage nearby, in the rugged Heddon Valley. They had two rooms to themselves, another for Cournos, and the use of the kitchen. They revelled in the rural life, H.D. making marmalade and Aldington cutting down trees and chopping them into firewood. H.D. wrote to Flint: 'The female prospers! She does a good "swat" of writing every Day – and in between poems scrubs the kettles & stew pans in our own trout-stream – it roars & gurgles down our valley across our road & all but into our front garden. You probably passed our house on your journeys from Hunters [sic] Inn up the valley – our stream is the Heddon – I believe you know its Mouth! A wonderful Mouth, too! R. & I have clambered along the edge of both the great hills that flank it. We will bathe there in the summer. London seems very far away. We are startled & furious when a carriage passes our door. This happens about twice a day. Once a motor flew past. We were sick!'[62] They worked in the mornings on translation and poetry and went for long walks in the afternoons, relishing the appearance of spring when, belatedly, it arrived. They enjoyed the company of the Fallases and Whitham, their 'confrères littéraires', on walks and at shared meals.[63] Cournos soon joined them and started work on his first novel. At Easter – a late one that year – Flint and his family came to visit. It seemed for a while to be an idyllic life.

Two factors intervened to spoil their peace of mind. First, they knew that the interlude would be short-lived; conscription (or the alternative, perhaps prison) threatened both Aldington and Fallas, although it was Aldington who brooded on the prospect. His letters to Flint make constant references to the pressing need for him to produce a book (he was working on one on French prose writers) and write some poetry before he was conscripted. Terrified as he was, he did not share Whitham's views and was conscious of the fact that others were serving while he was not. During Flint's Easter visit a terrible argument took place, concerning which Flint had the temerity to write subsequently, in a lengthy epistle of self-justification to H.D., 'Why in the world can we not argue out a question dispassionately?'[64] The disagreement had been principally between himself and Whitham, who had provocatively suggested that the British workman would be just as well off under

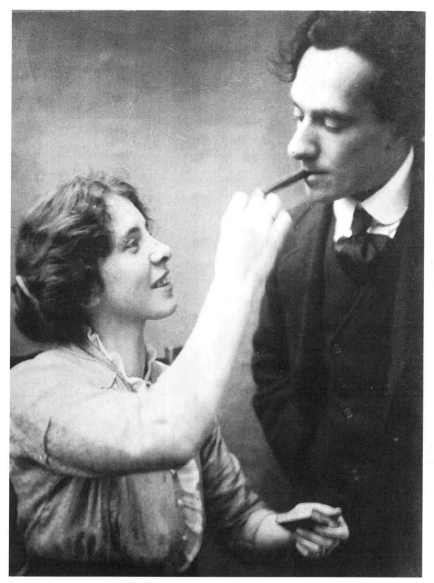

Carl and Florence Fallas, c. 1916

the Germans, but the intensity of the argument had clearly been heightened by H.D.'s sensitivity over American neutrality and by the fact that not one of the men around the table, other than Whitham, felt comfortable about his current non-combatant status. Flint had also become concerned about Aldington's proposal for H.D. to return to her family in the U.S. once he went into the army – or prison. It is a measure of Flint's devotion to both his friends that his own proposal was that H.D. should live with his family – or with just Violet and the children, if he too was called up. H.D. reassured him that she had no intention of leaving England.

It may well have been the strain of the war that precipitated the other catastrophe: Aldington was immediately attracted to Florence Fallas. Soon after moving to Woodland Cottage, he gave Flint a ribald account of her charms, but told him that he would not attempt an affair with her for fear of making H.D. miserable.[65] In a further letter a few days later he enclosed three poems, one of which, 'Blizzard', made Flint sure that his friend had abandoned his compunctions:

> The wind hurls snow against the hills,
> Piles it in hollows, against crags:
> The ice wind rattles like dying breath.
>
> The rush of hard white flakes blinds me;
> I am stunned by the whirring air.
> Yet I forget for a moment
> And think of your limbs in the firelight,
> The point of your breast
> Crushed under my cheek.
>
> Snow, wind, frost assail me;
> I am numb and desperate;
> But I grow warm – my face flushes –
> Remembering our keen forbidden caresses,
> The cleft of your body,
> Your closed eyes.[66]

In fact the poem was fantasy: it was two months before the affair was consummated. He wrote to Flint on 26 May:

> I ought to have foreseen it, but now I'm in, I'm in! Don't tell me I'm a scandalous rotter or I shall weep. You can trust me not to make anyone else unhappy.
>
> I *am* a damned sentimentalist.
>
> If you hit me with commonsense maxims I shall go and drown myself! But O Franky boy, what a red-hot lance of pleasure-pain and wild content a woman's lips thrust into one. For God's sake don't think I'm mad. I'm quite calm and cheerful, no-one sees anything.
>
> Don't pity H.D. – one learns to appreciate as [sic] I do – by compassion. And for heaven's sake utter silence about this. I am afraid I shall blurt it out to Kournos – be the patient keeper of my confessions! You shall know it all some time.[67]

With the letter he enclosed an untitled poem about the 'violence of [his] desire' that would appear – in a much abbreviated form – in the 1917 Imagist anthology under the title 'Images'. There would be more poems for Flint: on 2 June he sent him another untitled one and another entitled 'A Lost Day', both expressions of his current passion and neither of which he would publish.[68] On 12 June he wrote to Flint that: 'Double adultery has been "consummated" twice, *non sine gloria*.

Of course, I am calmer but damnably passionate.' He went on to tell Flint of how he had been in Florence's bed two days earlier at eleven o'clock in the morning when the bell had rung and they thought themselves discovered, but later learned that it had been merely a chance call from a neighbour. The experience, he said, had been quite 'eighteenth century'.[69]

That he could prioritise his own sexual desires over concerns for the feelings of his wife and his new friend may be an indication of the extent to which H.D.'s sexual reserve over the past year had affected him; but the reckless *carpe diem* tone of the letters to Flint suggests that the affair was just as much a manifestation of his fears about the war. Whether he consciously felt that he had a right to follow his instincts when he had only a short period of freedom ahead of him or whether there was a much more subconscious drive towards risk-taking as a form of displacement, anxiety and apprehension must have played their part. It was a pattern that would recur, but one he would never come to recognise. For him, sexual attraction was its own justification. 'Physical passion goes so deep that one is warped without it', he wrote to a correspondent in later years.[70] Although he and Fallas kept their affair secret from their partners (and there is no indication that Carl Fallas ever learned the truth), the acutely sensitive H.D. understood immediately what had happened, as her subsequent correspondence with Cournos revealed.

Meanwhile the creative output of the two poets was bringing them some notice. The 1916 anthology appeared in May. Its compilation had been difficult. When both Lawrence and Flint had been tardy in producing their contributions, Aldington had suggested approaching Williams, Moore, Upward or Cournos, but Lowell had refused to contemplate this. Then the contributors had been more critical – in a transatlantic divide – of one another's selections than in 1915. Flint's poem 'Evil' had caused the most controversy, with everyone finally accepting Lowell's veto. He and the Aldingtons were also unhappy with the tribute to Monroe's *Poetry* that Lowell insisted on including (Monroe now being perceived by them as in the Pound camp); and Fletcher's Preface had had to be virtually re-written by Lowell because it was too 'violent and militant'.[71] Aldington was dissatisfied with the final version, which was principally devoted to a defence of *vers libre*, but had been rebuked by Lowell: 'We [Fletcher and herself] both agree with your interpretation of Imagism but we are both intensely dramatic in our work, and I think both of us are willing to sacrifice some of the more astringent Imagist rules for the sake of vividness and life.'[72]

However, Lowell's tireless promotion of Imagism in the U.S. was paying off and the anthology received some encouraging reviews, notably that by William Stanley Braithwaite in the *Boston Evening Transcript* of 4 May. Braithwaite commented that there was 'something in the principles of the [Imagist] school which is vital to the substance and form of American poetry.' He judged the current anthology better than its 1915 predecessor and singled out Lowell's 'Spring Day' as 'the best study one can make of the new method of poetic expression.' Braithwaite had become a firm supporter of Lowell, through whom he offered Aldington the role of 'foreign correspondent' on his new (but short-lived) *Poetry Review of America*;

the war would prevent him from taking up the offer. Both Mary Aldis in *The Little Review* and Monroe in *Poetry* thought the anthology a valuable contribution to contemporary writing but found Aldington's poems less impressive than his previous work.[73] British responses were slower, but in January 1917 the *Times Literary Supplement* would open its review with the comment that: 'Imagist poetry fills us with hope.'[74]

Poetry was much more enthusiastic about Aldington's *Images Old and New*, which had at last appeared in America. The reviewer was Fletcher, now a supporter of Aldington, whom he felt had been badly treated by Lowell over the issue of starting an American journal. 'Recently,' he pronounced, 'there have been signs in England of a return to that simplicity and restraint which are the qualities of highest art. . . . Of this admirable tendency Mr Aldington is the precursor and the most shining example.' He went on to comment on Aldington's 'uniform technical excellence' and his 'style like a sword-blade, bright, keen, nervous and never exuberant.' 'He is,' he concluded, 'a poet as Simonides and Turgenev were poets.'[75] In the May issue of *The Little Review* the first part of an article by Fletcher entitled 'Three Imagist Poets' appeared, in which he called Aldington 'a poet for the well-read, intelligent, cultivated man or woman', a poet who 'never takes up the pen except when he has something individual to say.'[76]

Meanwhile, Constable had accepted H.D.'s first volume of verse, *Sea Garden*, and Lowell had been quick to place it with Houghton Mifflin in America. On 17 May H.D. wrote to Flint that the proofs for the English edition had arrived and that she, Aldington and Cournos were delighted with them. Constable had also expressed an interest in publishing the translation of Euripides' *Ion* on which she was working; but the real boost to her self-esteem came with a *TLS* review of the Poets' Translation Series in which the anonymous reviewer spoke of her as possessing 'an interpretative genius which is both provocative and stimulating.'[77] He was less complimentary about the other five translations but Aldington told Lowell that the review brought in a further five hundred sales of the series. Even T.S. Eliot's highly critical review in the November 1916 issue of *Poetry* would concede that H.D. had turned Euripides 'into English verse which can be taken seriously.'[78]

Lowell's promotion of the P.T.S. in America brought into the Aldingtons' lives a minister from Cleveland, Ohio with an amateur interest in printing. The Reverend Charles Bubb wrote to ask if he might publish some of the series on his small hand-press under his imprint of 'The Clerk's Press'. Bubb printed some seventy titles between 1908 and 1917, including five of Aldington's works and two of H.D.'s. It was a private arrangement, with no payment involved; the print runs never exceeded fifty copies, there were complimentary copies for the authors and they retained their copyright.[79] Both Aldington and H.D. were to be highly delighted by these attractive little booklets and Aldington wrote in response to Bubb's first letter: 'It is very pleasant to know that in these depressing months some of one's work has aroused interest so far away as Cleveland.'[80]

The anxiety about what lay ahead persisted, even turning into a form of panic, and Aldington received conflicting advice: Whitham argued for conscientious objection; Aldington's father advised him to apply for officer training, but there were no vacancies, and Albert Edward, although stressing the importance of his role in the Ministry of Munitions, was unable to pull strings. Randall suggested attesting for the Navy (Fallas's stories of life below deck soon made this option unattractive); and Fallas himself was as undecided as Aldington. H.D. voiced her concerns about her husband's state of 'melancholy' in letters to Flint and in conversations with Cournos. At the beginning of May, Whitham was hauled off to prison.[81]

On 25 May the Military Service Act (Session 2) was passed, extending conscription to married men. By now tension and anxiety had created in the group a wild gaiety, what Cournos in his autobiography describes as 'abnormal moods needing abnormal outlets'. His fictionalised account of events, *Miranda Masters* provides a more graphic, and perhaps exaggerated, account of the sexual tensions and of the nude bathing which was one of its outlets.[82] H.D. merely wrote to Flint: 'Every day we go to Heddons Mouth about 1:30, bathe, scamper about on the rocks, build a drift-wood fire and have tea.'[83] Since little Leonora Fallas was one of the party and would always remember the fun of bathing in a 'mountain pool' with H.D., the hedonism must not have been quite as unrestrained as Cournos portrays it.[84] However, it can be no coincidence that Aldington and Florence consummated their relationship in late May.

Forced to a decision at last, both men decided that they would not become conscientious objectors. In *Life for Life's Sake* Aldington writes: 'Carl was intensely curious to see the war, and pointed out that it would be a great shame to miss the greatest event of our lives. I saw that argument too; but it also struck me as a high price to pay for gratifying one's curiosity.'[85] It now occurred to them that if they enlisted promptly under the Derby Scheme, rather than waiting to be conscripted, they would have some choice about the regiment in which they would serve and would be able to remain together.[86] They must also have reflected that if they were going to serve anyway, it would be better not to go in under the slur of having been compelled to do so; they would become 'late-attested Derbymen'. They went off to enlist immediately and were given five weeks to set their affairs in order.

The June issue of *The Egoist* carried the following notice: 'Mr Aldington will shortly be called up for military service and during his absence the assistant-editorship of THE EGOIST will be taken over by "H.D."'

7. The Soldier: 1916

But O thou old and very cruel god,
Take, if thou will, this bitter cup from us
(Richard Aldington, 'Vicarious Atonement', 1916)

On Saturday 24 June 1916 Aldington and Fallas set off for the 11th Devonshire regimental base at Worgret Camp near Wareham in Dorset. H.D. remained at Woodland Cottage – with Cournos, who would later write in his autobiography:

> Psychically wrought up, immediately after his departure, [H.D.] impetuously walked over to me in the sitting-room we all jointly occupied, and kissed me. This revelation of confidence and its implication of the two of us being left to maintain the thinning thread of spirit in growing chaos, touched me, and I resolved to help her breach the emptiness of the days immediately before her. . . .
>
> An extraordinary thing happened a day or two after Richard left. We were in the sitting-room having afternoon tea, when suddenly we looked at each other strangely.
>
> 'Did you hear it?' she asked me. 'He called you!'
>
> 'Yes,' I said. 'Isn't it strange?'
>
> And, indeed, what we both heard, distinctly and unmistakably was Richard's voice calling me: 'Korshoon!'
>
> . . . It seemed to come out of the very air out of doors. We looked out, but saw nothing.[1]

This story also figures in Cournos's *roman à clef, Miranda Masters,* where the voice 'numbed his sense of action, wove itself into his devotion to Miranda, into the words of tenderness he spoke to her, into the very texture of the pages he was writing.'[2] It is unlikely, given H.D.'s fear of sex during this period, as well as Cournos's conscience with regard to his friend, that there was a full-blown affair, but his obvious attraction to her at a time when her sense of her own physical attractiveness and sexual appeal (never robust) was particularly low, seems to have led her into behaviour which encouraged his hopes and was certainly unwise, if not self-indulgent. Perhaps each exploited the other's vulnerability, but it seems clear that Cournos was genuinely in love with H.D. at this time.

Meanwhile, in Company E, Hut 8, private 24965 was finding army life tougher than even he could have anticipated. His initial letters to Flint attempted to make light of matters: 'Here I am in a "gun-fodder" regiment! We will be at the front in two weeks';[3] and 'If I haven't written to you it is only due to inoculation, vaccination and general exploitation.'[4] Only days later, however, his tone is utterly depressed and he complains of the 'obscene and offensive' nature of the men's language, the vileness of the NCOs, the filthy tasks, such as the scrubbing of a stone floor in the kitchen of the officers' mess, and the rigours of a day that lasts from 5.30 a.m. to 4.30 p.m. Aware that all this sounds like 'whining', he remarks that his life is 'made up of tiny things important enough to ruin your whole life'.[5]

To poor Cournos, fast becoming the emotional refuse bin for both Aldingtons, he allowed himself more self-pity. His more explicit account of the scrubbing of the kitchen floor (he only tells Flint that the task made him 'retch') runs: 'Yesterday I had a horrible experience, which please don't tell H.D. . . . . I was put to scrub the stone floor of one of the filthiest kitchens I ever saw in my life. It was deep with grease, soot and mess of all kinds. The bucket was greasy & the scrubbing rags so unspeakably filthy and slimy that it made me nauseated to touch them and I shuddered every time I had to plunge my hand into the pail of loathsome, greasy water. For a while it broke me, old chap, and I'm not too ashamed to tell you that for a moment or two I just bent my head & sobbed. It was so bitter a humiliation, so sordid a Golgotha.'[6] How much of his misery he did reveal to H.D. we shall never know: in late 1920 he would destroy all the letters she had ever written to him, along with his letters to her prior to late March 1918, the date when she left their London flat for Cornwall, leaving behind all their correspondence.

On Sunday 23 July H.D. joined him. She had taken lodgings in the village of Corfe Castle. In a letter to Cournos she spoke of falling out of the train 'into the salute of a very tall, strange person whom my mind told me must, of all his majesty's many, be only One!' She continues: 'It was R.A. – looking very well, taller, tremendously full chested with a cropped but not disfigured head.'[7] However, she saw more profound changes in her husband than his military demeanour, as she revealed in a letter to Flint: while he had 'changed superficially in to the "nice, clean young Englishman" type', what made her 'desperate' was 'the tragic eyes . . . the absolute foredoomed look'. She begged Flint to write 'silly, cheerful superficial anythings' to him as often as he could.[8]

She asked much the same of Lowell and Cournos. Lowell would manage to infuriate as much as console, writing: 'I cannot bear to have your brains and beautiful imagination knocked here and there in the rough duties of a private soldier's life.' Aldington clearly shared that sentiment, but the tones of the Boston patrician must have made him feel perversely that – for now at least – he would not attempt to join the officer class. She did not help matters by adding that, nevertheless, the war might prove 'a splendid experience' which would enlarge not only his 'outlook on life' but his 'suggestions for poetry'.[9]

Like H.D., Aldington wrote to Flint the day after her arrival, telling him how deeply affecting their reunion had been; but being with her had made life in the camp

Aldington the soldier, Autumn 1916

all the more difficult to cope with and his letter becomes an outburst of anger and disgust. 'This army life is stupid, boring and demoralising. The young ones learn to drink, and fornicate with disgusting whores – the old ones quickly become animals with an obscene tongue. . . . In all truth humanity is something disgusting. When I think about it I want to die.'[10] For all his sensuality, Aldington was a romantic and an idealist; his social world had also been very limited. (A few months later the young Wilfred Owen would react in a very similar way to his first close contact with 'other ranks' of men.)[11] And yet there were moments when his fellow soldiers surprised Aldington: only a week before the above letter he had written to Flint commenting on how touching he found it that on Saturdays they went looking for 'poppies, yellow and white daisies, and wild flowers' with which to decorate their tables. 'That's a simple act, which I'm very proud of. This love for flowers in the English lower classes is quite remarkable', he told Flint. We may find his remarks a little patronising, but they do reveal a genuine delight in his fellow men.[12]

Death of a Hero gives us a fuller picture not only of Aldington's experience of army training, but of the impact it had on him: 'It was not the physical fatigue Winterbourne minded. . . . He suffered mentally; suffered from the shock of the abrupt change from surroundings where the things of the mind chiefly were valued, to surroundings where they were ignorantly despised.'[13]

In 1919 Aldington would publish an article entitled 'Culture in the Army', which opens: 'Strictly speaking, there wasn't any.' It continues: 'The mind of the ordinary Englishman seems to be compounded of brutishness for which he can make no excuse and of sentimentality for which he can give no reason.'[14] Once in the front line, he would find (again like Wilfred Owen) other, perhaps compensating, qualities in his fellow soldiers. For now, however, the cultural desert that was army life and the minds of his companions appalled him.

His reactions both to the army regime and to the mass of civilian recruits were not unique or even unusual, particularly amongst those educated men who enlisted as private soldiers. The memoirs of Stephen Graham, the journalist and travel writer, another late volunteer, echo Aldington's letters and *Death of a Hero*. Graham tells us: 'We must not forget that for many the greatest ordeal was not the field of battle but the field of training, where men, infinitely diverse in character, originality and expression were standardised to become interchangeable parts in the fighting machine.'[15] He also recalls the ordeal of a fellow recruit who was a well-known composer: 'I don't think . . . anyone realised the strain and torture of the mind in a man whose heart and soul is given to Art, given long since, and the mind and body suddenly given to the army.' Like Aldington, Graham was also shocked to discover the level of education and culture in his fellow recruits.

In some ways ignorance and lack of imagination were a protection: 'those who could think most suffered most', Graham reflects.[16] The war itself continued to horrify Aldington – on moral, political and personal grounds. *Death of a Hero* again: 'The very apparatus of killing revolted him, took on a sort of sinister deadness. There was something in the very look of his rifle and equipment which filled him with depression. And then, in the imagination, he was already facing the existence for which this was but a preparation, already confronting the agony of his own death. . . . It was, perhaps, selfish . . . to worry about his own extinction when so many better men had already been obliterated. He felt rather ashamed and apologetic about it himself. But it is human to recoil from a violent death, even at twenty-two or three.'[17]

It is, perhaps, surprising to find how isolated Aldington felt. Although his childhood had been a lonely one, as an adult he had been universally regarded – almost from the time when he had gone to university and first found like-minded people – as lively, cheerful and companionable. Of course, there were no like-minded people here, and his obvious contempt for his companions must have alienated them. However, there was Carl Fallas. In *Life for Life's Sake* Aldington speaks of the two friends going out to tea at Corfe Castle on Sunday afternoons; they were to remain together right through their service at the front in 1917. Yet Aldington's letters to Flint and Cournos stress his loneliness and make little mention of Fallas. Of course, H.D. arrived only four weeks into the two men's training, after which point Aldington spent every moment of his precious Saturday and Sunday afternoons in her company. It is also probable that the two men had been assigned to different units. Since, according to *Life for Life's Sake*, they enjoyed nights out together once they were at base camp in Calais at the end of the year, it seems unlikely that Aldington's affair with Flo estranged the two men, or even that Fallas ever came to know of it.

Poet Aldington may have been, but he was also a robust and healthy young man: 'Winterbourne bore it better than most. His long walks and love for swimming had kept him supple. He did not raise weights like the draymen or dig like the navvies, but he could out-march and out-run them all, learn every new movement in half the time, dismount [*sic*] a Lewis gun while they were wondering which way the handle came off, score four bulls out of five, and saw immediately why you made head-cover first when digging in.'[18] Indeed, Aldington soon worked out that his only hope of escaping departure for the front within a few weeks was to show himself a quick learner and adept with a rifle, thus procuring a place on NCO training. He even tried to enlist Flint's help in this project, asking him to obtain copies of army manuals to send to him.

H.D. was not well-placed to help her husband through his ordeal. Not only was she called upon to provide him with emotional support just at the time when she felt hurt and betrayed, but their relationship continued to be drenched in deception. Putting his needs before her own, she tried to conceal both her own misery and her alarm at his state of mind. 'I feel so weak in the face of all this startling and horrible Hell! But don't think I give way when R. is with me!' she wrote to Flint.[19] Nor did they yet discuss his affair with Flo Fallas. His despair at his present and future circumstances must have been compounded by feelings of remorse and guilt. In any case he felt bound, as always, to protect H.D., and only revealed the depths of his anguish to Flint and to Cournos.

Meanwhile Cournos was also the confidant for H.D., who wrote him thirty-two letters during her three months at Corfe Castle. A reading of the Aldingtons' letters to him in this period shows us two people out of control, the one sinking into an almost clinical state of depression, the other spiralling into hysteria, a hysteria which would lead to disastrous misunderstandings in her relationships both with Cournos and with D.H. Lawrence, with whom she corresponded in the autumn in order to compile the next Imagist anthology. (Lawrence was as cynical as ever in his assessment of his friends: 'I can tell that the glamour is getting hold of [Aldington]: the 'now we're all men together' business', he wrote to Lowell.)[20]

Flint did more than send Aldington 'silly, cheerful superficial anythings': in early August he sent him a poem:

Soldiers
To R.A.

> Brother,
> I saw you on a muddy road
> In France
> Pass by with your battalion,
> Rifle at the slope, full marching order,
> Arm swinging;
> And I stood at ease,
> Folding my hands over my rifle,
> With my battalion.
> You passed by me and our eyes met.
> We had not seen each other since the days
> We climbed the Devon hills together;
> Our eyes met, startled;
> And, because the order was Silence,
> We dared not speak.
> O face of my friend,
> Alone distinct of all that company,
> You went on, you went on,
> Into the darkness;
> And I sit here at my table,
> Holding back my tears,
> With my jaw set and my teeth clenched,
> Knowing I shall not be
> Even so near you as I saw you
> In my dream.[21]

Aldington, who had commanded his friend to send him everything he wrote, adding, 'Je veux souvenir que j'ai rêvé d'etre poète', was moved to tears and told Flint, 'You are a good friend, old boy.'[22]

Quite soon, however, the tensions at Corfe Castle created a misunderstanding with Flint as well. Towards the end of the summer his wife and children were camping at Swanage, on the coast only four miles from Corfe Castle, and Flint was joining them at weekends. On the weekend of 2 September they came over to see the Aldingtons and Flint wrote afterwards to H.D. to ask if they might come again the following weekend. She felt that their visit had been rather overwhelming for her husband and suggested that it would be better if they didn't. She was also frustrated by her need for time to discuss the Flo Fallas affair with him. Flint was shocked by her letter and suggested in his reply that the fuss H.D. was making over her husband's circumstances and state of mind was not helpful for him. This was a response that tapped immediately into H.D.'s insecurity, and, as usual, she turned to Cournos: 'I am often unhappy to think that my complicated nature has led R. to think I am unhappy. That was why Frank's remark hurt me to the heart. I think of it and wonder if perhaps it would be best for me to leave England as R. first begged me to do. I wonder if I am not causing him pain by staying here.'[23]

Reconciliation with Flint was soon effected. Aldington valued his few loyal friends; he wrote to Cournos in August: 'I wish I could tell you how much I appreciate your devotion and that of Frank and Alec [Randall]. H.D. and you three seem to be all that are really left to me of my world; other people fade, become phantoms, vanish from one's life.'[24]

However, there were moments of calm. H.D.'s lodgings in Corfe Castle, beneath the crumbling ruins of the eleventh century castle itself, were a peaceful weekend retreat. For both of them the spot was a romantic one. Writing to Bubb in 1917, Aldington recalled: 'Last summer when I was at Wareham I had to get up at 4:30 (3:30 by the sun!) to get back from Corfe by reveille. In the autumn dawn when the wind moaned round that huge old ruin I used to scurry along in dread of the ghosts of Saxon kings.'[25] The distance between Worgret Camp and H.D.'s lodgings was about four miles; from Corfe it was only another five miles to the Dorset coast. This was the countryside Aldington had explored as a teenager on his walking expedition with William Hilbery.[26] He took H.D. to visit the tiny St. Adhelm's Chapel, knowing that its austerity and its isolated position above the sea would appeal to her.

And, as always, he responded hungrily to nature around him, as we see in poems like 'Field Manoeuvres: Outpost Duty' and 'A Moment's Interlude':

> One Night I wandered alone from my comrades' huts;
> The grasshoppers chirped softly
> In the warm misty evening;
> Bracken fronds beckoned from the darkness
> With exquisite frail green fingers;
> The tree-gods muttered affectionately about me
> And from the distance came the grumble of a friendly train.
>
> I was so happy to be alone
> So full of love for the great speechless earth,
> That I could have laid my cheek in the grasses
> And caressed with my lips the hard sinewy body
> Of Earth, the cherishing mistress of bitter lovers.
>
>   ('A Moment's Interlude')

In 'Leave-Taking', however, nature takes on the attributes of the war – even perhaps the death – that awaited him on the other side of the Channel:

> Will the world still live for you
> When I am gone?
> Will the straight garden poppy
> Still spout blood from its green throat
> Before your feet?
> Will the five cleft petals of the campion
> Still be rose-coloured,
> Like five murdered senses, for you?

In 'Vicarious Atonement', he saw himself in the role of a martyr – even of Christ.

At the end of August when the draft was due to embark for France, both Aldington and Fallas were promoted to lance corporal, which meant three months' N.C.O. training, just as Aldington had hoped. Their service in the 11th Devonshires was also at an end: from September 1916 all regimental reserve battalions were amalgamated into a 'Training Reserve', a pool from which individuals could be posted to any regiment needing new drafts.

No sooner were H.D.'s fears for her husband's safety eased, than she discovered in the *Poetry Review of America* 'two beautiful and intense poems' that convinced her that Aldington's feelings for Flo Fallas ran deep.[27] 'Images' and 'Inarticulate Grief' are both expressions of anguish, and clearly located in North Devon where they had been composed. That H.D. had seen neither poem before and had not known that they had been sent to the journal suggests that the two poets had ceased to share their creative lives. 'Images' is a poem of frustrated love, beginning:

> Through the dark pine trunks,
> Silver and yellow gleam the clouds
> And the sun;
> The sea is faint purple.
> My love, my love, I shall never reach you.

H.D. wrote to Cournos that these poems had made her realise that what he and she had seen as 'a mild and distracting flirtation' was in fact 'a very intense passion.' She was, she wrote, convinced that Aldington was still in love with Flo and wished he would talk to her about it, so that she could 'help more'. She even asked if she should invite Flo to come and stay at Corfe Castle. Her letter finishes dramatically: 'I am ready to give my own life away to him, to give my soul and the peace of my spirit that he may have beauty, that he may see and feel beauty so that he may write – as that is the ultimate desire of all of us.'[28]

We may find such self-abnegation remarkable. Helen Carr suggests that H.D. tried to live 'by the standards of unselfish womanly goodness and kindliness she had learnt from her Moravian mother.' Carr also points out that, idealising each other, husband and wife constantly tried to live up to each other's image of themselves.[29] H.D. also clung to her conception of the artist as set apart from the rest of humanity and attempted to use this notion to justify both Aldington's affair (as a quest for beauty) and her own suffering (out of which poetry would arise). 'The hurt I suffered has freed my song – this is most precious to me', she wrote to Cournos in her next letter, only a few days later.[30] It is clear from this letter that she has at last been able to communicate with Aldington about the affair, as she tells Cournos: 'R. writes – "Hang Flo & damn Carl. . . . For God's sake, love your Faun & don't be nobil [sic]."'

However, so fixated is she on her notion of the primacy of love that she also advises Cournos: 'And you – do not you deny your fate. If love of me – absolute and terrible and hopeless love – is going to help you to write – then *love* me. Do not let *ought* and *ought not*, two evil sprites, torment you.' Small wonder that Cournos was bewildered – and eventually bitter. Indeed, H.D. found herself having to back-track in her next two letters, telling him, 'When I said I could love you, you know what I meant. I meant if it would help R.' and, 'I do love you, Florentine, but you know the great and tender and bitter Greek love is beyond my love for you. . . . At the same time, one does not preclude the other.'[31]

Meanwhile in her poetry we find a more complex, less 'schematic' – and more human – response to her situation. Its publication history is revealing. Three poems, 'Amaranth', 'Eros' and 'Envy', were never published in their complete form in her lifetime; instead, portions of them, pruned of their most personal content, appeared in *Heliodora* in 1924, masked as expansions of fragments of Sappho.[32] Even purged of these personal references, the poems are strikingly different from those of *Sea Garden*: they are longer and, despite the Greek framework, more anguished and intimate. In all three the speaker has been rejected by her lover for a new love. In 'Amaranth' she tells her lover:

> I was not dull and dead when I fell back on our couch at night.
> I was not indifferent though I turned
> And lay quiet.
> I was not dead in my sleep.

and in the two withheld closing sections she wrestles with conflicting emotions: the self-sacrifice that H.D. expressed in her letters to Cournos:

> life is his if he take it,
> right. then let him take beauty
> as his

her anger and hurt pride:

> But I,
> how I hate you for this,
> how I despise and hate,
> was my beauty so slight a gift,
> so soon, so soon forgot?

and her desire for him to return to her:

> Turn for I love you yet,
> though you are not worthy my love,
> though you are not equal to it.

At the end of the poem, the goddess of love herself warns the fickle lover:

> Turn if you will from her path
> for one moment seek
> a lesser beauty
> and a lesser grace,
> but you will find
> no peace in the end
> save in her presence.

Here indeed is the poet as prophet! In 'Eros' she questions the very nature of love and loss:

> Is it bitter to give back
> love to your lover if he wish it
> for a new favourite,
> who can say,
> or is it sweet?
>
> is it sweet to possess utterly,
> or is it bitter,
> bitter as ash?

and she concludes:

> What need of a lamp
> when day lightens us,
> what need to bind love
> when love stands
> with such radiant wings over us?
>
> what need –
> yet to sing love,
> love must first shatter us.

The most harrowing of the three poems is 'Envy', which opens and closes: 'I envy you your chance of death' and asks, 'What can death mar in me/ that you have not?' The speaker recalls her lover's former tenderness in a passage which clearly refers to Aldington's visit to H.D. in the nursing home after the stillbirth of their child:

> You gathered violets,
> you spoke:
> 'your hair is not less black

> nor less fragrant,
> not in your eyes is less light,
> your hair is not less sweet
> with purple in the lift of locks;'
> why were those slight words
> and the violets you gathered
> of such worth?

and the with-held section of the poem contrasts this gentleness with his subsequent masculine physicality:

> Could I have known
> you were more male than the sun-god,
> more hot, more intense,
> could I have known?
> for your glance all-enfolding,
> sympathetic, was selfless
> as a girl's glance.

concluding poignantly:

> Could I have known?
> I whose heart,
> being rent, cared nothing,
> was unspeakably indifferent.

So in poems that, ironically, her husband would never read in their entirety and certainly did not see at the time of their composition, H.D. disclosed – and wrestled with – feelings that she refused, out of both pride and concern for his well-being, to reveal to him. Perhaps the outcome for their relationship would have been different had there been greater honesty between them. H.D. would eventually, although painfully, accomplish a capacity for openness through the writing of her novels and through psychoanalysis; Aldington's path would be harder.

Meanwhile, she was writing in a white heat: indeed, this is the image she uses to Cournos: 'you know I am living a curious imaginative life now. Everything burns me and everything seems to have become significant. . . . This is wonderful, this life for me – but I am torn and burnt out physically.'[33] In another letter she makes explicit the notion that runs like an undercurrent through the poems: that the personal suffering was the fuel for her creativity and therefore to be welcomed: 'I love Richard with a searing, burning intensity. I love him and have come to this torture of my free will. I could have forgotten my pride broken and my beauty as it were, unappreciated. I could have found peace with you. But of my own will I have allowed this fire to burn me. Of my own will I have come to this Hell. But beauty is never Hell. I believe this flame is my very Daemon driving me to write.'[34] In these weeks she also wrote 'The Islands', 'The God', 'Adonis' and 'Eurydice'.[35] She told Cournos that this work was 'a series that all runs on continuously but can be read as single poems' and that it would be 'very far ahead' of all her other work, if she could find the strength to go on with it.[36] Alone all week in her lodgings, she also busied herself with her new duties as assistant editor of *The Egoist*, commissioning and writing material, and with her translation of Euripides' *Hippolytus*.

On 20 September, Aldington was given six days' leave before beginning his NCO training and the couple went straight to London to resume something resembling their former literary life. Cournos was back in town, having initially stayed with the Randalls until he could again occupy one of the small attic rooms at 44 Mecklenburgh Square; and, after an absence of nearly two years, Fletcher had returned to England in July to marry his now-divorced mistress, Daisy Arbuthnot. He, Flint, H.D. and Aldington dined together in Soho. Flint wrote to Lowell that it was a 'comprehensive gathering of the clan . . . the absent ones being yourself on the bay where the tea was spoiled and Lawrence on some little bay in Cornwall.'[37] Fletcher told her how well Aldington looked: 'You would scarcely know he is the same, so completely has the army changed him. I find him much more human than he used to be and much more modest.' But he wrote of H.D.: 'I was shocked at the change; she looked so absolutely frail and wasted.'[38] He assumed, of course, that this was entirely attributable to Aldington's enlistment.

After his leave, Aldington returned to Wareham, leaving H.D. alone again at Corfe Castle. Her subsequent correspondence with Lawrence, which has not survived, has excited much curiosity, and her later elliptical and enigmatic references to her relationship with him (in 'Advent' and, in fictionalised form, in *Bid Me To Live*) have fuelled speculation. At the end of October she wrote to Cournos that she had started to see people as colours and that, while Cournos was blue and Aldington red: 'There is a yellow flame! bright, hard, clear, terrible, cruel . . . that sees in me its *exact* compliment [*sic*].' She tells Cournos: 'There is a power in this person to kill me. I mean literally. For the spiritual vision, his thoughts, his distant passion has given me, I thank God. . . . But . . . there is yet another side – if he comes too near I am afraid for myself. . . . You, no doubt, know in your heart of whom I write as a cruel-fire! I do not want that person to die. He has a great gift. He is ill! – But I must be protected!'[39] H.D. was by this time unwell herself and in a highly nervous state; but there must have been something in Lawrence's letters to excite this response.

In *Bid Me To Live* 'Julia' describes 'Rico's' letters as 'just ordinary letters that you could chuck across a breakfast-tray to any husband, but that yet held the flame and the fire, the burning, the believing'.[40] It seems clear that H.D. was sending Lawrence her work – work which she was not showing to Aldington and which was not destined for the anthology.[41] Although she probably did not tell him of her husband's affair, her poems would have left Lawrence in little doubt. They were poems of which he would have approved – much more subjective and intense than her *Sea Garden*. Indeed in January 1917, when 'The God' and 'Adonis' appeared in *The Egoist*, he wrote to Edward Marsh: 'Don't you think H.D. – Mrs Aldington – writes some good poetry? I send you an 'Egoist' for this month. It's nothing of a paper – but H.D. is good, without doubt.'[42]

Yet something about his letters frightened her, certainly confused her. *Bid Me To Live* again: 'That was funny about Rico, he shouted at her, "Kick over your tiresome house of life," he wrote, "our languid lily of virtue nods perilously near the pit;" yet when it came to one, any one, of her broken stark metres, he had no criticism to make.'[43]

Lawrence could never resist the opportunity to lecture his friends, and his view of the mass of humanity at the period of his retreat to Cornwall was savage. Paul Delany observes that: 'Misanthropy, sometimes to the point of mania, became Lawrence's predominant mood during 1916.'[44] H.D. may simply have been alarmed by his ranting. *Bid Me To Live* suggests, however, that he was offering her some kind of close relationship: 'He had written about love, about her frozen altars . . . "come away where the angels come down to earth"; "crucible" he had called her, "burning slightly blue of flame"; "love-adept," he had written, "you are a living spirit in a living spirit city." '[45] The invitation to 'come away where the angels come down to earth' seems to be an allusion to Lawrence's continuing plans for 'Ranamin', a community of like-minded people; H.D. was now one of those to be included. In a letter to Cecil Gray a year later Lawrence would write: ' . . . my "women", Esther Andrews, Hilda Aldington etc. represent . . . the threshold of a new world, or underworld, of knowledge and being.'[46]

The reference to an 'underworld of knowledge and being' links directly both to Lawrence's own preoccupation with the Orpheus myth and to H.D.'s poem, 'Eurydice', which she had sent him. However, the kind of relationship that Lawrence offered 'his women' was invariably that of disciples; it is not surprising that H.D. was terrified.('Frederico, for all his acceptance of her verses, had shouted his man-is-man, his woman-is-woman at her; his shrill peacock-cry sounded a love-cry, death-cry for their generation', Julia realises.)[47] In contrast, the Aldingtons' marriage had been one of equality and mutual respect, founded on a belief in each other as poet and as human being. Now, with the equilibrium destroyed by Aldington's infidelity and his enlistment so soon afterwards, H.D. had lost her sense of personal worth: 'I have all faith in my work. What I want at times is to feel faith in my self, in my mere physical presence in the world, in my personality, I feel my work is beautiful, I have a deep faith in it, an absolute faith. But sometimes I have no faith in my own self', she wrote in a touching postscript to Cournos.[48]

For his part, overwhelmed by the bleakness of his present life and by his fear of what was to come, Aldington was losing faith, if not in his powers as a poet, at least in the possibility of his ever again having the time – or the life – in which to write. Perhaps this was another reason why H.D. did not share with him the work she was producing. 'R. seems to double his concern for my "career" not [sic] that his has been more or less invalided', she wrote to Flint.[49] But her successes were all too apparent. *Sea Garden* was published in September and in August her Clerk's Press edition of *Iphigenia in Aulis* arrived. 'It will be an inspiration to us to go on with our work', she wrote to Bubb, knowing that she had no need of inspiration and that it would not be enough to inspire her husband, although he must have been pleased for her.

Her next poem was a further departure. 'The Tribute', published in the

John Gould Fletcher

November issue of *The Egoist*, is, despite its archetypal setting, a poem about the war, a political critique of the commercialism, ugliness and godlessness dominating society, and a tribute to the young men who have been sent to war. It is also a tribute to all those who seek for the old gods of beauty to replace the 'god of the lance' who reigns unchallenged over the city.

Meanwhile, Aldington's next published work – in November's *The Little Review* – was also a departure: sixteen short prose poems, the first of *The Love Poems of Myrrhine and Konallis*, a cycle of thirty-two such poems 'in the Greek manner' celebrating the love between a goat-girl and a hetaira, which would be published by the Clerk's Press in June 1917: heavily sensuous, Grecian, neo-Decadent pieces. He would describe them to Bubb as 'sterile and passionate and lovely and melancholy' and, tellingly, inform him that 'in those poems I have expressed more of myself than in *Images*, which is tinged with influences foreign to myself.'[50] The last of those published in *The Little Review*, 'The Last Song', gives some indication of his state of mind at the time:

> Along the shorn fields stand the last brown wheat-sheaves,
>   casting long shadows in the autumn sunset.
> White were the horses of Helios at dawn, golden at noon,
>   blood-red at night – and all too brief the day.
> So was my life and even so brief; night comes; I rise from the
>   glad feast, drink to the gods of Life, cast incense to the
>   gods of Death, to Love a shattered rose; and turn away.
> Hail, all! Laugh, this is the bitter end of life.

So, ironically, while he was turning away from contemporary reality, H.D. whom he saw so often as in need of protection, was engaging with it, finding for herself a purpose in the wartime world, though no less appalled by it. She dedicated her poem to her husband, and had Bubb publish it in book form for him in February 1917. Meanwhile, he was heartened to receive from Bubb towards the end of October copies of his *Latin Poems of the Renaissance*.

There was a new crisis in mid October. With Aldington transferred some twenty-five miles west to Westham Camp at Weymouth, H.D. fell ill. Aldington became concerned once again about her vulnerability, not only because she would soon be alone – perhaps permanently – but because, he argued in a letter to Flint, he anticipated that all women under thirty without children would soon be industrially conscripted. His plan for her to go back to America was revived; H.D. booked her passage and even asked Cournos to accompany her. By late November, however, she had first delayed her plans and then abandoned them. Instead, she moved back to London on 12 November, to their room at 44 Mecklenburgh Square.

Aldington's anxiety was compounded by his own miserable circumstances. In mid November he was transferred to Verne Citadel, Portland. A letter to Flint a few days after his arrival starts, 'My dear lad/ I feel rather depressed tonight, so you must pardon it if my letter is depressing.'

And indeed it is. He paints a stark picture of his new surroundings, 'a wild desolate spot with dispiriting associations'.[51] He speaks of the icy November wind, which 'shoots, as if through a tunnel, across the parade-ground and freezes face, hands and feet until we almost weep with the pain.' As for the surrounding landscape: 'Everywhere there are desolate quarries, everywhere the traces of the unhappy convicts in the prison here.'

As so often, he becomes aware that, when others are suffering far worse in France, his complaints must seem self-indulgent, but, rising to a crescendo, the letter continues: 'my pity explodes into hate for those imbeciles who pretend that there is anything fine and enobling or romantic in soldiering. It is simply dreary routine, dreary endurance, dreary 'heroism' of dying at the word of command! Somehow some of us will endure to the end, but what shall we be worth?'[52] By December, he was writing more cheerful letters, but the underlying pessimism remains: 'I would prefer to die than exist in this appalling postwar world. Europe is ruined – that is the definite truth.'[53]

On 20 December he was notified for the draft. He and Fallas were to go to the Leicestershire Regiment, with no guarantee that they would be NCOs, despite their training. Furthermore, they were to depart the next day; there would be no embarkation leave. Aldington and H.D. had a hurried farewell at Waterloo Station, as his train passed through.

And so to France. In *Death of a Hero* it is on board ship that Winterbourne starts to feel 'almost happy' for the first time since war was declared. The cause of this uplifting sensation is his sight of the 'real soldiers', the men going back to the front from leave. Listening to their conversations, he discovers that they have no more delusions about the war than he has, but that they 'went on with the business . . . because they had been told that it had to be done and believed what they had been told.'[54] That voyage seems to have been the starting point for Aldington's later conviction that those who went to war became a race apart.

He spent the last week of 1916 under canvas at a base camp near Calais. He told Flint that they were sixteen to a tent; by the time he came to write *Life for Life's Sake* it had become twenty-two to an eight man tent. They were to stay there, freezing cold and usually hungry, for almost three weeks, with little to do, apart from 'a little floundering about in marching order, going through the gas chamber, and throwing a couple of Mills bombs apiece.'[55]

On 9 January both men joined a draft of 106 other ranks sent to 11th Battalion of the Leicestershire Regiment, the Pioneer battalion of 6th Division, currently situated at the Cambrin-Hohenzollern Quarries front, south of La Bassée and north of Loos. Aldington's war had begun.

8. To the Front and Back: 1917

Were even the sweet grey eyes
Of Artemis a lie,
The speech of Hermes but a trick,
The glory of Apollonian hair deceit?

Desolate we move across a desolate land,
The high gates closed,
No answer to our prayer . . .

(Richard Aldington, 'Disdain', 1917)

The British Army Pioneer battalions were formed, one per division – sixty-eight in all, in response to the huge demand that the onset of trench warfare on the Western Front had created at the end of 1914 for manpower trained as infantry but with special skills and aptitude for earthwork. Their central tasks were entrenching and building track ways but others included wiring, road-making and bridging, felling trees, demolition, tunnelling, railway construction, grave-digging and burying bodies.

K.W.Mitchinson tells us: 'Digging . . . might seem inglorious but it was certainly dangerous and demanding. A War Diary might simply record that a certain yardage of trench had been excavated. What it does not so often mention is the circumstances in which that earth was dug: the consuming darkness, the energy-sapping mud, the loose tangled barbed wire which snagged and constricted movement, the marking tapes obliterated by shell fire, the shrieking arrival of splintering shells, the searching traverses of an enemy machine gun and the ever-present horrors of insidious, seeping gas.'[1]

Although jobs in the rear areas could be done during daylight, a great deal of Pioneer work had to be executed in the hours of darkness. Furthermore, men working at the front were bivouacked close to the artillery lines, their sleep disrupted by both their own guns and German counter-battery fire, while their camps could be shelled or bombed at any time.[2] While the dangers to Pioneers were not generally as extreme as those experienced by front-line infantry,[3] wastage through sickness and wounds was constant: for April 1917 alone, the 11th Leicestershire's War Diary records a total loss of 10 officers and 110 other ranks.

The Western Front 1914-1918

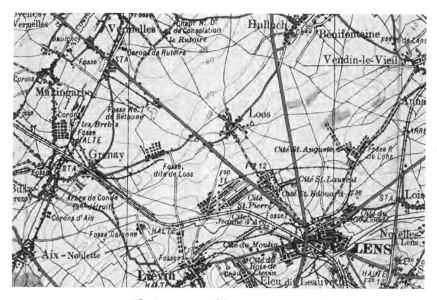

The Lens sector of the Western Front

Death of a Hero gives us a comprehensive picture of the pioneering experience: the extreme cold of January and February 1917 and the dreary hours spent digging and filling and carrying sandbags; either on the night shift, where the men dug saps out from the front line and 'were shot at, worked, and shivered with cold, went down the line, slept, tried to clean themselves, and paraded again', or on the day shift, where they worked on the support or reserve trenches. On the day shift they had 'to hack up the frozen mud, extricate the worn duck-boards, dig "sump-holes" and re-lay new duck-boards'.[4] Each platoon did a week's day-shift followed by three weeks' night-work.

Then there were the terrible moments when a working party received a direct hit from a trench mortar, smashing bodies to pieces,[5] or a camp was subjected to a phosgene gas-shell bombardment, with grim consequences for those caught without their gas-masks on.[6] Once the thaw set in, the work posed new difficulties, as the men spent their time 'plodging through interminable muddy trenches, up to the ankles, up to the calves, up to the knees; shovelling mud frantically out of trenches onto the berm, and then by night from the berm over the parapets, while the shells crashed and the machine-gun bullets struck gold sparks from the road stones.'[7]

The battalion was billeted in the cellars of the ruined coal-mining towns and villages behind the front line, like Annequin, Mazingarbe, Maroc, Vermelles, and Noeux les Mines. North-west of Lens, the notorious Hill 70, which the Allies would not capture until August, allowed the German artillery to dominate the region. *Death of a Hero* describes the landscape as 'flat, almost treeless except for a few shellblasted stumps, and covered with snow, frozen hard.' The novel continues: 'Every building in sight had been smashed, in many cases almost level with the ground. It was a mining country with great queer hills of slag and strange pit-head machinery in steel, reduced by shell-fire to huge masses of twisted rusting metal.'[8]

April saw the sector become dangerously active: the Battle of Arras got underway further south and 6th Division were involved in more or less continuous fighting consequent on the German withdrawal on their right. *Death of a Hero* describes the 'stupendous symphony of sound' that was the preliminary bombardment of the battle: 'The roar of the guns was beyond clamour – it was an immense rhythmic harmony, a super-jazz of tremendous drums, a ride of the Valkyrie played by three thousand cannon.' Meanwhile Mazingarbe was being pounded by German shells, 'smashing at the communication trenches and crossroads, hurling masses of metal at their own ruined village.'[9] 'Bombardment' gives powerful expression to the experience:

> Four days the earth was rent and torn
> By bursting steel,
> The houses fell about us;
> Three nights we dared not sleep,
> Sweating, and listening for the imminent crash
> Which meant our death.
>
> The fourth night every man,
> Nerve-tortured, racked to exhaustion,
> Slept, muttering and twitching,
> While the shells crashed overhead.

> The fifth day there came a hush;
> We left our holes
> And looked above the wreckage of the earth
> To where the white clouds moved in silent lines
> Across the untroubled blue.

For Aldington, as for his hero, there was 'a triple strain – that of his personal life, that of exasperation with Army routine, and that of battle'. We can guess the poet's misery through his account of Winterbourne's feelings: '[H]e felt a degradation, a humiliation, in the dirt, the lice, the communal life in holes and ruins, the innumerable deprivations and hardships. He suffered at feeling that his body had become worthless, condemned to a sort of kept tramp's standard of living, and ruthlessly treated as cannon fodder.'[10] Something akin to personal vanity was always part of Aldington's make-up; perhaps it is better construed as an Hellenic trait, a passionate belief in (male) physical beauty and the life of the senses. In some ways the life of the soldier, although he was reluctant to admit it (and only H.D and D.H. Lawrence detected it in him),[11] satisfied this impulse through its emphasis on physical fitness and prowess; but the 'degradation' to which the soldier's body was subject offended him deeply. It found expression in a prose poem he contributed to *The Egoist*, entitled simply 'Hands': 'I am grieved for our hands, our hands that have caressed roses and women's flesh, old lovely books and marbles of Carrara . . . our hands that were so reverent in beauty's service . . . so glad of beauty of bronze, wood and stone and rustling parchment. . . . '[12]

Ambivalence is apparent, too, in his attitudes to those around him, the physically present (his fellow soldiers) and the members of his circle at home. The 'them and us' mindset, so characteristic of the serving soldier by the middle of the war, found expression in irony: 'So the weather is cold with you? Imagine! Here it is sub-tropical. We live on iced champagne and salads. The R.F.A. wear nothing but their trousers and socks.'[13] Poor Flint must have winced at this response to his innocent report on the weather at home.

Nevertheless, Aldington's letters continued to display the contempt for the minds of his fellow-soldiers that he had acquired at Wareham. 'I would like to gaze upon that god-like man – as Psappho would say – who knows Mallarmé from a gas-alert, Chateaubriand from a beef-steak, and Gongora from a venereal disease', he wrote to Flint.[14] Yet we can detect the beginnings of respect and solidarity in an epitaph written for a comrade killed in May:

> You too are dead,
> The coarse and ignorant,
> Carping against all that was too high
> For your poor spirit to grasp,
> Cruel and evil-tongued –
> Yet you died without a moan or a whimper.

> Oh not I, not I should dare to judge you!
> But rather leave with tears your grave
> Where the sweet grass will cover all your faults
> And all your courage too.
>
> Brother, hail and farewell.
>
> ('Epitaph: To E.T.')

He was preoccupied with the war's victims. It would have been difficult not to be aware of them. *Death of a Hero* tells us that 'In all directions were crosses, little wooden crosses, in ones and twos and threes, emerging blackly from the frozen snow. . . . There were also two large British cemeteries in sight – rectangular plantations of wooden crosses. It was like living in the graveyard of the world – dead trees, dead houses, dead mines, dead villages, dead men. Only the long steel guns and the transport wagons seemed alive.'[15]

He wrote to Flint about discovering the graves of both Allied and German soldiers, and one letter ends: 'All wasted youth, broken hope, lost effort touches me deeply – and – you will think me very inhuman – I don't mind when I see older men 'clipped' and hear them moaning – it's the boys, the dear heart of youth stabbed – that's what hurts.'[16] The idea would take shape later in the poem 'The Blood of the Young Men'. Referring to his discovery of the graves of two little French girls killed by a shell, he wrote, 'I often go and stand by them & think many things.'[17] One of those thoughts must surely have been of his own dead daughter. The incident gave rise to another poem:

> Three little girls with broken shoes
> And hard sharp coughs,
> Three little girls who sold us sweets
> Too near the shells,
> Three little girls with names of saints
> And angels' eyes . . .
>
> (from 'Three Little Girls')

And, as with many of the combatant poets, his natural surroundings stirred in him conflicting feelings. One was a deepened appreciation: 'I had a talk with a fieldmouse in the trenches the other day – we got on splendidly! And there are hawks & crows & chaffinches & sparrows & owls & starlings & grey crows to look at & understand. They are so delightfully unorganised, such vagabonds!'[18] This relish of nature is apparent in many of his trench poems. Alongside it, however, is the terrible awareness, especially shocking for a Hellenist, of man's sacrilege:

> . . . each rush and crash
> Of mortar and shell,
> Each cruel bitter shriek of bullet
> That tears the wind like a blade,
> Each wound on the breast of earth,
> Of Demeter, our Mother,

> Wound us also,
> Sever and rend the fine fabric
> Of the wings of our frail souls,
> Scatter into dust the bright wings
> Of Psyche!

('In the Trenches' lines 6-16)

And yet the poems demonstrate trust in the ability of nature to heal and renew itself:

> Soon the spring will drop flowers
> And patient creeping stalk and leaf
> Along these barren lines
> Where huge rats scuttle
> And the hawk shrieks to the carrion crow.

('In the Trenches' lines 26-30)

Then there was the destruction of himself as an intellectual and an artist. He wrote sardonically in the April issue of *The Egoist*: 'I have not done any poems. I am having too good a time. Soon I will get miserable and write some more.'[19] *Death of a Hero* conveys the bitterness of the experience: 'He watched his mind degenerating with horror. . . . He was bitterly humiliated to find that he could neither concentrate nor achieve as he had done in the past. . . . After about two months in the line, he saw that intellectually he was slowly slipping backwards. Slipping backwards, too, in the years which should have been the most energetic and formative and creative of his whole life.'[20] Even so, there were moments when he knew that it was a blessing, rather than a curse, to be an artist: 'One's art, looked at selfishly, is less important for what it produces for others, than for what it adds to one's own life, making things poignant & strange & beautiful where otherwise they would be just ordinary', he wrote to Flint.[21]

He was also beginning to perceive, from his geographical and experiential distance, the pettiness of the London literary circles. Flint, still immersed in that world, was constantly incensed, generally by Pound's activities (and Harriet Weaver's continued support for him) but also by the conservatism of the London critics and reviewers, led by John Squire at the *New Statesman* and Naomi Royde-Smith at the *Westminster Gazette*. Being Flint, he had to put pen to paper to express his fury on every occasion. One letter informed Harriet Weaver that 'we are all tired of Mr Pound . . . body and soul, lock, stock and barrel; and those of us who were once associated with him and are so no longer for very good reasons, detest him with the heartiest of loathings.'[22] Flint ignored Cournos's advice not to send the letter on the grounds that: 'To have anything whatsoever to do with E.P. in a personal way is to step into a heap of dog's dung. You'll never get your boots quite clean of it afterward. . . . He is steering on disaster and ignominy without help from any of us.'[23] Aldington concurred, but from a much more lofty standpoint: 'Controversy is wrong for an artist, wasting energy wh. might have created something.'[24]

Even when Flint sent him a copy of Louis Wilkinson's novel, *The Buffoon*, with its malicious portrait of H.D., his response was merely that he would put a Mills bomb in Wilkinson's pocket after the war, and he confessed: 'I worry very little about all these literary squabbles – how can one trouble in the face of so much human misery?'[25] Back home in November, he would write to Lowell: 'I have lost a great deal, I am handicapped in ways you cannot imagine, but this abrupt withdrawal from the rapid current of my life into something alien & painful may, perhaps, be as salutary for me as prison for the author of 'De Profundis'. One sees the unimportance of the "literary life" and the supreme importance of literature, the one imperishable record of the human soul, the means of multiplying personality, the expression of destiny.'[26]

Nevertheless, he was not averse to using Flint's combativeness for his own ends. Eliot had criticised his *Anyte of Tegea* translations in *Poetry* and opined that there was no point in multiplying translations of epigraphs, which belonged to the art of 'epigraphy' rather than to literature. [27] 'Slay me this imbecile with a note to "Arriet"', Aldington commanded Flint.[28] Eliot was also in the process of rekindling the *vers libre* controversy, publishing two articles on the subject in the *New Statesman*, the second critical of Aldington's prose poems (*The Love of Myrrhine and Konallis*) because they 'hesitated' between poetry and prose, and asserting that the technical differences between the two genres had to be observed.[29]

Aldington's letters to Flint reveal a man more at peace with himself than the Aldington of Wareham Camp, despite the grim conditions he was experiencing and the separation from H.D. In a sense the war had taken him out of himself; the deepest emotion we find him expressing is compassion, not despair. H.D. told Lowell that he was 'quite happy in a philosophical way' and doing more work than he had done for some time.[30] He was sending her his scraps of *vers libre* to be typed up. Knowing that she had the company of Cournos, Flint and Fletcher and her work at *The Egoist*, as well as her own writing and translation, to occupy her, he ceased to worry about her so much. Jokingly, he suggested that Flint devise for her 'any sort of an "affaire" pour passer le temps'.[31]

He was closer to the truth than he realised. If we are to believe Cournos's *Miranda Masters*, H.D. was having difficulty setting the limits to her relationship with him, alternately encouraging his advances and rejecting them, while Lawrence, from Cornwall, continued to correspond with her and to send her his work; first the manuscript of *Women in Love* and then his poems, *Look! We Have Come Through!* In late April he came himself. H.D.'s priority, however, was her husband: in February she had Bubb bring out 'The Tribute' (and 'Circe') in book form, dedicated to Aldington, the poem having been written, she told Bubb, as 'an attempt to express for Richard what I felt his part in this soldiering to be!'[32]

Meanwhile, Aldington was made a runner – as was Fallas. The runner had to carry messages from his platoon commander both to the platoon and to the company commander. He also accompanied his officer on reconnaissance trips and needed to be familiar with the areas of the front line in which the platoon worked. Perhaps less physically onerous than digging trenches, it was a more dangerous job, particularly once the Arras offensive to the south began to 'heat up' the sector. Aldington tells us in his memoir of one occasion when he had his first night off in two months and a shell dropped on a group of officers and their runners, killing or wounding all except Fallas and his officer. At the time he wrote to Flint: 'You will be glad to know that I've had several very close shaves in the past fortnight & missed one particularly dirty do by a fortunate accident.'[33] Such incidents, however, far from provoking a sense of personal good fortune, only increased the soldier's sense of fatalism, as did the deaths of others: in the same letter Aldington indicates that he has heard of the death of Edward Thomas at Arras on 9 April.

In *Death of a Hero* Winterbourne develops considerable respect for Evans, his officer: 'He was exasperatingly stupid, but he was honest, he was kindly, he was conscientious, he could obey orders and command obedience in others, he took pains to look after his men.'[34] It is also from observing his officer that Winterbourne realises that constant exposure to danger over many months induced neurosis, 'a completely sub-conscious reflex action of terror': 'It is absurd to talk about men being brave or cowards. There were greater or less degrees of sensibility, more or less self-control. The longer the strain on the finer sensibility, the greater the self-control needed. But this continual neurosis steadily became worse and required a greater effort of repression. . . . Evans . . . had been in two big battles, had spent eleven months in the line, and had reached the stage when conscious self-control was needed.'[35] That he was an officer, tasked with setting an example to his men, only intensified his shame – and his neurosis.

Back in England for officer training, Aldington's fear of being under fire would intensify alongside his anxiety about his capacity for leadership. Added to this psychological pressure, he would cope for the rest of the war (and beyond) with the long-term effects of the heavy gas-shelling on the company's billets which took place intermittently throughout his tour of duty, but specifically at Maroc in the last ten days of April.

He returned to England at the end of May, after five months in the line, and as the Battle of Arras, a costly disaster after its initial successes, was being closed down. He was sent to Brocton Camp in Staffordshire for assessment, with a view to his undergoing training for a commission.

9. Interlude: 1917

You should have loved a god; I am but dust.
Yet no god loved as loves this poor frail dust.

(Richard Aldington, 'Prelude', 1919)

In London, Aldington was immediately thrown back into the world of literary
politics with the decision, engineered by Pound, but freely consented to by H.D.,
for Eliot to replace her (and Aldington) as assistant editor at *The Egoist*. She and
Weaver viewed this as a temporary arrangement until the war ended and her
husband could resume his duties, while Lowell and Flint, aware that this was an
unlikely eventuality, saw it as an alarming victory for the Pound camp. Knowing
that H.D. could not continue in the role if she and he were to have any time together
while he was at home, Aldington went willingly to the *Egoist* offices in Bloomsbury
Street to meet Eliot for the 'hand-over'.

Flint was further enraged to discover that the couple had accepted an invitation
from Pound to a dinner to mark the occasion. They were never able to share his
monumental resentment of Pound or completely break their early ties with him.
For Aldington, the dinner offered a welcome break from his life as a soldier. We
may not give credence to his fictionalised account of the occasion in *Death of a
Hero*, where, amidst the superficial gossip, Winterbourne feels 'like a death's head
at a feast' and, catching a glimpse of himself in one of the restaurant mirrors,
sees himself looking 'ludicrously solemn and distressed'. In the account Upjohn
(Pound) and Waldo Tubbe (Eliot) show a sublime indifference to Winterbourne's
recent experiences, the latter remarking that he had 'always doubted whether
[Winterbourne's] Vocation were really towards the arts', and felt that he was 'more
fitted for an open-air life'.[1]

Since Eliot had only recently met Aldington and was happy to print his trench
poems in *The Egoist* over the ensuing months, perhaps this fictional account is
less an accurate rendering of the actual event and more a product of Aldington's
growing self-doubt — and of his schism with Eliot a decade later. Nevertheless,
disenchantment with the 'frivolity' of life on the Home Front was a common feeling
amongst returning soldiers. Furthermore, writing–and the question of whether he
was still a writer – was a worrying concern for Aldington now. Pound would never
experience that kind of self-doubt – which is why he so infuriated Flint.

Aldington might not share Flint's animosity towards Pound, but he had no illusions and summarised him succinctly in a letter to Charles Bubb, the Ohio printer: 'Five or six years ago, when I first knew him, he was fascinating & electric; now, he is merely poseful & somewhat overfull of sneers. I think if a man *were* the greatest living poet he wouldn't tell you so every time he saw you. Mind you, I'll still defend Pound against the Philistines till my last gasp, but I don't believe in him & haven't for over three years.'[2]

In mid-1917 Pound was at the height of his influence in Britain and in America. With money put up by the American art dealer John Quinn, he had been able to buy himself in as foreign editor on Margaret Anderson's *The Little Review* and was still foreign correspondent for *Poetry*. Now he had Eliot running the literary side of *The Egoist* and had already persuaded Harriet Weaver to publish Joyce's *Ulysses* serially (a venture that would plunge *The Egoist* into financial ruin by 1919). He continued to publish a weekly column in *The New Age* and was about to become that journal's music critic (under the pseudonym 'William Atheling') and art critic (as A.H. Dias).

To Margaret Anderson he had been quite clear about his aims: 'I want an 'official organ' (vile phrase). I mean I want a place where I and T.S. Eliot can appear once a month (or once an issue) and where Joyce can appear when he likes, and where Wyndham Lewis can appear if he comes back from the war.' There might be the occasional poem from Iris Barry or John Rodker, he told her, but: 'The rest are clustered to *The Egoist*. I got Aldington the job several years ago. He hasn't done quite as well as I expected, BUT he was very young. H.D. is all right but shouldn't write criticism. The Lawrence-Lowell-Flint-Cournos contingent give me no active pleasure. Fletcher is all right now and again, but too diffuse in the intervals.'[3] He expanded on his position in a further letter: 'I don't think any of these people have gone on; have invented much since the first *Des Imagistes* anthology. H.D. has done work as good. She has also (under I suppose the flow contamination of Amy and Fletcher) let loose dilutations and repetitions, so that she has spoiled the "few but perfect" position she might have held onto.'[4]

That Aldington had been otherwise occupied for the past year does not seem to have occurred to Pound. Humphrey Carpenter suggests that his attitude to the war was 'as far as possible to pay no attention to it', and even the entry of America in April had not altered that stance.[5] He wrote to his father: 'I don't quite know what 'feelings' you want me to run up. It is of course pleasing to see the stars and stripes and the union jack amorously entwined on the same flag pole at the British Museum.' He does seem to have made some attempt to offer his services to his country but the American Embassy turned him down, leading him to remark loftily: 'As I am for the present definitely left out, through no act of my own, or through no neglect of my own, I think it would ill become me to go about shouting magniloquently about the glory of war,' and – even more loftily: 'An intelligent government would of course preserve people like Lewis and myself. Lewis is however in the thick of it.'[6]

Aldington had only a short leave in London; by the middle of June he was in a reserve battalion at Brocton Camp in Staffordshire undergoing assessment for officer training. For the first few weeks he was not allowed outside camp, but once he was permitted a weekend pass, he persuaded H.D. to join him. Perhaps recalling the bitter intensities of Corfe Castle, she was at first reluctant to disrupt her routine for what might be only a very short period, just so that they might be together at weekends, but she did take a room in the pretty village of Brocton, staying there until Aldington's transfer in early August. They were together for his birthday on Sunday 8 July: he would write to her the following year that of all his birthdays, his twenty-first (spent with her in Paris just before their marriage) and twenty-fifth (at Brocton) had been the happiest of his life.[7] Throughout their marriage the most idyllic times were those they spent in privacy; the presence of others always created tensions. In these summer months, away from the pressures of the front and the petty disputes of the London literary circle, he treasured his time with H.D. and their relationship was reinvigorated. Even army life was more tolerable than it had been at Wareham the previous year: Brocton, although a hutted camp, was large and well-planned with a bank, a post-office, shops and even a theatre; and H.D.'s lodgings, although they could only be together at weekends, were just minutes away. In his free time they took walks on the heath and in the woods of Cannock Chase.

However, his grim experiences at the front, his certain knowledge that he must return and his fear that his creative powers had fled all continued to burden him. The poem 'Apathy' almost certainly dates from this period. The poet and a female companion pause on a bridge in the course of a walk. The poet insists that, despite his mood of 'blank apathy':

> I have not lost all touch and taste for life,
> See beauty just as keenly, relish things.

and he proceeds to demonstrate this by detailed observation of the river below them. However:

> . . . there's always something else —
> The way one corpse held its stiff yellow fingers
> And pointed to the huge dark hole
> Gouged between ear and jaw right to the skull.

This recollection prompts a mirthless laugh, the reason for which he cannot share with his companion. Yet, throughout the walk, she shows a silent and compassionate understanding:

> You do not speak, you do not look at me;
> Just walk in silence on the grey firm road
> Guessing my mood by instinct, not by thought.

Brocton Camp, Staffordshire

That birthday weekend she reassured him and helped him take stock of his situation. He wrote to Bubb: 'I have been thinking over writing, translation & similar matters & under the encouragement of my wife I have begun to try to build up the ruins again!'[8] There follows a suggested programme for Bubb to print, ranging from completed work (some trench poems, translations of Latin poems of the Renaissance and of Remy de Gourmont's 'Saintes du Paradis') to new projects (translations of Meleager and of 'neo-Hellenic poems of modern France') and even including his Capri translations of the bucolic poets.

With H.D.'s support, he was tackling the problems the war had brought him as a writer: the lack of time for any sustained work, the limited opportunities for publication – and, worst of all, his 'writer's block', arising out of his not having the luxury (unlike Pound and Eliot) of being able to ignore the war and yet feeling that what he could write about it was weak and inadequate. When he sent work to *The Dial* in July (some of his trench poems and a prose piece that he had written since his return, the first of his 'Letters to Unknown Women'), he told Martyn Johnson: 'I feel rather like Mr Dick in 'David Copperfield' – though my King Charles' head is the war, which I am definitely trying to keep out of my work.'[9]

The letters he wrote to Charles Bubb over this summer and autumn are evidence of his huge struggle over these months not to give in to defeat and self-pity but to find ways around the impasse. His sense of failure is evident: 'Some people like the poems I wrote in the trenches, others hint that they are badly written. I can't help feeling that this is a true criticism. Often I had no real time to put down what I wanted and it is now too late to tinker with these poems . . . they aren't worth your time & type & paper! . . . I can write nothing. I have tried & tried, but am always dissatisfied.' The sense of his personal loss is complicated by his awareness of the wider tragedy and the feeling that he has no right to grieve: 'I can't complain; lots of other people have lost all they cared for in the war & I still believe with rest & freedom I could write again; but for a few years I am "napoo" first! I shall have to begin all over again.'[10]

He knows, however, that the loss goes deeply: 'Until I joined the Army I had lived with dreams, books and love – the shock of change was too abrupt and I still feel like a man gasping vainly for breath after being kicked in the stomach! . . . If I am over-pessimistic at present, you must remember that before I went to France I had never seen a dead man & since I went there I have seen too many.'[11] Yet he makes the effort to prepare the promised material – and to shake himself out of his depression; in August he writes to thank Bubb for his understanding, telling him, 'I'm very much cheered up and writing quite a lot – I was just weary with my hard winter and a little discouraged', and signs himself, 'Yours cheerfully'.[12]

We might wonder why an avowedly-pagan young poet – with little time for correspondence – should engage in an exchange of letters with a devout 41-year-old cleric whom he had never met, even daring on one occasion to venture into the field of religion ('I believe I like Christ more than scores of people who profess to be Christians').[13] It is clear from his letters that Aldington appreciated Bubb's kindness and his interest in him. They spoke of meeting up one day; Bubb's father had been born in Cheltenham and he was eager to hear about the West Country. Aldington warns, poignantly, 'I should always feel afraid to meet you lest I lost that kind opinion of me which you now have. You would find my mind a chaos bitten into by scepticism, & my opinion of the world appalling.'[14] Yet they shared a passion for the classics and a love of beauty; both Aldington and H.D. were delighted with Bubb's meticulously printed and exquisite booklets. Most of all, Aldington was grateful that Bubb had brought into the light of day his *Myrrhine and Konallis* poems; this private publication, which he could distribute amongst his friends, would protect him from 'the uncomprehension & perhaps contempt of the public.' (By 'public' he probably meant Pound and Eliot.)[15] He told Bubb, 'I have lived with them & loved them and from shadows they became so real to me that human beings seemed only shadows by comparison.'[16] His awareness that these pagan, sensual and lesbian poems might have shocked Bubb made him all the more appreciative. In this period, both he and H.D. used The Clerk's Press as a means of expressing their mutual affection, he through Bubb's publication in October of *Reverie: a little book of poems for H.D.* and she through her *Tribute and Circe*, dedicated to her husband.

Given that he would have little opportunity, even while in England, to visit the British Museum to check his source material, Aldington's decision to concentrate on translation may seem to have been an odd one. Nevertheless, there was a mixture of pragmatism and idealism in his thinking and that of H.D. It was partly a case of giving in to necessity: if the muse had deserted him, he must not brood on the loss, but must use his skills and creativity in other ways; and translation work could be attempted in the short and infrequent breaks that his army routine allowed him. But the translation project had always been an important one for them both, an opportunity to disseminate the classical literature they admired and to demonstrate its continuing relevance to a modern audience. Translation had brought them together in 1912 and could bring them a new closeness now. The Clerk's Press was not a commercial venture, but some of those beautifully-produced little books, judiciously placed, might excite the interest of an English publisher; and they had always planned a second series of the Egoist Press translations.

On 10 August Aldington was transferred to a cadet battalion at Whittington Barracks, some fifteen miles S.E. of Brocton, for officer training. H.D. returned to London, but by the end of the month she had taken lodgings in the market square in Lichfield (number 16), only three miles from the barracks, so that they could resume their weekends together: 'I am sick of single blessedness', she wrote to Flint as she prepared to leave London for the Midlands once more.[17]

Cournos may have been hoping that he, too, was done with single-blessedness. Before he had come to England in 1912, he had been in love with a young Philadelphian art student, Dorothy Yorke, eleven years his junior, who had at first encouraged his courtship and then blown cold, probably because her mother saw Cournos as too impoverished a suitor. After his move to England they had remained in touch and it was in response to renewed encouragement from Yorke that Cournos had made a voyage home in early 1914, only to have his hopes dashed again. When he returned to England, Dorothy and her mother travelled to Paris, where Dorothy found work as a designer and dress-maker. Now they were forced to leave for England as the war was beginning to make their circumstances precarious. By a remarkable coincidence, Cournos met the pair in London as they were searching for lodgings. Mrs Yorke had obtained a post managing an aircraft factory canteen outside London, with accommodation provided, but Dorothy needed to be in London to find work for herself. H.D., vacating her room for Lichfield, was happy to help Cournos by lending it without charge to Yorke: 'A beautiful lady has my room', she told Flint.[18] Cournos himself was now doing war-work for Marconi, translating Russian cables, so he had a regular income to protect him in these uncertain times.

Meanwhile, the war was having a further impact on the writers' success. The 1917 Imagist anthology had been published in America just as that country entered the war and sales of poetry slumped. As there was now a ban on the import of books into Britain, printing plates of the anthology were sent – and lost at sea. Then plates were banned too. It was all Lowell needed to bring her to the decision she had been contemplating for a while: there would be no further Imagist anthologies. It was quite apparent in the most recent one that the six poets had diverged from one another to the extent that the Imagist label was no longer appropriate for them all. She wrote to each of them explaining her decision.

Aldington's life, between Whittington Barracks and H.D.'s lodgings, was settled and pleasant. In what time he had available he worked on the translation of Meleager he had promised Bubb. Not that he forgot the war or that he would soon be returning to it. A September letter to Flint begins jovially: 'We are "at it" for umpteen hours a day here, dodging from one military subject to another with incredible rapidity,' but a few paragraphs later he acknowledges the 'sober fact' that he will be back in France before long, and confesses: 'I've got the wind up horribly. I think I shall just lie down and sob if I get into another artillery barrage.'[19] The news, at the end of September, that Hulme had been killed must have been a forceful reminder of the relentlessness of the war, particularly as Hulme had been serving (as a Marine Artillery officer) on the Belgian coast, which, until the commencement of the Battle of Third Ypres, had been a relatively safe place to be.

At the end of November he passed all his assessments and was commissioned as a second lieutenant in the Royal Sussex Regiment.[20] His next move would be to his new regiment's 3rd (Reserve) Battalion at Newhaven. First, however, he had a month's leave. He and H.D. returned to London. As so often before, their return from a life on their own to membership of a small and over-heated social group would place unbearable pressures on their relationship. Three people, in particular, would come between them. One was a familiar irritant, the other two new acquaintances whose entry into the lives of the couple would have a devastating impact on their marriage and their futures.

10. Betrayals: 1917-1918

There was a shape to their marriage, broken now, shattered actually, but there was a shape to it. It was Frederick who had taken her away (cerebrally), it was Bella who had broken across (physically), but all the same, there it was, the union, the two minds that yet had the urge, or the cheek you might say, to dare to communicate. For her, it was very simple.

(H.D., *Bid Me To Live*, 1960)[1]

The Lawrences had been in Cornwall since the start of 1916, and had settled at Zennor on the north coast, five miles west of St Ives. Lawrence had left their quiet retreat on only two occasions, for two weeks in April 1917 to visit his family in Derbyshire and friends in London, and on an even more fleeting visit to the capital in June to consult a Harley Street specialist when he was threatened for the second time with conscription.

Various acquaintances had made the pilgrimage to Cornwall, only to depart in disillusionment or acrimony; the most important of these – in terms of the mutual hopes both sides had had for the relationship – were John Middleton Murry and Katherine Mansfield, but others included the American journalist Esther Andrews and the volatile young composer, Philip Heseltine (later Peter Warlock) and his friend Dikran Kouyoumdjian (later Michael Arlen). Despite his split with the Lawrences, Heseltine returned to Cornwall in May 1917 to rent a house inland from Zennor, although he departed for Ireland three months later to escape both conscription and a despised lover.

Heseltine was followed to Cornwall by another young composer, his friend and former London flat-mate Cecil Gray, who found himself a house to rent on the cliffs at Gurnard's Head, only a couple of miles from Zennor. Like Heseltine, a man of independent means, the 22-year-old Gray appeared to be a calmer and more sympathetic individual, and he and the Lawrences were soon exchanging regular visits; it seems likely that Frieda embarked on, or at least contemplated, an affair with him.

From Cornwall Lawrence conducted the correspondence with H.D. that she found increasingly troubling.[2] It is probable that he visited her while in London in April 1917. She had become one of the few people he trusted with his draft manuscripts.[3] Her response to the *Look! We Have Come Through!* poems reminds us, however, of the essential differences between their work: 'Hilda Aldington says they won't do at all; they are not eternal, not sublimated: too much body and emotions', he wrote to Catherine Carswell.[4] Nevertheless, her respect for his critical judgement is demonstrated by a letter she wrote to Marianne Moore in August: stating her intention of sending Moore's latest poems to Lawrence, she writes, 'He has curious gifts of intuition and I wonder what he will say of your work. . . . Your work is more rare, more fine than any modern I know. But you puzzle me. Lawrence will send me the clue I am sure.'[5]

Meanwhile, the authorities were stepping up their surveillance of the Lawrences. Cornwall was a coastal defence zone and, despite the introduction of the British convoy system in June 1917, U-boat attacks sank two ships between Land's End and St Ives in August and six in September. As young men who were neither employed nor in uniform (Gray, like Lawrence, had a medical exemption)[6], who occupied houses with a view of the sea, and who were constantly visiting each other, Lawrence and Gray attracted the suspicions of local people and the attentions of the police and military intelligence. Frieda's German parentage, and, worse still, the fact that Manfred von Richthofen, the notorious 'Red Baron', was her distant cousin, made the Lawrences even greater objects of suspicion. Neither of them was prepared to be guarded or discreet: Frieda continued her correspondence with her family in Germany while Lawrence talked openly about how much he hated the war. They were watched and stopped and searched in a mounting campaign of intimidation.

One evening in late August when they were staying with Gray, his house was raided; he was subsequently charged and fined for negligence in showing a light.[7] On Thursday 11 October the Lawrences' cottage was searched in their absence and documents removed. Next morning an army officer, two detectives and the local police sergeant arrived to read them an order under the Defence of the Realm Act (DORA): they had three days to leave Cornwall and must not travel to coastal or other protected ('class 2') areas; within twenty-four hours of finding a new residence, they must report to a police station. No appeal was allowed.

That the couple were forced to leave was financially ruinous for them: they had been able to live extremely frugally in Cornwall; they had also paid for a further six months' tenancy of their cottage. They were virtually penniless. Far worse, however, as Paul Delany points out, was 'the moral shock of being expelled from the place that they had thought was a refuge from militarism and social disintegration.'[8] They had nowhere to go but London – to the small Hampstead home of their kindly friend, the poet Dollie Radford.[9] That could only be a temporary respite; they had to find accommodation of their own.

Fortunately, Lawrence had another generous poet friend – Hilda Aldington. A week after their flight to London the Lawrences moved into 44 Mecklenburgh Square. Cournos had departed for Russia in early October as an interpreter on the ill-fated Anglo-Russian Commission (an attempt to persuade the new Provisional Government of Russia to stay in the war) and Dorothy Yorke moved upstairs to his tiny top-floor room in order to vacate H.D.'s much larger one on the first floor. The Lawrences and Yorke took to one another immediately. Lawrence wrote to his friend Lady Cynthia Asquith, who invited him and Frieda to share a box with her at the opera: 'if you've not asked much other people, could we take with us Miss Yorke American girl – elegant but poor – lives in this house – usually lives in Paris – like her very much.'[10]

In mid-November, H.D. went up to London for a few days on business. At night, she, Dorothy and Frieda slept in her spacious bed-sitting room while Lawrence retired to Dorothy's attic room. In those few days, according to *Bid Me To Live*, the tensions in the relationship between H.D. and Lawrence came to a climax.

In H.D.'s narrative, Rico, sitting one evening with Julia and Elsa (Frieda), tells Julia that their relationship is 'written in blood for all eternity'. When the two are left alone to work in the apartment the next afternoon by the obliging Elsa, Julia responds to a clear signal from Rico: 'Now here was this track between them, written in the air, not fiery, but imbued with some familiar magnetism.' She moves her chair to sit beside him, 'a child waiting for instruction.' However, when she reaches out her hand and touches his sleeve: 'he shivered, he seemed to move back, move away, like a hurt animal.' Almost immediately, they are interrupted by the return of Elsa and Bella (Yorke). As she reflects on what happened – or failed to happen – between herself and Rico, Julia realises that he is 'tethered to the totem pole of Rule Germania', that he was able 'to dart out, make his own little excursions into any unknown dimension, because there, firm as a rock, was Elsa.'[11] Elsa herself, according to the narrator, has contemplated the growing intensity of Rico's connection to Julia without resentment, calculating that an affair between the two poets will leave her free to continue hers with Vane (Gray), who is due to return to London shortly.

That night, Julia shrinks from the final opportunity to consummate the relationship; she writes later to Rico: 'I'm trying to explain to you why I didn't climb up those stairs to your room.'[12] She tries out, and dismisses, several explanations: guilt towards Elsa – or respect for her; the fact that 'Miss Kerr' (May Sinclair) has warned her against Rico; fear that he has tuberculosis (he probably hadn't – yet) or that she may become pregnant. Eventually, she tells him: 'The thing that kept me from you wasn't only your genius. . . . I wasn't afraid – that is why I was afraid. . . . I was walking into a new dimension. It couldn't mean anything but death,'[13] and she reflects: 'It had all happened too suddenly. Life was lived to the very extreme edge of possibility, it was lived dangerously with danger taken for granted.'[14] Rico becomes entangled in Julia's mind with the magician Merlin and with Vincent van Gogh, indications of H.D.'s sense of Lawrence as a dangerous genius.

That the last chapter and a half of *Bid Me To Live* takes the form of the (unsent) letter to Rico demonstrates the importance of the relationship for H.D. The novel closes with Julia's memory of the morning after the failure: 'I can remember breakfast the next morning. I can remember how you said to me "You were singing in a dream. I woke and found my face wet with tears."'

There is little doubt that these events reflect actuality. Sixteen years later (and three years after his death) H.D. was dealing with Lawrence's impact on her in her consultations with Freud in Vienna. One version of *Bid Me To Live* (otherwise entitled *Madrigal*) came out of these sessions: she wrote to her friend Bryher in

May 1933 'I have been soaking in D.H.L. letters, not too good for me, but Freud seems to agree with me for once. Evidently I blocked the whole of the 'period' and if I can skeleton-in a vol. about it, it will break the clutch . . . the cure will be, I fear me, writing that damned vol. straight . . . then later, changing names and so on.'[15]

Not even this motivation, however, helped H.D. to complete the task. In 1949 she wrote: 'I had been trying to write this story since 1921. I rewrote [it] under various titles, in London and in Switzerland. . . . It is the eternal story of the search. In *Madrigal*, Julia Ashton finds a companion, creatively her equal or superior. But she sacrifices him or is sacrificed by him.'[16] Now she rewrote the ending of the novel – adding the letter to Rico. She told Aldington four years later that *Madrigal* 'was literally on the hob for thirty years'.[17]

So there we have it: in Lawrence, H.D. thought that she had found her creative equal – or superior, and she remained for ever unsure as to whether he had ultimately rejected her or whether it was she who had stood back at the edge of the pit. If it was the latter, then it was probably not timidity, but self-preservation that won out. H.D. always understood that her constant desire for a male mentor was in conflict with her need for creative autonomy; she told Aldington in 1953: 'I just had to do my own work and was from the first, even with Ezra, in danger of being negated by other people's work.'[18] In the case of Lawrence (unlike that of Pound) the erotic aspect of the attraction was difficult to resist; but she instinctively sensed both his fundamental Puritanism and the centrality of Frieda to his existence. She wrote to Bryher in 1935: 'How grateful I am that I never slept with D.H.L.'[19] It was probably never Lawrence's intention; with H.D., as Louis Martz recognises, he wanted a relationship of the sort that he formed with several other women, 'spiritual, poetic, emotional, erotic in part, but not carnal'.[20]

We may be less surprised by H.D.'s drawing back from physical intimacy with Lawrence than by the fact that she contemplated it at all, given the sexual problems in her marriage at the time. Physically, however, Lawrence intimidated her less than her husband. Her frigidity derived directly from the loss of her child and the fact that the couple had suppressed all the feelings that arose from that loss. Her insistence that, on her doctor's advice, she could not risk falling pregnant again was a simplification of these complex feelings: 'The surface was as the surface had been. Only colder. . . . If the wound had been nearer the surface, she could have grappled with it. It was annihilation itself that gaped at her.'[21] Furthermore, Lawrence had shown understanding of her feelings of loss and bereavement; Julia realises about Rico: 'he really cared. Tenderness. That was it. . . . '[22]

Since the stillbirth, other events had further weakened her marriage. One was Aldington's affair with Flo Fallas, which had shaken her already insecure confidence in her own sexual appeal. Here, too, a similar pattern had emerged: she had sought consolation from Cournos, and his compassionate response had awakened a physical attraction between them. Then there had been Aldington's enlistment: both his training and his war service had brought the horror of the war close to her, particularly as he was convinced of the certainty of his death and terrified of returning to the front. Lawrence represented a different world; the war

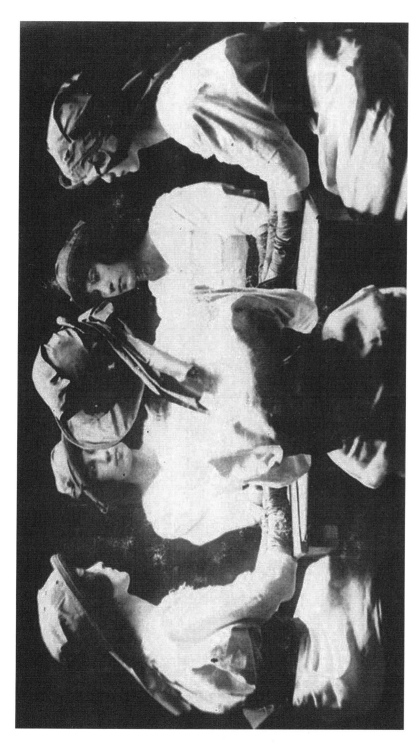

Dorothy Yorke 1916: a multiple image

might threaten him, but he was not 'of it': 'Rico was safe with his supreme, hard-won, valiant indifference.'[23] Lastly, the means that Aldington employed to disguise his fear from himself and others was to adopt a military bearing and attitudes, what Lawrence called his 'now we are all men together' stance.[24] ('Darrington was a soldier, but why if he now felt it that way couldn't he have gone in the beginning?' the narrator of *Asphodel* asks acidly.)[25] H.D. found this assertive 'masculinity' threatening; in *Bid Me To Live* (and also – literally – in *Palimpsest*) she expresses this through her representation of him as a Roman soldier. While Rafe is physically overpowering, 'a great over-sexed officer on leave', Julia sees Rico as 'the little man' even though she acknowledges that: 'He stood almost as tall as she when they stood face to face'.[26]

As for Lawrence, he seems to have been looking for a relationship to counter-balance, rather than to replace, his marriage. Only days before H.D.'s arrival at Mecklenburgh Square, he had written the letter to Gray concerning 'his women': 'You want an emotional sensuous underworld, like Frieda and the Hebrideans; my 'women' [Esther Andrews, Hilda Aldington etc.] want an ecstatic subtly-intellectual underworld, like the Greeks – Orphicism – like Magdalene at her feet-washing – and there you are.'[27]

For H.D., the dangerous aspect of all this was its emphasis on discipleship. She was not interested in playing Mary Magdalene to Lawrence's Jesus Christ, or, as she puts it in *Bid Me To Live*, in being 'used, a little heap of fire-wood, brushwood, to feed the flame of Rico'.[28] She would soon find herself used by Lawrence in another way, and ruthlessly: as material for his writing.[29]

It was in the immediate aftermath of this abortive affair that H.D. and Aldington arrived back in London from the Midlands at the end of November. The Lawrences moved into an apartment in Earl's Court Square owned by Gray's mother so that the couple could have their room back. But their Christmas leave was doomed: Aldington was in a *carpe diem* mood and almost immediately embarked on an affair with Dorothy Yorke. He was never one to waste time, once attracted.

There are descriptions of Yorke, both fictionalised and otherwise, in the writings of Cournos, Lawrence, H.D. and Patmore. Lawrence liked her and she comes off better than the rest of the group in his novel, *Aaron's Rod*: 'With her tight, black, bright hair, her arched brows, her dusky-ruddy face and her bare shoulders; her strange equanimity, her long, slow, slanting looks; she looked foreign and frightening, clear as a cameo, but dark, far off.'[30] Most accounts feature her slightly oriental appearance, her striking make-up and style of dress (her clothes designed and made by herself) and her reserved and self-contained manner. In H.D.'s view, however, 'her dark eyes pulled up at the corners were a mask . . . she was too taut, she was simmering inside.'[31] Both H.D. and Cournos compare her to a frightened deer: '[I]t was as though she were frightened of life and expressed her innermost fear in occasional revealing moments', says Cournos in his autobiography.[32]

D.H. Lawrence, late 1915

What is clear – and quickly became apparent to H.D. – was that this affair was very different from the last one, although the fact of that earlier affair made it so much easier for Aldington to repeat the pattern. Florence Fallas – the same age as Yorke (and Aldington) – was happily married with a child. Yorke was single, fatherless, with a very limited income, and her engagement to Cournos had probably not been her only failed relationship. She desperately wanted a husband. (In *Bid Me To Live* Rafe tells Julia that Bella also wants a child, *his* child.) She was both sexually experienced and determined. Furthermore, despite the picture presented in his self-serving novel and autobiography, it seems clear that she had never really been attracted to Cournos; but she fell in love with Aldington. 'Bella' tells Julia that she had been unable to help herself, that she had not meant 'to break across a man and his wife'.

What of Aldington? Once back in France in April 1918, he would attempt in his letters to H.D. to explain his muddled feelings: 'I suppose in a way I care for Arabella & in a way I care most terribly for you. . . . The truth is: I love you & I desire – l'autre. . . . Really I can never be happy without you; and very often it seems I couldn't be happy without her. . . . I would have been content if I hadn't made you suffer so much. And then, and then, I must look after A.'[33] The final comment seems to be a self-justification, but perhaps he was genuinely convinced of the emotional fragility of the brittle young woman who, like Patmore, appears to have suffered disappointment in all her relationships. H.D.'s sufferings, of course, would be less apparent to her husband; her pride saw to that.

At Mecklenburgh Square that Christmas, however, he flung himself into the affair, making no attempt this time to conceal it. Many years later he would confide to a correspondent: 'It wasn't until my fourth affair (at 26) that I achieved a really full physical satisfaction with a woman.'[34] Physical passion, not for the first time, seems to have warped his judgment. Miss James, the landlady, was forced to protest to H.D. about the way the conduct of the two lovers was affecting the reputation of the house. In *Bid Me To Live* there is a shocking moment for Julia when she returns early from an evening out with Morgan [Patmore] and discovers that the lovers' response to her warnings has been to appropriate her bed: 'Something went still in her and she knew they were there on the other side of the room, actually in bed together. . . . It was true, quite true that Julia had asked Bella to be careful, had said don't risk going up to your room if the munition girls are around. She had meant it but not meant it as literally as all this.'[35]

She could not protest. To an extent she felt responsible: her own sexual inhibitedness and her recent preoccupation with Lawrence made her feel guilty towards her husband. She even wondered whether her initial reaction to his attraction to Yorke had not been relief that an affair between the two might take the pressure off her to respond to him sexually: 'She had not so much condoned Bella and Rafe as actually encouraged them, against her human, actual intention.'[36] As with her husband's last affair, her lack of faith in her own attractiveness and her belief that people should be free to follow their emotions made her feel that she had no right to intervene. The moods of Corfe Castle were reversed: as Aldington's behaviour became wilder, H.D. sank into depression. One action in particular revealed quite how depressed she was: repeating the pattern of the previous occasion, she expressed her feelings in her writing – but this time she destroyed it. Aldington wrote to Amy Lowell: 'Unfortunately, she has burned some most poignant lyrics and a long poem of about 10,000 words. I can't forgive her for it, but she said that she thought them inadequate!'[37] As usual, of course, Lowell was only given half the story.

One passage in *Bid Me To Live* particularly reveals H.D.'s sense of inadequacy: 'They had talked of happiness. They had theorised of sex-expression and experience. This was. This was the deepest experience. All the same, if she had not so valiantly attempted and signally failed at their game, she would not be here. If she had not condoned (she believed the word was) Rafe's relationship with Bella, she would never have touched bed-rock of desolation. Morgan [Patmore] had helped. They seemed bent on demonstrating to her their sexual possessions. She had felt like a child left out of a game; left out of a game, a child crept slyly away to a corner of a large room, found a book on a shelf. Opened a book. Another world. Somewhere, somehow, she had been left out, Cinderella to dead ashes.'[38]

The allusion to 'Morgan' is also telling. Back in London, Aldington was in the mood for parties: 'She always felt that he wanted to see people, lighted up, laughing, with lots of people.'[39] One of the people he wanted to see was Patmore. Living – unhappily – in Brighton with her husband for the duration of the war, she was eager to come up to town and see her friends. It also provided her with cover for her current affair.[40] The flirtatiousness with which Patmore and Aldington conducted their friendship had always made H.D. feel deeply anxious (particularly as it was a style she could not imitate herself) and she must have suspected at times over the previous five years – as have various commentators since – that the relationship had gone further than flirtation.

There is some – admittedly scant – circumstantial evidence for this. During the autumn of 1914, when H.D. was at Selsey and Aldington on his own in London, he had written to Lowell: 'Hilda is staying in the country with the Hueffers. . . . So I am a bachelor for the time being', a casual but awkward comment, with a variety of possible interpretations.[41] Patmore's own short story 'Cyprian Brass' offers a suggestive parallel. Vesper, the central character, tells another character of how, 'a young man, nothing to me, but dear in his youth, and particularly because he adored a woman whom I loved extremely well . . . came to me in despair over his ignorance of women and his fear of hurting her . . . often he asked me to . . . teach him . . . and when I felt she would give herself to him I consented.' She goes on to say that, 'Once I went to have tea with him after he was married and found him alone . . . he so evidently was prepared for a love-meeting . . . I, half in a dislike of hurting, half, I suppose, because I wanted some love substitute. . . . ' When her listener interrupts to ask if she did not consider the wife's feelings, she replies, 'I hardly thought she would mind. We were so extraordinarily united . . . all three. . . . '[42]

In *Bid Me To Live*, Julia feels that 'it was the casual taking-for-granted of Morgan coming in and spending the night, of her way of throwing her arms about Rafe that had started the whole thing. She had thought when Bella came along, well, at least Bella is straight in her way; in her crooked definition, she is straight, while Morgan lolls about and you never know what it is she wants.'[43]

Patmore, Lawrence and H.D. all give accounts of a particular party at 44 Mecklenburgh Square; it may have been a farewell party for the Lawrences, as they moved out of London (to Dollie Radford's cottage in Hermitage, Berkshire) on 18 December. Given the complexity of the relationships amongst the group which gathered at the house – the Aldingtons, the Lawrences, Patmore and her lover, Yorke and Cecil Gray (now returned from Cornwall) – it is not surprising that the mood was one almost of hysteria. 'We all burned with a different incandescence,' writes Patmore in her memoir, recalling H.D. as 'a swaying slim sapling, almost destroyed in a forest fire' with 'all the blueness of flame gone into her large distracted eyes', while 'Richard flickered with the desperate gaiety of the soldier on leave'; Gray was 'a shaded candle' and Yorke 'smouldered under her polished hair'. But presiding over it all was Lawrence, 'as if he'd drunk fire'.[44]

And it was Lawrence who, revelling in the emotionally-charged atmosphere, arranged a 'charade' in which Aldington and Yorke played Adam and Eve, Frieda the

44 Mecklenburgh Square

serpent, H.D. the 'tree of life', Gray 'the angel at the gate' and Lawrence himself – God.[45] We might sense something more satanic than divine in this delight in playing with people's pain, and there is certainly cruelty in his subsequent portrayal of them all in *Aaron's Rod*. This may have been the party at which Rico tells Julia that she and Vane are 'made for each other',[46] the party which ends in an air-raid that shatters the windows of number 44 and brings books tumbling off the shelves, and the party at which Bella makes her bid for Rafe, kissing him passionately in the gardens outside. A pass which Rafe characteristically reports immediately to Julia ('What are you and she going to do about it?' she asks, knowing the answer.)[47] 'Changing partners, changing hands, dancing round, in a Bacchic orgy of war-time love and death', says Julia.[48]

We might wonder what had meanwhile happened to the more level-headed of the Aldingtons' friends, the Randalls, the Whitalls, George Plank, Frank Flint and John Gould Fletcher. Aldington's first letter to Flint after the end of his December leave refers to a recent conversation the two have had,[49] while a letter from Lawrence to Lowell indicates that he has met Fletcher for the first time, and this may well have been at Mecklenburgh Square, where five of the six 'post-Imagists' could now assemble.[50] Notes from Aldington to George Plank also reveal that he and H.D. were meeting up with both Plank and the Whitalls. No doubt they would have seen the Randalls too. However, as his leave approached its end, Aldington's accelerating infatuation with Yorke must have curtailed the couple's social life considerably and thrown them inwards to the hot-house of emotions that 44 Mecklenburgh Square had become. As always, they wanted to keep their lives private; none of these friends were aware at this stage of Aldington's affair with Yorke.

On 28 December Aldington's month's leave was up and he reported to the training headquarters of his new regiment, the Royal Sussex, at Newhaven. But H.D. was to have no reprieve; his weekend leaves were regular and he spent them almost entirely in Yorke's company, and chiefly in her bed. Mrs Yorke now returned to London and rented a room that had become vacant on the floor above H.D.'s, lending a kind of respectability to her daughter's situation. We might think Aldington slow to see the net closing in around him, but his physical infatuation blinded him; it was not until he was back in France months later that he perceived the scale of Yorke's possessiveness and determination. *Bid Me To Live* suggests that there were moments of remorse for the pain he was causing H.D. but he was unable to stop himself. However, the novel also features a scene in which Bella pleads with Julia to let Rafe go, because although he loves her body, Julia 'tyrannises his soul'. When Julia suggests that it is Rafe who has to resolve the dilemma, Bella tells her: ' . . . he doesn't face anything. He says wait till the war is over.'[51]

The poems that would appear in Britain as *Images of Desire* were written during this phase of Aldington's relationship with Yorke. [52] Contemplating publishing them in America, along with the war poems written in France in the first half of 1917, he acknowledged to Bubb that they might shock people 'accustomed merely to conventional expressions of emotion' and that Bubb himself would probably find them 'almost over-passionate, over in love with the beauty of the flesh'. He pleaded with Bubb to understand the 'mentality of the soldier – the profound shattering of the nerves, the over-wrought tension, the intensity of sensation which come to him. . . . '[53] And in the foreword to the American edition, *War and Love*, he attempts to excuse to Flint (to whom the book is dedicated) what the latter may see as 'the exaggerated passion or sensualism' of these poems, asserting that they express 'the soldier's mood; a reckless disregard of rules for conduct, a yearning of the flesh, a wild grasping at life.'[54]

When Lowell received copies of the poems, she was shocked, probably as much by the fact that they revealed – although neither Aldington nor H.D. had told her of it – that he was involved in an extra-marital affair, as by their sensuality. Her response was not prudish: it reflected both her own convictions about the nature of sexual love and her deep affection for the couple, particularly for H.D. As tactfully as she could, she remonstrated with him: 'If I had a criticism it would be, not that your poems are too physical in their expression, but that for the first time in your work you have entirely obliterated the other side of love – the spiritual. A little change here and there, a poem or two inserted to stress the love side in contradiction to the lust side would have made a truer balance, I think.'[55]

Searching for a tactic that would be sensitive to the situation, she sent the letter to H.D. – to read and then forward to her husband. H.D.'s response to Lowell is a touching insight into her moral dilemma and worth reproducing in full: 'About R.'s poems – I must leave the matter entirely to you and to him! I myself mildly remonstrated about some of the poems – But it was a delicate matter for me, as I have always maintained that no relationship can endure without mental frankness & freedom between two people. It seemed an encroachment on R.'s personal freedom (under the circumstances) – a criticising of his *actions* rather than of his poetry. At the same time, my loyalty to R. forbids my criticism (in this particular instance). I trust to your friendship, dear Amy, to us both – therefore what I say or imply is safe with you. But I do not like much in the poems, quite apart from who wrote them. Do insist on certain alterations and omissions.'[56]

However, Lowell's views had no influence on Aldington. 'His letter was as nice as it could possibly be, most friendly and sympathetic, but he clings to his own opinion, which is natural, after all', she told H.D.. She made one last effort: 'As his guardian angel you would do well to put a veto on some of those poems. I think he will thank you later.'[57] She had further reason to be critical of Aldington's judgment: without consulting her, he had given his poems to Four Seas Press, despite the problems that he – and Lowell on his behalf – had encountered with Brown over *Images Old and New*.

Now the third person to disrupt this marriage stepped forward, given his cue by Lawrence. Cecil Gray saw the extent to which her husband's affair and the wretched conditions of life in wartime London were making H.D. unwell and unhappy. He planned to return to Cornwall as he still had the lease on his cottage and could work better there – and he wanted H.D. to go with him. She was vulnerable to his kindness and consideration – as she had been to Lawrence's tenderness – and, like Lawrence, he did not give off the scent of the war. Lawrence unflatteringly describes 'Cyril Scott' in *Aaron's Rod* as 'a fair, pale, fattish young fellow in pince-nez and dark clothes',[58] but H.D.'s Verrus in 'Hipparchia', the opening story of *Palimpsest*, is a more distinguished figure, 'priest, scholar, young patrician'.[59] H.D. was always as appreciative of good breeding as she was of artistic talent. *Asphodel* has an even more revealing passage: 'She should have obviously married someone like Cyril Vane, great house, everything clear and clean and beautiful, walls lined with books, her own room and everything right, the house-keeper dignified, everything right. People like Vane didn't have to explain things. It was people like Darrington that had to bluster a little, say "the gov'nor you know, four quarterings but all faked." Faked or not faked, you did not hear of Vane's people, nor his quarterings.'[60] The source of Gray's attractiveness is clear: 'She loved his detachment, his aloofness, his very special appreciation of what in her was singularly aloof, untouchable and to the general taste, inadequate.'[61] Gray did not frighten her; he was cool; she thought that she saw a mirror-image of herself; and he offered her the admiration of which she felt starved.

She was already considering the move in a letter to Cournos in late January, and a week later she wrote again to him: 'I want to go to Cornwall & live very, very quietly for some time. I feel I can *work* there.'[62] She kept from Cournos the circumstances of this planned move, adding in a postscript, 'Dorothy is quite well – is busy & seems happy.'[63] (Neither Aldington can have looked forward to Cournos's return from Russia.) Aldington was equally reticent in a letter to Lowell in early March: 'Hilda has done a certain amount of work, but naturally feels unsettled through my being away for so long – two years now. She needs tranquillity for her work and the raids in town, though comparatively harmless, are rather noisy and disturbing to a person with fragile nerves. She will probably go to the country when I leave.'[64] Half the story, again.

Aldington's 'now we are all men together' frame of mind is well illustrated in a letter he wrote to Flint on the day he reported for duty at the depot of the Third (Reserve) Battalion in Newhaven from his eventful Christmas leave. While commiserating with his friend for having been called up, he writes: 'But you will have compensations. You will feel the implacability of destiny, the hard reality of war – wh. no civilian can know – you will have the spiritual gain of suffering, of a disruption of your life, of severed affections, of lost leisure. You will realise then how much you now enjoy. And, also, you will come to hate and perhaps to love men, as never before. With death immanent & threatening you will find courage to support terror, & in the gaps of liberty allowed you to grasp at life with a zest you never before had. Rosy, not legal lips will tempt you!'[65] Lawrence's observations of his friends were often devastatingly accurate; but we can also see here H.D.'s 'great over-sexed officer on leave' – or perhaps just an attempt on Aldington's part to justify to himself his own sexual conduct. (Small wonder that he is forced to add to Flint, 'Perhaps things will be very different for you. Certainly your psychology will not immediately & exactly follow mine, as I have sketched it for you.') We find here, too, the arrogance of what has come to be called 'combat gnosticism', but we can sympathise with Aldington's need to feel himself a member of an élite to replace the artistic élite from which he felt exiled.[66]

Two days later he wrote another dishonest, or perhaps merely understated, letter to Bubb: 'I have just returned to military duties after nearly a month of leave, which was a kind of intoxicating drama of life after so many months of deprivation. I saw many dear and distinguished friends, and though at first I felt a little gauche, a little out of touch with things of the mind, I soon got back all my gaiety and energy. And now alas! It has gone again.'[67]

Interestingly, he had given up on the Meleager translations and was working instead on 'the Greek songs in the manner of Anacreon', a development that he explains to Bubb: 'Somehow, as things are, I cannot bear the extreme loveliness of great passion or great beauty. It gives me too much pain. . . . Perhaps this sounds affected and neurasthenic – it may be so, but I cannot bear to torture myself with this beauty . . . that keen passion, that amorous delight, those perfect painted words, no, if I tried to live with them now it would be agony. So I fall back on the Anacreonetics, which are gay and fresh and lovely and yet are not too intense, not passionate in any way – immortal just because they are so easy and human, not because they touch high mysteries or fierce delight of the senses.' The sentiment is echoed in a letter to Lowell: 'Great poetry – Shelley and Euripides and Dante – moves me so terribly that I cannot bear it. I feel choked. For this reason I had to give up those burning passionate poems of Meleager. They left me unnerved & unstrung. I am reading a little Dante, but only a very, very little each day – it exhausts me with emotion.'[68]

This inability to cope with extreme beauty and passion in literature seems more than an 'affectation' and gives us some clues to both Aldington's state of mind and his conduct in this period. The other word he uses to Bubb, although equally disparagingly, is 'neurasthenic'. This seems to offer us some understanding of the impact on him of his war experience (and the expectation of its renewal) and of his loss of artistic confidence. Here is a man who hates – and fears – everything about this war but who, ironically, can only find self-esteem (as well as justification for his personal conduct) through asserting his identity as a soldier. A man, furthermore, who has chosen irresponsibility, sensuality, even callousness, as an escape from fear of death and who cannot allow himself to confront issues of either morality or mortality, or to assert spirituality over sensuality. While at first sight, his behaviour seems to have been uncontrolled, even dangerous, it was in an important sense an attempt to *avoid* danger – the danger of personal disintegration. 'I want Bella. Bella makes me forget. You make me remember', says Rafe to Julia.[69] This goes some way to explaining why his verses of the period are either the cloying love poems or the few casual satires of mess-room life, 'Minor Exasperations'. Only 'The Blood of the Young Men' – a common theme amongst the combatant poets – attempts to confront the 'horror and the pity' of the war, although it lacks the creative rigour that it needed to be entirely successful.

Meanwhile, at Mecklenburgh Square, H.D., in what Donna Hollenberg refers to as a 'grim web of action and reaction', was approaching a decision.[70] Shortly before leaving for Cornwall in early March, Gray wrote her a letter which suggests to us that her belief in their mutual aloofness was perhaps mistaken: 'If only I could feel sure of you. . . . You do not pretend to love me any more than you do. This is something at any rate, but it is not enough to keep me from being unhappy now and then. Why are you so elusive, so unapproachable?'[71] He left London on 11 March and wrote immediately from Cornwall: 'The only decided thing is that you must come, whether you want to or not, because I need you very, very much.'[72] These expressions of neediness may have been warning signals for H.D. but the attraction of the peaceful rural environment and her need to escape living in the same house with Yorke and Aldington, who had still not been recalled to France, were compelling; she left London on 23 March.

There were two repercussions, one inevitable and anticipated, though dreaded – and perhaps a further reason for H.D.'s flight from London; the other less expected, and perhaps therefore more shocking for her. First, Cournos returned to London at the beginning of April, the fall of the Provisional Government in Russia having made the Anglo-Russian Commission redundant. Calling immediately on Yorke, he learned the truth and wrote a furious letter to Aldington who had been transferred on 27 March to the 4th (Reserve) Battalion at Tunbridge Wells for final training. Aldington responded in his most patronising vein – a further demonstration of his unwillingness to scrutinize his own conduct and inability to empathise with others. 'It seems rather odd that we should be quarelling, but naturally it's up to you to take any line you choose & to dictate what our future relations should be. . . . You ask for an 'explanation' – what exactly does that mean? I suppose it really means that you want to say bitter things, perhaps contemptuous things to me. . . . I am not ashamed of anything I have done; I regret nothing. If I told you that I have suffered through this – suffered for you too – you would not believe me. . . . I am not excusing myself, Korshune, because there is nothing to excuse – we fell in love with each other, that is all.'[73]

No mention of H.D. – to whom Cournos also wrote and who replied from Cornwall: 'O it was so terrible – you can't imagine. . . . I suffered so for [Richard]. I think him very strange and unbalanced now – his actions were quite unaccountable. I pray for him – indeed they both need our pity – But you, dear, I always trust and believe in you – when everything else fails there is you. I trust in your greatness. Perhaps we shall meet soon. . . . Write me, John, as I am going to write you, with *no* reservations.'[74] We may find this letter disingenuous; H.D., too, seems to have lost her moral compass.

She was in a state of shock. The second blow was that Lawrence, her other close male friend, had expressed his damning disapproval of her decision to join Gray in Cornwall. How profound an emotional impact this had on H.D. is clear from 'Advent', written nearly thirty years later: 'I don't want to think of Lawrence. "I hope never to see you again", he wrote in that last letter.'[75] Lawrence's attitude was inconsistent with his apparent approval of the relationship between Yorke and Aldington – Yorke would spend a fortnight with the Lawrences in their new home in Derbyshire in June. Perhaps he guessed that H.D.'s feelings for Gray did not run deep and felt her decision to be dishonest. He had become disenchanted with Gray himself (there are no letters from Lawrence to Gray after July of that year and they never met again). Perhaps, too, there was a trace of sexual jealousy. (In *Bid Me To Live* Rico calls on Julia to beg her not to go to Cornwall – or to stay in the cottage on which he still held the lease, rather than with Vane.)[76] Whatever the reason, he never wrote to her again (apart from a cursory 'business' letter in 1929) and they never met.

Two days before H.D. travelled to Cornwall, events in the real world of the Western Front took a dramatic turn for the worse. The German Army broke through the Allied lines in a huge spring offensive, penetrating thirty miles in only two days. Aldington's unit, the 9th Royal Sussex, were in Gough's Fifth Army, which bore the brunt of 'Operation Michael', fighting four major defensive battles (at St Quentin, the Somme crossings, Rosieres and the Avre) over a fortnight, desperately trying, as it withdrew, to maintain its links with Third Army on the left flank and the French on the right. The line finally stiffened on 4 April, fifty miles back from its starting point.[77] Meanwhile, the German onslaught shifted to Arras and then to Flanders, where it continued throughout April. The already depleted British Army suffered 236,000 casualties, of whom 120,000 were taken prisoner. Every available man in England was drafted to France; Aldington left Tunbridge Wells on 18 April.

11. Back to the Front

He had reached a stage where he did not care whether he lived or died. All that was left of human in him was a tenacious determination not to lose his inner integrity, not to do anything which would lose his self-respect. Therefore he carried out all duties thoroughly, but with a sort of dull despair. His face was quite expressionless, his eyes dull but haunted — he had seen too much.
(Richard Aldington, from 'Farewell to Memories', *Roads to Glory*, 1930)[1]

The 9th Battalion of the Royal Sussex Regiment, exhausted and depleted from their recent prolonged ordeal, were in rest at La Comté, north-west of Arras when Aldington joined them on 21 April. He was posted to D company and, due to the battalion's shortage of officers, became acting company commander. At the end of the month they moved to billets in cellars in St Maroc; he was back in the very same area, facing the city of Lens, where he had spent the five months of 1917. There is a scene in *Death of a Hero* where Winterbourne walks over the top of Hill 91 [Hill 70] on a misty dawn, 'where probably nobody had been by day since its capture':[2] 'The heavy mist brooded about him in a strange stillness. Scarcely a sound on their immediate front, though from north and south came the vibration of furious drum-fire. The ground was a desert of shell-holes and torn rusty wire, and everywhere lay skeletons in steel helmets, still clothed in the rags of sodden khaki or field grey. Here a fleshless hand still clutched a broken rusty rifle; there a gaping, decaying boot showed the thin knotty foot-bones. . . . Alone in the white curling mist, drifting slowly past like wraiths of the slain, with the far-off thunder of drum-fire beating the air, Winterbourne stood in frozen silence and contemplated the last achievements of civilised men.'[3] Being back in the sector he had known so well as a Pioneer and a runner must have given Aldington an advantage in his new role, but it must also have brought back all the horrors of that winter and spring of 1917.

Now he assumed the regular pattern of infantry life, although the amount of time the battalion spent in the front line was extended, perhaps because of pressure on manpower caused by the crises the British Army was facing to the north and south of this region. He went into support trenches in the Hill 70 sector on 1 May and then forward to the front line a few days later for what the battalion war diary calls 'a quiet tour', spent wiring and improving firing positions. It must have been in this period that he took that solitary walk on Hill 70 fictionalised in *Death of a Hero*.

The novel paints a vivid picture of the experience of commanding a company in the line at this stage of the war, when 'most of them [were] frightened boys who had never seen any but practice trenches and never heard a shell burst':[4] 'The blunders, the mistakes, the negligences of his inexperienced men were legion, and all were visited upon him by the martinet Colonel. For days and weeks he got scarcely any sleep and never once even took his boots off. . . . The boys, suddenly released from button-polishing and saluting and drill (which they had been taught to consider all important) became deplorably slack in important matters. They lost portions of their equipment, dropped their ammunition, never knew their orders as sentries, went to sleep on sentry duty, shivered when ordered to go on patrol, cried when put in listening posts in No Man's Land, littered up the trench with paper, bully-beef tins, and fragments of food, urinated in the trenches, and 'forgot' perpetually everything they were told.'[5] Winterbourne is not much better off with his subalterns: his four section commanders 'were all good fellows, but three of them had seen no service whatever, and the fourth had been in Egypt only.'[6]

In the circumstances, Winterbourne is understandably sceptical about the practicality of the Army's new system of 'elastic defence' (or 'defence-in-depth'), whereby 'he had an outpost line of four listening and observation posts with a section in each. Three hundred yards further back he had his main defence line and his own headquarters. Behind that he had various isolated Lewis-gun positions.' He feels that: 'The defence scheme might be all very well on paper, and might have worked out with experienced troops, but it was hopeless under these peculiar circumstances,' and he realises after a couple of nights in the front line that, 'under any determined attack it would be impossible for him to hold his positions for ten minutes.'[7] On one occasion he goes up at dawn to inspect his listening posts, the four of them about a hundred yards apart in what had once been the front line, and finds that the occupants of the third post have all disappeared – captured in broad daylight (probably asleep at the time).

On 19 May, the 9th Royal Sussex were relieved and went into billets in Les Brebis, but B and D companies were back in the line only two days later and remained there until the end of the month, involved in what the battalion war diary darkly refers to as 'active patrolling'. On 31 May, the day after the companies changed over, there was a gas attack on their section of the line, with heavy casualties, so Aldington narrowly missed an experience with which he had been all too familiar in his days as a Pioneer. He wrote about it:

> Heavy scented the air tonight –
> new-mown hay – a pungent exotic
> odour – phosgene . . .
> And to-morrow there will be huddled
> corpses with blue horrible faces
> And foam on their writhed mouths.
>
> ('Landscape': Loos, May, 1918)[8]

The next day the battalion was back in the line north of Loos for five days, chiefly occupied with filling front trenches with wire and digging saps forward of the line of resistance to provide fire positions. It was work with which Aldington was very familiar–only now he was supervising it. It wasn't just a quiet time: on 3 June the battalion mounted a thirty man raid, with artillery, trench mortar and machine gun support, capturing two German soldiers, but with several men wounded and two missing (another incident that finds its way into *Death of a Hero*).[9]

Although Aldington wrote to H.D. as soon as he arrived in France, cheerful affectionate letters, starting 'Dearest Dooley', she did not at first respond. It was perhaps his postscript to his letter of 6 May ('I love you – too much') which finally prompted her to write. It must have been an encouraging letter, because in his reply he addresses her as 'my exquisite one' and tells her that he has recently been at the very spot where he wrote 'Reverie'. However, the letter goes on to reveal a nihilistic state of mind:

> No doubt things seem very tragic & bitter to you, but what seems to me the great bitterness is my own apathy. Back here once more everything goes; I ask myself often what am I living for? Why do I trouble to hide from a shell or bullets? Only the mere weakness of the flesh. There really isn't anything or anybody I care for. My loneliness is complete. It is not a beautiful loneliness. It is loneliness haunted with horror and regret.
>
> I suppose in a way I care for Arabella & in a way I care most terribly for you. But nothing is real; there is nothing I really want. Isn't that rather sad? O my dear Dooley, I would so like to be gay & witty, contemptuous of 'ordinary people' – how I envy Gray his contempt – but there are too many dead men, too much misery. I am choked and stifled not so much by my own misery as by the unending misery of all these thousands. Who shall make amends for it?[10]

Of course, he had been in the line for seventeen days when he wrote this letter; but nevertheless, the mood did not lift. Only three days later (on the two-day rest period at Les Brebis) he wrote: 'Out here I really don't know what one lives for. I don't pretend it is all misery and horror; there are moments of rest, compensation, gaiety even. But there is constant wear – & having lost somehow the pearl & essence of life there seems no point in keeping on. Je vis en bête. Do you think there is any point in keeping on? Twice last week I tried to get killed – and was unlucky or lucky, whichever you like.'[11] He wrote to Alec Randall: 'This life is brutish and tries my patience beyond endurance.'[12]

Yet, despite the undercurrent of apathy, there was a rekindling of his love for H.D.: 'It is more difficult not to love you when I am away from you than when I am with you. Really, it is true that one has many lovers but only one love. And I gave you everything, so that I have only desire and consideration to give to others.' Yet even he, after five years of marriage, found H.D. an enigma: 'But I wonder if I was your love or just one of your lovers?' And he was still torn between the two women, although his sense of moral responsibility revived now

Aldington the officer, July 1918

that he was some distance away – although it extended to Yorke as well as to H.D. 'Somehow, Dooley, I have made a great mess of my life. But I would have been content if I hadn't made you suffer so much. And then, and then, I must look after A.'[13]

He was starting at last to reflect about his own future too ('On remâche ses idées in the long nights of watching. The stars are very powerful instillers of truth,' he told H.D.): 'One goes over & over things – what am I living for? What do I hope? And then even if the war did end & I got out how could I live? I'm too [old] to learn a trade or profession now & I don't feel like writing any more. Even if I did it wouldn't amount to much.'[14]

Yet the relative calm of the front line and the open-air life were having a soothing effect: ' Cornwall must be very lovely now if the days are as full of sunlight there as they are here. Extraordinarily pitiless and ironic these bright days are here, but get more physically comfortable – no mud, & nights are warm. We have no blankets – just a trench coat. Yet I sleep very well.'[15] He was even writing: very different pieces from the poems of *War and Love*, prose poems like those he had attempted early in 1917 and which had been included in his *Reverie*.[16] They include accounts of his battlefield experiences of the year before ('Dawns'), of the night of the gas attack on the 9th Royal Sussex ('Landscape') and of his nights spent in the trenches ('Stand-To', 'In an Old Battlefield' and 'Escape'): vivid evocations of the scenes around him and of the scenes of his imagination, including that idealised world of the classical past.

Still in the trenches at the beginning of June, he received a letter from H.D. that warmed his heart and he wrote immediately – that night and the day after:

1 June 11.30 pm
      I have just sent you a little note saying how glad your letter made me: I wanted to get it off at once in case anything should happen to prevent my writing to you later.

      Ah yes, I do think of our days together. What strange despised creatures we were & yet what a treasure we had. At times I think of some statue we both looked at together or remember some book we both cared for. How could there ever be anyone but you?

      Maupin. It was in London, I think, that we read it. But how far, far away that time is. In such a way people spoke of The Golden Age. I wonder what is gained through this desperation and suffering? After all we have scarcely known each other for two years. It is a lot.

      'Friends' you say. Not verse now only prose? Once when I threw myself at your feet, I felt your heart beat so wildly I was frightened. Friends – I would like you to kiss me passionately just for one night, to realise once with you, my Beatrice, the great frisson with the woman I love best. How could there ever be anyone but you?

      Oh, I know the world is a queer place & those who love each other best hurt each other most. Perhaps it will be only 'friends', but I cannot bear to think it yet: I shall think 'lovers' until you tell me 'no' with your own lips.

But, as I told you I have changed, through misery, through routine, through the strain of things. Perhaps I may get back equilibrium, some sort of life, even write again, but 'never glad confident morning again'. One acquiesces in the death of a flower but it is hard to admit that the flower of one's unique life dies as surely & nearly as quickly as the summer lilac.

Isn't it strange? I know the date & what time it is; but none of us knows which day of the week it is. All days are alike. I think it is Friday or Saturday. But, really now, aren't days of the week a superfluity?

Do you get enough money, enough to eat & buy clothes and books? Won't you let me give you 'of my scant pittance'? (you can see, can't you, how hard I am trying to make up to you!) Ah, but I am nearly crying as I write, my wife my Dooley. I am so proud that you have my name – please, please won't you keep it, whatever happens, in memoriam as it were?

I shall go on writing until dawn if I don't stop. For a while thinking of you I forget the horror.

I never forget you.

Richard.

2 June.

My dear Dooley

I hope you don't mind my writing to you so often. You must tell me if it causes any difficulty in your new ménage and I will then abridge my correspondence. But I shan't stop writing until you tell me that you don't want to hear – & perhaps not even then! . . .

I think of you perhaps too much and wonder if I shall ever see you again. Arabella sends me very kind letters and seems genuinely grieved to have me gone. But I can't tell. In any event I don't really care, but sometimes I would give everything just to touch your little finger as I did that first day at Brigit's. It's queer to be living in memories so early in life.

I can't quite give up the idea that we shall be together again. There is of course the complication of Cecil and Arabella, but they seem – to me at least – to fade into the arriere-plan where we two are concerned. Oh Dooley, we have not been as happy as we might – somehow I have failed. Of course it makes no difference that we have had other lovers – though sometimes it hurts, hurts. But out of this present utter darkness of mine, the confusion and complete lack of direction and interest, there is one thing that seems to matter – you.

The little less and what miles away! Why didn't you love me passionately *before* Arabella and not after? Don't you know that it's you, you I wanted & want life, everything with? The bitter irony of it! Like St Augustine I repeat to myself bitterly: 'too late have I loved thee O pulcritudinem antiquam!' Infinite problems circle about us, but, dear Dooley, let us at least keep a certain tolerance, a certain tenderness for each other. Here am in this wretched dug-out & there you are in Cornwall. What the next year will do for us, god knows. Perhaps it is very wrong of me to write you love-letters – perhaps I ought not to disturb you. You are very reticent – you do not tell me if you are happy with Gray. It is a great consolation for me to know that there is someone to look after you now and in the future, if by chance I should not be able to do so.

How one wanders in words – half expressing half one's thoughts. I write rather my meditations than a letter – chiefly writing because for a time I concentrate on the memory of you, all I seem to possess now. Why should one agonise with hope? I won't ask anything of you, anything of some things I was going to ask. I'll just finish and go up and listen to the guns a bit.

Richard[17]

These are moving and remarkable love letters. The sense of change and loss has not disappeared, but is expressed in sonorous, lyrical prose – and most poignantly through the exquisite image of the lilac and the Browning quotation: 'Never glad confident morning again.'[18] The note of indulgent self-pity has gone; there is a playfully self-aware irony in 'I'll just finish and go up and listen to the guns a bit' – perhaps even a little irony at H.D.'s expense: reminding her gently that he inhabited a world the horrors of which she could not comprehend. Browning allusions pepper these two letters, most of them, significantly, from the mature love poem, 'By the Fireside': 'a little less and what miles away' . . . 'friends, lovers that might have been' . . . 'not verse now, only prose'. The Browning marriage had always been for Aldington and H.D. a model for their own: two great poets passionately, and permanently, committed to each other – and to each other's work, and sharing an equally intense love for Italy. H.D.'s letter had clearly been filled with shared memories, especially of their 'golden year'.

There is another note, however: the mention of the continuing correspondence with Yorke, even if the writer adds, 'I don't really care'. And what are we to make of 'Why didn't you love me passionately before Arabella and not afterwards?' The implication seems to be that Aldington has made a commitment to Yorke on which he cannot now renege – and which he would not have made, had H.D. made clear earlier how much she cared for him. Her diffidence, her unwillingness to intervene and her continuing physical reticence had appeared to him to be indifference; but there is also a suggestion perhaps that there had been some moments of renewed passion between them before she left for Cornwall.[19]

On the same day he wrote to Flint, who had still not been called up and who had written to enquire about the rumours regarding H.D.'s move to Cornwall. Cournos must have been dropping heavy hints amongst his acquaintances about the state of the Aldington marriage. Aldington was emphatically reassuring: 'We are parted to the extent that I am in France and she in Cornwall. But we are not 'parted' in any other sense. . . . You – et le monde – are very blind if you think anyone could ever part us two.'[20]

He went on to tell Flint that Constable had turned down *War and Love*, so that

Beaumont's publication of some of the war poems (with illustrations by Paul Nash) might be their only appearance in England, and he insisted: 'I know why. I have told the truth about love and about war. And I am not wanted. I offend prejudices about morals, but, deep down, I think I'm right.'[21]

When the battalion returned to their billets at Les Brebis on 5 June, he was sent on a five week course at XVIII Corps (from July 1918 merged into VIII Corps) Infantry School at Fressin, east of Montreuil. Although he was delighted at his good fortune in being sent away from the front for a long period in summer, he was also, surprisingly, slightly regretful: 'I don't particularly want to go – I am more or less at home now with this battalion,' he told H.D.[22]

Meanwhile, H.D. was overwhelmed by the beauty of Cornwall, finding its skies and cliff-tops more like Capri than England. Julia, in *Bid Me To Live*, feels that, 'She had walked out of a dream, the fog and fever, the constant threat from the air, the constant reminder of death and suffering (those soldiers in blue hospital uniform) into reality. . . . She was at home in this land of subtle psychic reverberations, as she was at home in a book.'[23] She also – for now – felt in tune with 'Cyril Vane': 'He was conditioned like herself, to some special way of feeling. He felt as she did, more like a bird or a fish. Feeling everything, they did not need to discourse fluently on feeling.'[24] H.D. was emotionally drained – and tired of the emotions of others; it did not – yet – occur to her that Gray was emotionally deficient. (Aldington refers in one letter to Gray's 'marmoreal calm.')[25] She went on long solitary walks and worked on Greek translation, but she also started writing the novel which, more than forty years later, would become *Bid Me To Live* (and another reason for Aldington's comment, 'Not verse now, only prose?').[26]

Away from the line for almost six weeks, her husband, too, was able to absorb the beauty of the early summer. He relished the charm of the little farming village of Fressin and his letters to H.D. and to Flint show that he was enjoying the increased leisure time, walking, reading – and writing. In a post-war article he wrote about visiting the ruined fifteenth century castle at Fressin, 'the one place in Northern France which was not devastatingly ugly, miserable and unfortunate', and which reminded him so much of Corfe Castle two years earlier. [27] The prose poem experiments continued.[28] He attempted to explain to Flint what he was trying to do: 'In these little fragments I have attempted to be healthy, to steer clear of this hatred against the war, death and the people who are responsible for both – a hatred that has seriously damaged my writings (my writings!) Without watering down this hatred, I want to show the mind that separates itself from all this confusion, this din, so as to stroll quietly in dreams which are truer, more real, stronger than all that, because no price or value can be placed on them!'[29] To H.D. he explained: 'I write on a sheet of paper a line of French prose upon which I 'meditate' until out of the confusion of my sensations & thoughts & emotions something definite frames itself. This I translate as briefly and clearly as possible in two or three prose paragraphs, upon which I work at odd minutes and half hours during a week or so. I've done 8 so far, 6 of wh. I sent to Flint with the remark that he might pass them on to you. I am trying to avoid 1. All complaints and self-pity, 2. All excessive depression, 3. Any lack of candour with myself, 4. Everything that is not at least abstractly true.'[30] Quoting a section from 'Escape', he tells her, 'I am rather proud of this paragraph'.

His desire to avoid self-pity and depression was well advised, but the Fressin pieces are more abstract than some of those he had written in the trenches at Loos only a couple of weeks earlier, more self-indulgent and self-conscious in their evocation of the classical world. We have heard all this before; it is a model he was falling back on just as he needed to outgrow it. Several of the other combatant poets experienced a comparable crisis in their search for new forms of expression to accommodate this terrible war, but Aldington was also attempting to tackle what he saw as a decline in his creative powers, and there is something poignant about his rationale for these prose-poems:

> For me silence; or if speech, then some
> humble poem in prose. Indeed I am
> too conscientious – or shall we say
> too impotent? – to dare the cool
> rhythm of prose, the sharp
> edges of poetry.
>
> ('Discouragement': Officers' Camp, Fressin, 1918)

However, Flint was critical of the six pieces his friend sent him, particularly of their detachment from the realities of the war.[31]

At Fressin there was a marked shift in Aldington's mood towards H.D., first a sense of irritation with the narrowness of her world:

I really want to scold you a little. Your letter seems to me a bit unhappy. But why on earth do you worry about things so? You are free, you have an amiable lover, you have – or so it would appear – a nice house, flowers, books, something to eat, more books, music – in sum, everything you need to make you happy. But I'm afraid lest Destiny is preparing you some dirty trick to make you miss these times. Ah, I well know that you are among those people for whom happiness does not exist. Do you know why? You ask of life more than life can give you. Really, your ardour for perfection is making you very unhappy, poor girl.

But I seem like a priest to preach thus to you. My child – for, above all, with all your beauty and sensitivity, you are only a child – how much I pity you. How I would like to make life sweet for you! You feel yourself uprooted. But which of us is not uprooted? One really needs to find some purpose in life or existence is nothing but a sinister farce.[32]

And he began a new theme. While insisting, 'I love you, I am going to love you for my whole life', and, 'you will never be able to break the bond that joins you to me. I don't mean the utterly legal and common bond of marriage – I mean rather that of the love we each have had for the other', he nevertheless represents the pair of them as ultimately incompatible: '[M]y body hungered for a woman who was earthy like me. And you, too, needed a spirituality that was less gross than mine. . . . Our union

Aldington and company, July 1918

Aldington and fellow officers, July 1918

which was perfect in so many ways was lacking in certain respects – as all unions are it would appear.' The cynical, off-hand note of that final observation appears elsewhere in the same letter: 'I know perfectly that all the wrongs are mine. It's true that I have treated you very badly. But, what do you want, men are absurd. I think that I have given you less pain than any other bloke you could have hooked up with. Do I flatter myself? [33] The bluff 'Now we are all men together' mood was re-emerging. H.D. must have responded tartly to it, to judge by the comment in his next letter to her: ' . . . un peu cinglant. But it is astonishing what a thick, thick skin one grows – dodging whizz-bangs, I suppose, helps one to this indifference.' [34]

Fortunately for H.D.'s peace of mind, the correspondence soon settled into what they both enjoyed most: a companionable exchange of ideas about literature and philosophy. Ensuing events would, however, effect further considerable shifts in his feelings. The first factor was illness. Between 11 and 23 June five officers and 350 men of the 9th Royal Sussex were hospitalised for an outbreak of 'flu; Aldington may have been harbouring the virus when he left for Fressin, although the outbreak seems to have worked its way through most of the officers at the training school too and he was one of the last to get it, succumbing on 23 June, but up and walking again, although clearly quite weak and depressed, by the 26. On 7 July he addresses H.D. as 'Dearest Dooley' and writes: 'I am tenderly and passionately in love with you as always', but two days later he writes harshly (although apparently in response to an observation of hers):

> . . . to some extent the history of an impulsive or erotic man is simply that of successive enslavements & exceedingly painful emancipations from different women. Unfortunately in seems as if another woman is the only means of escape. . . . Of course I see with astonishing clearness . . . that Arabella is trying hard . . . to enslave me completely. I see perhaps the working of her instinct more clearly than herself and am appalled, yes positively appalled, at the degree of subjugation she intends for me. . . . You are right; one must possess oneself. But that is exceedingly difficult, because one cannot be 'reasonably' in love – it would be tedious & bourgeois – and any 'amour-passion' at once betrays one into a state of abject submission. Therefore one must live entirely apart from women – which is absurd – or else engage in this perpetual warfare of passion versus freedom. I daresay this sounds devilish blunt – in any case, most of it doesn't apply to you – but I merely reciprocate. . . . You will see that the problem from the male point of view is thorny with difficulties. Though it simplifies itself eventually into the ancient problem of eating one's cake & having it.
>
> I foresee that you are going to hate me very much for this letter. Even with the best & greatest of human beings we should employ a certain amount of humbug. But we agreed to cut it out, didn't we? Dangerous, most dangerous. I wonder if even our love can endure perfect frankness? From 'color che sanno' I gather that is impossible. How does it seem from your angle of the triangle or perhaps one should say acute-angled rectangle? [35]

The certainty of his death, which had haunted him for the past year or more, also resurfaces, but the mood is one of resignation: 'It is perhaps there all the time – a sense of a destiny to be fulfilled. Quem dei amant, you know. But I have rid myself of morbidity and await what often seems the inevitable, tranquilly, almost with indifference. I do not despise my life, but I do not overvalue it. Perhaps something will set me free; perhaps not. In any case, I do not complain.'[36]

However, by the time his course came to an end and he was facing a return to the line, he was able to tell her how much he had valued her correspondence: 'Through your letters I got into touch once again with that world of ideas which is my world just as much as the world of 'stupid poor men' is my world. You have been an immense succour to me and I shall carry back with me a charming image of you in my heart.'[37] He also points out that he has, so far, been incredibly lucky, having 'just missed' four great battles.[38] Preparations for the fifth were just beginning.[39]

What would become the advance to victory did not involve 73 Brigade and its three battalions immediately.[40] Aldington joined his company for a 'quiet' twelve days in the front line on 17 July before going into reserve at Les Brebis to rehearse for the coming action. The 'quietness' of that front-line tour was offset by active patrolling of No Man's Land and the constant noise of the British artillery bombarding the German back areas.

Back in the line, his heart hardened once more. He continued to debate with H.D. the rights and wrongs of his affair with Yorke, his defence, as always, being the authenticity of acting on impulse: 'You spoke, I remember, of my losing all sense of responsibility with Arabella. Of course you are right, but then at least I can urge as an excuse that the times are out of joint, and if I am mad in my way other people are no less mad in theirs. Besides the very madness & extravagance of that passion is the one thing that redeems it from vulgarity. One must have the courage of one's illusions or else life is willed, a fit of "shame & loathing"'. His letter of 23 July continues: 'God knows I [am] not Sir Parsifal. I desired the woman (best be frank even if brutal, eh?) but I was not entirely selfish. Perhaps if you knew a little more of life, a little more of the brutality of men, you would not feel so contemptuous. . . . I maintain that there was idealism & poetry even in the absurdities & cruelties of this affair. I am not an insurance broker, nor am I a soldier. . . . '[41]

He concludes, 'Anyway here we are — you in Cornwall, A. in London, I in France. I don't know who's having the worst time', and gives way to exasperation: 'You speak of poverty – dear girl, try living in a hole 30 feet underground with a pint of water per diem for drinking & washing & bully & biscuit for food; do you think poverty really matters? And in any case if I survive the war the government will be bound to look after me to some extent. What really troubles me nowadays is the semi-drying-up of my impulses to work, though I think I would get them again with idleness & tranquillity.'

Perhaps aware of the brutality of the letter, he adds a postscript: 'The faun sends kisses to his dear Astraea, and never, never, NEVER forgets her, nor her girl laughter, nor all the sweet parts of her. When the faun is free again she will love him as she used to.' And the following day he wrote her a love-letter, prompted by his receipt of a letter from her in which she spoke of her sense of isolation as a woman on her own, an artist and an American:

Dearest Astraea

You must never feel discouraged because the social order of to-day has apparently no niche to offer you, because you appear to be a sort of outcast, 'déracinée' as you like to call it. Only in a very few short epochs has there been a place for the 'dreamer of dreams' & even then he has been counted for other things than his dreams. . . . You, who are purely a poet, would have felt the hostility of any age.

You lay too much stress on nationality – a thing invented by politicians. True, the traditions of one's race & people are immeasurably important, but less important than the tradition of one's soil which in turn is far less important than the 'tradition of free minds'. That universal 'Kultur' which belongs to any spirit wide enough to invent it is far beyond any limited 'Kultur' or a race.

Returning to a common theme, he asks her: 'To live according to one's character, to live against the world's way – isn't that to save one's soul?' What follows makes this perhaps the most passionate love letter he ever wrote to her:

Someday you are coming back to be my dear Astraea again and all these mad adventures we have been on will make us the richer for each other, make our love the sweeter & keener. You speak of not having a body – you are wrong; you have a beautiful and passionate body. I knew that the last times we were together. And someday you will come back to me with a passionate abandonment and we will live a most poignant adventure together.

You are more wise than nearly all women. Don't be too bitter against me. Someday we will walk along & talk of the clouds & the fields as we did. And the beauty of these things will enter us & feed our love. Ah, my Dooley, did you want me to be like 'Caesar's wife'? To shut out the world of experience? Because I do not hate Gray perhaps you think I do not love you? Should I fear the ice who am fire? No, no; I love you & you love me & I know well that the time will come – & soon – when we will be lovers together again, & you will come to me naked & passionate, with a richer abandonment. My dear, dear beautiful child-wife, you don't think that our love could end? One epoch in it has been broken off; we have both suffered, you especially, but there will be new epochs. I don't mind what you say now – I know you must love me as inevitably as I must love you. Other people are nothing to us – just toys on the way. You have never looked into anyone else's eyes as you have looked into mine & I have never looked into anyone's eyes as I have looked into yours.

Yes, have faith and – 'escape me? Never!'[42]

Richard

By a supreme irony, however, two events had already taken place in H.D.'s life which would doom all such hopes.

12. Complications

Literature is futile, unless one can produce 30 or 40 good lyrics or an original prose work in a lifetime; and I don't see clearly for myself that possibility.
(Richard Aldington to Ezra Pound, 14 September 1918)[1]

I think also that I am too restless
For the old life,
Too contemptuous of narrow shoulders
To sit again with the café-chatterers,
Too sick at heart with overmuch slaughter
To dream quietly over books,
Too impatient of lies to cajole
Even my scanty pittance from the money-vultures.
(Richard Aldington, 'Meditation', 1919)

On Wednesday 17 July, while Gray was away on a visit to London, a young woman came to call on H.D. She was Winifred Ellerman, the 23-year-old daughter of the shipping magnate Sir John Ellerman, reputed to be the wealthiest man in England. Loathing her name, and indeed her female identity, the young woman called herself Bryher, after one of the Scilly Isles. She lived a sheltered life with her parents and eight-year-old brother in Mayfair and Eastbourne. A self-made man, her father was reclusive in his social habits. Apart from a short period in a girls' boarding school, which she had detested, his daughter had not been allowed to leave home or pursue any kind of career, although her father had taken the family travelling. Her visits with her school-friend Doris Banfield to the Scilly Isles, which had started in 1911, were her only opportunity for escape from a family life which was loving but controlling, introverted and intense. She was desperate to meet writers – and to become one herself. Having read Amy Lowell's work with enthusiasm, she had entered into correspondence with Lowell and on her recommendation read H.D.'s *Sea Garden* – going on to learn by heart all its contents.[2] She was now desperate to meet its author – and she was a young woman who knew how to get her own way. Her father's friend Clement Shorter, editor of *The Sphere* (in which Sir John was a major share-holder), contacted May Sinclair and obtained H.D.'s Cornish address. Bryher, then staying in Newlyn with Doris – whose mother's illness that summer had prevented them from making their usual visit to the Scillies – wrote immediately.

That momentous first meeting of 17 July 1918 figures in the fictional writings of both women, as well as in Bryher's memoir, *The Heart To Artemis*.[3] Her autobiographical novel *The Two Selves* ends: 'A tall figure opened the door. Young. A spear flower if a spear could bloom. She looked up into eyes that had the sea in them, the fire and colour and the splendour of it. A voice all wind and gull notes said: "I was waiting for you to come."'[4] In 'Hipparchia' H.D. wrote: 'The head with its close cap of carefully wound sleek braids was a head out of some deserted Graeco-Phoenician temenos . . . small yet so closely wrapped with coils and coils of carefully braided dark hair that it seemed ennobled, like some half-Asiatic child-Hera standing at the entrance to some vanished shattered temple.'[5] Neither party mentions that Bryher was accompanied that day by her friend Doris Banfield.[6]

Aldington's letter of 28 July is both tender and hopeful ('I tremble with pleasure when I think that on the very day of my leaving this prison I shall kiss again the cool fragrant petals of your pale hands and hold against me the tiny points of your sterile breasts'), but we learn from it that H.D. was on her way to visit the Scilly Isles with Bryher, who had clearly wasted no time in bringing together the woman she admired and the place she loved. Aldington is amused: 'You must tell me more about this new admirer of H.D. She must be very wise since she can love your poems so much. Has she a name or is she just a belle anonyme? Is she truly of the sacred race or merely one to whom it is given to recognise the gods yet not be of them?'[7] He had not understood that the intentions of the young admirer were no laughing matter.

Much more immediately threatening for his relationship with H.D. was the news that he received from her six days later, as he was about to go back into the front line for another twelve-day spell. She was pregnant. His response, sent off that day, was reassuring, practical and concerned: concerned both for her reputation (since his absence from England for the last four months made impossible any pretence that the child was his) and for her welfare. The letter ends with a list of recommendations:

1. Stay in Cornwall until you know whether Gray is going to be enlisted . . .
2. When you are sure of your condition – which, by the way, you should establish at once by consulting a doctor – you must tell Brigit and get her advice & assistance.
3. You must then leave Cornwall. If you stay where you are there may be all sorts of unpleasantness.
4. I don't quite know where to suggest your going – Brigit can help here.
5. You must not worry about the situation – I will accept the child as mine, if you wish, or follow any other course desirable to you.
6. I enclose £5. I will send you as much of my pay as I can. Try & keep it by you for doctors &c. You will need it.[8]

By the next day, however, he had clearly had time to reflect on the long-term implications. His lengthy letter starts 'Dearest Dooley' and he tells her that he is anxious not to worry her, but he states what he sees as the dilemma calmly and logically:

Bryher in the early 1920s

. . . We assume, do we not, that each man & woman is free to live his own life, to ignore any ordinary rules of conduct when he so chooses. We assume also that men & women are at liberty to use this freedom in matters of sex. In sexual relationships a woman's part is curious and difficult (so is a man's). That is to say a man has one 'mate' & many mistresses; a woman one 'mate' & many lovers. But there is a difference here somehow, for a man only loves eternally his spiritual mate, whereas a woman's 'mate' is the man to whom she bears children. Am I wrong? Formerly I stood first with you & remained first however many lovers you might have had. But doesn't this event cause a sort of volte-face? Gray becomes your husband & I merely your lover; because the emotions that bind lovers together are exquisite & sterile like poetry, but a child is a more ponderous link than any beauty. It is there, it cannot be ignored or explained away; it is made out of two people's bodies, is they, cannot be distinguished from them. Therefore I feel most deeply that it is no solution of the difficulties involved for me to pretend that his child is mine. Certainly it solves some immediate social difficulties but it does not solve the natural one, which to us should be the more important. For if we take that step, not only are we all three committed to a lie for the rest of our lives, not only is your child deprived of a real father, but there is immeasurable humiliation for you, humiliation for Gray & even for me. (My dear, my dear, don't let this cold language repel you; I am agonising for you; I will do anything, everything for you, but we must see this thing straight.) Every moment that child is growing within you makes you go further from me & nearer to Gray. Inevitably, you must come to love him more – is he not the father of your child? Inevitably, he must come to love you more – are you not the mother of his child? Inevitably I must drift further from you both – what part have I now that you have come together?

Oh, it is sad, bitter, biting sad, when our love was so deep, so untroubled really by our other love-affairs. But a child! It came to me last night as I lay awake and thought out the situation. The thing I proposed in my first letter is wrong, impossible, cruel – Cruel to you, to Gray, to me, cruellest of all to the dear baby-thing you will bear. You have become Gray's; you have ceased to be mine.

Best be honest and say what's happened and say that I'm eccentric enough not to commiserate but to applaud you, that even this makes no real difference to us. Damn it, Dooley, I am fed up to have lost you. I was an idiot to let you go away with Gray, but the omens were unfriendly. I never really thought you would have a child with him. And Dooley, I can't ever really love this little one – there's our own sweet dead baby I'll never forget. I should always hate this one for being alive. No, no: we can't act this lie. I won't. You are a free woman; act as such; be brave and tell the truth; you loved Gray because I had a mistress & you two have had a child. You have a right to have a child with any one you want; but don't let's act this lie. Always, always I will be devoted to you; I will do all I can with my money &c. But this other life-long lie I will not act. I will not.

Write me freely, & never doubt my love.

God bless you, dear.

Richard[9]

This stance was evidently arrived at through much heart-searching, and over the next few months he would waver on whether the child could take his name (particularly once it was clear that Gray would not accept any responsibility), although he was adamant that H.D. must not have an abortion – the example of Patmore's operation in 1913 was vivid in his mind. Nevertheless, he was convinced that the three of them could not become a family unit; the memory of the loss of their own child was still too painful. Even on this issue, however, he was not completely consistent, writing H.D. a one-sentence letter on 19 August which reads, 'I love you, I think of you, I want you – wait for me',[10] and telling her two days later: 'I will try to care for it for your sake – if you want.'[11]

He was agonisingly aware that it was his behaviour that had caused this mess: 'There are nights when I simply writhe with shame and anguish thinking of the poignancy of those moments last December when you sat alone by the fire singing softly to yourself. That was terrible, terrible, Dooley. . . . And that night my spirit was yours though my body was another's. I never deserved such love; but I pay a little for it every day with tears I shed inwardly, with pangs I do not speak of . . . ' Either in remorse or as a case of special pleading, he adds: 'but there is a side of me, which as you know, goes hankering after unredeemed sensualism.'[12]

He had no-one, apart from H.D. and Yorke, with whom he could – or was willing to – share his dilemma. A letter to Flint on 25 August, commiserating with the latter for having finally been called up, is silent on his own problems and jokily impersonal, as are subsequent letters written on 15 and 16 September. Roland Bate, who was a fellow officer in the battalion and became friendly with Aldington, wrote in 1971: '[He] was a healthy, likeable pagan, sociable and agnostic', clear evidence of Aldington's adeptness at keeping his emotions to himself and maintaining his privacy without appearing 'stand-offish'. [13]

The battalion was also on the verge of a major battle; they were inspected by General Daly, 24th Division commander, at Les Brebis on 22 August – and the town was heavily shelled that same day. The time was out of joint: he had a job to do – and one that gave him responsibility for the lives of others as well as a need to conduct himself well. This context makes understandable the facetiousness of his letters to Flint, as well as the contradictoriness of those to H.D. On 24 August he was back in the front line at Loos, and three days later the battalion moved to Lens to take part in the battle for that town on 28 August, a successful advance but one that took place under severe gas and shell fire.

On 5 September they were relieved and went into the support lines. The next day, Aldington departed to the VIII Corps Signals School for a month's training in signals and intelligence. He explained to Flint that it had been deemed necessary to train up another member of the battalion in case their 'present genius [went] to Blighty in the six months show'. [14] By now he had arrived – impulsively and melodramatically – at the decision that he would see neither H.D. nor Yorke ever again. How much he was influenced by Yorke herself, and his feelings for her, is hard to tell. He admitted to H.D. that he had been duplicitous: 'I have been very much at fault, weak and over-anxious not to wound. To you I have under-estimated my passion for A., to A. I have under-estimated my tenacious devotion to you. You might if you choose, call me a liar & a blackguard; I should not feel it truthful to dispute it. I have said passionate and intense, no doubt foolish things to A. and have led her to expect more than it is in my power to give. To *want* to give everything is not the same as having the power; my nuances were not precise. I have made a mess of things. You, poor darling, are up against it; A. will be very angry with me (which I shall dislike) and will say bitter things (which will hurt me very much) and I shall feel lonely & lost. But the only straight thing is to quit and see neither of you.' [15]

Yorke was determined to prevent him from accepting paternity of H.D.'s child.

Somewhat naively, he assumed that it was *his* interests that she was protecting: 'A. writes rather fiercely that she won't let me accept the child as mine! (Gesture of tigress preserving her young.) Good girl. But suppose I insist? It is rather charming of her, though, don't you think?'[16]

Meanwhile, H.D. followed his instructions to take care of herself. Gray had returned to London, to his mother's flat, at the beginning of August, not in order to avoid his paternal responsibilities – H.D. did not tell him that she was pregnant until much later in the month – but to head off Cornwall's zealous military authorities. H.D. herself returned three weeks later. A meeting between them established that he wanted nothing to do with her child; she seems to have expected this, perhaps even to have been relieved. ('Hipparchia was tired of Verrus. Facing him, she saw with no illusion, a peaked face finely intellectualised but petulant.')[17]

She also wrote to tell Lawrence of her pregnancy by Gray. He did not respond. Clearly he had meant every word of his last letter. Aldington wrote: 'I am sorry about the Lawrence business for your sake; but people are like that. I suspected the Gray business too. Artists! My God, *quel canaille.*'[18] Evidently, he dissociated himself from the class. Nor did he understand how devastating for H.D. was the impact of Lawrence's final rejection.

Aldington had no need to worry about her, however; she proved extraordinarily successful – or fortunate – in providing for herself. She gave up the Mecklenburgh Square apartment, although Miss James agreed to store all the Aldingtons' possessions, including their large library of books.[19] Flint was in the army but he, Cournos, Pound and Fletcher were 'out-of-bounds' anyway; they would all realise that Aldington could not be the father of her child. The only friends she could stay with in town were the Randalls, still living at Christchurch Place. She may not even have told them that she was two months pregnant; she certainly wouldn't have revealed that she was expecting an illegitimate child. Following Aldington's advice, she did, however, turn for help to Patmore, who undertook to book her into a suitable nursing home when the time arrived. Patmore had always cared deeply for H.D. and her sympathies would have been aroused by this further confirmation of the faithlessness of men.

H.D. could not remain indefinitely with the Randalls and wanted the peace and privacy of the country while expecting her child. At this point she was helped by another old friend, the actress Daphne Bax, wife of the playwright Clifford Bax.[20] The Baxes and their seven-year-old daughter lived in the village of Speen in the Chiltern Hills in Buckinghamshire. The cottage next-door to them, promisingly called Peace Cottage, was available to rent. H.D. contacted her girlhood friend Margaret Snively (now Margaret Pratt), also married to an English army officer serving in France and the mother of a one year-old daughter, and suggested that they share the cottage.[21]

Her friendship with Bryher was also starting to give her a new circle of support; that circle might be limited, but Bryher knew how to use it. H.D. spent her thirty-second birthday on 8 September dining at May Sinclair's house with Clement Shorter.

(Bryher and her family were mostly at Eastbourne during the summer and early autumn.) The 61-year-old editor of *The Illustrated London News* and *The Sphere* was suffering from loneliness, having been widowed earlier in the year.[22] His country house at Great Missenden was only five miles from Speen, and once H.D. was settled into her new home in October, he sent a car to fetch her and Margaret over for tea.

Maintaining the Aldingtons' tradition, H.D. wrote Lowell a letter of half-truths, but one that does reveal the importance of Bryher and Shorter in her new life:

> . . . got back from Cornwall + am hoping to go away again somewhere nearer London. . . . I am writing Fletcher – have not seen him yet. Will give you news of him. I dined with Clement Shorter last night – He is a fine old man – very generous + open-minded, though, of course, a bit conservative + old-fashioned. I think your book gave him his first impulse toward modernity. He thinks a lot of you, as you already know. I met the Bryher girl in Cornwall. She is about 24. I think, too, shows great promise. She simply worships you + your work. I go to see her this afternoon + will write you further of her. She comes from wealthy people. Do not tell her I told you as she is very queer about it. But her wealth could make no difference to you, nor to any real friend. She imagines any kindness + interest come only because her father is reputed the richest man in England. Of course, one can understand, but if she is any good at all, her father's position won't hurt her. (Her name is not Bryher.) Of course, did not know this when I met her, and my interest was genuine. Yours, too, I am sure is. – She was worried: Did I think Miss Lowell was offended etc. I assured her you would be pleased by her appreciation + now I will tell her I have heard direct from you. She wants to meet people who write. Clement Shorter + H D. is the extent at present of her literary acquaintances. I will try to find people but you know how disappointing most 'writers' are – and everyone is in the war almost. I told her if she went to America, I was sure Miss Lowell would be very kind to her. She is wild to go away. But it seems impossible now – and her people are dead against it.
>
> The Lawrences are in the country. You probably hear from Lawrence. Flint is in the army I don't know anything about him. I am forwarding the letter. R. has a jolly job now, back of the lines in signal work.[23] No doubt you will hear from him. I have not seen the Pounds. London is rather more lively than when I left – more hope in the air, and food problems not so serious.
>
> Well, good luck. I will write again.
>
> Love to Mrs Russell + to you.
>
> from
>
> Hilda.[24]

Out of the line, Aldington's feelings hardened once more, perhaps influenced by his realisation that H.D. was managing to look after herself perfectly well, perhaps also by the removal of the constant fear of death – and with it the feeling that each letter he wrote to her might be his last. His letter of 27 September is one of the most brutal and self-righteous he ever wrote:

So far as you & I ever being lovers again or living together as husband & wife, you must understand that it is fini, fini, fini. Now I am not trying to force you into anything. I am proud that you should bear my name; glad if you correspond with me on matters of art & literature & life; happy to meet you as one meets an old friend. You are quite free to make any kind of 'liaison' you choose, providing some sort of elementary social camouflage is used; I don't wish to interfere with you in any way. Be as 'free' as you can in a world of slaves, If you care to give & accept friendship upon these terms, I am only too happy. It is purely up to you. But I cannot have you being pleasant to me if I feel there is any idea in your mind of the old relationship being renewed. Because that is now impossible. You may think me idiotic and affirming more than I can carry out. But women are not so essential to life as they imagine; and in any case – well, there's no need to be offensive, is there?

I think I've made my point clear, and made it so with as much consideration as is consistent with precision.

It is no use our being humbugs, my dear. Things? I have at last 'sorti mon beau tranchant', as you see & cut the Gordian knot of this affair. Arabella knows precisely how I stand & we have now ceased to correspond except at rare intervals. But there is no necessity for you & I to adopt this severity, unless you are anxious to eliminate so eccentric a person from your circle. We have many points of common interest not at all affected by the state of our hearts. You don't need any reiteration of my admiration for your work (though, since we are being so devilish frank, it wouldn't hurt for you to improve your spelling & punctuation!) or for your personality and fine mind. So, as I have said, if you care to carry on, on this purely friendly basis, I am delighted. If not, it is up you.

Now then; I believe this is really the last postscript to this almost year-old affair. I am conscious of being less pleased with myself than I could wish, yet on the whole I have been fairly frank & not altogether inconsistent. Your going off with Gray was of course a mistake – never, in future, have an affair with a man if you are not both in love with each other. If you had been in love passionately with G., all right; but just slipping off like that – wrong, dead wrong. Probably you will now write & say that you *were* passionately in love with G. In which case I shall just note down that all men are liars, especially women.

For myself, as I wrote you, there seems to be no particularly brilliant future. There is nothing I particularly want, and that is very dull. Yet I have gained a certain balance a certain possession of myself, and a measure of certainty that no person in the world is essential to me. That is a great gain, for to put one's happiness into the hands of another is indeed a handing of hostages to the future.

You will, I hope, pardon the frankness and perhaps offensiveness of this letter – it is for the truth's sake. I hope to hear from you.

Ever yours
Richard[25]

It is illuminating to skim through the salutations and valedictions of his letters to her during these months. From April to late August he generally addressed her as 'Dearest Dooley' or 'Dearest Astraea' and closed with 'Your Richard' or 'Love from Richard', but from September she became '(My) dear Astraea' and the letters end with 'Affectionately, Richard' or even 'Yours, Richard'.

There is a palpable air of relief as the subject matter of their correspondence changes to their writing interests. H.D. put Bryher in touch with her husband so that he could comment on her work. He was impressed by the passages Bryher sent him from the fictionalised memoir she was writing about her childhood and life at boarding school.[26] He told Flint that her prose was 'young (& foolish) in parts' but that 'she has a superb gift of realisation of beauty & a clear imagist method of writing.' He sent his friend some extracts, characterising them as 'prose H.D.'[27] There is no indication that he was writing himself, however; perhaps this time the course was more demanding—and perhaps he felt more need to relax and socialise with his brother officers.

By 8 October he was on his way back to his battalion. It had moved. 24th Division was now in XVII Corps and ready to take part in the final battle of the Hindenburg Line, the Battle of Cambrai. From bivouacs near Cantaing, the battalion had moved forward to a position east of the St Quentin Canal:

> Winterbourne was back on the Somme, that incredible desert, pursuing the retreating enemy. They came up the Bapaume-Cambrai road by night, and bivouacked in holes scratched with entrenching tools in the side of a sandy bank. The wrecked countryside in the pale moonlight was a frigid and motionless image of death. They spoke in whispers, awed by the immensity of desolation. By day the whole landscape was covered with the debris left by the broken German armies. Smashed tanks, guns with their wheels broken, stood out like fixed wrecks in the unmoving ocean of shell-holes. The whole earth seemed a litter of overcoats, shaggy leather packs, rifles, water-bottles, gas-masks, steel helmets, bombs, entrenching tools, cast away in the panic of flight. By night the sky glowed with the flames of burning Cambrai, with the black hump of Bourlon Hill silhouetted against them.[28]

Writing to his friend Eric Warman on the eve of Armistice Day forty years later, Aldington used much the same language to recall this scene, which '[bore] witness that at last "the advance" was a reality and not paper propaganda'. He added: 'Having seen that, I know what Death is. In that desolation nothing lived. Even the rats had been killed by the gas, and if birds drank the water of the shell-holes, poisoned with mustard gas, they died.'[29]

He rejoined D Company and at six o'clock the next morning the battle began, with the Royal Sussex in the lead of the brigade. Crossing the Cambrai-Caudry Road by eleven o'clock, they attempted to occupy the village of Cauroir, meeting some resistance. It was six o'clock in the evening before the village was taken.

The advance resumed the following day and by 9.35 a.m. the Royal Sussex and the 7th Northants were east of the village of Cagnoncles. While the 13th Middlesex now 'leap-frogged' through them, one company of the Royal Sussex had to support the left flank of the Middlesex attack and met with heavy machine gun fire and considerable shell fire and gas shelling. By eight-fifteen in the evening they had reached the western outskirts of St. Aubert, but in the course of the attack Lieutenant Paul, the battalion's signals officer had been severely wounded. Aldington now stepped into the post for which he had just been trained, becoming Battalion Signals and Intelligence Officer, and an acting captain. Meanwhile, on their left, two Canadian divisions had taken Cambrai itself. The German Army had retreated to a line along the River Selle.

Even now, the full implications of this steady advance were not apparent to the soldier on the ground – or perhaps he did not dare to hope. Aldington wrote to H.D. on 14 October to tell her that he had just seen his first newspaper for several days and was stunned to read talk of 'terms accepted'. He demands: 'What does it mean? Can it be? Dare we hope? Is this torture, this age-long nightmare ending?'[30] Even on 23 October he was writing: 'At least there now seems some chance of a solution . . . I scarcely think it will last more than another year.'[31] He was picking up mementoes from the battlefield for H.D., to remind her of the terrible waste the war had been: a book of German songs and a German testament. He advised her: 'There will be people about you speaking foolishly & haughtily of "victory". Turn from them – remember, as I do, the myriad dead and give them, if you can, your tears, as I do.'[32] He went out and stood leaning his head on the cross over a dead German's grave, crying for the loss and the waste – an action that would become the central incident of a short story ten years later.[33]

The battalion was not engaged in the Battle of the Selle between 17 and 25 October, an attack that pushed the German Army back still further, to a line between Valenciennes and the River Sambre. Instead, it was at Cauroir, rehearsing strenuously for the next stage of the advance. This included, as their war diary tells us, learning such skills as 'how to envelop a strong point which is holding up an advance'; after four years of positional warfare, such tactics were new. On 1 November, however, their orders came through: the brigade was to relieve 184th Brigade of 61st Division in the front line. Aldington sent H.D. a blank cheque to draw against his account in the event of his death.

At five-thirty on the morning of 4 November, the 9th Royal Sussex had to move through the 13th Middlesex to take high ground north of Wargnies le Petit and Wargnies le Grand and to make good the crossings over the Rhonelle River. Aldington's job during the advance was to ensure that his battalion headquarters remained in constant contact with the HQs of both flanking battalions and with the brigade headquarters. Heavy enemy machine gun fire caused casualties even before zero hour. The advance was successful but two of the companies were held up by machine gun posts on both sides of the river until the enemy were forced to retire. All along the line, but with varying rates of casualties, the Battle of the Sambre had been a success.

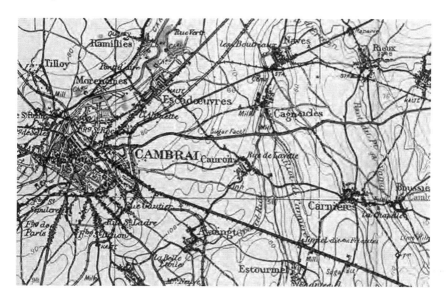

Map of 73 Brigade front at the Battle of Cambrai, October 1918

Over the next two days 73rd Brigade remained at Wargnies-le-Petit, as support and then reserve brigade, but subject to heavy enemy shell-fire. On 7 November they marched to Bavai. Aldington had found the whole experience exhilarating: 'This is very interesting and exciting – new towns & villages every day, enthusiastic welcomes by French people &c &c.,' he wrote to H.D. on 8 November. Knowing that he was due for leave later in the month, he continued: '[I] don't want to come specially. . . . what have I to come home to? . . . I am the only man in this battalion who is not anxious about leave.'[34]

Meanwhile, the advance continued, the brigade going into the front line again on 9 November. 9th Royal Sussex reached their objective – the Mons-Maubeuge Road – by midday. Relieved the following day, the whole brigade marched to billets at Les Vents. The next day – 11 November – they set off at six o'clock in the morning for Louvignies-Bavai, and it was here – at ten o'clock – that they were told that all hostilities would end at 11.00.: 'It was like the gift of another life! It *was* another life. Instead of living from minute to minute with the menace perpetually staring at you, instead of getting up and lying down with death. . . . Incredible. . . . A thrill of almost painful exaltation went through him, as if the first rush of returning hope and vitality were a hurt like blood flowing back into a crushed limb. Then with a worse, almost unendurable pang, he thought of the millions of men of many nations who would never feel that ecstasy, who were gone for ever, rotting in desolate battlefields and graveyards all over the world.'[35]

13 November

Dear Astraea

    I go on leave tomorrow & hope to reach London about the 16th or 17th. If you will write me and fix a date, place & time for meeting, I will be there. Only address will be 68 Queensborough Terrace, London, W2.

      Affectionately

        Richard

17 November

Sunday

    I am not seeing *anyone* to-day. Excuse my breaking appointment.

      Richard

This correspondence tells us all we need to know. That Aldington had to address the problem of his personal life only days after the sudden ending of the war exacerbated his unpreparedness. By the time he wrote to H.D. from Cambrai on 13 November, he had already travelled uncomfortably in several army trucks from Louvignies. A train the following morning took twenty-four hours to reach Boulogne. He arrived in London late on Saturday 16 November. It is not surprising that he felt unable to face H.D. the next day. His journey is described both in his memoir and in the short story 'Farewell to Memories':

> The train which was taking Brandon back to England . . . started from Cambrai before dawn. About eight miles from the town, in the Somme battlefield, it halted for nearly two hours. Brandon stared out of the window, still wearing his full equipment, with his rifle mechanically clutched between his knees. The colourless winter dawn hovered mournfully over a desecrated land, over a wreckage and sorrow that were beyond tears or outcries. Nothing can express that pitiable frozen silence, that awful symbol of the hatred of men for men. There stood a broken tank, poised on the verge of a huge shell-hole, just as it met disaster months before. There still lay the debris of battle. Guns, cocked sideways on broken wheels, showed where men had died. The frozen landscape was a tumult of shell-holes. Everywhere stood little groups of crosses; and to the south was a large, neatly lined cemetery. That was the symbol of the youth of a generation – lines of crosses. That was the symbol for all of them, living or dead – a graveyard on a battle-field.[36]

H.D. arrived in London on Friday 15 November and booked into the Lancaster Hotel in Bedford Place. The next day she dined at the Ellermans' home in South Audley Street. Quite when she and her husband did meet – and how frequently – we cannot know, but it was a difficult time for them both and we can only speculate about whether he kept his promise not to meet with Yorke. H.D. had only just heard of her brother's death; that she had not seen him since she left America seven years previously only deepened her sadness. A letter written to Bryher a few days before her visit to town suggests that she had hoped for much from her meeting with her husband: ' . . . once I hear from R., I will know

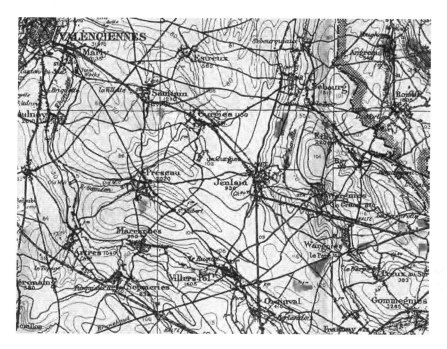

Map of 73 Brigade front at the Battle of the Sambre, November 1918

definitely about my future work and life.'[37] Aldington was evidently introduced to Bryher, and probably her family, during the first week of his leave, since he wrote to Amy Lowell on 8 December that Bryher 'seems a person of decidedly fine temperament'.[38]

By the end of his first week, however, the two had separated amid much bitterness, H.D. leaving London and returning to Speen. The discrepancy between two surviving letters reveals the failure of the couple to resolve their differences. A letter from H.D. to Shorter, written on Saturday 23 November, apologises to him for the fact that 'R. was suddenly called away', expresses her disappointment that they will not therefore be seeing Shorter and continues: 'I am feeling so tired with the continued rushing about we had last week that I will return at once to Speen.'[39] Nevertheless, a letter from Aldington to H.D. written a week later shows that he was still in London; its tone hints at the fraught nature of their meetings: 'I haven't forgotten you, you see. I was sorry you left town so suddenly, but I have no wish to interfere with your movements. Nor am I going to remonstrate any further with you on the subject of provision for your future; it is really up to you. No more than Cain am I my brother's keeper.' Characteristically, he moves quickly on to safer ground: 'I am planning to restore the P.T.S. Are you willing to collaborate?'[40]

Apart from probable meetings with Margery and his father in London and with his mother and the younger children in Rye, the only other person he seems to have encountered was Lawrence, who wrote to Lowell: 'I was in London in November – saw Richard, who was on leave. He is very fit, looking forward to peace and freedom. Hilda also is in town – not so very well. She is going to have another child it appears. I hope she will be all right. Perhaps she can get more settled, for her nerves are very shaken and perhaps the child will soothe her and steady her. I hope it will.'[41] This is a display either of Lawrence's indifference to his friends' feelings or of his tendency, like the Aldingtons, to tell Lowell a specially tailored version of events. Perhaps it is both. More cruelly, and revealing where he stood in relation to Yorke's campaign to win Aldington, he wrote to Mrs Yorke: 'Poor Hilda. Feeling sorry for her, one almost melts. But I *don't* trust her – other people's lives, indeed!'[42]

Aldington left London on 5 December to rejoin his battalion, which had moved west to Mouchin just inside the French border. On 18 December it moved again, to its final rest area in the Belgian village of Tantignies, five miles south-west of Tournai. The next two months were grim ones. First, he found the bitter cold and the bleak environment difficult to endure:

> This land is tedious as a worn-out whore;
> Faded and shabby
> As her once bright face
> Grown tarnished with disease,
> Loathsome as her grin which shows
> The black cubes of the missing teeth;
> The very sky is drab and sear
> As her lifeless hair,
> The earth itself rotten and foul
> As her dishonoured flesh.[43]

The routine into which the British Army had settled bored him utterly. Demobilisation had, perforce, to be a slow process. Meanwhile, from 9 December, the troops were subjected to educational classes in the mornings, football and other recreational activities in the afternoons, and entertainments – from card tournaments to concerts – in the evenings: 'By way of a contribution to the ease and comfort of the heroes of Armageddon under its command, the British War Office blithely issued instructions that all junior officers were to act forthwith as schoolmasters to "other ranks" in an education scheme concocted by somebody who evidently had a lot of second-hand school books to sell. Anyone acquainted with the ways and habits of men who go down to the sea in ships or up to the trenches with rifles will fully comprehend how deeply this kind thought was appreciated, and with what ardour we all returned to the three R's, the use of globes, music and dancing.'[44] Aldington wrote in an article that appeared in *The Sphere* in May 1919 that the experience confirmed him in his belief that: 'our people have a very sketchy idea of their religion and they are almost totally ignorant of their laws, their institutions, their geography, their history and, of course, their literature'.[45]

He was desperate to be demobilised, terrified that he would be drafted into the Army of Occupation. After longevity of service and 'essential' trades and occupations, priority for demobilisation was given to those whose pre-war employers wrote to indicate that they intended to re-employ them at a living wage on their return. Aldington knew himself to be disadvantaged on all counts. 'Were I wealthy, like the Sitwells, or merely syphiletic like Lewis, the case would be different!' he wrote to H.D.[46] He enlisted her help in persuading Harriet Weaver to give an assurance that she would employ him; when Weaver either misunderstood what was required of her or was wary of over-committing herself, his already-frayed temper erupted:

> Your letter of Jan 1st arrived. And from Miss Weaver. My God. All I can say is, My God. I am surrounded by fools and super-fools. Does she, do you, does *any* sane person imagine that the Govt. will release an officer to take up an appointment of *£36 a year*? Are you mad? Couldn't she have the sense to put a reasonable figure? I told her that there was nothing binding in it. Do you know what this means? That the application will certainly be rejected, that no effort on Hutton's part or my part or anyone's can alter it, that I shall be sent to the army of occupation & not be released, perhaps, for years?
>
> Well, I suppose it's not your fault; but it is the last straw. It's no use grousing is it? But my only chance of life is gone, wrecked. What a blasted fool the woman is. Tell her and her bloody paper to go to hell, will you. I have [not] the patience to write to her.
>
> Another two years of this hell!
>
> Cheerio; be good.
>
> R.[47]

He had the grace to apologise the next day and in a later letter to ask her not to worry or 'to stand in queues' on his behalf; but meanwhile the Yorkes had seized the opportunity and Mrs Yorke ('a good common-sense woman,' he told H.D.) had 'offered to help', so he sent her the forms 'and precise directions'.[48] However, he asked H.D. to see if Shorter could give him any freelance work on his demobilisation – and received assurances on that account.

Interspersed with these anxious letters were others, responding warmly, though rigorously, to the poems and translations H.D. was sending him. (Throughout her life, as Barbara Guest, points out, 'her creativity actually accelerated during periods of trial'.) Most of all, however, he was preoccupied with his plans for the new Poets' Translation Series. His aim was to involve all the original contributors, H.D., Flint, Storer and Whitall, as well as Cournos, Fletcher, Randall, Lowell and Bryher. He constructed an elaborate proposal and asked H.D. and Bryher to take his plans to Shorter to request that the latter approach Edward Hutton at Constable on his behalf. He was thinking bigger than the Egoist Press this time.

Meanwhile, he was picking up his translation of Anacreon, translating Alciphron and trying his hand at some journalism. He was sending his work (as he tactlessly revealed to H.D.) to Yorke for typing. It included some 'dialogues about books', and he told H.D. on 24 December that he had also written 'several poems and poems in prose' since returning to the battalion. Most of these poems would be published in *Images of Desire* and they reveal that by now he was planning a life with Yorke, but they also indicate his fragile emotional state. He told H.D. on 7 January that he was 'on the verge of a complete mental collapse' and complained two days later of having 'such extraordinary head-aches these days' that he could scarcely write.[49] Recalling this period in *Life for Life's Sake*, he wrote: 'It was at this time that I began to notice some of the after-effects of the war. I slept badly, was subject to meaningless but unpleasant moods of depression, and was in a frenzy of impatience to get out of the army. And it seemed to me that my mind had deteriorated, because of the difficulty I found in concentrating on mental work.'[50]

The obsessive plans for the P.T.S and the exasperation with H.D. and Weaver over his demobilisation indicate how close to the edge he was, terrified of being retained by the army but also of what the future held for him, still haunted by the war and dogged by the ill-health it had brought him. His final letter to H.D. before his demobilisation in early February reveals his inability to cope with his own situation and his unwillingness to take any responsibility for hers:

You've got to consider that I am probably fixed here for many, many months to come; & you must organise your life without any thought of me. I will send you all the money I can; beyond that I can't do anything. Life has not treated either of us too well, but you've got to realise, which you still haven't, the utter soullessness of the military machine, and the impossibility of an artist securing even bare justice from it. And the harshness of that machine is the reflection of the harshness of commercial civilization; you must secure some means of providing for yourself & your child. I am helpless and I am poor: you knew that six years ago; whatever chance I had of 'making good' has practically disappeared, and you can only rely on me for a very few pounds. When, eventually, I am discharged, I shall be scarcely able to earn a pittance for myself, as this harsh system has robbed me of whatever gifts I had. What on earth do you think I shall be worth after 2 or 3 years more of this?

There are the bare facts & you must face them. If Gray cannot or will not help you, then you must get work of some sort through your friends. What I can give will be totally inadequate.

I wish you the best of 'luck' in your coming ordeal; this time you go over the top while I watch helplessly. If it is any good saying it I would ask your forgiveness of the pain I have caused you, as freely as I forgive the pain you have caused me.

Richard.[51]

In adversity he had always had a tendency to both self-pity and priggishness. However, his worst immediate fear was not to be realised: he was demobilised on 8 February.

13. The Poet of War and Desire[1]

I would like to get rid of them – they cling to me and if I could publish them and forget them it would be a relief.

(Richard Aldington to Amy Lowell, 2 January 1918)[2]

It may seem to you that I have been almost wantonly morbid in these war poems, almost over-passionate, over in love with the beauty of the flesh, in the love poems. You cannot know, you cannot understand, where you are, the mentality of the soldier – the profound shattering of the nerves, the over-wrought tension, the intensity of sensation which come to him. One is like a man in a trance, moving & walking & talking mechanically, but yet exquisitely sensitive to every shock or touch of the senses. When I speak of 'soldiers' I do not mean the gay, careless, healthy fellows you see in your camps, fellows who've never seen a shot fired in wrath; I mean the men who've done weary months in the trenches, who know what death is, who have tasted to the dregs the bitterness of hell, who time & again have renounced all things. You will find we have a queer indifference to many things, & a great equally queer love.

(Richard Aldington to Charles Bubb, 8 February 1918)[3]

The first war poems Aldington had published were the nine that made up the Clerk's Press booklet, *Reverie: a little book of poems for H.D.*, which he sent to Bubb on 3 August 1917 and fifty copies of which were printed by the end of that month.[4] He had chosen carefully; they celebrate the Hellenic values the couple shared: love, nature and beauty. The long title poem, the poet's thoughts of his wife during a quiet moment spent in the line, proclaims the victory of love over death. Alec Waugh, writing in the journal *To-Day*, thought 'Reverie' the most beautiful example of both Aldington's philosophy and his poetic form: 'Each change of feeling is conveyed as much by the sounds of the words as by their sense. Theme and cadence are at one.'[5] Waugh was still praising the poem over forty years later, describing it as 'tender, wistful, nostalgic, uncomplaining'.[6] The short 'Epilogue' also celebrates the power of love, but more fiercely:

> We are of those that Dante saw
> Glad, for love's sake, among the flames of hell,
> Outdaring with a kiss all-powerful wrath;
> For we have passed athwart a fiercer hell,

Illustration by Paul Nash accompanying the poem 'Bombardment' in *Images of War*

> Through gloomier, more desperate circles
> Than ever Dante dreamed:
> And yet love kept us glad.

Aldington was not the only combatant poet to use the conceit of the descent into Hell as a metaphor of war and death, but, characteristically, he is the only one to use it to explore the role of *eros* in the soldier's life.[7] Of course, Dante's lovers were in the second circle of hell *because of* their (illicit) love, while for this poet love is what makes it possible to survive the hell of war. Of *Reverie* as a whole, but of this short poem in particular, Harriet Monroe wrote: 'Out of his despair, out of his hunger for beauty, comes a lyric note clearer and richer than anything we have heard from him since those earliest poems, and an exaltation of spirit as noble and impassioned, and perhaps more humane.'[8] The other seven poems explore the threat the war posed to love, nature and beauty: 'The Wine Cup' and 'Ananke' are accounts of the bitter anguish caused to the poet and his lover by their forced separation and the risk of death; 'An Earth Goddess' is a hymn to Nature, ravaged by war but still offering comfort to suffering humanity; 'Sorcery of Words' and 'Our Hands' are prose poems, the first celebrating the beauty of winter, as experienced by the soldier despite his physical discomfort, the second grieving for the state of his hands, once 'so reverent in beauty's service'. The remaining two short poems, 'Disdain' and 'Proem', express the poet's doubt or despair, his fear that the gods have betrayed him and that there is no meaning to all this suffering, nor salvation from it.

From Newhaven five months later, when he was putting together the selection that would be published in America (by Four Seas of Boston) as *War and Love*, Aldington wrote to Lowell that he had about sixty or seventy war poems.[9] In fact his output at the front in 1917 was less than forty poems, of which thirty-two appeared in *War and Love*.[10] Perhaps the figure he gave Lowell included the more recent love poems inspired by his affair with Yorke; these would eventually total twenty-eight, of which eighteen were included in *War and Love*. Significantly, Aldington had the tact to omit from this volume 'Reverie', 'Ananke' and 'Epilogue', all love poems to H.D., but much to his frustration, the book would not appear until September 1919.

He also tried to obtain a British publisher, but Constable turned him down. (*J'ai dit la vérité sur la guerre et sur l'amour. On ne veut pas de moi*, he told Flint.)[11] He would not find a publisher until after the war had ended, and then only by separating the war poems from the love poems: while Allen and Unwin finally accepted the former, which were published as *Images of War* in December 1919, it was Elkin Mathews, the small specialist poetry publisher, who took on *Images of Desire*, which appeared in June of that year.

However, shortly before he left England for his second tour of duty in April 1918, Aldington negotiated with Cyril Beaumont the publication of a limited edition of some of the war poems, *Images of War: A Book of Poems*, to be illustrated with wood-cuts by Paul Nash.[12] There would be two hundred copies, of which thirty were to be signed by author and artist and printed on vellum. Aldington again excluded 'Reverie', 'Ananke' and 'Epilogue', along with two further poems from *Reverie*; the handful of other omissions included another tribute to H.D., 'Time's Changes', which recalled their 'honeymoon' in Italy. Publication was again delayed, although this was the first edition of the war poems to be published either side of the Atlantic – in April 1919. Thus, while Aldington intended immediate publication for his war poetry, it is important to note that it did not make an appearance – in America or England – until at least six months after the Armistice.[13]

When he came to assemble the Allen and Unwin edition of *Images of War* in 1919, the omitted poems would all be reinstated.[14] One further poem would be added ('Insouciance'), but another six from *War and Love* discarded, including all the prose poems.

A note of defensiveness is apparent in his letters as he put together the creative outcome of his service in France.[15] He wrote to Lowell: 'Personally I think I have lost a delicacy of technique, a sureness of form, but that I've gained a wider outlook & a more direct appeal to people who are not enthusiasts for poetry . . . I've written honestly what I've seen, what I've felt. There is no lie, no sort of pose in the book.'[16] In his foreword to *War and Love*, dated February 1918 and addressed to Flint, he wrote: 'Even you may feel that these notes on war are overstrained, morbidly self-conscious, petulant perhaps.' However, the foreword continues: 'They represent to some degree the often inarticulate feelings of the ordinary civilised man thrust suddenly into these extraordinary circumstances – feelings of bewilderment, bitterness, dumb revolt and rather piteous weakness. Poor human flesh is so easily rent by the shattering of explosive and the jagged shear of metal. Those of us who have seen it will never be quite happy again.'

Setting aside the strain of military elitism here, ubiquitous in his dealings with Flint in this period, we need to take account of Aldington's insistence that his perspective is that of 'the ordinary civilised man'. It is this angle of vision which constitutes the appeal of the best of his war poems, and its achievement is all the more remarkable given that he was a product of a highly-intellectualised artistic elite. Amongst those who would become the published British combatant poets of the First World War, he was the only one, apart from Hulme and Manning, who had even come to the war as a professional writer.[17] However, his class identity had been destroyed through his enlistment as conscript and ordinary soldier and his artistic identity – and personal confidence – fragmented by his miserable months of training. All that he had left to cling to was his passionate sense of himself as a lover: of H.D., of the natural world and of 'civilisation', which was not for him a political or nationalist concept; it meant the values of classical Greece: order, reason and beauty.

Furthermore, the emotional range of this body of verse far exceeds the notes of 'bewilderment, bitterness, dumb revolt and rather piteous weakness' to which he refers. Self-pity, petulance and sentimentality are not totally absent, as they were not from the poems written during his training (or from *Images 1910-1915*). They appear in 'The Wine Cup':

> Cold terrible, unseen hands
> Have dragged the cup from us.

or 'Doubt':

> Ah! Weak as wax against their bronze are we,
> Ah! Faint as reed-pipes by the water's roar,
> And driven as land-birds by the vast sea wind.

or 'A Young Tree':

> And every keen dear lad that's killed
> Seems to cry out:
> 'We are so few, so very few,
> Could not our fate have been more merciful?'

or 'Disdain':

> Desolate we move across a desolate land,
> The high gates closed,
> No answer to our prayer . . .

However, his marriage and his love of nature did prove resilient supports. We have already noted the quiet certainty of 'Reverie', even if, for the modern reader, the poem seems a little 'over-written'. The more compact lyric, 'Time's Changes', shows Aldington's verse writing at its most successful, the memory vividly realised, the danger and uncertainty conveyed, not discursively, but in sharp visual images, the whole structured through an implied contrast:

> Four years ago today in Italy
> I gathered wild flowers for a girl –

> Thick scented broom, wild sword-flowers,
> The red anemones that line the ways
> And the frail-throated freesia
> Which lives beneath the orange boughs
> And whose faint scent to me
> Is love's own breath, its kiss . . .
>
> Today in sunless barren fields
> I gather heads of shells,
> Splinters of shrapnel, cartridges . . .
> What shall I gather
> Four years from today?

And in 'Bombardment', parallelism is used again, this time to celebrate the inviolability of nature:[18]

> Four days the earth was rent and torn
> By bursting steel,
> The houses fell about us;
> Three nights we dared not sleep,
> Sweating, and listening for the imminent crash
> Which meant our death.
>
> The fourth night every man,
> Nerve-tortured, racked to exhaustion,
> Slept, muttering and twitching,
> While the shells crashed overhead.
> The fifth day there came a hush;
> We left our holes
> And looked above the wreckage of the earth
> To where the white clouds moved in silent lines
> Across the untroubled blue.

Such tight lyric achievements show the poet applying his Imagist craft to the new context. In 'Bombardment', as in 'Picket', 'Machine Guns' and 'Battlefield', we get the 'direct treatment'[19] which enables the poet to render the trench experience concretely and precisely.

However, Imagism was not adequate for all he wanted to do. His pre-war writing showed him, with very limited success, trying to find the language and forms for a more expansive and reflective kind of poetry. What his war poetry reveals is that the problem was not just one of form and language; it was also a problem of *voice*. 'Time's Changes' and 'Bombardment' succeed most of all because, from within the Imagist framework, an authentic voice, that of the lover or the soldier – that 'ordinary civilised man' – emerges. The first person plural of 'Bombardment' is hugely important to its impact – the poet speaking as one of a unit of infantrymen. Once Aldington tried to employ a more discursive form, voice became more problematic. On the one hand he adopted – in such poems as 'In the Trenches', 'The Wine Cup', 'Terror', 'Defeat', 'Doubt' and 'An Earth Goddess' – the formal, usually plural, first person voice of Greek drama, along with the verse form, rhetoric and imagery of the Greek chorus:

> White goddess of beauty,
> Take these roses –
> It is our blood that colours them;
> Take these lilies –
> White as our intense hearts;
> Take these wind-flowers –
> Frail as our strength spent in your service;
> Take these hyacinths –
> Graven with the sigh of our lost days;
> Take these narcissus blooms
> Lovely as your naked breasts.
>
> ('Defeat', lines 17-27)

The result is generally, as in this extract, disappointing. The form now starts to seem escapist and artificial, the tone self-indulgent, the language stylised, the imagery *fin-de-siècle* – and inadequate to express a response to the experience of industrial warfare. More interesting are the attempts to produce reflective poetry with a *personal* voice, such as 'Reverie' and 'A Village'. Here the poet's strengths – his realism, his love of nature, his appreciation of contrasts – are deployed effectively: the physical surroundings are conveyed with immediacy and the voice is that of the ordinary soldier:

> Today the larks are up,
> The willow boughs are red with sap,
> The last ice melting on the dykes;
> One side there stands a row of poplars,
> Slender amazons, martial and tall,
> And on the other
> The sunlight makes the red-tiled roofs deep orange . . .
>
> And we have come from death,
> From the long weary nights and days
> Out in those frozen wire-fringed ditches;
> And this is life again, rich life –
> This poor drab village, lovely in our eyes
> As the prince city of Tuscany
> Or the crown of Asia, Damascus.
>
> ('A Village', lines 44-57)

The first person plural – the identification with his fellow pioneers – is one of the strengths of this poem. That the piece represents Aldington's emergence (and it is actually poised at the emergence of the landscape from winter) from self-pity and isolation is evident from its opening lines:

> Now if you saw my village
> You'd not think it beautiful,
> But flat and commonplace –
> As I'd have called it half a year ago.

The possessive adjective is illuminating: this poet, never a nationalist (or only fleetingly so in 1914), has come to see this drab, and now half-ruined, French village as his home. He also perceives himself as an equal member of its temporary community of soldiers, whereas the first person plural of the formal choruses proclaimed his separation from both his physical surroundings and his real-life companions.

A logical development of a move towards realism was experimentation with informal expression. This was a characteristic of some of his earlier discursive poems, such as 'Eros and Psyche', 'Childhood' and 'Daisy', and, as has been remarked earlier, often caused a loss of rigour and cadence or the emergence of a strain of sentimentality, even vulgarity. In some cases this continued to be true, particularly in a longer poem, even an otherwise impressive one like 'A Village':

> But when you've pondered
> Hour upon chilly hour in those damned trenches,
> You get at the significance of things,
> Get to know, clearer than before,
> What a tree means, what a pool,
> Or a black wet field in sunlight.

Thomas MacGreevy observantly remarked that the use here of the word 'damned' 'breaks in discordantly on the emotional essence as well as on the technical excellence of the passage.' He continues: 'It constitutes an indubitably threadbare epithet placed amongst words that are themselves charged with new meaning by the intensity of the perception behind them.'[20]

However, in some of the shorter poems, the approach is more effective in creating a realistic tone and, precisely because they *are* shorter, a coherent idea. 'Machine Guns' (an account of an occasion when a group of soldiers come under fire) begins as an imagist poem, but ends:

> Only we two stand upright;
> All differences of life and character smoothed out
> And nothing left
> Save that one foolish tie of caste
> That will not let us shrink.

A simple and shrewd observation, neatly expressed. Like Owen, Sassoon and Gurney, Aldington experimented with the use of colloquial language to convey the characters and attitudes he observed around him. The speaker in the two 'soliloquies' confides to the reader:

Illustration by Paul Nash accompanying the poem 'Picket' in *Images of War*

> But – the way they wobble! –
> God! That makes one sick.
> Dead men should be so still, austere,
> And beautiful,
> Not wobbling carrion roped upon a cart . . .
> Well, thank God for rum.

We are reminded of Robert Graves's attempt to shock his readers with the reality of death in 'The Dead Boche' (although Graves might not have allowed himself the clumsiness of the repetition of 'wobble'). However, the second of the two soliloquies begins:

> I was wrong, quite wrong;
> The dead men are not always carrion.

The language is already more restrained and the gap between speaker and poet narrower; it has disappeared altogether by the end of the poem when Aldington characteristically describes the 'dead English soldier' he finds on a fire-step as

> More subtly coloured than a perfect Goya,
> And more austere and lovely in repose
> Than Angelo's hand could ever carve in stone.

'Trench Idyll' again uses colloquial language to convey class and character and to shock the reader:

> 'Well, as to that, the nastiest job I've had

> Was last year on this very front
> Taking the discs at night from men
> Who'd hung there for six months on the wire
> Just over there.
> The worst of all was
> They fell to pieces at a touch.
> Thank God we couldn't see their faces;
> They had gas helmets on . . . '

And the piece is closed, neatly and ironically, with the poet's own voice:

> I shivered;
> 'It's rather cold here, sir, suppose we move?'

The eleven months that lapsed between Aldington's homecoming from his first period of front-line service and his return to France as a commissioned officer were, as we have remarked, an unproductive period, apart from the frenzy of love poems that occurred at the turn of the year in response to his affair with Dorothy Yorke. However, there are two other published poems from this time. The first, 'Apathy', written while he was at Brocton Camp in the summer of 1917, was discussed in chapter 9 and shows the poet juxtaposing the quiet reflective style of 'Reverie' or 'A Village' with the graphic realism and colloquialism of his first 'Soliloquy' to expose his own dysfunctional state.

The second, 'The Blood of the Young Men', written in January 1918, demonstrates acutely the difficulties Aldington was facing in trying to find poetic expression for his feelings about the war. Away from the front, he was no longer directly observing the impact of the war on himself, his companions and the natural world. Like Sassoon back from the front a year earlier, he was becoming angry on their behalf; like Sassoon he targets the complacency of civilians, specifically women and 'the old men'.[21] Unlike Sassoon, however, he could not find the appropriate form through which to express his anger with satirical force; the result is a poem that is rambling (seventy lines long), repetitive (the word 'blood' alone recurring fifteen times) and hectoring. He was not in a state to recognise its imperfections. Not only did he include it in *War and Love* (and subsequently the Allen and Unwin *Images of War*), but he also submitted it to Beaumont and Michael Sadler for inclusion in *New Paths,* the attractive anthology of verse, prose and pictures which Beaumont brought out in May 1919.[22] (Since his other contribution was 'Soliloquy I', the anthology did not display him at his best.)

The only other work from this period is three short 'Minor Exasperations' written at Newhaven (and never published, though printed in *Coterie* in September 1919) which show him attempting satire with some limited success. The problem with satire is that it requires humour as well as the motor of anger, and Aldington's personal and military life over the previous months had taken its toll on that sense, among others.

With the exception of the prose poems, which will be discussed shortly, Aldington's second period of service at the front, up until the Armistice, was as creatively unproductive as his months in England. While his increased responsibilities and involvement in what had become a war of rapid movement go some way to account for this, he did have two extended periods away from the front line on courses. He sent three poems in letters to H.D. and possibly more love poems to Yorke (since *Images of Desire* includes ten that did not appear in *War and Love*). Only one of the three poems he sent H.D. was ever published, 'The Faun Captive'.[23] Like 'The Faun Complains' of the previous year, the poem trades on the role that Aldington had played to H.D.'s 'dryad' since the early days of their relationship. In both poems the faun bewails the loss of the Greek idyll but in the later poem vows:

> One night I shall break these thongs
> And kill, kill, kill in sharp revenge.

Then, he tells us, he will escape: 'to the unploughed lands no foot oppresses'. Norman Gates considered this one of Aldington's finest poems, since it 'integrates the idea and symbol so well' and 'the emotion that the poem develops is valid both on the level of the faun and on the level of the poet.'[24] However, for many readers the poem may seem misanthropic, its voice petulant, the conceit too precious to engage with the devastating effects of the war.

More interesting, although a less 'finished' work (and never published by Aldington), is 'Deaths of Common Men', written in the late summer of 1918, a further attempt at the reflective mode of 'Reverie', 'A Village' or 'Apathy'.[25] As in the latter poem, Aldington treats the actualities of the war in language that is shocking:

> I have seen the good flesh cut, the white bone shattered,
> Seen the red face turn like a yellow leaf,
> The firm mouth wobble;
> Watched it all, taken it in.

and the ideas in the poem are well-tried ones: death the leveller and the Hardyesque notion that:

> We are made of the infinite dead,
> And, dead, we make the infinite living.

However, the evocation of the rural setting and the mood of acceptance almost, if not entirely, make the poem's didacticism palatable:

> Now, while the sun is hot
> And they gather the grape harvest,
> And the leaves are gold, and life splendid,
> Let me speak once more of the end, the parting–
> How simple it is, how natural.

The voice is not 'right', but at least it is authentic:

> Have no fear of the subtle man,
> The man of affected speech and brains;
> You and I will make just as good corpses,
> Our clay is sweeter.

At the end of 1916, when he reached France fresh from his *Myrrhine and Konallis* experiments, Aldington's first writing had consisted of two prose poems written at base camp, 'Fatigues' and 'Sorcery of Words', followed up, while he was on active service, with two others, 'Our Hands' and 'The Road'. When he returned to France in April 1918 he took up the form again – almost exclusively, even providing a self-deprecatory justification:

> Now I am good only to mimic inferior
> masters. My thoughts are stifling –
> heavy grey dust from a scorched road.
> For me silence; or if speech, then some
> humble poem in prose. Indeed I am
> too conscientious – or shall we say
> too impotent? – to dare the cool
> rhythm of prose, the sharp
> edges of poetry.
>   (from 'Discouragement': Officers; Camp, Fressin, 1918)

It may be that Eliot's *New Statesman* article had made him defensive about his use of the form.[26] Tellingly, he excluded all of his prose poems, the four from 1916/17 and the ten he wrote in 1918, from the Allen and Unwin *Images of War*; 'The Road' and the 1918 pieces would not appear between book covers at all until 1926.[27] Several of the 1918 pieces confirm the rightness of this decision, although he did send them to Harriet Munroe.[28] 'Fantasy', 'Reaction', 'Prayer' and 'Escape' are stylised, self-indulgent hankerings after the lost Greek world and they betray their origins in the verbal exercises he described to H.D.[29] It is not surprising that Flint was critical. However, the battlefield pieces, particularly when they confine themselves to the concrete circumstances of a moment's experience, have a compelling beauty and pathos:

> Only last night, in the midst of a
> Raid – searchlights, menacing hum of
> planes, soft thuds of anti-aircraft
> guns, deep rapidly-nearing crashes
> of bombs, no cover – I found three
> boys sitting in darkness, softly
> singing old tunes.   (from 'Song': Divisional Camp 1918)

>   For a
> moment each group was silhouetted

> against the whitening east: the steel
> helmets (like those of medieval
> men-at-arms), the slung rifles, the
> strained postures of carrying, the
> useless vacillating corpse under its
> sepulchral blanket – all sharply edged
> in black on that smooth sky.   (from 'Dawns', Loos, 1918)

Comment is achieved not by assertion, a weakness in so many of the longer poems, but implicitly, through ironic juxtaposition. 'Dawns' concludes:

> And as
> the groups passed they shouted the
> names of the things they carried –
> things which yesterday were
> living men.
> and I forwarded my report through
> the usual channels.

'Landscape', which begins with a description of a moonlit night, in which 'the air blows cleaner and sweeter', continues:

> Heavy scented the air tonight –
> new-mown hay – a pungent exotic
> odour – phosgene . . .
> And tomorrow there will be huddled
> Corpses with blue horrible faces
> And foam on their writhed mouths.

When Aldington allowed himself to discard poeticisms and Hellenic imaginings and to use the prose-poem as a form closer to prose than to poetry, he could achieve an elegiac, even apocalyptic, vision of war:

> And just before dawn when
> the last limber rattles away and the
> last stretcher has gone back to the
> line, then the ghosts of the dead
> armies march down, heroic in their
> silence, battalion after battalion,
> brigade after brigade, division after
> division; the immeasurable forces of
> the dead youth of Europe march
> down the Road past the silent sentry,
> past the ruined house, march back,
> march home.   ('The Road', Maroc, 1917)

Over a decade later he would recognise this achievement by incorporating the majority of the prose poems, as passages of elevated prose, into the short story

'Farewell to Memories', which closes the collection *Roads to Glory*.[30] There they bring to the war story of the soldier Brandon that elegiac quality which enabled the writer to achieve the closure that *Death of a Hero* had not given him.

Norman Gates called *Images of Desire* one of Aldington's best volumes of poetry, because 'it deals with the life of sensations', Gates being of the opinion that this was Aldington's great strength as a poet.[31] Of the twenty-four poems in the Elkin Mathews volume, fourteen (and an additional four, which were not carried over into *Images of Desire*) appeared in the earlier volume, *War and Love,* prepared for publication in January and February 1918. The majority were therefore written over a period of a few weeks, since Aldington's affair with Dorothy Yorke did not begin until some time in December 1917. This accounts for a feature which Gates identifies, their homogeneity of form, style and mood. [32] Most are quite short and several show Aldington employing rhyme, metre and traditional lyric form.

For the most part, they read, unsurprisingly, as the poems of a new love affair, focusing on the physical attributes of the poet's mistress, the agonies of desire and separation and the pleasures of fulfilment. Titles such as 'Possession', 'Gain', 'Her Mouth', 'Daybreak', 'Sleep' and 'Before Parting' as well as the variations on 'Song' ('Song for Her', 'A Soldier's Song', 'An Old Song') give some indication of this.

In both his *War and Love* foreword to Flint and his February 1918 letter to Bubb, Aldington attempted to defend the sensualism of these poems by asking his correspondent to visualise the emotional and mental state of the soldier. In fact, the poems are extremely 'conventional' in their adherence to the tradition of erotic verse, that is in their expression of desire, ecstasy, joy and agony. However, their sexual frankness would certainly have shocked Bubb. It is linked to an explicit rejection of religious faith:

> But we who do not drug ourselves with lies
> Know, with how deep a pathos, that we have
> Only the warmth and beauty of this world
> Before the blankness of the unending gloom. (from 'Epilogue')[33]

Furthermore, the poet relishes the illicit nature of the love affair. In 'An Old Song' the poet compares the Virgin Mary unfavourably with his mistress and vows:

> Into uttermost hell shall I go
> For sweet sin with this lady.

In 'Images of Desire', he sees his mistress as both 'sister and lover' and concludes:

> Would that we had one mother indeed
> That we might be bound closer in shame.

Indeed, he re-uses the image of Dante's second circle of hell, which had informed his 'Epilogue' in *Reverie: a little book of poems for H.D.,* but this time for its original meaning:

> There shall be two spirits rived together
> . . . in the icy whirlwind that is hell
> For those who loved each other more than God.   ('Possession')

Gates regretted the separation of the love poems from the war poems; in his opinion, 'by issuing two different volumes, Aldington has given us, in each case, only a partial view of his wartime poetry'.[34] Yet there are two considerations to weigh against this judgement. The first is the fact that the majority of the love poems were written at Mecklenburgh Square and at Newhaven, when Aldington was, although separated from Yorke for short periods of time, not in France or in immediate danger. Of course, he was dealing with both the effects of his time at the front and his certain knowledge that he was to return there shortly. However, the intensity of the poems derives not from the writer's identity as a soldier, but from the physicality of the relationship and the extent to which it was being conducted in a spirit of defiance towards the outside world (both characteristic themes of erotic poetry). Secondly, few of the poems, other than those that we can deduce (both from internal clues and because they do not appear in *War and Love*) were written later in France, address the issue of the war. Exceptions are 'Before Parting':

> Though I return once more to the terror of battle,
> Though perchance I be lost to you for ever –
> Give me, O love, your love for this last brief season,
> Be mine indeed as I am yours for ever.

and 'Prayer':

> Lord, you know not her or love
> If you let death take me.
> . . . No God, no nation, no cause,
> No life of any man, no person,
> Nothing created or living
> Do I love as I love her.

while the use made of the war in 'Daybreak' seems shocking in its triviality:

> Not all the blood of our dead, the bright gay blood so gaily shed,
> Shines with so clear a glow as gleams your breast-flower peering
>   from our bed.

This quotation brings us to another problematic aspect of the love poems: for the most part the poet fails to find a language to express sensuality and eroticism that is not cloying or overblown. The constant references to breasts as flowers or (in 'Loss') as 'two-fold amorous breasts' are an instance of this. H.D. brilliantly classed these poems as 'that hyacinth-myrrh poetry'.[35] (If we are to believe *Bid Me To Live*, he showed them to her – with characteristically brutal honesty – while putting *War and Love* together in January 1918.) For the most part, they reveal that Aldington the artist could not distance himself from the obsession of Aldington the lover. In 1919, as they were due to be published, he would confess to Flint that he hated their 'vulgarity',[36] but at the time he was incapable of such detachment.[37]

Among the additional poems that appeared in *Images of Desire* are a handful which appear to have been written during the dead period between armistice and demobilisation, and in which the voice is that of the soldier as well as the lover. These are 'Cynthia', 'Reserve', 'Odelette', 'The Winter Park' and 'Meditation'. The first of these is a traditional love lyric:

> Day droops on stems of pallid light
> Over these sodden northern fields,
> And I am lonely, thinking here,
>   Cynthia of you.
>
> Here life is but a phantom of himself
> And limps and mutters by these war-worn paths,
> And I could weep to waste my youth,
>   Cynthia from you.
>
> O rose that filled my mouth with life!
> Wine of your lips, your budded breasts!
> How could I serve another god,
>   Cynthia but you?

While it slips finally into the erotic clichés, the poem effectively uses the lyric form to evoke the winter landscape of war-torn Belgium and the poet's weariness of spirit. In 'The Winter Park' the dreary setting is described in more realistic detail but becomes a foil for the poet's dreams of his lover. In contrast, in 'Odelette' and the four-lined poem, 'Reserve', love cannot console the soldier for the losses he has experienced:

> Now I regret
> The fervour that has gone from me,
> Stolen by circumstance,
> Leaving me lassitude –
> A deserted temple with no god.   (from 'Odelette')
>
> Though you desire me I will still feign sleep
> And check my eyes from opening to the day,
> For as I lie, thrilled by your gold-dark flesh,
> I think of how the dead, my dead, once lay.   ('Reserve')

'Meditation' abandons the dominant forms and style of *Images of Desire*, for the personal voice and extended reflective manner of 'A Village'. It begins with a jarring description of the poet's physical surroundings:

> Outside the young frost crisps the grass

Illustration by Paul Nash accompanying the poem 'Trench Idyll' in *Images of War*

> And bends the narrow willow boughs
> And flecks the dyke with little spears of ice;
> The huge moon, yellow and blotched,
> Like the face of a six days' corpse,
> Stares hideously over the barren wood.

However, the poet, alone in a small Belgian house, 'untroubled by crash of guns or tramp of men', can now start the process of 'purging out bitterness, effacing miseries', and look forward hopefully to what he has 'yearned for', his 'chance to live [his] life out to the end', his relationship with his mistress, travel, reading and social companionship. Yet the second part of the poem deals with his fears; he knows that he still has trauma and bitterness to deal with and that the old life may no longer satisfy him.

And so the poem ends on a subdued note:

> Perhaps, then, this is my happiest moment,
> Here in this little cold Belgian house,
> Remembering harsh years past,
> Plotting gold years to come,
> Trusting so blithely in a woman's faith;
> In the quiet night,
> In the silence.

It is Aldington's 'Frost at Midnight', and it gives us the clearest picture of the state of mind of the poet, the soldier and the lover at the end of two years of war.

PART THREE
Exile

14. The Aftermath: 1919

I am utterly weary now that it is over,
weary as the lost Argonauts beating
hopelessly for home against the
implacable storm.   (Richard Aldington, 'In the Library', 1919)

It was a world of tired people, trying simply to exist.
                                    (Bryher, *The Heart to Artemis*, 1963)[1]

Aldington arrived at Charing Cross Station late on Tuesday evening, 11 February. There was no-one to greet him. Carrying his kitbag, he walked up Charing Cross Road and entered Mario Massaglia's Italian restaurant at the shabby Hotel du Littoral on Moor Street, across from the Palace Theatre. There he ate a meal and booked himself into a room. Drained and exhausted, he spent most of the next day sleeping.

The rest of the week was spent searching for work, reporting to Crystal Palace to complete his demobilisation and visiting his bank to sort out his finances. The first two weekends he spent in Rye with his family; but, even there, he continued the hunt for work with a stream of correspondence, writing to Charles Bubb to ask for the return of any manuscripts that Bubb did not intend printing,[2] to Martyn Johnson at *The Dial*, offering him four articles, to Amy Lowell for help in finding an American publisher for the planned translation series and to Harriet Monroe with material for *Poetry*.[3] He met Clement Shorter over dinner at the Littoral on 20 February; Shorter accepted two poems and commissioned Aldington to develop the comment pieces he had written in Belgium into a series of articles for *The Sphere*.[4]

There are no surviving letters from Aldington to H.D. between 29 January and 24 February; perhaps the bluntness of his last one had left them with nothing more to say. She left Speen at the end of January for lodgings recommended to her by Margaret Pratt at 2, Hangar Lane, Ealing, near to St Faith's nursing home, into which Patmore had booked her for her confinement. She was already envisaging throwing in her lot with Bryher: in letters she wrote to her in December and early January she had made it clear that she saw their futures as together and had even suggested a furnished flat they could take in Woburn Buildings (where Yeats lived).[5] The two women had seen Shorter as a useful ally in Bryher's attempt to break free of the stranglehold of her family, and thus to overcome her near-suicidal depression, and H.D. wrote to him in January: 'I think Winifred Bryher must take her flat. I have written her that later I shall be glad to be with her almost entirely, if she would like, and I could arrange for my child's being cared for nearby.'[6]

Aldington himself, having made clear his refusal to take responsibility for H.D. and her child, spent February attending to his own prospects and had few emotional reserves left to consider anyone but himself. There may, however, be a less bleak interpretation of the absence of letters between himself and H.D. (not even one to let her know that he was back in London). She was taken ill shortly after her move to Hangar Lane. 'Flu was now an epidemic throughout the country and especially serious for someone in her condition. It quickly turned into pneumonia. Bryher went to visit her and found the doctor there. According to Bryher, the landlady said to her, 'Do you know the woman? She is going to die. Can you pay the funeral expenses?'[7] Bryher contacted Patmore, who immediately made arrangements for H.D. to be admitted early into the nursing home. H.D. was 'dangerously ill for several days'. (It was at this point that Bryher vowed to take her to Greece as soon as she was well enough.) In the anxiety and confusion of the moment, H.D.'s mail may well have been mislaid.

Aldington's letter of Monday 24 February certainly indicates that he has heard of her illness; perhaps Bryher or Patmore had contacted him at the Littoral. He wrote:

Dear Astraea

I hear you are not feeling too famously; you must keep strong and hopeful, for I think you will have a good chance of a fine literary career. Let me know if I can do anything for you in the way of sending out ms.s &c.

As to type-writer, I intend buying another second-hand so you had better keep the one you have. It still goes, doesn't it?

No news particularly. I see few people – they are all so very discouraging. But I'm sending quite a deal of work to U.S. Dial has promised more pay. As soon as you are well I want you to write some articles for them—I know I can get them to print them.

Keep cheerful & courageous. I know there is happiness & a fine life for you. This is a harsh test, but remember your Greeks at Marathon!

Richard[8]

His tone is bluffly friendly, staying on firm ground, the bond between them as writers. By the following Saturday, he writes more personally: 'Please get well soon; I feel very miserable when I think of you lying ill. There is so much for you to come back to; everyone speaks so admiringly of you & your work. On Friday I saw Massingham and he asked me for work by you. I said I would ask you to let him see your Hippolytus; so if you will ask Brigit to send it to me I will retype it & send it to him. Could you make her send it soon? This week I have some Anacreon in the Nation; but you should be there too. You must let me do anything I can for your work – it seems all I can do.'[9]

That day, 1 March, he had moved temporarily to a studio at 52 Doughty Street, lent him by an acquaintance. Away from the dingy room at the Littoral and in his own lodgings, at least for a while, he was more cheerful, and the letter continues: 'I'm very happy to be back. Please forgive my being happy when you are so ill. And please keep brave – you have a wonderful life to come back to and all the really worthwhile people will stick to you.' However, the letter is revealing for its omissions; it is only her *work* for which he offers support. The final reassurance clearly alludes to the dubious social status she will acquire as a single mother, rather than to her literary prospects; and here he makes no pledges of his own.

Aldington was having a hard time finding the 'really worthwhile people' for his own support. Flint was still in barracks in Cornwall, miserable, unable to work and with no immediate prospect of release. Aldington's letters to him were mostly devoted to his attempts to pull strings for Flint's demobilisation; in any case, he could not confide in his friend, as the paternity of H.D.'s child was a secret. He entertained Flint and Violet to dinner at the Littoral on 12 April (by which time the baby had been born), but it is hard to guess how much of his personal situation Aldington was able or willing to impart to them.

Moor Street

By some irony, Cournos was lodging not far from Aldington, in St Martin's Street, off Leicester Square, but these two former friends had nothing to say to each other; Cournos's closest companion now was Fletcher. Lawrence, who had barely survived a severe case of 'flu, was alone in his Derbyshire cottage, Frieda having refused to leave London. Hueffer, shell-shocked and gassed in France and Flanders, was now farming in rural Sussex with his new lover, Stella Bowen. Two obstacles prevented Aldington from seeking the companionship of other former friends such as Whitall or Randall: the need to keep his complex personal circumstances private and his instinctive aversion to the company of those who had not seen combat. Only five weeks after arriving in London he wrote to Shorter: 'I wonder if you realise what a gulf there is in my generation between the men who fought and those who didn't? It's a strain being with them; I feel as if I was calling across an enormous ravine to them. Of course I've got used to meeting them, but honestly I shrink from it. I can't quite tell you why, except perhaps that we others have seen all the misery & pain & hunger & despair & death of the world & they, in their comfortable England, have not.'[10]

There was still Pound. Aldington had written eagerly to him from Tournai: 'I should with luck be free on Friday. Will trot along to see you. I have got a chance of one or two jobs in town, but I want to come and talk things over with you and, if possible, to recommence our ancient war on les cuistres.'[11] But, affable as he was for old times' sake, Pound had moved on. Aldington had been filed as an Amygist; Pound's new protégées were Joyce, Lewis and Eliot, the true modernists. He was more than ever engaged in the 'ancient war' but did not see Aldington as a worthy ally. He was also about to move on in another sense: he had developed such a dislike of London (and much of London, it has to be said, for him) that he would soon be abandoning it. 'London, deah old Lundon, is the place for poesy', he had written airily to William Carlos Williams exactly a decade earlier.[12] Such was apparently no longer the case. Twenty-two years later Aldington would write: 'Ezra started out in a time of peace and prosperity with everything in his favour, and muffed his chances of becoming literary dictator of London – to which he undoubtedly aspired – by his own conceit, folly and bad manners.'[13] Pound and Dorothy would depart for France and Italy – for a few months in April 1919 and again in April 1920, then permanently at the end of that year. Lawrence would turn his back on England even sooner (November 1919) and Hueffer in 1922. Aldington himself would follow towards the end of the 1920s.

The kindly Sinclair could not be a confidante, but continued to be a firm friend and a supporter of Aldington's writing. The depth of her actual feelings is revealed in her 1919 autobiographical novel, *Mary Olivier: A Life*, in which he is almost certainly the model for her hero, Richard Nicholson. Towards the end of the novel the narrator, reflecting on her loss of her lover, speaks of the painful occasions when she finds herself near him: 'that horrible evening at the Dining Club when the secretary woman put her as far as possible from Richard, next to the little Jew financier who smelt of wine. She couldn't even hear what Richard was saying; the little wine-lapping Jew went on talking about Women's Suffrage and his collection of Fragonards and his wife's portrait by Sargent. . . . She tried . . . to be kind to him and listen and smile . . . ; not to attend to Richard's voice breaking the beat of her heart.'[14] (We note here the casual anti-Semitism, shocking in the mouth of such an otherwise tolerant woman, but ubiquitous in so much writing of the period.) The incident may be based on the dinner at the Albemarle Club to which Sinclair invited Aldington on 16 April, so that he could meet some influential people. It is even possible that the model for the financier was Clement Shorter, already Aldington's sponsor.[15]

Certainly, the establishment, of which he had always been so critical, was now essential to Aldington's advancement. This did not make him less iconoclastic. In 1941 he wrote of this occasion: 'What estranged me was the sense of futility emanated by these gentle amiable people. They seemed so hopelessly out of date, so unaware that earth's foundations had trembled and that nothing would really be the same again. It was as if we were making vain gestures to each other across a river of death.'[16]

He soon discovered that the 'camaraderie of the trenches' would not provide him with a replacement for the 'old bohemian camaraderie' of pre-war London that he so missed. He tells us in *Life for Life's Sake* that he went on to a battalion reunion immediately after Sinclair's dinner. It did not help matters that he therefore arrived in evening dress; the Colonel was the only other officer so attired. To the others, jobless and alienated, he must have appeared, ironically, to have landed on his feet. 'We did our best to be friendly,' he writes, 'but there was something forced and hollow about it. With the end of the war the true reason for our old feeling of union was gone, and by trying to revive it we were flogging a dead horse. We were no longer one hundred per cent soldiers, but subtly and inevitably turning back into civilians, with different aims, hopes and antipathies.'[17]

May Sinclair

There were a few new or recent acquaintances. One was Herbert Read. They met in Cyril Beaumont's bookshop at 75 Charing Cross Road.[18] Read, a captain in the 10th Battalion of the Yorkshire Regiment (and recipient of the Military Cross and the Distinguished Service Order), had been demobilised in January. Since June 1917 he had been co-editing, with the art critic Frank Rutter, a journal called *Art and Letters* but, unlike Aldington, he was about to take up full-time employment (in the civil service), a move necessitated by his forthcoming marriage. Read considered himself an Imagist and Aldington praised his *Naked Warriors* in his *Sphere* article on war poetry, writing that, 'The psychology of the infantryman has nowhere been put down with such stark earnestness.'[19] They quickly established a warm professional and personal relationship. 'He was', wrote Read later, 'one of the most stimulating friends I have ever had — easy in conversation and very frank, full of strange oaths (mostly in French), his mind darting about rapidly from one aspect of a subject to another.'[20]

Another ex-subaltern, Alec Waugh, sounds a similar note: 'His talk did not scintillate, but it was sound, varied, entertaining. It stimulated talk in others. Parties went better for his presence. He enjoyed good company and good wine. I have never heard him speak spitefully or enviously of another writer.'[21] Waugh had already shocked the establishment with his sensational novel about public-school life, *The Loom of Youth*, published in 1917 while he was at the front. He shared the same birthday as Aldington, although six years younger, and they became friendly; but Waugh's dilettante lifestyle was not one to which Aldington aspired, or which he could have afforded.

Osbert Sitwell, who had become a third partner in *Art and Letters*, was another ex-soldier and poet whose company Aldington could enjoy. He was attracted by Sitwell's 'wit and honesty' and in *Life for Life's Sake* remarked that at the time he had had 'a slightly romantic feeling' about Osbert, his brother Sacheverell and sister

Edith 'because they seemed to be carrying on the tradition of the cultivated English aristocrat', reading, writing, travelling widely and being 'tireless investigators of Europe's known and unknown beauties'.[22] The social divide would prevent them from becoming close friends, however.

One member of the establishment with whom Aldington was achieving some form of reconciliation was his own father. At the end of the war, Albert Edward had lost both home and job: his Civil Service post in the Ministry of Munitions had come to an end and he had taken on what amounted to not much more than clerical work in Malcolm Hilbery's chambers in Holborn; and May had installed her lover, Vivian Arthur Watkins (whom she had met when he was serving in the Canadian forces and was billeted on her), at The Mermaid.[23] It was at his father's instigation that Aldington now joined the Authors' Club; Albert had been a member since the family moved to London in 1909. His son was able to use the club as a postal address and he found its rooms in Whitehall Court a more peaceful and attractive setting than his small dingy room at the Littoral in which to work and conduct his correspondence. He and his father took to meeting there quite regularly.

There were two parties at the Poetry Bookshop in Devonshire Street to offer Harold Monro advice and support for the planned *Monthly Chapbook*, the successor to the pre-war *Poetry Review* and *Poetry and Drama*. Here Aldington met up with Read, Waugh, Sitwell, Fletcher, Wyndham Lewis, Douglas Goldring, Edward Shanks and the Australian poet, Walter Turner.[24] The first of the chapbooks came out in July, with twenty-three new poems, each by a different author. Aldington was represented by 'Freedom' (a rather premature celebration of his release from 'hate and pity/ Desire and anguish') and H.D. by 'Leda'. However, the poems were printed anonymously, with contributors' names simply listed on the contents page; the selection was catholic, ranging from imagists to Georgians and to modernists like Read and the Sitwells (but not Pound or Eliot).[25]

Monro was already a workaholic, running the bookshop and preparing the chapbooks and the fourth Georgian anthology, as well as trying to write himself. (In August he would have a nervous breakdown which would put him out of action for over two months.) Perhaps it was this shared characteristic which would draw him increasingly into the company of Aldington – and Flint – over the next few years. Their troubled personalities and complex emotional histories were other attributes they had in common.

Aldington was already driving himself to his emotional limits. Financial necessity impelled him to over-work, but, as in those last months in Belgium, work was also a distraction from his miserable personal circumstances, which demanded decisions that he felt poorly equipped to make. Heartened by his success with *The Sphere*, he visited the offices of the *Pall Mall Gazette* and the *Daily Express* to offer them some pieces of 'rank journalism'.[26] At a guinea a time, such articles could provide some immediate cash, if little artistic satisfaction.[27]

His other immediate hope of income – and recognition – was translation.

Harold Monro, 1919

Nevertheless, he abandoned his elaborate plans for the new Poets' Translation Series. Edward Hutton at Constable must have responded negatively to the idea and a letter from Aldington to Amy Lowell indicates that Shorter, Bryher and H.D. were no longer 'so keen on it'. He agreed with Lowell that 'the whole project would be more trouble than it is worth', but his observation that the attempt is 'probably beyond my power to carry to a successful conclusion' suggests his recognition that his fragile emotional state ill-suited him for a major editorial role.[28]

However, his own translations could earn him much-needed cash. Following the publication of 'Letters to Unknown Women', *The Dial* took the Anacreon translations; now Aldington needed British publishers.[29] Meetings with Henry Massingham, editor of the radical weekly *The Nation*, and Holbrook Jackson of the pocket literary monthly, *To-Day*, met with success: six of the Anacreon translations appeared in *The Nation* on 1 March and nine in the July issue of *To-Day*. A further nine were published in *The New Age* on 31 July. *The New Age*, however, was now firmly under Pound's influence: he appeared in his own right and in the personas of 'B.H. Dias' (art critic) and 'William Atheling' (music critic).

What Aldington most needed was regular reviewing work. The *Pall Mall Gazette* agreed to take him on as their poetry reviewer, but he wanted recognition from literary journals. On 28 February he lunched with Edward Hutton, who, in addition to his role at Constable, edited the *Anglo-Italian Review*, and who promised him work. In early March he met with Henry Davray, editor of the *Anglo-French Review*, who took him on as reviewer of French poetry, immediately commissioning a study of Duhamel.[30] Meanwhile, he heard that Middleton Murry was giving up his post as reviewer of French literature for the *Times Literary Supplement* in order to revive the literary weekly, *Athenaeum*.

Aldington tells us in *Life for Life's Sake* that he immediately wrote to *The Times*, expressing an interest in succeeding Murry; he heard nothing. However, meeting Bryher on 10 March and dining with the Ellermans two weeks later, he imparted this information and was rewarded with a letter of recommendation from Sir John, a significant stake-holder in *The Times*, to Henry Wickham Steed, the paper's new editor. Steed told him that the job was his and immediately sent him along to Bruce Richmond, the *TLS* editor, who was understandably annoyed at having Aldington appointed over his head. It was an uncomfortable lesson in the way to succeed in this post-war world. Fortunately, the two men would develop a good professional relationship over the next ten years.[31]

By May he had replaced Murry. This post at last gave him some financial stability, but it is a measure of his personal modesty and his loyalty to Flint that by early June, when the latter was finally demobilised, he suggested to Richmond that he and Flint should divide the reviewing of French literature between them. Richmond, who had heard the poet laureate, Robert Bridges, speak well of Flint's understanding of French poetry, readily agreed. This was not to be the only occasion during his tenure when Aldington would attempt to share with his friends the benefits of his situation on the *TLS*.

He was primarily a poet, however, and had to promote his poetry of the last two years if he was to achieve recognition in the post-war literary world. Cyril Beaumont's limited edition of the war poems appeared in April 1919. Allen and Unwin's fuller mass-market edition not until December. Meanwhile, Elkin Mathews published *Images of Desire* in June, and in September the Egoist Press brought out a new edition of *Images*, with the addition of the poems from the later Imagist anthologies.

Only the literary journals could give his poetry the high profile it needed. At *The*

Egoist Eliot continued to accept his work: seven poems appeared in the March/April issue, with notices of the imminent publication of the Beaumont edition of the war poems and the Elkin Mathews *Images of Desire*.[32] However, the *Egoist* was struggling in its efforts to serialise Joyce's *Ulysses* (which entailed constant battles with the printers over obscenities), was appearing irregularly and by the end of the year would cease publication altogether. Aldington dined with Shorter and Austin Harrison of *The English Review* on 27 March, but the only result was the appearance of 'Reverie' in the May issue. That month another love poem, 'Cynthia', appeared in *To-Day*.

In May, a new literary quarterly began publication: *Coterie*, edited by the young Chaman Lall. By then Aldington was writing for the *TLS* where he gave a half-hearted welcome to the new journal with the observation that the first issue's presentation of the work of eleven poets had no real coherence and exhibited 'neither the solid achievement of the Georgians, the definite experimentalism of the Imagists nor the rebelliousness of *Wheels*'.[33] He singled out only Aldous Huxley and Eliot for praise.[34] However, his four 'Minor Exasperations' would appear in the September issue; a recent poem, 'Bones', in December (prefaced by a tribute to Aldington by Flint); and before the end of the year he would accept a place on the magazine's editorial committee.[35]

Walter de la Mare's *TLS* review of the new edition of *Images* in October was critical: 'This volume proves, we think, with its remote images at one extreme and its emphatic veracity or similitude at the other – that Mr Aldington has not yet found himself as a poet, though he can be a delicate craftsman.'[36] Alec Waugh's article on Aldington in *To-Day* that same month touched on a problem which Kerker Quinn would pinpoint nearly twenty years later ('[Imagism] was temporarily beneficial to [Aldington]. . . .Yet when Imagism slipped its moorings and drifted far from popular favour, most of us overlooked that he wasn't still aboard.')[37] Waugh argued that 'collectivism in art brings its own revenge' and that Aldington was suffering from the fact that Imagism had become to a large extent discredited. He felt, however, that the poet had now discovered his medium and also had 'something definite to express.'[38] He praised 'Reverie' highly; for Waugh, Aldington was 'the only genuine modern love poet'.

In the American journals, perhaps because Pound was still foreign correspondent for *Poetry* and London editor of *The Little Review* (and would soon become foreign agent for *The Dial*), Aldington had an equally low profile. Certainly *The Little Review* was primarily home to Pound's modernist protégées – Eliot, Lewis, Joyce – and his other allies, Yeats and Hueffer, although it had started to serialise Sinclair's *Mary Olivier*. Aldington contributed an essay on Remy de Gourmont to the February/March issue, which was devoted to that writer, but his three pages were preceded by an eighteen page article by Pound and further pieces by Manning, T.T. Clayton and John Rodker, hardly recognition of the fact that Aldington had been Gourmont's chief British champion and translator before the war. His essay ended on a note of loss that says as much about his own mental state as about Gourmont's importance: 'We have lost almost the last of the true critics. We get new prose but no more prose like his; new thoughts but never his clear thought again.'[39]

In September's *Little Review* William Carlos Williams wrote a scathing critique of the poems by Aldington (and by D.H. Lawrence) that had appeared in the July 'After the War' issue of *Poetry*, asserting that Aldington had 'gone backwards'. (Aldington's choice had been infelicitous: five rather inconsequential short poems grouped under the heading 'In France 1916-1918', only two of which he ever published.)[40] Williams complained: 'I do not ask for cannon in a poem but I do ask for more than a drugged swig of loveliness. I ask for existence, for wide open eyes into which shells pass and explode with all their havoc sucked from them for secret purposes. . . . Poetry is not a despairing cry of defiance. It is not a bottle to nurse. It is an assertion: I am here today in the midst of living hell! I, equal to any hell of gas or noise or sniper's bullet or disease and its filth.'[41]

Williams had the grace to concede: 'It is easy for me to write. I have never been in the trenches', but the gist of his article was that the two prose writers currently being serialised in *The Little Review*, Joyce and Dorothy Richardson, were superior artists to Aldington and Lawrence because 'they plunge naked into the flaming cauldron of today'. Williams had clearly nailed his colours to Pound's mast. Aldington responded in a letter to Harriet Monroe: 'Did he – a doctor – imagine that artistic calm, detached vision, were possible to men who were reduced by inadequate diet, sleeping in wet clothes out-of-doors, months of physical torment and mental stagnation in a desert of mud, broken walls, hell?'[42] The tone is quavering, rather than angry, reminding us how close to breakdown the writer is. Fortunately, Rodker (who replaced Pound as foreign editor in May) contributed a more enthusiastic review of *Images*, and of the first three issues of the new Poets' Translation Series, to the October issue of *The Little Review*.

Harriet Monroe and Pound had been mutually disenchanted for some time and she would soon ask Aldington to replace Pound as *Poetry*'s foreign correspondent. Following the appearance of his prose poems, 'Prayers and Fantasies', in the November 1918 issue of *Poetry*, and the five poems so sharply criticised by Williams in the 'After the War' number in July 1919, Aldington contributed to the October issue a review of six recent books of French poetry. In the September *Poetry*, however, Marjorie Allen Seiffert's review of *War and Love* was harsh. Although she liked the love poetry ('It is of the flesh, yet delicate, rare, torturingly beautiful'), she was critical of the war poems: 'Aldington's genius could not use the crude, painful and bitter experience he was forced to undergo. . . . The war poems in this book are only bitter, muffled plaints of rebellion.'[43] While Aldington was falling short of *The Little Review*'s modernist standards, *Poetry* seems to have been regretting his abandonment of classical imagism.

A short anonymous review of *War and Love* in *The Dial* in May was much more positive: 'Whatever he has lost of the cold fire and chiselled form of the Images is richly returned in a warmer passion and a new humanity. Always the honest artist, he is now the honest reporter of war – and of love in wartime, though it drives him to metre and rhyme and an intensification of sex that recalls Donne. There is ecstasy and exquisite suffering in these poems, but not sentimentality. The war has produced no more genuine poetry.'[44] The poet could not have asked for better appreciation of how his art had changed.

15. Separation

Proserpina, Lady of Hell, in whose
Keeping are the great sombre rivers,
Grant me I beseech one draught of
Lethe to purge my spirit of horror,
To make me worthy to mingle with
Sane men once more.   (Richard Aldington, 'Lethe', 1919)

Yesterday is not a milestone that has been passed, but a daystone on the beaten track
of the years, and irremediably part of us, within us, heavy and dangerous. We are not
merely more weary because of yesterday, we are other, no longer what we were before the
calamity of yesterday.   (Samuel Beckett, *Proust*)[1]

By March 1919 H.D.'s pregnancy was nearing its full term. Despite his declared
position at the end of January, Aldington did not know his own mind. His continuing
love for her was in conflict with his conviction that he could not accept her child.
Nor was his relationship with Dorothy Yorke resolved; the physical attraction
between them was still strong. His response to her possessiveness had always been
ambivalent. On the one hand, it alarmed him; he had written to H.D. in October:
'I heard from Arabella yesterday; she is "touchante", but I can see she still dreams
of "possession". And that will not be. I will not sell my tatters of freedom, my mind,
my love of beauty, for any other passion. No doubt she would be an excellent wife;
but that is precisely what I don't want.'[2] However, it also flattered his vanity.[3] Now,
Yorke's persistence struck him as a demonstration of loyalty which must have been
appealing in his present isolated circumstances.

    Unfortunately for the future of his marriage, there were puppeteers on the scene
whose own minds were much clearer, who were well-versed in the art of manipulation
and for whom neither he nor H.D. was a match. One was Selina Yorke, as sure as
ever of her daughter's interests, and determined that Dorothy would have Richard.
He cannot have seemed much of a match, but she was now unlikely to find a better.
Moreover, Selina Yorke's role in achieving his demobilisation, when H.D. and her
contacts had failed, made Aldington beholden to her, an advantage which she pushed
home. He was further obligated to Dorothy for having typed all his work for the last few
months. Both mother and daughter had also reinforced his uncertain feelings towards
H.D.'s child by telling him that he must not be forced into accepting legal paternity.

It seems probable that he was continuing to see Yorke regularly, at least until the point at which he wrote to H.D.: 'I've told her. It was very hard and I suffered very much, because – well, you understand. As usual after a 'scene' I can't sleep – have just made a meal of eggs & tea at 4 am! Shall go out when the light comes and get breakfast. Dooley, I feel terribly responsible. Do you understand. But deep down I feel calm. I wish I could go away for weekend in a motorcar. Don't worry about me. I shall be all right. Only *live!'*[4] The letter is undated, but was written some time in March.[5] It suggests that at this point Aldington did attempt to end his relationship with Yorke and make a commitment to his marriage.

He visited H.D. at least once in the nursing home in Ealing before the baby was born: the reassurance of her improving state of health in the letter that he sent to Shorter on 8 March may have been based on reports from Patmore and Bryher, but he tells him in a letter of 17 March that he has been to visit her 'in her new place'. It may have been during this visit that he promised to make the break with Yorke. H.D. recreates the occasion in *Asphodel*: 'Darrington lifted heavy eye-brows and his hands stopped fingering the ebony stick, looked across at Hermione, smiled across at her and smiling, his smile with a conjuror's magic brought back camellias, white and red, red rosettes and white rosettes that they had gathered, scraped from the clean sand of the paths to lay on the stone of Shelley.'[6] 'Hermione' forgets her fears over the baby's birth:

> Something had happened more strange, more miraculous than anything that could ever happen. Darrington was with her, beside her, a Darrington had crept out of the brown lean khaki, like a great moth, elegant in shape, still a little foreign in his bronze but all different. . . . The smile Darrington smiled had nothing to do with rows and rows of livid dead, with barbed wire, with the flare of red or green blazing above broken trenches, with the drone of planes, with the sudden flare and drop of bombs . . . Darrington smiled a smile that erased all that, the smudged out image of the war, of terrible things that had happened, of Louise and Florient and Merry.[7] . . . He had forgotten. She had forgotten. He was going to take care of her and he had come back and he was so happy and everything was going to be all right. Clear out of the years of terror the past rose, rose and cleft the years of terror like white lightning, a black storm cloud.

There seems to have been a mutual re-enchantment. Out of uniform, Aldington seemed to H.D. his former pre-war self, not the rough, over-sexed soldier he had become. There was warmth, humour and understanding between them. She could not know how close to the edge he really was; perhaps he himself did not realise it. Meanwhile, they could enjoy their new-found contentment in each other's company; and he was able to comfort her when she received the news of her father's death in Philadelphia on 3 March. The war had prevented her from seeing her parents since her marriage in 1913, but she had always felt great respect and affection for her father.

Amidst all this, she had an unexpected visitor – only the day before her baby

Clement Shorter with Charlie Chaplin, 1919

arrived: 'He hurtles himself into the decorous St. Faith's Nursing Home. . . . Beard, black soft hat, ebony stick – something unbelievably operatic – directoire overcoat, Verdi. He stalked and stamped the length of the room.'[8] Pound told her, 'My only real criticism is that this is not my child.'

The child arrived on 31 March, like the 'daffodils / That come before the swallow dares and take/ The winds of March with beauty.'[9] 'Richard had brought

me many daffodils, that English Lent-lily', H.D. wrote years later.[10] She named the
little girl Perdita, after Shakespeare's heroine, but perhaps also in memory of the
daughter she had lost. It shows the continuing understanding between them that it
was Aldington who suggested her other name: Frances, after Gregg.[11] He visited
the mother and daughter in the nursing home the day after the birth (which was
also the day he had to surrender the Doughty Street studio and move back into
the Littoral) and wrote affectionately the following day: 'I like your daughter quite
well; she is very attractive with her long hair and oriental features. I think you
like her more than you say.'[12] Two weeks late arriving, the baby was strong and
healthy with a mass of dark hair. Aldington visited the nursing home on at least
four occasions during the three weeks after her birth,[13] writing to H.D. on 5 April:

> Dear Astraea
>   Thanks for your note for £1. There will be lots of change!
>   I think it would be better for me to come along later next week. May S.
> [Sinclair] wants to see you. She has sent me a cheque saying 'Will you get H.
> some little thing with enclosed, considering me for the time being as a sort
> of aunt.' It is very charming of her. So I don't think you can refuse, especially
> as you'll need *all* the money you can get. Will you drop May a line & tell her
> when to come see you? Why not make it Tuesday? I'm seeing her this pm &
> will arrange that tentatively.
>   I will come see you Thursday if that will suit.
>   You are not in Nation this week. Will be next I suppose.
>   Yrs
>   Richard.[14]

Waiting in the wings, however, was the puppeteer *par excellence*: Bryher. 'The
vengeful, she understood, and she understood the possessive instinct: for money
and for people', Bryher's first husband, Robert McAlmon, would write in 1938.[15]
McAlmon was not the most impartial of commentators; he and Bryher entered
into a marriage of convenience in 1921, which ended in divorce six years later.
However, he was one of the few people who ever had the opportunity to observe
the Ellerman household from the inside. He referred to Sir John as 'a man who had a
monomania for planning his family's life to the minutest detail';[16] this was Bryher's
model for intimate relationships. In 1933, when H.D. showed him photographs
of Bryher, Freud commented that she looked 'so decisive, so unyielding'.[17]
    As she learned what H.D. had kept from her throughout the six months of their
acquaintance – Aldington's infidelity (though not yet the fact that he was not the
father of H.D.'s child) – Bryher became emboldened.[18] Throughout most of March
and April she was forced to be with her family at their country home in Eastbourne,
but her letters show her mounting an escalating attack on Aldington to undermine
H.D.'s confidence. It was also Bryher who insisted that Perdita must go to a nursery
as soon as H.D. was well enough to leave the nursing home. H.D. began to waver
on this, writing to her on 19 April, 'Perdita is so very good. She stays with me most
of the day. I am relieved about her 'home' but don't know what I shall do', and just

as she was about to leave St Faith's: 'I *will* be so glad when tomorrow is over. I grow weaker as the parting comes – but I know it is best to leave Perdita for the time. She gets more charming – that is the trouble . . . I am torn between the desire for a little place with Perdita+ fairy books + Noahs [*sic*] arks and dolls, and a wild adventure.'[19]

Bryher was unrelenting: 'I hope you will be sensible over Perdita and remember that you were not given poetry to sit and worry over an infant in a solitary cottage. I am very jealous for your poetry and I will even fight Perdita about it. She will be much healthier and happier for the next year or two in a home.'[20] Here spoke a young woman eight years H.D.'s junior, who had been kept in a state of child-like dependency throughout her life and had little experience of children, of loving relationships or of the wider world. In contrast, when H.D. was in the early stages of her pregnancy and had mooted the possibility of having her child reared in a nursery, Aldington had written: 'I don't know that I like the farm idea. A mother ought to suckle her child if she can and have it live near her.[21] You would have fits all the time thinking it would get hurt if it was away from you. I know what mothers are.'[22]

If Bryher saw Perdita as a rival, then she was in no doubt of the threat that Aldington was beginning to pose. H.D. asked him to book her into a room at the Littoral as soon as she left St Faith's. His letter of 17 April was solicitous: 'I will of course try to get you a room. Will a week be long enough? Try to get a feeling of *leisure*. It is excellent after these years of worry. There is time enough. Anyhow, I'll see what can be done.'[23] On 18 April, H.D. wrote to Bryher: 'R. comes tomorrow after all – so I can get future plans more definite with his help',[24] and on 19 April, Easter Saturday, and only three days before she was due to leave St Faith's, she wrote: 'R. came. He was in such a strange state of duality. He is so puzzling. But I want to see more of him. I can't rest now till I understand.'[25]

A letter from Aldington to Lowell makes clear what the couple's plans were at this stage: 'Hilda is better of her pneumonia and has a little daughter – very delightful little creature. But Hilda is terribly ill and thin – the strain of all these years has told on her. She comes out of hospital on Tuesday and will stay with me in town, but she will soon go into the country, probably with W. Bryher. I have to stay in town for the purpose of 'getting into' these infernal periodicals.'[26] While he had to hide from Lowell his own infidelity and the paternity of the child, we can see here his concern for H.D. and her child and also how unresolved and open the situation still remained.

Bryher knew that her biggest obstacle was Aldington's admiration for H.D. the artist and his wife's dependence on his guidance and encouragement. She had herself benefited from his advice on her work; but now H.D. was her mentor. H.D.'s letters throughout March and April were filled with encouragement as Bryher worked in Eastbourne on a further draft of *Development*. Bryher was beginning to resent Aldington's more critical approach and expressed this resentment to H.D., who wrote to her on 13 April: 'You must not let him discourage you. He is really so interested and grateful for any intelligence – as you + and I – he feels the general futility of most people + feels someone who knows Greek + Elizabethans is really a trouvaille.'[27]

Bryher tried to undermine H.D.'s reliance on her husband's artistic judgement, writing on 21 April 1919: 'I am most disturbed that Mr Aldington is applying the pedantic method to your poems. To my eyes, at least, it lowers his mind. . . . Please don't alter a word to please him. . . . He has no right to do other than accept thankfully your poems.'[28] By the next day, when H.D. left St. Faith's, Bryher was writing with more open hostility: 'I have had an amusing letter from Mr Aldington. I have evidently annoyed him very much. (This relieves my mind.) He takes refuge in saying that I shall grow wiser with age which is no right weapon to use and one feels his extreme contempt curling about the lines. But I won't give in to his theories and he can't afford to talk about wisdom increasing with years and to publish 'Images of Desire' on top of it. Also one would imagine from his letter that I had never taken pen in hand before.'[29] Clearly, by this stage Bryher's hostility was so intense that she was even prepared to hurt H.D.'s feelings by alluding to her husband's infidelity.

On 23 April the Ellermans returned to London. H.D. was now resident at the Littoral, while Perdita was in a nursery in Hampstead found by the ever-supportive Patmore. H.D. visited Bryher that afternoon. What happened over the next two days is unclear, but by the end of them the Aldingtons had separated permanently.

Maybe the temporary reunion was only ever intended to give an outward impression of respectability to H.D.'s recent confinement and time for her to reassure herself that Perdita was settled in her nursery before she and Bryher departed for the west country. H.D. wrote to Pound a decade later: '[H]e had said he would look after us, up to the point at least, of seeing me on my feet again.'[30] *Asphodel* suggests, however, that H.D. had expected more. She describes her room at the Littoral 'with its narrow sordid proportion and its one narrow meagrely curtained window looking over the Soho back street' as being 'like the tube of the Indian mystic, self-made from which, or at the end of which, he projects images of marvellous reality':

> At first the room containing Darrington had contained Italy, the slopes of Monte Solaro, anemones blooming pre-war Easter red and the blood red of the foot steps of Adonis that had been the atrocious wooden image that they had carried to the songs of pre-Hellenic old volcanic southern gypsy chanting. Christ had died and Christ was to be born again. Red anemones had flowered against the dim shabby paper of the narrow room and red anemones had fallen beneath her feet and had burned the very soles of her feet as she had stepped tentatively out of her bed cold mornings, mist cold early spring mornings, mornings over Soho like a bride's veil for she was that in her renewed love of Jerrold. The narrow room with the stained sulphur coloured paper had been wide tunnel toward enchantment.[31]

Then came the terrible row between them. Aldington told her that she must register Perdita and that she must name Gray as the father. H.D. was bewildered. *Asphodel* again: 'What was Darrington after? What was it all about? . . . "I will look

H.D. and Perdita, 1919

after you" and "now register it as Vane's" didn't go together.'[32] She had taken it as understood that, at the least, Aldington was intending to accept paternity of the child, for Perdita's sake as much as for her own. In letters written a decade or so later to close male friends from the early years of their marriage – Pound, Cournos and George Plank – she would go over and over those moments when her marriage ended, still searching to understand, and perhaps to justify herself.

She knew the reason why her shock turned to anger, and it was not simply her sense of yet another betrayal: 'I was quite unprepared for the experience. I mean the terror of feeling that wadge of bird-feathers and petticoats HAD to be protected.' Worn out by all the strains of the last few years, by her illness, her confinement and her recent separation from her child, she nevertheless found reserves of strength for Perdita's sake, as *Asphodel* portrays: 'Hermione, worn past endurance, found words she had never dreamed she had the strength to utter, forming somewhere white bullets, white searing lead, in the inside of her now cold head, and white bullets, white searing lead, projected outwards, out and out into a void where Darrington was, where Jerrold was. . . . Turned into a monster, a Minotaur when Hermione had thought he was one of the youths of Athens.'[33]

Her hopes shattered, the Soho hotel room becomes its sordid self: 'The room had grown narrow, it appeared, while she regarded it. . . . The wallpaper, Hermione saw it for the first time, was faded with a smudgy uneven spottiness that let show through the mustard like spots, the egg-stain like spots of singularly mal-formed tuberous yellow rose buds. The room became a room in Soho and the paper sordid as she saw it.'[34]

But what was her husband thinking and feeling? Had he shared, or even appreciated, the hopes that H.D. had been entertaining? And why was he so insistent that the child should not be registered as his? Caroline Zilboorg suggests that this behaviour was the manifestation of a trait of character that had been intensified by his precarious state of health and the fact that his emotional and professional lives were in chaos: 'Aldington, always and particularly in times of stress, was a martinet about order and detail.' 'It appears,' she writes, 'that he wanted insistently to do the right thing, morally and legally, and they were not the same.'[35]

However, we must factor in the influence of the Yorkes. Had Aldington already decided that his future was with Dorothy? H.D. told George Plank ten years later, 'He appealed to me, "I shall go mad between the TWO of you, It MUST be one or the other."'[36] Her letter to Pound implies that Yorke was present for at least some of the time: '[S]uddenly they were howling at me, screaming illegitimacy and what not, and they started it.' However, there is no suggestion in *Asphodel* of the physical presence of a third party – not, that is, until Aldington, as H.D. later told Cournos, 'literally called up Bryher and said "Hilda must get out of here at once."'[37]

So Bryher arrived to carry H.D. off to the luxury and comfort of 1, South Audley Street; only now, if we are to believe *Asphodel*, did H.D. tell her that Aldington was not the father of her child. Bryher was, of course, delighted. In June, with Perdita moved to the prestigious Norland Nursery in Kensington (at Bryher's expense), she would take H.D. to the Scillies. In the interim, with the Pounds having left for Paris on 22 April, H.D was able to borrow their flat at Holland Place Chambers, the address that appears on Perdita's birth certificate. The certificate further tells us that that Frances Perdita's father is Richard Edward Godfree Aldington, journalist. *Asphodel* tells us of Hermione's terror, as she made the bus journey to the registrar's office in Ealing, that her 'crime' would be discovered: 'Darrington' had threatened her: '[O]f course, you know if you make a false statement it's perjury and five years' penal servitude.' That she put off that bus journey until 6 May reveals the extent of her trepidation.

She might well be frightened of him: she thought him mad, and Bryher did not disabuse her. H.D. told Pound in 1929: '[I]t was madness . . . to see him look out at me through a strange great hulk of passion and disintegration.'[38] The day after she left the Littoral, Aldington wrote her one of his bluff self-justifying letters:

Dear Dooley

Herewith that letter that came for you.

I am sorry you feel ill; but things could not go on as they were. No doubt you think me selfish and unkind. I can't help it if you do. I've done my best to be amiable all round & the result has merely been chaos. I shall see a lawyer & hand the matter over; if you do the same with HA [her married status], it will save us both much worry.

Meanwhile old thing, don't take things too damn seriously! I'm not going to have my existence poisoned by too much scrupulosity. And I *do* seriously want you to be happy in your own way.

Yrs

R.[39]

Neither of them would see a lawyer; but the mere mention of the law intensified H.D's fears. When she and Bryher returned from the Scillies, H.D. came back to Kensington – to be on familiar territory and to be close to Perdita. She rented a flat at 16 Bullingham Mansions, just off Church Street, where Bryher was permitted by her family to join her. The two women had embarked on what was to be the most permanent and lasting relationship of their lives.

One of the group of short poems by Aldington that had been savaged by Williams in September 1919 was entitled 'Beauty Unpraised':[40]

> There is only you.
> The rest are palterers, slovens, parasites.
> You only are strong, clear-cut, austere;
> Only about you the light curls
> Like a gold laurel bough.
>
> *Your words are cold flaked stone,*
> *Scentless white violets?*
>
> Laugh!
> Let them blunder.
> The sea is ever the sea
> And none can change it,
> > None possess it.

Aldington was forced to remain at the Littoral for the rest of the year, since lodgings were at a premium. His emotional state was more fragile than ever. He wrote to Flint on 17 May:

What you say about my writing is most kind, but my friend, I am going through a really desperate crisis. I have serious doubts about my talent. Everything I've written, everything I am writing, seems to me bad, spoiled, foolish. My poems seem stupid; my prose cliché-ridden. I must carry on writing in order to live. But I've lost any confidence. It's awful. I blush each time I see my name printed on work I deem to be pathetic. My *Images of Desire* poems I rate as vulgar. I despair when I think they are going to be publicly presented in a few days. My war poems – pooh! What rubbish! If I had your knowledge of French literature at least I could feel less ashamed of the work I do for the *Times*. But all my pleasure writing about French authors is ruined for me by the thought that there exist certainly several people who could fulfil this role with more skill and knowledge than me. To sum up, I look like someone taking advantage of the public. I'm nothing but a mediocre poet, and a less than mediocre critic.[41]

That this ran deeper than a lack of professional confidence is made clear by the following passage from the same letter: 'Two days ago I was strolling with a woman friend along the paths at Hampton Court. There were lilac and apple trees in blossom, wallflowers, all the trees were covered in fresh, fragile foliage, the birds were singing. I thought of your poem "Fragment" and, I don't know why, but I was overcome with a great sadness. It was the immense futility of life that brought a lump to my throat and I had the awful thought that by escaping death in the war I have perhaps missed my true fate. It's ridiculous but since it exists how can I disown it? Maybe I'll write a poem about it.'[42]

He was deeply traumatised by his war experiences and suffering from the syndrome familiarly known as 'survivors' guilt'. That he wrote to Flint so frankly about his feelings is a measure of his desperation: he was not prone to intimate revelations, even to his closest friend, and there were to be no more such confidences. Perhaps if there had been, his recovery would have been a swifter one. What he did not admit to Flint was that he was also suffering from the break-up of his marriage.

Inevitably his depression began to manifest itself in physical symptoms, and the physical symptoms in turn increased the sense of victimhood. He had written to Lowell at the end of March: 'I think in some ways you are not quite fair to me, Amy. Of course, I don't expect non-combatants to understand; they can't. But you see I'm not at all well; my nerves have got into such a state that I have a sort of 'sympathetic' neuralgia in my neck and arms; I sleep badly; I have a 'trench throat' & cough; I have ague, directly I get cold.'[43]

He was seeing Dorothy, even inviting Flint to dine with the two of them at the Littoral on 24 July. He was also coping with professional pressures less and less well and by August was on the verge of a complete breakdown. In September he went off on his own for a break in the country, writing jovially (and in English) to Flint: 'As the morrow be prosperous & the rogues and footpads not stirring I look to be a wayfaring to the west, yea upwards of a hundred mile.'[44] His choice of locations, however (Corfe Castle and then on to Cornwall), tells us a great deal about his feelings.

He wrote to Lowell on 11 October: 'In September I had to go away. I had no holiday after demobilization, the Govt. did not pay me my gratuity for three months & I had to work like a slave to keep going. The result was I nearly broke down mentally, though my physical health is excellent. Since I got back I have only been able to work three days a week; if I work more I get horrible pains in my head, due, people say, to a sort of deferred shell-shock. But I am rapidly getting better & shall be able to attend to things.' The tone, as so often in his letters to Lowell, is self-absorbed, almost petulant. In the same letter he tells her that because it is impossible to find anywhere to live except a room in a Soho restaurant, 'Hilda is living with the Ellermans.'[45] Clearly he could not bring himself to tell Lowell the true story.

The September holiday had not significantly benefited his state of health. Since he had spent it revisiting sites with painful associations that may not surprise us. He wrote to Monroe in October, when apologetically sending her some poems: 'No doubt you will be disappointed with them. But I think you'll know that they are real and that they expose a common psychology of the time, the 'lostness'& bitterness of my generation. . . . I am getting over this phase. I am hoping to get away from London to forget the bitterness in work & I think the next lot of poems will be sweeter and more happy.'[46]

Perhaps, too, he felt that it was only out of London that he could set up a household with Dorothy Yorke without gossip and condemnation. In November Lawrence came to see him and told him that he and Frieda were leaving for Italy. He offered Aldington the opportunity to take over the tenancy of Dollie Radford's cottage in Hermitage, Berkshire, where he and Frieda had lived from December 1917 to April 1918. In December Aldington left his room at the Littoral for the Berkshire countryside.

In the Aldington archive in the Morris Library of Southern Illinois University lies the undated typescript of a poem Aldington never published:

> It is bitter, watching the bright leaves fall,
> To think: 'Now I shall not see her ever,
> Never once, never hear her soft voice call
> My name, and clasp her hand in mine never.'
>
> As the leaves fall I dream that you sit alone,
> With hands empty and resigned, and the light
> Gone from your eyes and hair, still as a stone,
> And a dream face haunting your inward sight.
>
> Time drifts with the leaves, and murmurs: 'Too late.'
> If we met we could but turn with a sigh:
> 'Too late,' O lost love hidden by Fate
> And haunting my bitter heart till I die.

16. Retreat: 1920-1925

O friend, why is it that the fields have peace
And we have none? I press my hands
Sadly against my aching eyes and feel
How hot they are with scanning many books;
My brain is dry with thoughts of many men,
My heart is faint with deaths of many gods.
I know I live only because I suffer.
I know of truth, only because I seek,
Only because I need it know I love.

(Richard Aldington, 'At a Gate by the Way', 1923)

Hermitage was not quite the idyllic country retreat that its name had suggested. It was 'a nondescript straggling hamlet without charm or antiquity in rather featureless country', and the two drab Victorian semi-detached 'two-up, two-down' farm-workers' cottages were at a right angle to the approach road, so that the occupants of number 2 had to pass the front of Aldington's cottage to reach their front door.[1] While Dorothy Yorke was present for much of the time, she did not immediately take up residence.[2] She and her mother remained in the small flat (at 4 Holland Place Chambers) for which they had left Mecklenburgh Square in early 1918. On 28 January Aldington wrote his final letter to H.D., whom Bryher was now taking on the promised trip to Greece: 'This is just to wish you "bon voyage" and some peace in the sunlight of your Hellas.' He asked her what she was working on and told her to bring back poems from Crete and never to forget that she was 'the grandest of the rebel poets'.[3] Desperate to preserve a link, he offered to try to find a publisher for her latest collection if Constable did not want it.[4]

Nevertheless, he did not miss London: 'The contrast of silence and untroubled darkness was healing.'[5] A contrast not only with London but with the Western Front of 1917 and 1918: '[N]o rumble and roar of night-fighting, no shell-burst or rattle of machine-guns, no trampling and cursing of transport columns and working parties, no sinister sudden glare of Very lights showing a landscape bristling with barbed wire.' Memories of the war and thoughts of what it had cost him, personally and artistically, were easier to put behind him – or to suppress – here. He appreciated the rural simplicity of his neighbours: Mr Brown, 'a genuine *terrae filius*, as close to the earth as the placid cows and elms of the landscape . . . would sometimes drop in of an evening, and we would smoke our pipes and drink ale from blue earthenware mugs, and talk of essential things.'[6] Turning his hand to cultivating vegetables, he was grateful for Brown's expertise. That this kindly man subsequently became a model for several characters in Aldington novels indicates the impression he made.[7]

There was work to be done, but the volume of poetry Allen and Unwin published in 1923 was a slim one and many of the sixteen poems in the first section had been written—and appeared in journals – as early as 1919, while those in the second section were principally pastiches and 'metrical exercises'.[8] An article Aldington wrote for *Poetry* in May 1921 on 'The Poet and Modern Life' seemed to say more about his own dilemma than that of others: 'How can poetry, which is essentially order, affirmation, achievement, be created in an age, a *milieu*, of profound doubt and discouragement?' The essentials for poetry, he argued, were 'deep spiritual enthusiasm and energy, disinterested thought, unfettered intelligence [and] profound culture.'[9]

The problem was a practical one as well as one of mood and inspiration. He told Monro: 'I suppose you can see the problem I'm struggling with, which is to get a little thought and some ideas into my verse-writing. Obviously I had to close down on the impressionism of Images and look for something else. You said some of my recent things were 'thinking aloud' and I thought when you said it, "Good, the cohesion will come later." But I confess to you I feel more uncertain than ever.'[10]

Putting poetry to one side, he adopted a punishing routine of reading, translating and reviewing. 'I knew enough to know how little I knew', he wrote in *Life for Life's Sake*.[11] He would tell Flint in 1924 that he had 'learned to read' over the previous five years and considered it the most important acquisition he had made.[12] Conscious of his poor academic credentials, he knew that if he was to hang on to his position as reviewer of French literature in *The Times Literary Supplement,* he had to immerse himself in that literature; it was *The Times* that earned him a living. After demobilisation in February 1919, Clement Shorter had been his initial life-line, the articles for *The Sphere* paying him £67. 4. 00, but by the end of a year his income from *The Times* was already double that figure. Grateful to be able to turn his back on the popular press (and only occasionally irked by the constraints imposed by the conservative *Times*) he, nevertheless, still needed to place articles elsewhere, for the purposes of both income and reputation; *TLS* reviews were anonymous.[13] His accounts reveal that he was contributing to almost a dozen journals, English and American, every year until at least 1924. He had also taken over from Pound as *Poetry*'s 'London correspondent', although this was an unpaid position and one he would surrender by August of 1921, telling Monroe that he could find little in the English poetry scene for which he could express unqualified admiration.

Translation offered him the possibility of book publication (Alfred Knopf brought out an American edition of his collected translations in 1921 under the title *Medallions in Clay*) and enhanced his academic status but it also continued to serve two other important functions: making him feel productive, even creative, at a time when the poetic muse seemed to have deserted him; and transporting him to that more attractive culture of the past.[14]

His diagnosis of the state of the nation was profoundly gloomy: for him it was a time 'when the whole of Europe is in an ungodly mess as a result of the war; when the most superficial observer must notice a sharp decline in general morals and manners; when even wealthy England is on the verge of bankruptcy; when almost the whole life of the nation has become commercialised; when art and artists are in a lamentable state of disorder and neglect.'[15] He construed the modern world as one which 'conceives of man as an animal which eats, drinks, is clothed, travels and needs to be entertained.'[16] In 'The Poet and His Age' he placed much of the blame for the fact that most contemporary poetry was (in his view) either ordered but effete or vigorous but shapeless, on 'the ignorance, conceit and snobbery of audiences.'[17] He found himself on the horns of a dilemma, wanting to reject the increasing intellectual elitism of Pound or Eliot, but out of tune with wider society.

'The Influence of Mr James Joyce', written originally for *The Dial* but which appeared in *The English Review* in April 1921, is a revealing essay. While he defended Joyce vigorously to Lowell ('I don't mind his obscenity because it is intellectual'),[18] he argues passionately here that the philosophy of *The Dubliners* and *Ulysses* is 'a tremendous libel on humanity.' Commenting on the 'repugnance for humanity . . . abhorrence of the human body, and particularly of sexual relations' which he finds in *Ulysses*, he is driven to share with his readers his own experience of life in the trenches. Describing in detail the squalor of that existence, he goes on to ask: 'But were we despicable? Had we poor infantry cannon-fodder—apt symbols of humanity in a world whose misery seems to have neither purpose nor justification – had we nothing to set against our grotesque sufferings?' He continues: 'Let those answer "No" who never saw the comradeship of the front line, who never saw a man give his life for another, who never shared that dumb profound kindness of common men under a mutual disaster. . . . I say that such things, obscure, unknown, show that men are not wholly debased even by the disgusting savagery of war, that they can be equally superior in the disgusting vulgarities of daily existence.' He is clinging on to his 'religion of beauty', to a belief in the life of the senses, and also to a faith in humanity which contrasts sharply with the pessimism of much of much of his own writing of the time, including his poetry.

The essay is also critical of Joyce's *style*. While conceding that 'he has done daring and quite wonderful things with words', and supporting this assertion with an analysis of Joyce's gifts, he is anxious about the writer's influence: 'He is disgusting with a reason; others will be disgusting without reason. He is obscure and justifies his obscurity; but how many others will write mere confusion and think it sublime?'[19] Defending the essay in a letter to Eliot, he insisted that 'a classic style – sobriety, precision, concision – is and must be the most beautiful thing in literature and all deviations from it are retrogression.'[20]

In 'The Poet and Modern Life' he suggests, harking back to the example of Matthew Arnold in an earlier age of doubt, that 'now, if ever, must be an age of criticism, of pure conservation.' It was this belief that drove his own work but also that attracted him to Eliot. Back in 1919 he had written to tell Eliot that he considered him 'the only modern writer of pure criticism in English' (although bluntly adding that he disliked his poetry because it was 'over intellectual and afraid of those essential emotions that make poetry').[21]

Displaying his usual eagerness to support those in whom he believed, he had gone on to arrange a meeting between Eliot and Bruce Richmond, the *TLS* editor, in the hope that Richmond would offer Eliot reviewing work. (Eliot's first review for the *TLS* appeared in November 1919.) He praised Eliot's 1920 collection of criticism, *The Sacred Wood*, in reviews that appeared in both *Poetry* and *To-Day*.[22] For him, Eliot was 'a critic with principle, not impressions; a critic whose perceptions have been stimulated by the best literature of the past, whose appreciation of the present is equally keen and just; a critic without fads, personal vanity or affectation.'[23] He persuaded Monro to devote a whole issue of his *Monthly Chapbook* to a debate on the controversial topic of prose poetry (thus revisiting Eliot's March and May 1917 articles in the *New Statesman*), with Eliot and Manning (another critic he admired) stating the case against the form, and Aldous Huxley and himself advocating it. The issue appeared in April 1921, although without the hoped-for contribution from Huxley.[24]

It was not just Eliot's *writing* that Aldington admired. In June 1920 he told Lowell, who had little time for Eliot's work: 'As a literary personality he is fascinating. His manners are charming and ironical, his conversation really witty, his point of view always finished and sometimes profound; he is a really polished American and I know of no greater praise to give a man.'[25] A year later he is still telling her how mistaken she is, remarking on how Eliot has 'that charm and vigour of the early Ezra, plus a soundness, a coolness, an urbanity, Ezra could never have. He is quite unprovincial, which is perhaps the highest praise one can give an Anglo-Saxon writer. He is certainly the most attractive critical writer ever produced by America; I for one am extremely grateful to him for living in England and not a little proud that he prefers to.'[26] In a further letter he goes so far as to say: 'He is the one friend I have made since my return.'[27]

Aldington desperately needed friends to replace those he had lost – Pound (now in Paris), Cournos, Fletcher, Plank and Whitall – and the early 1920s show him working hard at the relationship with Eliot, but he never quite seems to have broken through his own awe or Eliot's natural reserve. Interviewed by Selwyn Kittredge in 1963, Yorke commented: 'They got along very easily indeed, although Aldington was always a little formal with him. Eliot is the sort of person one *is* a bit formal with.'[28] Certainly, although Aldington might tell Lowell that he and Eliot agreed 'in so many of [their] tastes and lines of thought,' the friendship between the hedonist and the Puritan was unlikely to be a lasting one.[29]

There was still Flint. The two men corresponded regularly, shared out the *TLS* work and tried to meet up when Aldington was in London. Flint, however, was advancing his Civil Service career and finding it increasingly hard, with his family commitments too, to produce translation, criticism and creative work. On 9 April 1920 Violet Flint died in childbirth, along with their baby daughter. 'Sweat[ing]

for some word or phrase or thought. . . . Not so much to help as to show him/
That all comradeship is not dead', Aldington remembered the poem Flint had
sent him when he was suffering in camp in 1916 and wrote him one entitled 'The
Walk', expressing the hope that his friend would find his silence 'beneficent and
comprehending'. The poem concludes:

> It is not grief that dares not speak
> But pity which can find no words.[30]

Four months later Flint quietly married Violet's older sister, Ruth, thus ensuring
a mother for his two children; Aldington wrote to congratulate him – and to tell
him not to pay any attention to what others thought of his actions. Flint's third (and
final) collection of poems, *Otherworld*, was published by Monro in July and Aldington
reviewed it warmly in the October issue of *Poetry*, praising 'its melancholy, love
of beauty, essential sweetness, homeliness and good sense, [its] gusto for ordinary
human life.'[31] However, once an admirer of Flint's scholarly familiarity with French
literature, Aldington now saw him as the critical inferior of Manning and Eliot.
He confided to Monro: 'Frank never gets beyond the state of giving information
about new writers; he is just incapable of writing an interesting essay on Keats
or Lamartine, whereas Eliot & Manning are really profound, their intelligence is
constantly at play.'[32]

One contact Aldington made in this period indicates how much he missed the
pre-war world and its close literary ties. In 1919 Sturge Moore had published a
collection of essays entitled *Some Soldier Poets*, which included an essay on Aldington.[33]
The essay focused on the pre-war imagist poetry, the war poems not having been
published when it was written. While making some of the same criticisms as
Monro would make in his 1920 *Some Contemporary Poets*, for example of the poet's
over-use of colour adjectives or 'inelegancies of syntax', and remarking that he was
at his best when prompted by 'admiration and delight' rather than by 'personal
antagonism', Sturge Moore praised him for his 'love of beauty that mounts almost
to passion'.[34] Aldington wrote to him and a correspondence ensued.

A reading of Aldington's side of the correspondence shows him hungry for
disinterested criticism and seeking the kind of sponsorship that Yeats had given
Pound in the earlier days – or perhaps that Pound himself had provided for him.
(He told Monro at this time, '[Sturge Moore] is the only one of my elders and
betters who condescends to take an interest in mes ouvrages.')[35] He tells Sturge
Moore of his distress: 'I can't find any security, any serenity, and I waste half my
time in a wholly fruitless "febrility"'.[36] He begs the older poet to tell him whether
he finds the war poems 'an advance or a retrogression', telling him what 'a dreadful
fizzle' they had been, with only eighty or ninety copies sold. The correspondence
ceased in early 1922 and it is difficult to know why: the last letters concern an
invitation from Sturge Moore for Aldington to visit for a weekend and the younger
man's postponement of the visit. Perhaps Aldington was becoming painfully aware
that he had little creative work to submit for Sturge Moore's criticism; perhaps he
simply became too busy to maintain this friendship.

Meanwhile there had been problems at Chapel Farm Cottage which Aldington found himself ill-equipped to deal with. Dollie Radford was only a lease-holder; widowed in 1919 and anxious about the state of health of her daughter, she had neglected to pass on Aldington's rent payments to the owner, a local builder. After Dollie's death in March 1920, Aldington found himself in danger of eviction. Not for the last time, he solicited the help of Malcolm Hilbery to sort out the mess, but he had to be out by the end of the year, when the lease would expire. He now decided to stay in the area – for its convenient distance from London, for the peace it offered and because he could live there cheaply. David Wilkinson has identified an advert in the *Newbury Weekly News* of 14 October 1920 which must surely have been placed by Aldington: '4-6 roomed cottage wanted in any village of Newbury district, within two miles of station; permanent tenant; good rent paid. Box 312.'

What he found was Malthouse Cottage at Lower Padworth, half-way between Newbury and Reading: a cottage attached to the end of a working malthouse on the bank of the Kennet and Avon Canal and only a few hundred yards from Aldermaston Railway Station. It was another two-up, two-down, with a further staircase up to an attic and a lean-to kitchen at the back. Reached by a lane that ran between the brewery and the canal, it was quite secluded. The cottage was only a few feet from the canal but the front door was on the side of the house, facing osier beds and fields. It had been empty for a year and the rent was 11/6 a week (raised in September 1923 to 12 shillings). 'Permanent tenant' he intended to be – spending a large proportion of what little money he had on furnishing the cottage.

And he made other decisions about his lifestyle. Yorke came to live with him, to all appearances as his wife, even appearing eventually as such on the electoral register (as Mrs H Aldington). On leaving Hermitage in December, he asked Mrs Brown to burn the contents of a trunk: the correspondence that H.D. had left at Mecklenburgh Square when she left for Cornwall in March 1918 – all their letters to each other up to that date and other correspondence, including Lawrence's and Cournos's letters to H.D.. (It is interesting to note that, despite making this decision to cut off the past, he could not bring himself to light the fire.)[37] That this break in his life was a momentous and troubled one can be inferred from the fact that he left Yorke to carry out the move on her own and went off by himself for three weeks. Just as he had done the previous year, he chose a location associated with his life with H.D., not only going to Martinhoe, but actually staying in Woodland Cottage.

Ominously, he would write to Flint shortly after his move had taken place, 'I could never be sure if I was happier with or without a woman. Each state has its good and bad side. One is more at peace, more intelligent when one is on one's own; one is more comfortable, more human, more foolish with a woman. Why are we so determined to have 'our own little woman'? How stupid!'[38] However, he came to like his new home. He wrote to Lowell in early April: 'It is simply the most flowery place imaginable – it would delight you with its freshness and extreme richness.'[39] *Life for Life's Sake* devotes several pages to the walks he enjoyed in the Kennett Valley and along the Ridgeway and to the history he discovered.[40]

He wanted to share his pleasure. Flint, either alone or with Ruth and the children, made several weekend visits to Berkshire over the next few years, staying at the nearby Butt Inn. Yet Aldington was aware of a gradual cooling of this friendship, of letters unanswered and invitations unacknowledged. He wrote to Lowell in August 1921 that he hadn't seen or heard from his friend for three months: 'Flint is in a strange humour . . . a nervous crisis. . . . He writes no poems. . . . He scarcely answers his letters and lives without ever seeing his friends. . . . He is really quite ill, but doesn't know it.'[41] Richard Church, who was both a colleague of Flint's at the Ministry of Labour and a fellow writer, describes Flint in his memoirs as 'a furnace of nervous passion'[42] and Aldington would tell Herbert Read in 1925: 'Yes, Frank is a hopeless topic. I have done best and so have all his friends. There is no more to do.'[43] From time to time he would come up with inventive ways to keep the friendship going: a regular exchange of sonnets or working in tandem on Latin translation and sending each other their efforts; but these schemes petered out, more as a result of Flint's professional and family commitments than from a lack of inclination. Flint was also, as ever, prone to take offence where none was intended; on one occasion the cause was Aldington's disparaging remarks about current practitioners of free verse. Yet it was to Flint that Aldington sent the manuscript of his long poem, *A Fool i' the Forest*, in 1924; and it was to Aldington and Padworth that Flint came when he suffered a breakdown from overwork in early 1925.

A letter from Aldington to Flint records Eliot's first visit to Malthouse Cottage in May 1921. The tone is playfully self-conscious but his pleasure is unmistakeable: 'One, Master Thomas Eliot (my singular good friend) hath honoured me with his presence this Pentecost. We had right pleasant and godly discourse together, wherein Master Eliot most sweetly and learnedly took part. I am right well affected to him & beseech you to cherish him in your thoughts as a marvellous towardly young gentleman & one that shall honour His Majesty by residence in his dominions.'[44] Eliot was accommodated not at the humble Butt Inn, but at The Hare and Hounds, the coaching inn on the Bath Road. He came alone. His marriage to Vivien Haigh-Wood, whom he had met while at Oxford in 1915 and married three months later, was already very troubled. Reserved and sexually repressed, he had been attracted by her vitality, not initially recognising the nervous instability which lay behind it.[45] While Aldington dined at the Eliots' flat occasionally during the 1920s, the two couples never met socially.

The very first weekend visitor to Malthouse Cottage, in March 1921, was Albert Aldington, who had also visited his son at Hermitage. On 21 April, however, Albert died of a heart attack; he was fifty-six years old. May Aldington wanted nothing to do with the sordid business and Aldington was left to identify his father's body, attend the coroner's inquest and organise the funeral. His mother did not attend. He told Flint: 'I must have lost all my sensitivity in the Artois and near the Somme, for I was present

Chapel Farm Cottages

Malthouse Cottage

at my father's burial without too much feeling. . . . For me the dead are yellow faces, pools of blood, muddy khaki, hurried burials under shell-fire . . . I became addicted to wholesale death; so retail death, although it touches me closely, cannot move me greatly.'[46] While these remarks reveal the extent to which his war was still with him, they probably conceal the extent of his affection – and pity – for his father.

He told Lowell in September that the education of his brother and younger sister was a cause of anxiety, but he seems to have involved himself very little in the lives of twelve-year-old Patricia and ten-year-old Tony. Such involvement would have brought him into too close a contact with his mother and Watkins, who were married exactly six months after Albert's death. Patricia told David Wilkinson in 1982 that she had only once visited her brother at Padworth: she had been put on a train to London and he had met her there and taken her down to Malthouse Cottage for a stay of two or three days.

However, he did play an active role in his sister Margery's life during this period. Before the war, she had been even more of a victim of her parents' misfortunes and carelessness than her brother. At first, she had been sent to a cheap convent boarding school outside Brussels; but she had been brought back to look after her father in London when May Aldington moved to Rye, before her mother decided that she would make a useful nursemaid for her younger siblings. When war broke out and May had forty army officers billeted at The Mermaid she felt it politic to send her daughter back to London, where, for a while, she attended a drama school. Realising what a fine singing voice she had, her teacher sent her along for an audition at Covent Garden where she joined the Royal Opera House chorus for a whole season – at seventeen years old, the youngest member, as she proudly told David Wilkinson nearly seventy years later. This was 1915 and shortly afterwards the Opera House closed and became a furniture depository until the end of the war; Margery found work in the chorus at the Gaiety Theatre on the corner of Aldwych and the Strand. After her father's death she shared a flat with a friend, but they struggled to make ends meet and in 1922 Aldington decided that the two young women, now approaching their mid-twenties, would be more easily able to manage – and live a healthier life – if they came to Berkshire.

He found a cottage for them to rent on the outskirts of the village of Oare, a mile north of Hermitage, and about ten miles from Padworth. Here Margery and her friend Olive Salter threw themselves into rural life, forming an ensemble called 'Mr Gay's Players': they found two local violinists, a viola player and a cellist (three of them from the same family) and Margery sang while Olive played the piano. They performed in local village halls and also gave music lessons, while Olive wrote articles and short stories for periodicals. Life was still a struggle and eventually they had to return to London to find more regular work, but for a year or more they were frequent visitors at Malthouse Cottage, spending Christmas of 1922 with Aldington and Yorke – along with Mrs Yorke, of whom Aldington was not over-fond. He even secured (through Eliot) an audition for his sister with Helen Rootham, Edith Sitwell's former-governess and present companion, and Margery went up to London twice a week for singing lessons with her.

Speaking to David Wilkinson in 1982, Margery had fond memories of that period, of the long walk between Oare and Padworth and of Yorke, whom they nicknamed 'Dolkins': 'funny little thing; looked rather like an Indian – wore a hand-cut black bang of hair and short cut hair and walked with a funny tottering walk but she did that sixteen [sic] miles that we used to do between Oare and

T.S. Eliot, early 1920s

Padworth, we with our long English legs and little Bun [Salter] scuttling along and Dolkins scudding with her and Budge the dog behind.' According to Margery, Aldington still had nightmares about the war at this stage and would wake up 'lashing about apparently and shouting.' She admired Yorke for dealing with these problems, and it is clear that Yorke submerged her own life in Aldington's in this period, taking on most of the household tasks, including the cooking, and doing much of his typing.[47] In a letter to Flint in October 1921 Aldington refers to Yorke's visiting London to sell her drawings; in 1920 she had provided the hand-coloured illustrations for Cyril Beaumont's study of the dancer Lydia Lopokova.[48] However, there is no extant evidence of any further work.

In the summer of 1921 the couple took a three-week break, a walking holiday in the West of England and Wales. In Devon they stayed with John Mills Whitham, with whom Aldington had renewed his acquaintance during his stay in Martinhoe six months earlier. While engaged in enforced labour in 1916, Whitham had met and married the artist Sylvia Milman and they had settled in a cottage at Holdstone Down near Combe Martin, about five miles from Martinhoe.[49] Here they lived a frugal life similar to Aldington's at Padworth, but without his regular contact with the London literary scene, and Whitham continued to produce his pessimistic novels.

Back at Padworth after this holiday, Aldington undertook an errand of mercy. Frederic Manning's mentor and friend, Arthur Galton, had died, leaving Manning not only without emotional support, but actually homeless; he had had to move out of the rectory at Edenham and was living in temporary rented accommodation in the village. The death in July of Eva Fowler, the American literary hostess, who had been Manning's close friend and another mentor, had been a further shock. Fowler was only forty-one years old and had died of a heart attack. In desperate need of money, Manning had accepted a commission from John Murray to write a biography of Sir William White, the late nineteenth-century naval architect, and now felt overwhelmed by the task. Aldington went to Lincolnshire to visit him and undertook to do the bulk of the research. It was an undertaking that would subsequently destroy the relationship: both men being in straitened circumstances, there would be acrimony over payment. At the time Aldington merely told Lowell that his own work was delayed because of 'having to rush off from time to time to save people from nervous breakdowns.'[50]

Indeed, no sooner was he back at Padworth again than another friend's needs laid claim upon him. Eliot was on the verge of nervous collapse, the pressures of his marriage and a recent visit from his family, as well as his demanding job at Lloyds Bank, having taken their toll. He came to stay at Malthouse Cottage for a few days in September but, shortly afterwards, was advised to take three months off work and travelled to a clinic in Lausanne. Aldington's concerns about Eliot's situation coincided with those of Pound, who in February 1922, when Eliot was showing further signs of stress, devised his 'Bel Esprit' scheme. Thirty people were to be approached to pledge £10 a year for Eliot's financial support, so that he could 'devote his entire time to literary work'. Pound and Aldington themselves were the first to pledge. 'I want T. out of bank by end of October, if not before', Pound wrote in characteristically imperious fashion.[51] He made Aldington and May Sinclair the British trustees of the scheme, while Virginia Woolf and Ottoline Morrell were Aldington's fellow signatories on the bank account.

Lowell, whom Aldington approached for a pledge, showed a scepticism which stemmed as much from her shrewd common sense as from her dislike of Eliot's work. She wanted to know why Eliot's own family could not give him financial help and told Aldington that she regarded the scheme as a 'strategic blunder'[52]. And so it proved. Pound's arrogance and Aldington's naivety landed them in difficulties, not least with Eliot himself, who was extremely embarrassed when he discovered that he was to be an object of charity. Pound's article in *The New Age*, in which he explained that the sponsorship of Eliot was only the first on which 'Bel Esprit' would embark and told the world about Eliot's 'recent three months absence due to complete physical breakdown', caused the very private Eliot public humiliation.[53] The scheme was eventually abandoned and Eliot remained at Lloyds until he was offered a post in the publishing house of Faber and Gwyer in 1925.

Other friendships occupied Aldington's time. Harold Monro, another melancholy man troubled by an unsuitable marriage (his second), made several visits to Malthouse Cottage in 1921, one of the few visitors to be accommodated in the cottage itself. In March of that year, Aldington told Monro: 'Your nerves are in a bad state altogether. Take yourself in hand and struggle against this damned despair which is choking us all.' He advised his friend: '[Y]ou mustn't let yourself be beaten down. You didn't make this world and you're not responsible for it – a little less Huxley and Marx – and a little more Epicurus and Keats! Eh?'[54] He seems to have been taking his own advice as he tells Monro that he has enjoyed this spring more than any since he was a boy and remarking that although he rather envies Monro his Mediterranean retreat (Monro was spending three months at his villa on Cap Ferrat), he really likes his 'little cottage'. In a further letter he explains that his current mood of cheerfulness comes: '1. From active liver. 2. No alcohol or tobacco. 3. Daily cold baths & walks. 4. Discreet use of veney [wine]. 5. Plenty of books. 6. No newspapers. 7. £7 a week.'[55]

Apart from the books, none of these habits figured in Monro's life. In *Life for Life's Sake* Aldington writes of one occasion when Monro came for a weekend's visit and became very drunk, knocking himself out on the garden path, but a letter to Flint reveals that this particular visit took place in May 1924.[56] Although this was another friendship that would fade, Aldington liked Monro and respected his integrity. He told Herbert Read, after Monro had been to stay at Padworth for a weekend in 1925: 'We had a most pleasant time, for he is a delightful and quite different personality in the country.' He felt a loyalty to the older man, commenting in another letter to Read: 'He was very kind to me in the past when I greatly needed kindness.'[57]

A new friendship was formed with the playwright John Halcott Glover, older than Aldington by fifteen years, but who endeared himself to the latter not only by his cheerfulness, but because he had served in the Royal Flying Corps in the war. In September 1922, Glover made possible Aldington's first trip abroad since demobilisation, when he lent the couple his flat in the Piazza Margana in Rome for three weeks. Ten years on from his last visit to Italy, the holiday must have brought back poignant memories for Aldington but he wrote about his return to Rome and Florence in glowing terms in *Life for Life's Sake*.

Meanwhile he was still working hard on reading, reviewing and translation. In 1922 Beaumont published a limited edition of his translation of Goldoni's *The Good Humoured Ladies*. Then he had a stroke of good fortune: his *TLS* review of a new edition of Cyrano de Bergerac brought him to the notice of Routledge, who commissioned him to write a translation of Cyrano's *Voyages dans la Lune et du Soleil*.[58] Over the next six years he would produce eleven books for the publishing house, ten in their Broadway Translations series and a book on Voltaire as the first critical biography in their new Republic of Letters series.[59] Most of these works were also published in America. Another French translation commission, *Sturly*, which came his way from Jonathan Cape in 1924, was a surprising one: a work by the oceanographer Pierre Custot. The task had initially been given to T.E. Lawrence but he had found the technical language too difficult. Aldington managed by the laborious two-stage process of finding the Latin names in French scientific textbooks and then looking them up in equivalent English books. Lowell arranged for Houghton Mifflin to bring out an American edition.

Allen and Unwin continued to publish Aldington's original work, bringing out *Exile and Other Poems* (which included 'The Berkshire Kennet', a long poem he also had published in a limited edition of fifty copies) in 1923. They also produced a compilation, *Literary Studies and Reviews*, in 1924, which consisted of twenty-one articles that had originally appeared in the *TLS* and other periodicals (including *The Literary Review* and *The Dial* in America); most were on French writers but there was also the delightful essay 'Theocritus in Capri', his 1922 *To-Day* article on 'The Poetry of T.S. Eliot' and the April 1921 *English Review* one on Joyce, along with 'The Poet and His Age' from the September 1922 *Chapbook*.

In October 1922, Eliot, with the financial backing of Lady Rothermere, the estranged wife of the newspaper proprietor, was able to start his own literary quarterly, which he named *The Criterion*. ('The Waste Land', chiefly written during his stay in the Lausanne clinic the previous year, appeared in the first issue.)[60] By the following April, Aldington was involved in the journal, producing reviews of French periodicals. In May he became Eliot's 'secretary and managing editor' (at £50 per annum) and also in charge of the foreign section. He found himself on two occasions – in July and October 1923 – having to over-see issues of *The Criterion* through printing because either Eliot or his wife was indisposed. Not only was this consuming of his time and energy, it also prepared the way for his disenchantment with Eliot, whom he felt was taking him for granted. The partnership had started promisingly: Eliot told Charles Whibley, who had become something of a literary mentor to Eliot, that Aldington's 'principles, political and literary' were nearer to his own than those of anyone else he could have approached.[61] Yet the seeds of discord were there from the start, both in Eliot's rather patronising view of Aldington and in his whole concept of the 'Criterion Club' of contributors. He explained to his mother in October: 'I have aimed to get together people whose bond should be myself, so that the power should remain in my hands. Richard Aldington is very useful and hardworking and more suitable for my purpose than anyone else I could have had.'[62]

Herbert Read, 1934

Perhaps in recognition of the risks he was taking with his physical and mental health, Aldington and Yorke had a July holiday with the Whithams in Devon and then, in November, he resigned from his post as Eliot's assistant on *The Criterion* and they went off to Italy for three whole months. The trip was made possible by payments from *The Criterion* (£35), his income from Routledge (£25) and a belated £50 from Manning for his work on Sir William White, along with the offer of Glover's apartment again. In Rome Aldington met a friend of Glover's, the dramatist, translator and journalist George Gribble who lived in a tumbledown mediaeval tower with his French wife and small daughter.[63] Fluent in French, German and Italian and blessed with an easy-going temperament, he was a man Aldington could admire, 'a good European'.[64] (In November 1924, the Gribbles would visit England, where, apart from entertaining them at Malthouse Cottage, Aldington would arrange for them to meet Eliot and Edith Sitwell.) Edward Storer was also now living in Rome. 'He is a very good chap and improves the more you know him', Aldington told Flint.[65]

His long stay out of England did not, however, make him restless. He wrote to Monro: 'It is fun to be in Italy, but I shan't be sorry to return to England. Italy isn't really alive – it's only pretending to be.' Nevertheless, he did not intend to return to Eliot's fold: 'I intend to go my own way and to hell with coteries and to hell with intellectual snobbery!'[66] On his return in early February 1924, he began work on a new long poem, a departure from anything he had ever attempted before. In his poem *The Berkshire Kennet*, a year earlier, he had described a Wordsworthian recovery of tranquillity, the Kennet doubling for the earlier poet's Derwent. In this Berkshire valley he had found solitude, peace and silence and these:

> Have cleansed the wounds of war away,
> And brought to my long troubled mind
> The health that I despaired to find. . . .

His critical writings and many of the poems in *Exile* had suggested that it was not that easy. Now *A Fool i' the Forest* was his depiction of 'a man of our own time . . . shown at a moment of crisis . . . as he struggles to attain a harmony between himself and the exterior world.'[67] And the conclusion is deeply pessimistic.

He was working simultaneously on a monograph on Voltaire for the Routledge Republic of Letters series. A glance at its bibliography give us some idea of the massive amount of reading he undertook to produce what is a comprehensive and scholarly, but very readable and concise, work of biography and criticism amounting to only 60,000 words. He admired Voltaire the philosopher for his understanding that injustice and intolerance were 'the great enemies of human happiness', that 'war is the result of both, and war is the destroyer of civilisation', and for his rejection of Rousseau's optimistic faith in man in a state of nature, which, in Aldington's opinion, led to 'the abandonment of rational self-discipline and the paradoxical assertion of the aristocracy of the plebs.' He admired Voltaire the writer because 'in his hands French prose became one of the most supple, elegant and precise instruments of expression ever framed by civilised men.' However, he saw Voltaire's poetry and literary criticism as hampered by an insistence on taste and elegance and an absence of 'high poetic passion and imagination': 'Good sense, vraisemblance, sobriety, precision, elegance, clarity, are the qualities Voltaire admired and possessed. The greatest poetry demands in addition profound passion, a towering imagination, an eloquence which rushes from the depths to the heights and back again; those qualities Voltaire did not possess and underestimated.'[68] It is Aldington's objection to Eliot's verse again.

He did not resume working for *The Criterion,* complaining to Monro in May 1924: 'I did a hell of a lot of work for it, gave suggestions, procured authors, acted as secretary, tried to get subscriptions, got people interested in it, all for a pound a week! I had continually to put aside other work to answer Eliot's letters for him, I found him difficult to work with and I also found I was absolutely paralysed mentally by the snobbish attitude of *The Criterion*. My reward was a piffling little "attack" on something I said about Joyce, and the growing realisation that I was a "useful hack journalist" whose plodding habits might be of use to the superior intellectuals with whom I was graciously permitted to come into contact.'[69]

He was regularly reviewing for *The Nation* and *The Spectator* as well as the *TLS*.[70] *Vogue* had commissioned him for a series of articles on poetry and he still had his translation work to do. The combination of his demanding routine and the emotional toll taken by writing *A Fool i' the Forest* (his 'subconscious life getting a chance to express itself') was perhaps inevitable: in February 1925 he collapsed from nervous exhaustion.[71] A fortnight in bed, a visit from Flint and a walking holiday with Yorke in North Wales appeared to remedy the situation, but it had shown him how near the abyss he was: '[T]he writing of this poem had been accompanied by moods of depression which were quite alarming. I disregarded these warnings, and set them down as after-effects of the war. . . . I failed to see that by devoting myself to literary studies to the extent of over-work I was frustrating a whole series of impulses and condemning myself to a life of unnecessary monotony.'[72] The true state of his emotional health would reveal itself more devastatingly – for others as well as himself – a year later.

On their return from Greece in May 1920, H.D. and Bryher had spent time in Cornwall before returning to the Bullingham Mansions flat, but in September they embarked, with Perdita and a nurse, on a six-month visit to America. They were met on their arrival in New York by Lowell and Russell. And it was in New York, at the end of their tour, that Bryher was married to Robert McAlmon, a young American writer to whom Williams had introduced them.[73] It was a marriage of convenience, providing McAlmon with financial support and the opportunity to move to Europe and Bryher with freedom from her family. By the summer of 1921 they had all settled in Switzerland, where Mrs Doolittle joined them, becoming an established part of the household there until her death in 1927. McAlmon, often accompanied by Bryher, spent more time in Paris; but in their apartment in the Riant Chateau in Territet near Montreux, H.D. settled down to write her fictionalised accounts of her troubled life, *Paint It Today* and *Asphodel*. She spent time in Italy, and she and Bryher had one more long tour – to Egypt in 1923.

She visited London occasionally, although not renting an apartment again until 1925; for now, the Hotel Washington in Curzon Street was her London base. 'I get awfully homesick for England at times,' she told Plank in November 1922, 'but I know I am best out of it.'[74]

Her relationship with Bryher was a close and affectionate one. Each woman knew that the other had 'rescued' her, H.D. from the poverty and isolation of single parenthood, Bryher from suicidal depression and a claustrophobic family life. The gratitude and loyalty that recognition brought never vanished. In the early years the letters written when they were apart are tender, longing, even passionate, with H.D. addressing Bryher as 'Dear, dear boy', 'Baby love', 'Dearest baby' and 'Darling child', but it was only for a short while a physical relationship. H.D. told George Plank in 1935: 'I had a very lovely relationship with Bryher in Greece. It did not last long, she was utterly unresponsive and these things, you know *must* interact.'[75]

Throughout these years she was hungry for news of Aldington. With Pound in Paris, her contacts with Aldington's circle were limited, but she used them. Once she heard of his friendship with Eliot, she asked Patmore and two other close women friends, Doris Oppenheimer ('Oppy') and Dorothy Cole ('Cole'), to obtain information from Vivien Eliot about him.[76] In February 1922 Patmore wangled an invitation through Hunt to the Sitwells' home to hear Aldington read from *Hymen*. (Patmore herself was living in much reduced circumstances; Deighton Patmore had been declared bankrupt and they were occupying rented rooms.) '[Richard] looks common somehow – coarsened – an inclination of middle waistcoat button to protrude,' she wrote to Bryher, feeding the latter just the kind of comment she wanted to hear.[77]

Then in November 1924 Patmore wrote to H.D. of a 'sighting': Aldington coming into the British Museum, 'carrying a very neat little attaché case, clothed in light tweeds and a smallish black hat'. He looked, she said, 'rather subdued . . . not the old time *con brio*.' She did not know whether he had recognised her and had been too taken-aback and nervous to speak to him. She sought reassurance from H.D. that she had done the right thing.[78] H.D.'s disappointment that no more had come out of the encounter – and her true feelings about Patmore – surfaced in a letter to Plank: 'She did not need or ask my sanction in the old days for any relationship she wanted with Richard.'[79] She went on to ask Plank if he ever heard anything of the Randalls, as they might know something about Aldington.

Part of her interest was self-preservation: encouraged by Bryher to mistrust her husband and to see him as a possible threat to Perdita, she wanted to be armed for any legal proceedings he might institute. That that was not the whole story, however, is clear from an earlier letter to Plank in which she stresses the need for circumspection in their enquiries: 'if R.A. finds out he will either make himself altogether scarce or come to see me.' She felt unable to cope with either outcome: 'Of course, *au font*, I should like to see R. but things being at present so difficult with money, my mother, my baby etc., I don't dare think of seeing him. It wouldn't be fair to myself, nor to my friends who did so much to help me.'[80]

She knew that her interest was being mirrored by Aldington's. She told Plank in the same letter that Aldington had been asking Harriet Weaver for information: 'That

Dorothy Yorke (right) and Babette Plechner Hughes at Malthouse Cottage, 1925

he has been to see her several times, she says, asking for news, begging in fact, just to hear "where H.D. sleeps", "not for her sake but for his own" etc.' H.D. had been well-briefed by Bryher, however. She told Plank a few months later that it could all be 'some lawyer's trick'; she could be too easily trapped, though it might well be 'the most innocent and heart-rending of attempts' to get in touch with her again.[81]

Her fears seemed to be confirmed in February 1925, when Cournos called on her in Switzerland and warned her that Aldington was likely to sue for divorce on the grounds of desertion in order to marry Yorke, and would probably demand custody of Perdita, as he was legally entitled to do. In the ensuing panic, there was a flurry of letters between Bryher and Patmore, who was enlisted (as she had been a few years earlier – and without success – to procure promises of financial support for Perdita from Gray) to make legal enquiries of an intimate lawyer friend. One of the options to be explored was whether Bryher and McAlmon could adopt Perdita. (Bryher, ever the shrewd businesswoman, told Patmore, 'I will not spend a lot of money on the infant's education and have R.A. stick his nose in, in the middle.')[82]

The ambivalence of H.D.'s feelings towards her husband is clear from a May 1925 letter to Plank: 'No, I long ago decided that well enough was best let [severely?] alone. After all, it is only sentiment, a desire to link up with the past & I might loose [sic] even the illusion of that past if it were broken across. If things happen they happen! That is again different. But I don't see that there can be any possible move this end, considering my temperament. I am really supremely happy in my present state. Naturally we all have "moments" of sorts'.

That same month the news of Lowell's death from a cerebral haemorrhage must have prompted poignant memories of pre-war London for both H.D. and Aldington. Her correspondence with them both had been intermittent over the last few years as she struggled with ill health and devoted all her time to her biography of Keats. The task completed (Aldington acknowledged receipt of a copy in March), she had planned a lecture tour in Britain for April. 'However silent I may be as a correspondent, you must not ever think that I change in my affection for you', she had written to Aldington in April 1923, 'because that never alters.'[83] Shortly after that letter, Harriet Monroe had come on a visit to London and Aldington and Flint had taken her out to lunch, another glimpse into the vanished past.

In late June 1925 H.D., with her mother and Perdita, came to London for a five month stay. By the time she returned to Territet she had found herself an apartment in Sloane Street which would become her permanent summer residence.

At *The Criterion* Eliot had brought together a group of collaborators and contributors mostly of a similar age and some of whom had been friends or acquaintances for a long time: Monro, Aldington, Flint, Randall, Herbert Read, Bonamy Dobrée, Richard Church, J.B. Trend, Orlo Williams, Humbert Wolfe and Frank Morley. When they were in England, Fletcher and Aiken were also participants.[84] During 1923 Aldington had generally managed to attend the group's weekly lunches and their more formal monthly meetings.[85] Despite his strong reservations about Eliot, he now began to feel isolated and made steps to heal the breach, contributing an article on Francois Villon for the April 1925 issue.[86]

It was through the *Criterion* lunches that his friendship with Herbert Read developed. While an admirer of Read's war poems, *NakedWarriors*, Aldington had objected to the intellectual quality of his 1922 collection, *Mutations of the Phoenix*, seeing it as under the influence of Eliot. He told Monro: '[O]ur [the Imagists'] poetry was the poetry of the emotions and beauty, of instinct and sudden impulse . . . Read (and others of his school) try to create poetry from thought and the operations of the intelligence; psychology and character interest them; beauty is a phenomenon not a passion; they analyse love, they don't overflow with it. . . . Their style is allusive and elliptic; their vocabulary abstruse and ponderous; their meaning tenuous and remote. We were sentimentalists; they are anatomists.'[87] He felt very differently about *In Retreat*, Read's 1925 prose memoir of the 1918 German Spring Offensive, which Aldington would refer to in later years as 'a classic of the World War'.[88] At the time it inspired him with the idea of writing a companion volume on 'The Advance' (of the final months of the war) and he told Read: 'I should try to tell it as coolly and truthfully as you did. . . . My great difficulty is to refrain from giving in to angry emotionalism. I feel we wasted men's lives up to the last hour.'[89] In a further letter he told Read: 'I am going to try to do that Advance sometime, and to model myself on your perfect restraint. I don't know if I can. I get excited and angry and almost hysterical when I think about it. . . . It needs to be a series of sharp images and impressions.'[90]

Read came to visit at Padworth and plans were made for him to bring his wife and two-year-old son for a weekend, but these foundered on the problem of accommodating under the same roof the Reads' dog and the cat to which Aldington and Yorke had given a home.[91] The two men had much in common, their intellectual and imaginative powers matched by a determination to succeed in the literary world and a capacity for hard work. 'We missed a good few years by our absurd capers in Picardy, Artois, Flanders &c.,' Aldington told Read, 'but I believe we learned there the importance of a pertinacious production of energy long after all energy has gone! This literary game is not worth much but we ought to be able to play it as well as the best.'[92] Neither had fully grasped that their war experiences, coming, as they had, after unresolved childhood challenges, had put them under an enormous emotional strain which hard work and literary success would not alleviate. However, Read's move in 1922 from the Ministry of Labour to a curatorship in the Ceramics Department of the Victoria and Albert Museum had opened up to him the world of the visual arts, which would later sustain him professionally and imaginatively.

They shared not only their ideas about literature but their resentment of Eliot's arrogance. 'Put not your trust in princes', Aldington warned Read. ' . . . we are a mere chorus of Theban old men useful as celebrators and disciples. . . . I do most vehemently suspect him of condescension to us all. . . . We are his claque, his suite, his ladder, his footprints in the sands of Time, his stepping-stones to higher things, his duniwassal's tail, his Persian eunuchs, his trumpet-blowers, his pipers of Penzance, his good friends Suckfist and Kissbreach.'[93] He was keen to help Read succeed in his literary aspirations and, as he had done six years earlier with Eliot, he introduced his friend to Bruce Richmond, with the result that Read became a reviewer for the *TLS*. He also tried to interest him in contributing to the two Routledge series, the Republic of Letters and the Broadway Translations, presenting his usual justifications for the time he spent on such work.

Another old friend now enlisted his help and guidance: Pound, now settled in Rapallo, near Genoa, wanted to get himself noticed again on the British publishing scene. Aldington's advice was to 'get out something in the erudite line; just as the reviews of that are dying down, burst out with the Cantos [which Eliot had been publishing in *The Criterion*] or a book of shorter poems (new) and, if possible, follow that up in six months with a book of essays or a critical biography.'[94] Pound seems not to have followed this advice but continued to ask for Aldington's opinion, for example on what to include of his earlier work in his *Collected Poems*, which Boni and Liveright brought out the following year.

As 1925 drew to a close, Aldington was feeling confident about his status in the literary world. Glenn Hughes, the American academic who had taken an interest in the Imagists and who, with his wife, visited Padworth in September 1925, wrote in November to offer him a lecture tour to the U.S.A.[95] Aldington expressed his appreciation but declined the invitation. 'You must remember', he told Hughes, 'that my interests are as much literary as poetic.' A nine-month absence would lose him his regular reviewing on the *TLS*, *The Nation* and *The Spectator* and the 'influential (behind the throne) position' it gave him. They were, he asserted, 'the three best and most solid literary papers in England [which] touch the whole, or nearly the whole, of the cultured classes throughout the Empire.' He confided that he was about to be offered joint editorship of the Routledge Republic of Letters imprint, as well as sole editorship of a series of eighteenth century French translations in the firm's Broadway series. 'You see,' he concluded, 'I am playing for a fairly big thing – nothing less than the position of the accepted English authority on French literature. The two acknowledged authorities, Dr Saintsbury and Sir Edmund Gosse, are both very old men. Dr Whibley has other fish to fry. I don't fear any of my contemporaries: those who know more about French than I do cannot write so well, and those who can write better, do not know so much.'[96] He was, he said, preparing lists of books and authors for the two Routledge series and lists of translators and scholars to undertake the work. He himself intended to bring out 'at least fifteen more books, translations, monographs, essays, new editions of French literature' in the next five years. He concluded: 'I have already put in six years strenuous work on these lines and it would be madness to abandon it in mid career.'[97]

Only days later, a great blow struck. Routledge had indeed encouraged him to hope that he would soon be appointed as joint editor with W.K. Rose of the Republic of Letters series as well as editor of a section of the Broadway Translations series. Meanwhile, however, Eliot had left Lloyds to become literary adviser to the new publishing firm of Faber and Gwyer and proposed to set up a translation series and a series of monographs on foreign writers. He had actually invited Aldington to provide a Gourmont monograph. Aldington had declined the invitation, recognising that it would constitute a conflict of interests, but was unworried: 'I think the wise thing will be a sort of unspoken gentleman's agreement to leave the historical figures to Routledge and let Tom take the moderns,' he had told Read.[98]

Routledge, however, now came up with an alternative solution: making the Republic of Letters series a joint imprint with Faber and Gwyer, with Eliot sharing the editorship with Rose. Initially, Aldington was generous towards Eliot, telling Read that he assumed that Eliot had started his own series in all good faith, not realising that he himself was 'sweating' for the editorship of the Routledge imprint. He felt obliged to support the scheme, aware that if it did not come about, Routledge would be forced to limit their own series and would not be able to afford the joint editorship he had been craving. However, the more he brooded on his bad luck the more bitter he became. The result was two letters to Read in which he blamed not only Eliot but Read and others who had declined his own invitations to contribute to the two Routledge series but had accepted those from Eliot: 'This affair is the biggest setback I have had since the war and loses me the fruit of years of work', he told Read. 'I shall, of course, withdraw from any further collaboration with either series and probably from the Broadway.'[99]

Two days later he begged Read to destroy the letters: 'I must say that Tom has acted in the most straightforward and decent manner and has done his best to arrange matters amiably.'[100] Eliot (and Faber and Gwyer) had turned down the collaboration proposal, but both firms had accepted the 'gentleman's agreement' which Aldington had initially proposed. There would be no joint editorship of the Republic of Letters, but Aldington was given the editorship of the eighteenth century French translations. Eliot's charm and Aldington's *capacity* for reflection had brought him back from the brink of personal and professional isolation, but it had been close. Nor could he face the next few years with quite the confidence he had expressed to Glenn Hughes only weeks previously.

The year ended, as the previous one had, with a Christmas visit to his family. Relations with his mother had improved when (as he told Eliot) she had begun 'to do the right thing', by transferring to him his father's books, some old pewter and some shares. The transfer of investments must have been considerable, since he informed Eliot that it was 'the first step towards some economic independence', but his chief pleasure was the receipt of Albert Edward's library.[101] He told Flint about having a new bookcase put up in the front room of the cottage 'to take the new books from Rye', adding 'I must be getting well on the way towards 3000 by now.'[102] It is a measure of the improved relationship between Aldington and his mother that in the letter to Flint he writes: 'My mother is coming down here on Thursday and will probably want to take us "riding abaht in 'er motor-cah" for a few days.'

However, the 1925 Christmas visit was not to Rye. May and her husband had sold The Mermaid Inn and moved back to the Dover area, where she was now running the Bay Hotel at St-Margaret's-at-Cliffe: Aldington and Yorke spent Christmas 1925 in the village where he had spent his adolescent years.

17. *Exile* and *A Fool i' the Forest*

I say, pox on your intensities and essences; know what you know, feel what you feel, think what you think, and put it down, write, write, write.

(Richard Aldington to Herbert Read, 1924)[1]

Ghosts and nightmares stalk Aldington's post-war poems, as they do those of Sassoon, Blunden and Graves. He tells us in 'Eumenides': 'I have lived with, fed upon death/ As happier generations feed on life;/ My very mind seems gangrened.' When the speaker in 'In the Palace Garden' tells us:

> It was enough not to be dead,
> Not to be a black spongy mass of decay
> Half-buried on the edge of a trench . . .

What we respond to is not the sense of relief but the grim recollection. In 'Eumenides' we are given some of the 'thousand images' he sees and struggles with 'and cannot kill':

> That boot I kicked
> (It had a mouldy foot in it)
> The night K's head was smashed
> Like a rotten pear by a mortar . . .

And so 'Le Maudit', in the poem with that title, 'stands alone in the darkness/ Like a sentry never relieved.' The solitary figure of the sentry appears in the poems of many of the survivors, but what distinguishes Aldington's poetry of the aftermath from that of Blunden, Sassoon or Read is the absence of any nostalgia for the war.[2] There is no ambivalent hankering after those 'lost intensities of hope and fear' of which Blunden speaks, none of the regimental pride or poignant memories of companionship that we find in Sassoon, Graves, Read or Gurney.[3] Aldington had not entered the war with any illusions and, both as private soldier and as junior officer, had been a loner. Unlike Graves or Blunden, he had pursued a peacetime career before the war, and the loss he so poignantly felt was of that pre-war life – and of the creative power he had then possessed.

At least initially, the inability to forget the horrors of war is linked to a strong sense of survivor guilt:

> Happiness hissed into nothing —
> Metal under a fierce acid —
> And I was whispering:
> 'This happiness is not yours;
> It is stolen from other men.
> Coward! You have shirked your fate.'
> ('In the Palace Garden')

In the later poems of this 1923 collection the memories have been suppressed:

> At last, after years, I am saturated
> With pity and agony and tears;
> At last I have reached indifference;
> Now I am almost free — . . .
>
> The dead may be myriad,
> But my nostrils are sweet with crushed leaves . . .
>
> I have passed through hate and pity,
> Desire and anguish, to this:
> I am myself,
> I am free.   ('Freedom')

Yet we can see that 'indifference' is no solution, and satire and irony, when he employs them, as in 'Bones' and 'Having Seen Men Killed', strike us as tactics of avoidance. In 'Eumenides' the poet tells us how hard he has 'striven for health':

> Lived calmly (as it seemed) these many months,
> Walked daily among neat-hedged fields,
> Watched the long pageant of the clouds,
> Loved, drawn into my being, flowers . . .
> Noted the springing green
> Of white ash, birch and heavy oak,
> Lived with the noblest books, the noblest friends,
> Looked gay, laughed free, worked long.

'Retreat', with its prayer:

> Let there be silence sometimes,
> A space of starless night —
> A silence, a space of forgetfulness
> Away from seething of lives,
> The rage of struggle.

must have been written in response to the 'silence and untroubled darkness' he found at Hermitage.[4] And yet he is still haunted. At the end of 'Eumenides' he comes to the realisation that the ghost that rises up to torment his nights is his own 'murdered self':

> A self which had its passion for beauty,
> Some moment's touch with immortality –

This is the loss that he mourns: the loss of his creative spirit. In the blank verse 'At a Gate by the Way', the poet stands with a friend (probably Flint), looking at the 'silent garnered fields' of early Autumn, which, from his characteristically Hellenic perspective, are 'like huge-limbed country gods'. He is struck by the contrast between their 'long task fitly ended' and his own lack of productivity. He tells his friend:

> We have hunted, you and I, these many years;
> Either the game is scant, the luck is thwart,
> Or we are mole-eyed or the gods are cruel,
> For what we seized, breathless with joy
> Turned rotten in our hands and what we missed
> Seemed ever the one quarry that we sought.

Exile and Other Poems consists of two sections: the sixteen free verse poems that constitute *Exile* are followed by a group of skilled and generally pleasing pastiches of seventeenth and eighteenth century verse, perhaps evidence of this loss of creative inspiration. The murdered self would continue to haunt the poet and we meet it again two years later in *A Fool i' the Forest*.

Aldington wrote to Harriet Monroe on 22 September 1924, 'Only four people beside myself and the publisher have seen it . . . and all agree that it is by far the best thing I have done.'[5] The four people included Flint and Eliot–but not Read, to whom he finally sent a copy of his manuscript in December. Read's praise was qualified and prompted an outburst from Aldington: 'I am, of course, delighted to know that you think The Fool has expressed some of the general feelings of the men of our generation who have had our experience. . . . [but] if The Fool strikes you as loose in structure, texture and idea, I reply that what you call "loose" I call ease, fluidity, clarity. . . . Ten years, five years ago, I should have said Amen to your denunciation. Now, I take it as a compliment! I abandon, cast off, utterly deny the virtue of "extreme compression and essential significance of every word". I say that is the narrow path that leads to sterility. . . . I say, pox on your intensities and essences; know what you know, feel what you feel, think what you think, and put it down, write, write, write.'[6]

A Fool i' the Forest:A Phantasmagoria represented a complete departure for Aldington: a free verse poem in thirty-four sections comprising some 1350 words. While the picaresque narrative ranges over place and time, there is a central consciousness – a first person narrator – and two additional 'characters'. Aldington explains their significance in an introduction: 'I' 'is intended to be typical of a man of our own time, one who is by temperament more fitted for an art than a scientific civilisation. He is shown at a moment of crisis, and the phantasmagoria is the mirror of his mind's turmoil as he struggles to gain a harmony between himself and the exterior world.' Mezzetin 'symbolises the imaginative faculties – art, youth, satire, irresponsible gaiety, liberty', while the third character, the Conjuror 'symbolises the intellectual faculties – age, science, righteous cant, solemnity, authority'. We guess that these last two are the Touchstone and Jacques of *As You Like It*. The poem represents, as the note on the original dustcover indicated, 'the contest between the ideals of the old Art civilisation and the new Trade civilisation'. More importantly, it is a contest for the soul of the narrator and it becomes clear that, although 'I', the narrator, is attracted much more by Mezzetin than the Conjuror, he needs both to achieve fulfilment.

The journey of the three characters takes them to Athens and the Parthenon. There a severe scrutiny of the classical world and its values takes place, occupying eighteen of the thirty-four sections (almost half the entire poem), but the dramatisation of the debate and the variety of poetic genres and moods employed ensure the poem's continuing pace and vitality. The narrator asks:

> Did they truly reach that harmony we hear of?
> Balance of thinker, athlete, artist?

Mezzetin argues that 'Their world was clear and reasonable, / Yet not excluding beauty', and for the narrator the Parthenon represents 'Science and beauty reconciled with health', whereas in the modern world:

> We have beauty that's diseased and wanton,
> Art that plays with ugliness and fantasy,
> Science heavy, technical and mystic,
> Stupid health for some – the rest imperfect.

The critique of the contemporary Western world is sustained throughout the poem, but the Conjuror questions the narrator's Hellenism:

> What are these myths but half-truths, quarter-truths,
> Dreams of semi-barbarous children
> With an exquisite aesthetic tact?
> Art is primitive and precedes true knowledge . . .
> The glory of Hellas is her thinkers
> Not her poets and her artists.

and he subjects the narrator to 'monstrous visions of lust' to persuade him that Greek culture became in the end 'an art of death, / A stimulus to perverse and jaded senses.' The narrator does not accept this view, arguing that 'Even these wildest and most perverse excesses / Are disciplined by a sense of beauty'.

Eventually the Parthenon vanishes and the narrator finds himself and his two companions undertaking a grim underground journey across time and place. They arrive in northern France where the Conjuror explains to the narrator that he cannot reconcile his two companions and must choose between them, while the narrator insists: 'If I lose one of you, I'm incomplete; / If both it's mental death.' There follows a long reflective and autobiographical passage, in which he recalls the Italy of 1913:

> . . . at twenty, I beheld the Bay of Naples;
> All my being towered into a splendid flame –
> Sunlight sparkled on the sea
> Odyseus cut with carven prow,
> And the sirens still were siging.
> Every rock-cleft blossomed with narcissus,
> Every slope with broom and vine and lemon;
> Every hill was sacred to a goddess.

He wishes that he had died then:

> When the flame goes, man's a husk, a ghost,
> Herding miserably with other ghosts,
> Sunk in apathy or shrieking at his memories.

We are back with the ghosts of *Exile* – and the war:

> What's to do then?
> For to lament is pitiful,
> Most unbecoming men who strove with Kitchener.

Now we understand why the journey has ended in France. We are back in the trenches of the Western Front and there follows a dramatic scene in which the Conjuror, now their sergeant-major, takes the other two, privates in his platoon, out on patrol. Through incompetence, the Conjuror causes the death of Mezzetin. His reaction is to tell the narrator, 'Now he's gone, we'll make a man of you.' This is the climax of the poem, the narrator's loss of his creative self:

> Then I knew that Mezzetin
> Was as much to me as life itself;
> I wished a bomb would fall into my shell-hole,
> For I felt too numb to stand up to the bullets.

In the closing sections of the poem, the narrator and the Conjuror return to London, where they work in the British Museum ('Ennui of knowledge without wisdom/ Soaked into my flesh and numbed me') and tramp the streets at night while the narrator contemplates doing 'Something rather sudden and bloody', but finds that his 'inbred scepticism' makes him inactive. Finally, he throws the Conjuror off Waterloo Bridge one night.

With both his other selves destroyed, the narrator becomes, in a section entitled 'The Good Citizen', a decent working man, 'a loyal English husband' and a devoted father:

> At the office I am dilgent and punctual,
> Courteous, well-bred, and much respected . . .
> Everything I do is wise and orderly.

Yet at times he is haunted by 'pangs of the forgotten years' and finds himself asking:

> Need I fall so low as this?
> Need I prison up my spirit
> In so meek and regular a cage?

He knows that it would have been different had both Mezzetin and the Conjuror survived; memories of 'a life once vowed to truth and beauty' pierce him with anguish. The poem ends with a choric chant, reminiscent of 'Choricos'.

Commentators at the time made comparisons with Eliot's *The Waste Land*, which had been published three years earlier. The shifts in time and place in *A Fool i' the Forest*, the range of poetic genres employed (from Swinburnian hexameters to ragtime), the literary allusions and the use of languages other than English (with one whole section written in French) certainly convey some of the eclecticism of the earlier poem, and both works represent the contemporary world as fragmented and sterile. The essential difference lies in the central organising consciousness of the two poems: *The Waste Land* has a variety of unidentified and shifting narrative voices and no continuous narrative, whereas *A Fool i' the Forest* has one narrator and one narrative. There are certainly passages, particularly those relating to London, that may remind us of Eliot's *Preludes*, 'The Love Song of J. Alfred Prufrock' or 'Portrait of a Lady', but the presence of autobiographical content indicates that Aldington's poem is an account of a personal journey.

The large amount of philosophical reflection in the poem constantly threatens to become an aesthetic weakness; but the dramatic representations of the conflicting characters of Mezzetin and the Conjuror, the pace of the narrative and the variety of scenes and visions give the poem a compensating imaginative immediacy. This was the crux of the argument with Read about whether the poem is too loose in structure, texture and idea. In 1921 Pound had helped Eliot to reduce *The Waste Land* to half its length – and to about a third of the length of Aldington's 'phantasmagoria'; we might wonder what Pound would have done with *A Fool i' the Forest*. As with *The Waste Land*, the degree of erudition in the poem also undermines its accessibility; we may recall Aldington's accusation that Eliot's poetry was 'over-intellectual'.[7] However, while the foreign language passages in *A Fool i' the Forest* in particular seem at times self-indulgent, it is again the narrative drive that prevents the poem from becoming obscure. The *TLS* reviewer recognised the achievement, referring to the poem as 'a most engaging and suggestive allegory . . . at once ribald and poignant' and claiming that, without becoming didactic in tone, it '[struck] at the very roots of modernity'.[8]

In 1921 Aldington had asked how poetry, 'which is essentially order, affirmation, achievement', could be created in 'an age, a *milieu*, of profound doubt and discouragement'.[9] The resolution of *A Fool i' the Forest* is deeply pessimistic, but the artistic achievement of the poem is that it refrains from self-pity. This is partly because of the wit and humour that constantly leaven its grimness. It is also because our final picture of the narrator is a satirical one. Despite the earlier closely biographical references to Italy and to the Western Front, the poet avoids portraying his own circumstances at the end of the poem. His narrator leads a life that his creator had rejected: a clerical job, a suburban home, a wife and children. The writer's own existence was not quite 'so meek and regular a cage'. Nevertheless the fact that he produced out of his own self-doubt and disillusion with the post-war world a lively and readable poem is a paradox.

In the process he had opened a Pandora's Box. He tells us that the writing of the poem had been accompanied by 'quite alarming' moods of depression. It was followed by a nervous breakdown and it would be several more years before he was able to deal, artistically and personally, with the ghosts of his past.

18. The Cracks Appear: 1926-1927

What ails thee, lad?
(D.H. Lawrence, letter to Richard Aldington, 24 May 1927)[1]

Memories of Athens and of Naples,
Of a life once vowed to truth and beauty,
Pierce me till I start and gasp with anguish . . .
(Richard Aldington, *A Fool i' the Forest*, 1925)

Aldington and Yorke had now lived in Padworth for five years. His occupation and limited means had enabled them to avoid the conventional way of life of the middle-classes in a feudal home counties village without sparking disapproval or undue curiosity. Their choice of privacy was tolerated; their frugal way of life set them apart from the wealthier inhabitants and their culture from others who also lived a simple life; they had need of neither church nor school, although Aldington did make sparing use of the local public house, for the occasional beer and for accommodating his visitors. The couple were assumed to be man and wife and Aldington's regular trips by train to London to see his editors gave an aura of respectability to his work. The village was used to artists anyway: the painter Christopher Strange, cousin of the local brewery owner, lived not far from Aldermaston Wharf.

In Aldington's 1931 novel *The Colonel's Daughter*, the daughter of the wealthy retired industrialist (and war profiteer) remarks that, 'if you live in the country, you've got to know everybody or nobody.'[2] After five years in Padworth Aldington and Yorke had moved from the anonymity of the latter position to something resembling the former. The novel's events and characters are closely modelled, as David Wilkinson found, and Aldington tells us, on Padworth's inhabitants in the 1920s.[3] Aldington is savage in his portrayal of the hypocrisy, selfishness, prying and censoriousness of the middle classes. However, the victims of this society, generally young women, are the objects of his pity, and while the ne'er-do-wells are caricatured, his representation of working class life and characters is affectionate and sympathetic.

More surprisingly, both in the novel and in *Life for Life's Sake*, he is reasonably benign, although never sentimental, towards the gentry. This is chiefly because he saw them as dinosaurs and less pernicious than their successors, the capitalists, the commercialists and the war profiteers. The squire, and owner of the Padworth estate, Major Darby-Griffith (formerly of the Grenadier Guards), was in his late sixties, unmarried and the last of his line.[4] He was parsimonious, neglectful of the estate and a shrewd manipulator of the stock market, but Aldington found his eccentricity entertaining.[5]

Closer to hand, as Aldington's nearest neighbour, at Bridge House by the canal, was the larger-than-life Brigadier General Mills, an elderly retired career soldier of limited means (the 'colonel' of the novel's title).[6] The General's household consisted of his wife and daughter, then in her late thirties (and the model for Aldington's protagonist), and his older, unmarried brother. The brigadier had come to the village at the end of the war, buying Bridge House and its grounds, which included the malthouse (leased to the brewery) and its cottage; he was thus Aldington's landlord. David Wilkinson's interviews with three former maids at Bridge House, the Roberts sisters, established that Yorke and Aldington were frequent dinner-guests and that the two sets of neighbours 'got on very well together.' In *Life for Life's Sake* Aldington refers to him as 'my old friend, General Mills'.[7] To judge from the novel, conversation would chiefly have consisted of the brigadier's tales of his experiences in India and in the Boer War, although he had re-enlisted in 1914, serving on Fourth Army staff throughout the war. Since *Who Was Who* lists his interests as racing, shooting, hunting, fishing, polo and pig-sticking, there can have been little meeting of minds, although for the seventy-year-old impoverished brigadier such entertainments — except perhaps the fishing — were only faded memories.

There were plenty of reminders of the war in the village. Most of the younger men had served, many of them in the service battalions of the Royal Berkshire Regiment, and there were several with wounds to show for it. A memorial to commemorate those who had died was unveiled on 4 August 1926 and we can guess that Aldington and Yorke attended the ceremony.[8] This memorial, outside the church on Padworth Common, would prompt his 1930 story, 'The Lads of the Village'.[9] Another prominent figure in village life, Major Draper-Strange, the owner of Strange's, the family brewery, had served in the Berkshire Yeomanry and been awarded a D.S.O., while his cousin the artist was also a veteran, although of the Army Service Corps, a body for which Aldington, as an ex-infantryman, had little respect.

The chief pleasure of Aldington's life at Padworth was still its rural surroundings, and with Yorke or with one of his visitors he walked the countryside for miles around. The Roberts sisters recalled, 'They [Aldington and Yorke] were marvellous. They were always out walking together. We'd see them constantly.' The rural beauty of Padworth is evoked with a light touch in several passages of *The Colonel's Daughter*:

> The horizon . . . was a mass of broken drifting clouds, superb vapour effigies of a ruined Troy collapsing in fire. Starlings waddled greedily over the cropped green meadow-grass, and a young cart-horse colt with absurdly

hairy fetlocks gambolled heavily before the fatuous maternal gaze of an adipose mare. The sallow blossoms had lost their bright pollen, like little gold women past their prime; but there were young green leaves dipping and shaking in every copse. Only the great cautious oaks and black-budded ashes still withheld their leaves from the peril of late frosts. And oh! Those bird voices singing under the wide cupola of the sky! Lovely shrill notes, so pure, so clear–blackbird singing against blackbird and thrush against thrush, heedless of the hungry generation to be hatched and laboured for. The lovely northern spring, which is so cool, so rain-drenched, so virginal, so unlike the sudden sensual warmth of a southern April where all the songbirds have been killed. . . . [10]

This is spring; but the winter of 1925/1926 was a severe one. In January the snow lay so deeply that all communications were cut off and the school closed. David Wilkinson tells us that 'life in the village and surrounding countryside was paralysed by the bad weather.' When the snow thawed the river flooded; miraculously, Malthouse Cottage was not affected, although the river was only a few hundred yards to its rear and the canal feet away from its front; but with the meadows awash, walks were severely limited. Small wonder that at Easter Aldington and Yorke took themselves off for a short visit to Italy, on what in *Life for Life's Sake* he describes as 'a carefully planned tour of Tuscan and Umbrian hill towns.'[11] Lawrence and Frieda were now living in Italy but at this time they were on the Italian Riviera at Spotorno, south-west of Genoa.

Shortly after Aldington's return normal proceedings were again disrupted, not this time by the elements but by the ten-day General Strike of May 1926. Both his accounts of his actions during the strike, that in his memoirs and the fictionalised one in *All Men Are Enemies*, betray his later embarrassment. On receiving a telegram from *The Times* asking him to help ensure that the paper was distributed, he immediately hitch-hiked to London; his job involved loading bundles of the paper into private cars, helping to protect the cars as they left the *Times* offices and wrapping up copies for mailing to subscribers. 'I suppose I ought really to have been on the other side', he admits in *Life for Life's Sake*, 'for I had no particular liking for Mr Baldwin and his friends or what they represented.' 'On the other hand', he continues, 'a dictatorship of wooden-headed trade union leaders seemed no great happiness; while contact with Labour-minded intellectuals [among them, of course, Frank Flint] had made them positively distasteful to me.' Rather weakly he concludes: 'I suppose my real motive was dislike of inactivity in a crisis, and as I couldn't get on with my own job the best thing to do was to take on somebody else's.'[12]

The protagonist of *All Men Are Enemies* is more conscious of the inappropriateness of his actions: 'Another bloody war, and on the wrong side.' When his 'patriotic' wife urges him to volunteer, Anthony Clarendon tells her that he 'has had enough of helping Governments in crises', and when he does volunteer, it is to give reluctant support to his young brother-in-law who works on *The Times*. During the course of events he saves his former friend, the socialist Robin Fletcher, from being arrested. Nevertheless, he is not on the side of the workers either; his individualism is threatened by the strike: 'This strike has reminded me unpleasantly of how utterly helpless one is – how at the mercy of the social machine . . . it was . . . becoming more and more difficult to prevent other people from interfering with your life on some more or less crass pretext, and thus making it impossible; which perhaps explained why so many people of all sorts of nations wanted to live out of their own country.'[13]

Lawrence could have told Aldington this a long time ago. By 1926, however, Aldington had tied himself into institutions from which he could not afford to cut loose. This was not simply because they were his livelihood, but because, somewhere along the line since 1919, his goal had changed (as his letter to Hughes of 26 November 1925 shows): the wish to become an influential critic and an authority on French literature had replaced his desire to be an artist. He had written nothing since *A Fool i' the Forest*. This may partly have been a consequence of its luke-warm reception, but the writing of the poem had also opened the flood-gates to feelings that he had subsequently been trying to dam up.[14] At the end of the poem, the narrator cries:

> Need I fall so low as this?
> Need I prison up my spirit
> In so meek and regular a cage?

He was unable, or unwilling, to acknowledge that this was what he had come to. His correspondence of this period with Read, Monro, Pound, Dobrée, Hughes and others focuses almost entirely on the subject of the Routledge translations series and the Republic of Letters monographs: persuading his friends to take on projects, asking them to suggest suitable texts and other authors and translators, telling them about his thinking and plans for the two imprints. There is very little humour in these letters – and not a great deal of interest in the lives and affairs of his correspondents. The letters closely resemble those he had written from Belgium in the months following the Armistice when his emotional state was fragile and plans for an earlier translations series consumed all his thoughts.

He was as busy as ever with his own translations; he produced four in this period.[15] Allen and Unwin also published his *French Studies and Reviews*, a companion volume to his 1924 *Literary Studies and Reviews*, consisting this time entirely of articles that had previously appeared in the *TLS,* apart from his 'Francois Villon', which came from *The Criterion*. The book was published simultaneously in New York by Schofield Thayer's *Dial* Press. He was getting noticed by those whose esteem he craved. His *Voltaire* had prompted a personal letter of admiration from Edmund Gosse himself and Aldington was delighted with Arthur Waugh's review of the monograph in the *Daily Telegraph*.[16] A further boost to his self-esteem came in April, shortly after his return from Italy, when J.C.Squire, editor since 1919 of the right-wing *London Mercury,* brought Crosby Gaige to visit him at Padworth.[17] Gaige was a wealthy American theatre producer and director with the expensive hobby of book-collecting, and he wanted first editions of Aldington's work. He was also in the process of setting up a private publishing company to print fine quality limited editions of unpublished work by major authors; Aldington, of course, had nothing new to offer him.[18] By the end of the year, however, he would have a proposal for Gaige.

It may not be chance that there is no extant correspondence with Flint from this period onwards: both men were submerged in their own pursuits, although they did meet in town at lunches with Read, Dobrée and others. Aldington had lost his faith in Flint, as critic if not translator – and Flint must have known it. Aldington told Read in January 1926 that Flint had taken 'a rather lofty attitude' and demanded a different Routledge contract from anyone else's on the grounds that Squire had called him 'a Harley Street specialist in French translation'. He considered this as evidence of Flint's 'inferiority complex'.[19]

Between March and June 1926 there was no correspondence between Aldington and Read either, although this can be explained by the fact that Aldington was in Italy in early April while Read departed on a trip to Spain on museum business in late April, not returning until the end of May. Aldington had favourably reviewed Read's first book of criticism, *Reason and Romanticism* (one of the first publications by the new Faber and Gwyer), in the *TLS* in February, but by July he was writing to Dobrée: 'What a dreary old stick Herbert is becoming! The pater familias of criticism, the pedagogue of poetry, switching the buttocks of poets with a ferula of relativity.'[20] While these comments spring from his passionate belief, which he had already debated with Read at length, that, 'Literature, like human life, is far too varied and curious to be imprisoned by any but the widest and most general formulas,' they also suggest that pressures of over-work and professional jealousies were beginning to isolate him again. He would tell the novelist James Hanley in 1929: 'Men like ourselves are always lonely in every walk of life. The only hope is to find a few congenial spirits.'[21] At various points over the years he had found such spirits, first Pound and Flint, then Eliot, then Read, but, one by one, they had failed him.

He was no happier with *The Criterion*, published now by Faber and Gwyer as *The New Criterion*.[22] Although he had been impressed with the first issue in January, he told Dobrée in April: 'I feel confoundedly restive about The Criterion. Positively, it is a mere hodge-podge of conflicting views and personalities, in no way greatly superior to other quarterlies; negatively, it diffuses an odour of pretentiousness, pedantry and bad temper. I don't like it, I feel uneasy about it, I feel as if it committed me to what, in Gibbon's phrase, "I sincerely deprecate." '[23] James King, Read's biographer, suggests that this 'unease' was widespread among the *Criterion* circle and explains the reason for it: partially freed from the tastes of Lady Rothermere, Eliot began to allow political, theological and non-literary matters to dominate. More importantly, as far as Aldington was concerned, Eliot's severely classical critical standpoint, favouring literature which displayed 'a more severe and serene control of the emotions by Reason', was less and less contested.[24] Aldington was tempted to withdraw yet again from the *Criterion* circle, but was aware that it gave him his only literary contacts.

His irritability was jeopardising his livelihood too: in July he submitted a scathing review of Hugh Walpole's *Reading: An Essay* to *The Nation*. (His subsequent account of the affair to Read was that he had written 'a nice slap-dash attack on a miserable journalist-novelist who published a soi-disant book of essays of a contemptible kind'.)[25] Walpole was an important establishment figure and the journal's editor, Hubert Henderson, refused to print the review, calling it 'a personal attack'. While Leonard Woolf, the literary editor, had not supported this action and tried to achieve a reconciliation with Aldington, it was December before he received another book to review for *The Nation*.[26] Interestingly, when it did come, he told Read loftily that he would be returning it because he did not have the time and felt contempt for the book itself; it would be 26 February 1927 before he had a review appear in *The Nation* again and by the autumn of that year he would have parted company with the journal.

By the beginning of August he was telling Read: 'I am very, very tired, more tired than I have ever been in my life and wondering if I am going to collapse. In fact, I feel damned ill. We have arranged to go to Italy on the 25th and the space of three weeks which must elapse seems like a vast desert. However, I have got to turn out some articles before I go, so there we are.'[27]

What happened only two days later rescued him from what could well have become another nervous breakdown. On 6 August the Lawrences came to visit. After leaving England at the end of 1919, the couple had spent two years in Italy and Sicily. At the end of 1921 they had moved on to Ceylon and thence to Australia, but from 1922 until September 1925 they had lived in New Mexico and in Mexico. In the long term Lawrence's health was worsening and his tuberculosis had finally been diagnosed, but he had periods of intermission. He had made one brief visit to England from late 1923 to early 1924, but Aldington and Yorke had been in Italy then. In September 1925 the Lawrences had left America for Europe, probably aware that, because of his health, they would not be able to return to their ranch in New Mexico. They settled in Italy, first in Spotorno and then on the top floor of an old villa at Scandicci, about eight miles south-west of Florence. In August and September 1926 they visited England once more.

The Lawrences had always felt affection for Yorke and the two couples enjoyed their long weekend together. In *Life for Life's Sake* Aldington recalls being spell-bound by Lawrence's tales of his travels: 'Lawrence had the remarkable gift – in his writing and especially in his talk – of evoking his experiences so vividly and accurately that his listeners felt as if they had been present themselves, with the supreme advantage of being gifted with Lawrence's unique perceptions.' They went out walking together and Aldington was struck by the other man's capacity to respond to natural beauty: 'No man I have ever known had that awareness of nature which was one of Lawrence's gifts.' He read his friend's recent work and realised that he had previously under-rated him. It was on this visit, and Aldington's subsequent visit to the Villa Mirenda, that he formed an opinion of Lawrence from which he would never depart: 'Of all human beings I have known he was by far the most continuously and vividly alive and receptive.'[28] He would shortly begin the first of his critical accounts of Lawrence's work, a pamphlet for Glenn Hughes.[29]

On 25 August Aldington and Yorke set off for their planned holiday, and included in their itinerary a five-day visit to the Lawrences, who returned to the Villa Mirenda in late September.[30] Telling Read about their holiday, Aldington remarked: 'We saw a good deal of Lawrence in Italy – cantankerous and amusing as ever. He is hideously narrow-minded and too self-centred. But I like him very much. He is someone.'[31] Clearly, close acquaintance with Lawrence had reminded him of the latter's more irritating traits. (He would write in his 1950 biography of Lawrence, 'He needed cool handling and not too close an intimacy.')[32] However, his essential view never changed.

The revival of the acquaintance had, moreover, forced him to recognise the contrast between his own 'parasitic and unadventurous life . . . with one leg chained to a library and the other to the London literary press' and Lawrence's physical and artistic freedom. He saw that, in part, the difference was a result of their backgrounds: 'A bourgeois strain prevents me from taking drastic steps until and unless I have good reason for supposing the new adventure will succeed', he wrote in his memoir; but he went on to acknowledge that he 'had so energetically dug [himself] into the "literary" world"' that it was going to be 'astonishingly difficult' to dig himself out again.[33] An unpublished poem, entitled 'To D.H. Lawrence', and which must have been written at this time, includes the lines:

> I came back to England
> Filled with an ecstasy
> Creative,
> As if I had risen from the dead.
> My vital processes were running at top speed
> Like a good motor on a smooth road,
> I felt that at any moment
> I might say or do something interesting,
> Something with an enormous life-value
> For me at least.
> I was ready to sell my library
> And start on any adventure.
>
> And ever since I returned,
> The machine has been running down,
> Slackening down,
> In spite of my desperate efforts.

He puts the blame on others, on their 'gentle unexpressed disapproval':

> I can't see into people's minds
> As you are able to see.
> All I know is that I gradually become alive
> When I go away from them,
> And rapidly go dead again
> When I come back to them.[34]

In November 1926 he was warning Read that the latter's museum work and review writing would wear him out, but went on to say: 'I want to see you very much but how to do it? I have just reduced myself to a state of imbecility by writing a lecture on Remy de Gourmont which I must deliver at Newcastle on the 6th . . . I go direct from here to Newcastle, then I have promised to go direct to the south coast to see my mother who wants my help in her business affairs. Then I must scurry back here and slap off some wolf-scarers, and on the 21st I go to Devonshire [for Christmas with the Whithams].'[35] The Newcastle Literary Society paid him fifteen guineas for his lecture and he was able to deliver it again to the Cambridge University Heretics Society the following spring, but he was certainly not slowing his pace.

When the American publisher Pascal Covici approached him about bringing out a new edition of *The Love of Myrrhine and Konallis, and Other Prose Poems*, which had only so far appeared in the small Clark's Press edition, he was delighted, but asked if Covici might also be interested in publishing a two-volume anthology of Gourmont's output. Covici accepted the proposal, thus giving Aldington another weighty translation task for the months ahead. En route from Newcastle to Dover in December he met up with Crosby Gaige in London and out of that meeting came another translation project: having no original work to offer Gaige, he suggested a collection of mediaeval and Renaissance French and Italian lyric poems, with translations and introductory comments. Thus began Aldington's second (but not last) collaboration with a private printer.[36] He also undertook to translate Julian Benda's *La Trahison des Clercs* for Gaige's press and to produce another chapbook for Hughes, this time on Gourmont.[37]

He earned £500 in 1926, but by the end of the following year his income was nearly £700, chiefly because of his publishing projects with Covici, Gaige and Routledge. Yet none of the work was original and he was no nearer extricating himself from his routine and demanding life-style; he wanted not merely the income, but the status, that both translation and reviewing gave him, although his recent encounter with Lawrence had left him wondering if such status was worth the effort and, indeed, if it was simply an illusion. Lawrence displayed the perspicacity which was his marked characteristic, when he wrote to Aldington in May 1927 on receiving a copy of the Hughes chapbook, and asked him:

> Why do you write on the one hand as if you were my grandmother – about sixty years older than me, and forced rather to apologise for the *enfant terrible* in the family? Why will you be so old and responsible? . . . And on the other hand why do you write as if you were on hot bricks? Is the game worth the candle? Make up your mind. I mean the whole game of life and literature. . . . You don't believe it's worth it. . . . Well then, don't worry any more. Be good and commercial. But don't, don't feel yourself one of the pillars of society. My dear chap, where did you get all this conscience of yours? You haven't got it, really. . . . I never knew a man who seemed more to me to be living from a character not his own, than you. What is it that you are afraid of? – ultimately? – is it death? Or pain? Or just fear of the negative infinite of all things? What ails thee lad?'[38]

A great deal 'ailed' him. Repeating the pattern of his past, his response to feeling unable to take control of his life was to start an affair. Across the other side of the Kennet and Avon Canal, within view of Malthouse Cottage lay a six-acre chicken farm and the timber bungalow inhabited by its owners, Athol and Jessie Capper. Capper was a year younger than Aldington; he had served in the 1ˢᵗ Battalion of the East Kent Regiment in the war and been badly wounded; a shell splinter had rendered him partially blind. On returning home he had set up his chicken farm and in 1925 married Jessie Brodie, who was two years older. Their son, John, was born in October 1926. Around this time Jessie Capper and Yorke struck up a conversation on a bus journey; the outcome was that the Cappers were invited for a meal at Malthouse Cottage and a friendship between the two couples developed. What happened subsequently is dramatically fictionalised in the *roman à clef* Jessie Capper published in 1932 under the pseudonym Jennifer Courtenay. Its title, *Several Faces*, alludes to the male character's conduct during the affair and is drawn from Lawrence's poem, 'The End':

> And oh, that you had never, never been
> Some of your selves, my love, that some
> Of your several faces I had never seen!

If there is any doubt about the fidelity of the account, we can find confirmation in Walter and Lilian Lowenfels' unpublished 1964 interview with Yorke and in the correspondence which passed between Havelock Ellis and both Capper and H.D. in the early 1930s and between Capper and H.D. in 1937.[39] In any case we can recognise our characters straightaway. Valentine Somerville [Yorke] walks 'with tiny brisk steps as if her feet had never known anything but pavements and high-heeled shoes', yet she and her husband walk long distances and 'know their Berkshire intimately.' She is blonde, but we are familiar with that hairstyle, 'clipped like a mediaeval page's', and the 'nearly imperceptibly slanted' dark eyebrows. Barbara Buxton, the protagonist, admires Valentine's dressmaking and culinary skills and observes how efficiently she does the washing and the ironing, acts as her husband's secretary and still finds time to read. Altogether, the Yorke character comes out of the story very well, is ignorant of the affair until it is over, and then very sympathetic towards her friend. Anthony Somerville looks 'the typical Englishman . . . tall, broad, blue-eyed and fair-skinned'; he resembles a footballer or a boxer, except that there is a 'curious conflict between the heavy jaw and fine forehead, and between the brooding expression of his eyes and the satiric twist of his eyebrows, as pointed as were his faun's ears.' His dislikes include 'suburbs, "sport", public schools, English novelists (except D.H. Lawrence and George Moore) and tea-table gossip about servants and babies, and parsons, and the cult of Sir James Barrie in general and of Peter Pan in particular . . . and the Gilbert and Sullivan craze, and "white men", and jazz and Americanisms, and the Oxford accent, and the smugness of "Punch" and the English breakfast, and Kipling.'[40]

Barbara is quick to spot 'the manifest pleasure' the couple take in each other, even after seven years of marriage. Nevertheless, Anthony soon starts a passionate affair with Barbara, making love to her on a walk in the woods and taking advantage of an occasion when Valentine is visiting her mother in London.[41] Although in her mid-thirties, Barbara has never experienced such skilful love-making or known a man so sophisticated, and she falls in love. She is anxious about hurting Valentine for whom she cares, but Anthony tells her: 'I loved a woman once, before I knew Valentine – not just a passing affair – she filled every channel of my being. When we parted, I thought I should die. Something did die in me. I can never give that love to anyone again. I don't give it to Valentine. She doesn't know, she must never know. . . . Valentine does not fill the whole of my life. She is my dear friend and companion and lover, but – do you understand?' While this sounds like the calculated speech of an adept seducer, we can, nevertheless, recognise its veracity. He also reassures Barbara that, 'Valentine and I respect each other's freedom! The cardinal sin in love is not infidelity, but jealousy.'[42] A persuasive argument, which we have heard before, and which by now we might have hoped the speaker would have learned to distrust.

Anthony ends the affair almost immediately, telling Barbara that he has realised that, 'after many years of perfect happiness with one woman, [he] could have nothing but friendship to give to another.' He insists that it is not an issue of morality, as he 'accept[s] no conventional standards', but that the relationship is not making him happy. The reader is left with the distinct impression that he has decided that the rewards of this affair do not warrant the risks. Five months later, however, he picks up the relationship again, suggesting that they have 'just a modern pagan affair'. Barbara, desperately in love, will accept any form of relationship. He tells her that, 'Love is an art with a technique to be mastered like any other art.'[43] She is disturbed when friends of Somerville, a playwright and his French wife (who bear a marked resemblance to the Gribbles), come to stay at the inn for two weeks and she realises that there is – at the least – a flirtation going on between 'Louise Oldershaw' and Somerville.

At the end of March 1927, his fifty poems for Gaige translated and dispatched, Aldington made his first bid for freedom. He and Yorke rented a tiny apartment on the east side of the Jardin du Luxembourg in Paris. In 1912 he had stayed on the west side, on the border of Montparnasse, but with the post-war influx of young expatriate English and American intellectuals and artists, this area was now prohibitively expensive. The humble little cafés he remembered had 'monstrously expanded' and multiplied, so that 'in one place and in one moment of time were gathered together nearly as many specimens of the genus would-be artist as all Europe had produced of the genuine article since the fall of Troy'.[44] Nevertheless, Paris also offered the 'genuine article', along with a vitality and tolerance of artistic innovation that was less prevalent in post-war London. And it was *French* art and literature in which Aldington was primarily interested.

He and Yorke probably visited Natalie Barney's Friday evening salon in the Rue Jacob, since Barney and Pound had been close friends. Certainly, back in Paris a year later, Aldington persuaded Barney to give Covici first refusal of three books she had in manuscript.[45] He also introduced himself to Jean Paulhan, the editor

Jessie Capper and son, 1930

of *La Nouvelle Revue Francaise* and called in at Sylvia Beach's and Adrienne Monnier's bookshops in the Rue de l'Odéon. He and Yorke enjoyed the theatre and the café life and meeting up again with George Gribble, but Aldington was still bound to his work for the *TLS* and the translation of Gourmont, and he and Yorke were back in England by May. He also had an appointment to meet the American publisher

George Doran in London. Keen to 'get back to poetry', as he informed Gaige, he wanted the U.S. copyright of all his poems gathered together in a 'Collected Poems' edition and had asked Gaige to suggest a publisher. Unfortunately, Doran was not willing to offer satisfactory terms and Aldington found the encounter humiliating.[46]

Paris – and Lawrence – had made him restless, but in the Gourmont project he had taken on a major task. He declined an invitation from Randall who, since the end of 1925, had been living in Rome as ambassador to the Holy See, regretting that he couldn't afford the time to visit him because of his 'big translating job for America.'[47] By September he would tell Dobrée, who had taken up the chair of English Literature at the University of Cairo: 'I think I have only been once in London this past two months and then accomplished a superhuman round of calls on publishers and editors. . . . I have been hammering away here like a frantic gnome on my typewriter, producing enormous masses of translation for an American who promises dollars in relative abundance.'[48]

The strains of work, and, presumably, of managing his affair with Capper without Yorke knowing, began to tell. In August he told Pound, 'I have withdrawn from the Criterion on what I consider excellent grounds, i.e. that T.S.E. is employing that ghetto guttersnipe Cournos. I have told Tom that I won't appear in the same periodical with said C.'[49] Aldington and Cournos had never repaired their friendship but the level of venom it had now reached was motivated by Cournos's publication of his *roman à clef*, *Miranda Masters*. Miranda is H.D. and the events of 1916 to 1918, Cournos's failed relationship with H.D., and Aldington's 'theft' of Yorke, form the plot of the novel. Cournos is more savage in his treatment of H.D. than of her husband and much of what she wrote to him from Corfe Castle is reproduced verbatim. It was this 'betrayal' of H.D. that so enraged Aldington.

However, the timing of his withdrawal from *The Criterion* is puzzling.[50] Cournos's novel had appeared in 1926 and his contributions to *The Criterion* – on Russian periodicals and literature – had also started that year. Nevertheless, having chosen to make a stand, Aldington made it violently, as his comment to Pound indicates, and in such a way that he drove himself into a corner – unless this was, in fact, the pretext he had been craving for dissociating himself from the Eliot circle. Pound tried to dissuade him from his action. 'Your private lives are of no importance in the eyes of Athene,' he told him.[51]

The correspondence concerning the incident makes fascinating reading. He issued an ultimatum: either Cournos or himself. Eliot was not particularly keen to keep Cournos and would have gladly 'chucked' him to keep Aldington but, as Read pointed out (Eliot having consulted him on the matter), Aldington was 'in effect, compelling his friends to take up his personal quarrels.'[52] Eliot agreed: he could not 'honourably get rid of Cournos on this count.'[53] That Eliot should have consulted Read on the issue is perhaps understandable: he was a friend of them both; and Read's advice to 'attempt to reason with Richard' seems appropriate. What is staggering is the extent to which Read has become disillusioned with

Aldington: 'You might think it worthwhile to sacrifice your editorial probity for the sake of Richard's friendship. But I should think twice about the value of that friendship. People like Richard work themselves up into a passion and in that state their professions of friendship are of the same value as their resentments.'

Read's letter also suggests a reason for the absence of any correspondence between Aldington and Flint between 1926 and 1929. Acknowledging Cournos's betrayal of loyalty, Read continues: 'Richard himself has on a smaller scale done the same thing by making criticisms of Frank which were based, not on his work, but on his knowledge of his personality. Although the occasion was a smaller one, the intimacy that has subsisted between Frank and Richard makes the indiscretion almost equal to the Cournos affair. It took Frank a long time to get over it.'

Whether Aldington's conduct was unreasonable or calculated, it is hard for us to feel sympathy. Nevertheless, we receive the uncomfortable impression that he is not the only one feeling resentment. Seeking Read's counsel on Aldington's final letter on the matter, Eliot wrote on 30 August: 'I don't propose to acquaint anyone else of this affair, but if you would agree I should like to expose the whole business to Flint and get his advice also. It has really worried me very much.'[54] While Eliot's concern is clearly genuine, we might feel that any involvement of Flint was probably going to aggravate matters.

But Eliot had already aggravated matters: his attempt to 'reason with Richard', although kindly meant, must have seemed patronising. In his letter to Aldington he explained why he felt unable to comply with the latter's demands, but tried to shift the ground by suggesting that his friend would feel much happier if he and Yorke came out of their retirement in Berkshire and spent a winter in London. He clearly interpreted Aldington's wariness of London as arising from the fact that he and Yorke were not married, and told him: 'George Eliot was no better off and yet George Eliot lived in London and enjoyed the respect and friendship of the society she wanted.' He stressed that all Aldington's friends desired to see more of him and that his own advice was offered out of 'genuine solicitude and affection.'[55] Eliot reported to Read:

> I have urged him to come to London for six months. His position is not in the least unique, and anyway nobody is the least interested except his private friends who know that Richard would like to have children and can[']t. He would find that all the people whom he wanted to see would receive him and Dorothy. My own social circle has been considerably restricted in the last year or two, but I would guarantee him the Woolfs and the Morrells, and the Fabers (who are highly respectable) if he liked.
>
> I feel in general that this respectability obsession has spoilt his work: has ruined his verse, and has made him run to these tedious adacemic[*sic*] scholarly essays and editing. But (except for the children part of it) it is all a delusion; and, apart from that (and I really don[']t know how much that counts with him) there are plenty of people suffering from much more *real* torments than his own.[56]

There is a great deal to untangle in this letter. It is the only mention, anywhere in this period, either that Aldington would have liked to have children or that he and Yorke were unable to do so. Yet it is clearly an allusion to a private conversation or conversations that at some point he must have had with Eliot, and probably with Read too. Eliot would have been unlikely to share this information with Read if it had not been common knowledge amongst Aldington's 'private friends'. If we assume that he would have liked to have children, we are prompted to ask why he could not; it seems unlikely that straitened material circumstances would have been the only impediment. Since Aldington had already fathered a child, the problem may have been Yorke's infertility. In *Bid Me To Live* 'Bella' tells 'Julia' that she 'had been slashed about by unauthorised abortionists' in Paris, but in her interview with the Lowenfels in 1964 Yorke expressed anger at the insinuation that she had ever had an abortion, which assertion she deemed libellous. Nevertheless, this does not preclude the possibility that she was infertile and we know that she never did have a child. In *Bid Me To Live*, 'Rafe' tells Julia that Bella wants to have his child.[57]

Other than on the basis of Eliot's comment to Read, there is no reason for us to assume that parenthood was the desire of either Aldington or Yorke. However, if either partner *did* want a child and they were unable to have one, this would have put a strain on the relationship and might offer some explanation for Aldington's sexual restlessness. However, there is another dimension to this issue of parenthood and this is linked to Eliot's reference to Aldington's 'respectability obsession'. Eliot confuses two kinds of 'respectability'. We are likely to agree with his verdict on the damage Aldington had done to himself as an artist by his desperate need to achieve *academic* respectability. *Social* respectability is another matter. How important was this to him? Certainly he and Yorke had pretended to legal marital status in Padworth; but a village in southern England was not the same social environment as an artistic and intellectual circle in London, even, as Eliot pointed out, in Victorian times. We cannot think that this would have been an issue to keep him away from London, if London was where he wanted to be.

However, Aldington may have felt that in the social climate of the day it was not fair to bring an illegitimate child into the world. (He had not seen this as a concern in his battle with H.D. over the registration of Perdita's identity in 1919, but he had then been in a highly fragile state.) Why, during the eight years since he and H.D. had separated, had he not sought a divorce in order to marry Yorke? There were several powerful reasons and a lack of commitment to Yorke may not have been amongst them. Anthony Somerville's account to Barbara in *Several Faces* of the woman he had loved and lost suggests how strongly linked to H.D. Aldington still felt; he may have dreaded the thought of formalising their separation. In any case, divorce proceedings would have been painful for them both and he knew this; protecting H.D. always had been, and always would be, important to him (despite Bryher's poor opinion of him). Furthermore, as both H.D. and Bryher feared, divorce proceedings, brought by either of them and whether on the grounds of adultery or desertion (the only two grounds the law allowed), would have provoked sensational publicity and raised questions about Perdita's paternity and even perhaps the relationship between Bryher and H.D.

Eliot's kindly-meant comments had simplified the problems. In his letter of 30 August he conceded to Read that his 'exhortations' might have been 'tactless', but he had lost patience. He told Read, 'The man is full of false pride'. Given that Vivien Eliot had been in and out of sanatoriums for the last few months, we might sympathise with him and understand why he had commented that, 'there are plenty of people suffering from much more *real* torments than his own'. We may feel less understanding towards Read, who remarked that the affair only showed 'what a mess these people make of life when their only basis is an emotional one.' He did add that 'Richard might well say: "Wait until you yourself are up against such a situation"', but concluded, 'I honestly don't think I should act in such a fashion.' We might wonder whether he recalled this comment five years later when he himself was prompted to act from his heart and sought Aldington's advice.[58]

By October, however, Aldington's correspondence with both Eliot and Read was relaxed and friendly again and Eliot even dared to come up with a suggestion that Aldington might like to give a course of lectures on English Literature at the University of Madrid, an offer he turned down. Even Eliot's rejection of the Gourmont translations for Faber did not cause conflict between them. Meanwhile, a figure from Aldington's past made a welcome re-entry into his life: Henry Slonimsky came on a visit to Europe.[59] He entertained Aldington and Yorke in London and visited the couple in Padworth, staying at the Fox and Hounds. By the end of 1927, however, although his relationships with his colleagues were calmer, Aldington was still no nearer solving his problems as an artist and was losing control of his personal life.

19. The Walls Fall Down: 1928

I missed most of my twenties, when most people have a lot of fun. . . . [T]here was a repressed young man under my sedate exterior clamouring to be heard. I let him be heard. And why not?   (Richard Aldington, *Life for Life's Sake*, 1941)[1]

On 17 September 1927 Aldington's 'old friend' and landlord, Brigadier General Mills, died. The imminent sale of the Bridge House estate now pushed Aldington towards resolving the problem he had been debating for some time. Was he to move to Paris? In *Life for Life's Sake* he tells us: '[I]t seemed to me that I had completely recovered from the effects of temporary heroism at the front and that retirement was no longer indicated as the proper treatment.'[2] Whether he was also contemplating other changes in his domestic circumstances we cannot be sure. He told Hughes in March: 'I don't feel like buying the cottage; first because I haven't got the money; second, neither Dorothy nor I want to own property; third, it is in a damnable state of repair.'[3] In the event, he was able to postpone his decision as his lease on Malthouse Cottage was extended for another year.

His first step was to try Eliot's solution. After their second Christmas at Combe Martin with the Whithams, he and Yorke spent most of January in London, at a borrowed flat at 3, Mecklenburgh Square. (We may wonder how helpful it was for the couple to return to a spot so fraught with memories.) He told Pound: 'It is amusing to be in London again, but with people dropping in, and oneself going out, and concerts to hear, and pictures to see, work goes by the board.'[4] He enjoyed seeing Monro, who, he felt, seemed happier than for a long time, but Read was out of town the whole month, attending to the new home he was having built in Buckinghamshire.[5] Nevertheless, the experience confirmed him in his conviction that London was not for him and he was irritated by the assumption amongst the *Criterion* circle that in returning 'belatedly but repentantly to the one true source of wisdom, knowledge and fame; viz., themselves', he 'had at last recovered [his] senses.'[6] He consulted Pound, who was unhelpful: 'Damnd [*sic*] if I know whether to urge you, violently, to GET OFF THE DAMNED ISLAND for at least six months, or whether such deracination wd. utterly wreck you and make you forever after incapable of earning a living on it.'[7] He did add: 'Put the question: If England cease to exist?' and asserted a week later: 'It seems to me I lengthened my life by ten years when I went to Paris, and that I added another ten moving here [Rapallo].'[8]

Aldington seems to have repaired his friendship with Flint while in London, as he spent some time trying to obtain a publisher for his friend's unpublished and uncollected work, telling Samuel Putnam, the American critic and translator, who had recently set up a publishing house in London, that Flint had 'never had half the recognition he deserves'.[9] Pound, whom Aldington approached for help, was discouraging: 'Frank don't appeal to scholarly snobbism, nor to the modern moderns. falls [*sic*] between two bales of hay.' He did promise to try Boni and Liveright, but Flint never would publish another collection.

Back at Padworth, Aldington made plans to spend three months in Paris. He asked Pound for introductions and was sent addresses for some of the 'decent people', who included painters and sculptors like Constantin Brancusi, Francis Picabia and Fernand Leger, and writers such as Louis Aragon, Jean Cocteau, Jean Giradoux, Philippe Soupault and Pierre Drieu La Rochelle. 'Do try to see some of the active spurits [*sic*],' Pound counselled him, 'Not that they are very effervescent or howeffer [*sic*] you spell it.'[10] Aldington had plenty of work to keep him going, principally the translation of Boccaccio's *Decameron*, which was his next commission from Covici; Samuel Putnam had agreed to publish it in England. There was also *La Trahison des Clercs* to complete and he was starting work on Gourmont's *Lettres á l'Amazone*, dedicated to Natalie Barney. His income, with royalties from Gaige, Covici and Routledge and continued work for the *TLS*, should suffice.[11]

From Combe Martin came Whitham's shocked response to the news: 'We were astonished and even a little alarmed to hear that you were on the eve of an elopement to Paris, for I thought the notion of such a change was only vague though alluring in your mind. Now what precisely do you mean to do? Leave England finally, as if you were going into exile? And if that is so, what of your present cottage, your books, your this, that and t' other, including your reviewing, lecturing and so on? . . . If you do leave this country we shall feel lonely and chilled.'[12] On 26 March, nevertheless, Aldington and Yorke left England. In Paris they first borrowed the apartment of Walter and Lilian Lowenfels, the young American poet and his wife whom they had met on their last visit, but then found one to rent at 17, Rue Vauquelin, again on the east side of the Jardin du Luxembourg.[13]

In Padworth the 'this, that and t' other' included Jessie Capper. In April she was overjoyed to receive an invitation to join Aldington and Yorke for a fortnight in Paris. In *Several Faces*, Barbara's visit is a disaster. Anthony is courteous but distant throughout her stay, finally losing his temper when she finds an opportunity to reproach him for his indifference: '[Y]our sort of temperament, your emotionalism, reminding me so forcibly of the woman I hate most in the world – my mother – upsets me and makes me wretched. . . . You are jealous of my freedom. . . . '[14] Again, there are features we recognise. It is interesting to note, however, 'Anthony's' equation of the behaviour of mistress and mother. Negative experiences, particularly where women were concerned, always led Aldington back to childhood and adolescence – and his mother. There had been some kind of rapprochement between them in the mid 1920s but, if Capper's novel is accurate, he seems by 1928 to have reverted to his more common feelings of contempt and resentment. Towards the end of the year they would have an outlet in his writing.

It is what happens next in the novel, however, that shocks both Barbara and the reader. When the Somervilles return to the village two months later, it is clear that all is not well between them. Anthony tells Barbara that he is passionately in love with someone else. He tells her his version of the events: '[Valentine] wrecked it, deliberately wrecked it in the name of her wonderful modern principles. Pretending all the time to be so broad-minded, she went to – the woman I love, before I myself had spoken a word of love to her or made any suggestions, and coldly, cold-bloodedly agreed that this woman and I should have an affair together, all with her (Valentine's) sanction and approval. Naturally, the other revolted from the idea. It was an insult, put like that.'[15]

Valentine, however, has a different story: 'You see, he wouldn't discuss it with me reasonably. He just laid down his challenge: "I love Yvonne Desseignet!" and I was to take it or leave it. He couldn't seem to see how I felt. He seemed to resent my being hurt. . . . He kept on saying that I was making an infernal fuss about nothing, he felt the same to me – but all the time he acted as if he resented my presence there at all.'[16] Valentine had spoken to the woman to ascertain her feelings in the matter and the woman had told her that she did not want Anthony, or any lover, because she loved her husband.

In Paris in the early summer of 1928 the woman with whom Aldington fell in love, his Yvonne Desseignet, was Valentine Dobrée, the wife of his friend Bonamy. The couple were in Paris on vacation from Dobrée's post at the University of Cairo. It is probably not chance that Capper chose to use the name Valentine in her novel, transferring it to the Yorke character to avoid the risk of libel. 'Valentine' (like 'Richard' in Aldington's case) was actually an assumed name. Its bearer was christened Gladys May Mary and she was the daughter of a baronet, Sir Augustus Alexander Brooke-Pechell. The Dobrées had married in 1913. Bonamy had been an officer in the Royal Field Artillery both before and during the war and had studied at Cambridge for an M.A. afterwards.

Valentine Dobrée was everything Aldington could admire in a woman: a year younger than himself, she was beautiful, aristocratic, self-assured and a talented painter who had turned her hand to writing. (Aldington told Putnam that June that she was 'a damned clever novelist', and he may himself have been responsible for placing her first novel with the American publisher Alfred Knopf, since Bonamy had sought his advice on the matter in early 1926.)[17] Furthermore, she had led a bohemian lifestyle in the early 1920s and the painter Mark Gertler had been her lover for a while: Aldington must have seen her as both sexually experienced and approachable. Describing her own feelings about Dobrée, who was a close friend from their days together at the Slade, Dora Carrington wrote to her lover Gerald Brennan in 1921: 'She has given so much of herself to the world, lived so fiercely it is splendid. Then I admire the ways she has no preconceived conception of how a woman and an artist should live. She is as worldy as she feels wordly. She is business-like and generous, gay and very melancholly [sic], uprincipalled [sic], and yet virtuous, and does not think it wrong to bake good cakes, and trim a hat with ribbons, and yet paints five hours a day, and will not be interrupted for all the men in the world.'[18]

Valentine Dobrée

The extent to which Aldington was infatuated can be discerned by a reading of *A Dream in the Luxembourg*, the long narrative poem which he wrote that early summer in Paris – and sent to Valentine. It concerns a dream that comes to the poet as he sits in the Luxembourg Gardens, a dream about the woman with whom he has fallen in love, 'a laughing tree-nymph, crisp-haired like the ilex'. He tells us that he had only spent four days in her company:

> And all that time my mind was in confusion,
> For there were many reasons why I should not love again
> And so many reasons why I should not love her.

He had fought against his feelings, 'trying to be "honourable"', but on the second day he had let himself 'taste the happiness of being near her':

> For a moment my eyes met hers, and for a moment
> I gazed into the loveliest of human minds.

The rest of the poem is devoted to the dream, in which she summons him from England to be with her in a small country house she has taken on the south coast of France. When he arrives, she tells him that she had sent the summons to three men, all of whom had sworn they loved her; now he has arrived, she telegraphs the other two not to come. We are given the realistic (and mundane) details of how he is shown to his room, dresses for dinner, dines with her and goes for a walk and then of how he goes to her room that night and they make love. The dream experience continues over days and weeks in which there are 'days of hard work' (the implication is that they are both writers) 'and merry playing', and nights when she reads to him 'in her clear voice' and in which they lie together 'In that mysterious communion of love.' The dream, of course, ends and the poet feels 'all the bitterness of the real':

> And I said to myself: 'She does not love me,
> It was only a dream, a fool's dream, a fool's paradise.

The poem includes familiar themes. One is the presentation of love as something sweet and transient, to be tasted when it is offered:

> Why cannot we be like the Epicureans
> Who thought not of possession but enjoyment?
> . . . All we have's today.

and:

> It is madness to mortgage the whole future
> Even in the delirium of love,
> Only in spans of a few months do we live
> And the lover of yesteryear is next year's friend.

and:

> How faint grow the memories of the old loves!
> But then how sweet, how sweet is the new love!

This *carpe diem* philosophy is linked directly to his war experience:

> How many yellow dead men have I seen?
> Carried how many stretchers?
> Stood by how many graves – of young men too?
> Reported how many casualties?

His lover, 'brave and frank and honest and herself', is clearly drawn. Whether portrayed as wood nymph, troubador's mistress or independent modern woman, she is the initiator of events; her lover, the poet, is rendered speechless at 'the tenderness in her gaze' and, except in going to her room on the first night of his stay, follows her bidding at all times. He sees her, in the dream narrative, waiting on the station platform for his arrival:

> So straight and trim in her neat spring dress
> With the brim of her hat just wide enough and curved enough
> To bring out the sweetness
> As well as the gaiety in her face.

He tells us:

> The only fine vivid characters are those like her

> Who are not the epitome of an education, a culture or a class
> But are keen enough and strong enough
> To work through prejudices and customs
> And to give themselves directly to life and those they love.

Charles Prentice of Chatto and Windus, reading the poem in 1929, found it 'a charming and unforced poem . . . agreeably light and fresh', and there are certainly passages of the dream sequence which display these qualities.[19] When the poem was published in 1930, however, the *TLS* reviewer found it 'self-conscious and self-pitying' and commented that 'it is lacking in the imaginative penetration which gives a new and universal meaning to personal sentiment and physical desire.'[20] Glenn Hughes's verdict was also that, although 'here and there a line flashes fire', many passages were 'dull prose', and 'the intensity of emotion which evidently inspired the poem is by no means communicated to the reader.'[21]

We are back with the problem behind 'Childhood' all those years ago: when self-pity or romantic passion motivate his writing, Aldington can lose the critical rigour that shapes the finest verse – particularly free verse, which can so easily slip into prose. As in 'Childhood', the best lines in *A Dream in the Luxembourg* are those in which 'compression and intensity' are evident, where an image is finely and aptly drawn. There are two recurring motifs, which, along with the dream narrative, give the poem its shape – and the only moments of intensity it achieves. One is the Luxembourg fountain, which is an image both of the way a poem springs up in the poet's mind and of his heart 'pouring out tenderness and devotion and desire'. The other is the making of 'a miraculous slender glass bowl' which is immediately filled with poison so that it collapses 'and crumble[s] to a little dust', a representation of the lover's hopes and their destruction. At the end of the poem, these two images are brought dramatically together:

> At that moment the tall white fountain jet
> Fell from its height, crumbled like dust of water;
> Like dust of water it fell to a faint bubbling.
> Light faded from the Luxembourg
> As a heavy cloud from the north engulfed the sun,
> And a chill breeze ran over me.
> The dream was broken, fallen into dust
> Like the white fountain, like a Venetian glass
> When the poison is poured in it.

After the four days spent at some point that early summer in the company of the Dobrées in Paris, Aldington, in the words of his own poem, 'lost the sense of the thin boundary/ Between what is and is not.' It is hard to tell how much encouragement he received from Valentine, but he and Yorke were invited to stay for a week with the Dobrées in London on their way home to Berkshire. They left Paris on 2 July. By the time they reached Malthouse Cottage on the 10th, the 'dream' had 'crumbled into dust'.

Alone at the cottage a few days later (Had Yorke sought temporary refuge with her mother?), Aldington wrote to Valentine: 'It will take a long, long time for me to stop loving you.' He had experienced for her, he claimed, 'the most wonderfully intense feelings of tenderness and devotion' he had ever felt. Resorting to the familiar Hellenic and troubadour models, he called her his wood nymph and his lady of Provence, and, using an image that would re-surface in his 1929 poem, *The Eaten Heart,* told her she had made him feel like Philoctetes grasping the hand of Neoptolemus.[22] 'There are many rooms and corridors of me,' he wrote, 'that no-one has entered, there are others which have been in solitude since H.D. left them. . . . It seemed as though you could fill those deserted rooms and corridors with your presence.' He told her that he had tried to write from Paris to decline the Dobrées' invitation, but that he had not been able to keep away: 'I was so eager to fit with your 'new republic', to accept any part you chose to allot, so that at last I was in your world, so that at least I had some communication with you.' In a further letter, written two days later, he asks, 'Is it possible to save anything, Valentine? Do you want to save anything?'

From these letters we can piece together what had occurred. Aldington writes: 'It was a mistake to say anything to Dorothy. Her intervention by letter to you was unpardonable. I am too easy and cherishing with women. If I had slapped her – but I couldn't.' He tells Valentine, 'I have been in solitude since Friday.' By the time he writes the second letter, 'a cool but nice letter from Bonamy' has arrived and a letter for Yorke in Valentine's hand.[23]

He was clearly unwilling to give up and tries to persuade her that this is about minds, not bodies: 'Even intellectually, this is the most important thing I have found since I 'got' Tom's [Eliot's] mind. Good God, can't I see and write to you as I do and did to Tom, Herbert, Frank, Pound, H.D., Lawrence, Bonamy, Harold and all of them? Can there not be free communication between us? Are you afraid I shall pester you with signs, supplications, protestations, scenes, despairs? Well, Paris should have proved to you that I can control very violent emotions.' He begs to be allowed to see her alone somewhere before the Dobrées return to Cairo, so that they can 'quite calmly talk' of 'where [they] stand'. He concludes, darkly: '[D]on't tell Dorothy . . . I shall not entrust anything to Dorothy again, so you will not be torpedoed from that side. If I can see you, I will among other things try to tell you how I am organising that relationship.'

Setbacks in Aldington's life, as we have seen, were prone to bring back what he calls in *A Dream in the Luxembourg* 'all the old unhappy things', prompting a bitterness and resentment that he found hard to control. Yorke was now placed in that category of women which included his mother, women who are possessive and 'purely instinctive' (the term he uses to describe her to Valentine Dobrée) – and therefore dangerous. In *Several Faces*, Barbara, faced with her friend Valentine's misery, confesses to her that she also loves Anthony (but not that she has had an affair with him) and then feels morally bound to admit to Anthony that she has done so. In a 'carefully indifferent voice' he tells her: 'May I give you a word of advice? I shouldn't trust Valentine if I were you. Personally, I don't intend ever to trust anyone, or give myself to anyone, any more.'[24] Yorke returned to Malthouse Cottage but there was now little trust on either side.

Meanwhile, there was a task to perform for Lawrence. In June *Lady Chatterley's Lover* was published in Florence by his bookseller friend Pino Orioli, and a thousand copies printed.[25] No official ban could be imposed in Britain, as it had not been published there, and there were very few reviews, but word of mouth sped fast and bookshops began to order copies. Jackson's Bookshop in London, who had ordered seventy copies, were horrified when they saw the book and wanted their copies removed immediately; other bookshops followed suit. Lawrence enlisted Aldington and another friend, Samuel Koteliansky ('Kot'), to retrieve these copies and store them.[26] The book was soon added to the list of pornographic publications to be seized by customs authorities should they be discovered, so Aldington, Kot and another friend of Lawrence's, Enid Hilton, soon became active in distributing it. British orders received by Orioli in Florence could be despatched from London or Padworth with less risk of detection.

Aldington was also in close correspondence with Pound concerning the overview of Imagism which they intended to give Glenn Hughes. Hughes had been awarded a Guggenheim Fellowship for the 1928-1929 academic year to enable him to visit Europe and write a book on the Imagists. Pound was, perhaps understandably, keen for his own role in the movement to be acknowledged: '[P]ore ole farver was heard of before the mouvemong. Without which bit of oil on the axle the wheel wouldn't have turned.' He was as scathing as ever about the 'second phase', what he called 'the dilutation': 'It passes the point of energy and becomes backwash.' Fletcher's contribution had been negligible: '[N]either he nor Lawrence ever got aboard save for the cakes'. The second of the three original rules ('[t]o use absolutely no word that did not contribute to the presentation') was what mattered. Nevertheless, he admitted that 'We probably purify our intentions in retrospect', and agreed that they must each submit their own versions of the history to Hughes. However, and probably perceptively, he felt that any account of the movement H.D. might provide would be 'nebulous', and suggested that it might be more productive for Hughes to send her a carbon copy of his account which she could annotate with her comments.[27]

Mention of H.D. prompted Aldington to confide in Pound a piece of information he had recently received: 'H.D. won't know me because (so I'm told) she thinks I want to harm her – Christ knows why, since I feel perfectly benevolent & wouldn't hurt her for anything.' 'Are you allowed to know her?' he asked.[28] Pound's reply was caustic: when she was in Paris, H.D. had been constantly 'chaperoned' by Bryher and he had not been allowed to see her alone. Aldington replied: 'I think it pretty goddam bloody that even you aren't allowed to see her. She seems cut off hopelessly from the old gang. . . . Try to rescue [her] if you can.'[29]

If we are to believe Capper's novel, there was now another development at Malthouse Cottage: 'In September Rachel Armitage the novelist spent a fortnight with them. She was about forty-five and rather startling in appearance with her brilliantly henna'd hair and her dusky circled eyes, but she had great charm of manner and immense vivacity which gave the effect of wit to her scintillating conversation.' Valentine tells Barbara that, 'Rachel looks like a whore, and some people think she lives like one, but she isn't at heart. She's had a hell of a life ever since she was twenty-two with a vile husband who drank and gambled and knocked her about. She stuck to him till her two sons were old enough to stand alone and then she left him. She hasn't a penny of her own and no relations. She earns a precarious living by writing an occasional novel, and persuades the lover of the moment to use his good influence with reviewers and publishers. Her boys adore her. All young men do. Anthony knew her years ago, when he was quite young.'[30]

The current reader will have had no difficulty in recognising Brigit Patmore. Even the 'novelist' part has some truth as Patmore had published her first novel in 1926.[31] In *Several Faces*, 'Rachel' is not merely visiting the cottage; she is sleeping with Anthony, and with Valentine's tacit consent. '[S]he was his first mistress when he was a boy of seventeen and she was twenty-six or twenty-seven – she has no illusions. And she's decent too, she wanted to help him to be sane again for my sake as well. She did seem to cure him, for all the time she was with us I felt Anthony loved me too, as he used to do. I was happy. Rachel didn't take him away, she gave him back to me. Now that she has gone I've lost him again. The silence, full of hate. . . .'[32]

Whether or not this bizarre arrangement did take place, Aldington and Patmore were certainly lovers at this time. Aldington told Pound in December that the relationship had been going on since July, which would suggest that it had been a rebound on his part from the Dobrée fiasco. However, there had been an exchange of letters between them as early as February 1925, which Patmore had reported to H.D., suggesting that 'it might not be a bad thing for me to see R. and perhaps find out about A. [Yorke] and so on.'[33] That spring, her husband being bankrupt, Patmore had taken a job as a programme-seller at Wyndham's Theatre and in the September she had left him, finding a flat for herself and her older son, Derek (her younger son, Michael, being away at school) at 4, Millman Street in Bloomsbury. She had also begun an affair with the young Stephen Haden-Guest, twenty years her junior, who had been engaged to her friend 'Oppy'.[34]

Aldington would later tell H.D. that Patmore had contacted him at the time of her separation from her husband, asking him for help, and that he had arranged for her to translate the *Memoirs of Marmontel* for Routledge; but had not seen her until 1928. Contact between H.D. and Patmore had ceased in 1925. H.D. had never fully trusted Patmore and her 1926 story 'Murex' concerns Patmore's 'theft' of Haden-Guest ('Martin') from Oppy ('Ermy') and the painful memories this incident brings back of her similar behaviour regarding Aldington ('Freddie'). Of course, it was Yorke, rather than Patmore, who had 'stolen' Aldington, but H.D. had never seen it that way, considering herself partly responsible for the events at Mecklenburgh Square (which constitute the plot of 'Hipparchia', the first of the *Palimpsest* stories). Bryher disapproved of Patmore too: McAlmon refers in a later letter to H.D. to Bryher's having offered him 'the mangy Brigit' in the early twenties, as an attempt to keep him 'in leash', and H.D. told Pound in early 1929 that the reason why she hadn't seen Patmore for a long time was that Bryher could not stand her.[35]

Patmore's translation commission for Routledge had caused a curious exchange of views between Eliot and Aldington in February 1926. In what seems to have been an entirely inappropriate intervention (since Routledge business was not his concern), Eliot mentioned that Patmore had spoken in Vivien Eliot's presence of having a commission from Routledge. He asked Aldington, 'Is this credible and true?' adding that he 'should hardly have thought that she was up to the standard.' Aldington had felt obliged to explain the circumstances, prompting Eliot to reply: 'I quite understand the difficulties you are in with the Patmore case and think that you behaved with great magnanimity, but I cannot feel that your obligations to her, whatever they are, are as great as you imagine.'[36] Clearly, Eliot shared Bryher's distaste for Patmore.

Patmore's own version of her reunion with Aldington is that 'some American friends' brought him along one evening to a party that she and Derek were giving. She writes: 'I noticed that he had grown more handsome with the years. He was tall, broad-shouldered and so healthy that he looked exultant and his blue eyes were full of light.'[37] She does not say when this meeting occurred, but tells us that it was shortly afterwards that he offered her the translation project. This would date their meeting to 1926, but she seems to have been mistaken. The fact that in August 1928 Aldington had only just heard (as he revealed in his letter to Pound) of H.D.'s fear of him suggests that his reunion with Patmore was recent, since she would undoubtedly have been his source for this information. Certainly, at a time when his infatuation with Dobrée, if not the earlier affair with Capper, was signalling the death-throes of his ten-year relationship with Yorke, his resort to Patmore after the ugly scenes that terminated both affairs seems to have arisen, as Capper's narrative suggests, from a desire to be comforted and approved – even adored.

Lady Chatterley's Lover was proving a financial success and bringing Lawrence commissions in the popular press for topical articles, but he had been severely ill in the summer of 1927 and was by now a very sick man. He and Frieda had spent the first three months of 1928 with Aldous and Maria Huxley in Switzerland, before returning to the Villa Mirenda. The heat of the summer, however, had driven them back to Switzerland, this time in the company of their other close friends, Earl and Achsah Brewster.[38] There they had decided to give up the villa. He wrote to Yorke in early August: 'I *knew* you really like us both – but I felt a bit doubtful about Richard. Men so easily seem to have a mysterious grudge against me – I'm always up against it. But now I think that R. really likes us too – without that reserve which I felt before.'[39] On 17 August he suggested to her that the two couples spend the autumn and winter together somewhere warm and congenial, perhaps Egypt or the Spanish Mediterranean. Aldington contacted Jean Paulhan in Paris and obtained the loan of Paulhan's rented *vigie*, a fort on the island of Port Cros just off the French Mediterranean coast, twenty-five miles east of Toulon.

Aldington was expecting Glenn Hughes to arrive in England in mid September on his research tour. Now he was able to offer Hughes the use of Malthouse Cottage in his absence. They would have a fortnight together before Aldington and Yorke set off for the south of France. At the end of August, however, something happened to make an urgent change to his plans – another plea from a friend. This time it was Amy Randall who approached him. Aldington had not seen the Randalls since they moved to Rome in 1925 but knew that Alec had been seriously ill with typhoid earlier in the year. At the time the children had been sent to England with an Italian nurse to stay with Amy's parents. Now that Alec was convalescing at the Hotel Foresta in Vallombrosa, near Florence, she wanted to fetch the children, but was anxious about leaving him alone. Aldington and Yorke immediately set off for Italy. Aldington had to make hasty arrangements for the Hughes's reception at Padworth (Mrs Stacey in Mill Road, who would cook and clean, and the Cappers, who would give them 'any assistance' they might need) and in London, where Flint and Eliot would welcome him and be his guides to the poetry scene. Patmore would help in finding nursery facilities for their daughter. There was also *Lady Chatterley's Lover* to take care of; he had posted out twenty-seven copies and had to return the remaining five to Enid Hilton before his departure.

Randall never forgot Aldington's kindness in coming to his immediate help and would recall after Aldington's death that he was the ideal companion for a convalescent – 'so thoughtful and adaptable, so gay and cheerful.'[40] Aldington was working on his Boccaccio translation, and they would discuss Italian vocabulary. From Vallombrosa, they all travelled back to Randall's villa in Rome, where they stayed until the end of September. Aldington had not visited Rome since 1926 and he told Pound that he noticed many changes and was finding Italy 'both dear and unsympathetic'.[41] He knew, of course, of Pound's enthusiasm for the Mussolini regime: Pound had written to him the previous year that Italy was 'the best governed state in Europe and where the goodam [sic] shits least bother one.'[42] To Aldington's great pleasure, Pound came to Rome to see him – their first meeting since Pound had left England in 1920. However, for Aldington the most exciting aspect of Pound's visit was that he introduced Aldington to Nancy Cunard, who was also in Rome.

The 32-year-old Cunard was the heiress to the Cunard shipping line. Her American mother had separated from her husband and was a leading society hostess in London. Cunard had married at the age of twenty, but the marriage had been short-lived, and in 1920 she had moved to Paris where she had become a prominent figure on the literary scene. She was a talented poet, but her reputation was based more on her patronage of other avant-garde writers and on her unconventional, bohemian lifestyle. Tall, slim, fair-haired and pale-skinned, her appearance was

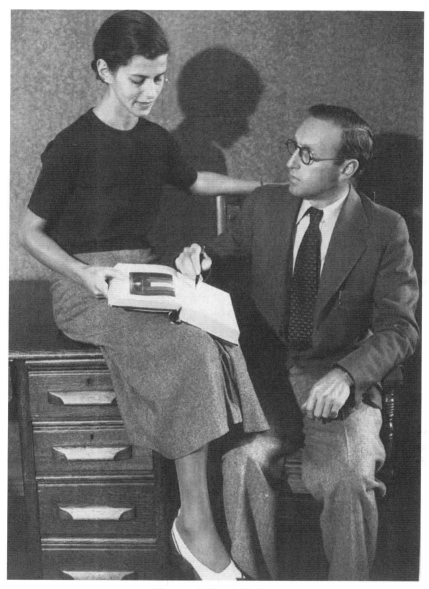

Glenn and Babette Hughes

flamboyant and dramatic. When Aldington met her in Rome she was embarking on a new project: she had acquired The Three Mountains Press from the American journalist, and friend of Pound, William Bird, and had moved it to her farmhouse in the village of La Chapelle-Réanville, sixty miles from Paris.

Aldington was immediately attracted by Cunard's vitality, intelligence and disregard for convention. He saw her as an entrée into the bohemian world of Paris and perhaps also as a potential lover. Cunard however, although she had had plenty of lovers, had been in a serious relationship with the Surrealist poet Louis Aragon since 1926 and would soon move into a new one with the African-American jazz musician, Henry Crowder, whom she met when she moved on from Rome to Venice. She would write of Aldington in her memoir, *These Were the Hours*: 'To me he looked the typical Englishman and not the type I find particularly comely. His hair was cider-red, his cheeks rosy, not large, and he was shy and arrogant at the same time.' It is not quite as flattering a portrait as Patmore's. She does, however, go on to recall 'a delightful afternoon' they all spent in the 'strikingly beautiful Roman countryside' and we can guess that he would have enjoyed being her guide.[43] Perhaps what she represented for Aldington was simply the courage to flout convention and live according to one's own lights. From Naples, where he and Yorke were awaiting the boat that would take them to Marseilles, he wrote to tell Pound how happy their reunion had made him; but his enigmatic comment that, 'You (unwittingly? intentionally?) gave me back life', perhaps refers to his introduction to Cunard.[44]

In the meantime, Lawrence had been looking forward to Port Cros. He told Huxley that he felt he could be happy there and that he liked Yorke and Aldington very much.[45] Frieda went alone from Switzerland to close up the Villa Mirenda and pack their possessions, but she also used the time to meet up with Angelo Ravagli. Ravagli was the Italian army-officer husband of their landlady at Spotorno, who had secretly become her lover in 1925. Lawrence proceeded alone to the south of France where he met up with his sister-in-law and her partner and the Huxleys, who accompanied him on an exploratory trip to the island. Despite his initial enthusiasm, his poor health had made him nervous and he had never been a great lover of islands. He was reassured by the trip, writing to Earl Brewster: 'It is rather lovely, all tangled forest like Corsica – but the hotel is 'chic' – quite a lot of high-browsh people there – and the whole place a bit artificial. The Vigie – fortress – is an hour's stony walk uphill – no way except to walk.' By 5 October, he was alone in his hotel at Le Lavandou and still undecided whether he and Frieda would go to the island or stay on the coast, which he found 'very pleasant'.[46]

The next day, Aldington and Yorke arrived, but they were not alone. Aldington had invited Patmore to join them and she had taken leave of absence from her job at Wyndham's Theatre in order to do so; they had met up with her at Marseilles. Aldington, who had not seen Lawrence for two years, was shocked by his fragile condition. Still undecided about joining his friends on the island, Lawrence wanted to wait for Frieda. The other three went ahead, wiring him once they were on the island to tell him how pleasant it was and how much they were looking forward to his joining them. It was a week before Frieda arrived at Le Lavandou and she brought with her a streaming cold, no doubt picked up from Ravagli. Lawrence immediately caught the cold, but they travelled over to the island on 15 October. The *vigie* was isolated and six hundred feet above the sea with wonderful views; Lawrence was exhausted from the long walk up from the harbour and took to his bed.

'For sheer natural beauty and climate,' wrote Aldington in his memoir, 'I know nothing to equal this island.' They bathed every day in a remote uninhabited bay, 'fringed on the landward side by wild canes and blocked on either flank by steep wooded cliffs'. He continues: 'The walk down and back was under tall, feathery

Port Cros (The vigie can be seen at the top of a hill to the left of the photograph.)

pines and strawberry trees, thick with clusters of round fruit which pass through a whole range of colour from clear lemon to orange to a rich red.Through gaps in the branches we had glimpses of the island, the sea and distant coastline.'[47] Lawrence, of course, could not take part in these outings and remained in the *vigie*, the others taking it in turns to stay with him. He was quite taken with the fort, describing it in detail to his correspondents: its moat, the sitting room and four bedrooms inside the south wall, the big dining hall, kitchen and pantry and 'the little room we use for eating in' on the north-east side, the open fire-places and large supply of wood to burn in them, the young man-servant and the donkey that brought their supplies up from the other end of the island.[48]

In spite of these idyllic surroundings, however, the tensions amongst the group would soon begin to tell. Frieda's affair with Ravagli, although kept secret from Lawrence, had become central to her life, and her infatuation with him at this time might seem to have parallels with Aldington's for Dobrée. John Worthen sees the immense strain of Frieda's life with the dying Lawrence as another important factor: 'She felt trapped; she wanted more freedom; and she seems to have determined on maintaining a relationship with Ravagli while remaining married to Lawrence.'[49] Lawrence's state of health was sobering for the rest of the party. Aldington remembered him in those weeks as 'sharp with the reckless hatred of those about to die', but Patmore is kinder: 'Lawrence never complained. He seemed to approve the place, its loveliness and quiet and being with friends with whom he could say what he liked and do as he pleased.'[50] Aldington was, however, impressed, when the bundle of British press cuttings on *Lady Chatterley's Lover* arrived from Lawrence's agent. Lawrence 'went tranquilly on with his writing although he was so ill, and was angry and bitter about the attacks on him in England.'[51]

They were all writing, apart perhaps from Frieda; even Yorke tried her hand at some free verse. Patmore was working on her second novel, another *roman á clef*. Lawrence was working on translation and on the first of his *Pansies*. And Aldington, while still finding time for work on *The Decameron*, had begun a new project. It was the task he had spoken about to Read in 1925, the account of his war experiences. He had begun this narrative in the cold little cottage in Belgium after the Armistice but then destroyed it. Read's *In Retreat* had prompted further brief but discarded attempts. He had failed to realise, he tells us in his memoir, that time was needed 'for the assimilation and arrangement of these experiences'. He had also been far too preoccupied with work that would earn him his living. In 1925 he had told Read that his greatest difficulty would be 'to refrain from giving in to angry emotionalism' and that he wanted to model himself on Read's 'perfect restraint'.[52] Now he saw things differently. It would be a novel and his aim was clear: 'I wanted to give free expression to the feelings and ideas of one very minor actor in that great tragedy, but I wanted to do it in terms of satire.' He tells us that as soon as the opening sentence of his narrative came into his mind, 'the whole book began to flow with irresistible force'.[53] He wrote the prologue and part one in ten days, 'and then stopped dead'. Lawrence hated it; the women were more encouraging.

Lawrence's hostility may not have been entirely prompted by Aldington's writing. Sexual tension at the *vigie* was high, with Aldington leaving the room he shared at night with Yorke to sleep with Patmore. The Lawrences were fond of Yorke and intensely aware of her misery. The high spirits and the nude bathing parties covered up a great deal of hurt and pain (a scenario we may recall from an earlier era). And the misery was not all Yorke's. 'Whether they meant to or not', argues John Worthen, 'Frieda, Brigit and Aldington (and in her own way poor Arabella) were making horribly clear to him the continuing importance of sexual desire in their lives.'[54] Yorke, according to her own account, sought comfort from Joseph, the Sicilian servant, while Aldington, apart from making love to Patmore, wore Nancy Cunard's beads about his neck.[55]

In Capper's novel, 'Valentine' writes to 'Barbara': 'It has come to me lately like a revelation that Anthony has no more idea than a child what he wants out of life. Even I, with my tears and scenes . . . am far more able to *bear* life, to live life than he. He just doesn't know what he wants and I don't know what will teach him. Just now he fancies himself in love with an Englishwoman here, a member of the aristocracy and one of the loosest most scattered people – drinks and takes drugs, and boasts of her fifty lovers. He doesn't love her really one atom. Anthony only loves himself! Oh it is bitter to say this, but I feel as if I were living with a stranger! Hyatt [Lawrence] says that all Anthony's amorousness is really cerebral. He gets a tremendous kick out of thinking himself in love with this woman.'[56]

Aldington himself would write to H.D. a few months later: 'Up in that lonely Vigie, a mile from the nearest house, it was like a series of demented scenes from some southern Wuthering Heights. Most fortunately I kept my head and my temper and a certain aloofness; but I emerged with a conviction that Lawrence is really malevolent and evil. I hope I never see him again. He is merely a Cournos of genius.'[57] These remarks say more about the emotional state of the writer than about Lawrence. In the grip of sexual passion, Aldington could be ruthless; he certainly resented any criticisms from others, however implicit, of his own

Nancy Cunard, 1929

conduct. While he always claimed to be a liberated human being, free of 'a sense of sin' (writing in *Life for Life's Sake*, 'Extensive observation of those who suffer from remorse induces me to believe that they suffer less from being sinful than from being found out in what local opinion considers sinful'), he was not wholly insensitive to the pain he inflicted, as his letters to H.D. in 1918 bear witness.[58] Unable to accept moral responsibility for his behaviour – indeed to accept that it *had* a moral dimension – he needed scapegoats, a function that both Yorke and Lawrence served.

In writing to H.D., he was also influenced by the jealousy he had always felt of her feelings for Lawrence. More importantly, Lawrence was the most remarkable man he had ever known, and to be the object of his disapproval was difficult to bear. In his 1950 *Portrait of a Genius, But* . . . he is kinder in his recall of that time: 'Night after night, I listened to his deep hollow cough . . . Only then did I realise how frail and ill he was, how bitterly he suffered, what frightening envy and hatred of ordinary healthy humanity sometimes possessed him, how his old wit had become bitter malice, how lonely he was, how utterly he depended on Frieda, how insanely jealous of her he had become.'[59] Nevertheless, the phrase 'ordinary healthy humanity' seems to be an insistence on the normality and acceptability of his own behaviour on Port Cros.

With one exception, Lawrence's letters from the island convey none of these tensions, a fact that suggests that the antagonism was to a large extent in Aldington's mind. In all his correspondence, Lawrence remarks on how much he likes Aldington, Yorke and Patmore, how kind they are and how well they all get on together, and in the early letters he states his intention of staying until 'about Christmas'.[60] What is increasingly apparent, however, is how ill he was becoming. On 26 October, he told Lawrence Pollinger, the literary agent, that he had been in bed for a week with a 'flu cold' and two days of haemorrhaging, and that he felt 'rather rotten'. He adds: 'I don't think we shall stay here very long. I don't believe it suits me.'[61]

Perhaps there was a showdown in the end. Things must certainly have come to a head by 28 October (after two shared weeks on the island) when Lawrence wrote a letter to Huxley that is a unique outburst of anger towards both Huxley himself and Aldington. Responding to Huxley's *Point Counter Point*, which he had been reading (and which contains fictionalised portraits of – amongst others – Huxley himself, Cunard – with whom Huxley had had a bruising affair, and Lawrence and Frieda), he began with praise: 'I do think that you've shown the truth . . . about you and your generation with really fine courage'; but he proceeded to attack his friend:

> [I]f murder, suicide, rape is what you thrill to, and nothing else, then it's your destiny –you can't change it *mentally*. You live by what you thrill to, and there's the end of it. Still for all that it's a *perverse* courage which makes the man accept the slow suicide of inertia and sterility: the perverseness of a perverse child. – It's amazing how men are like that. Richard Aldington is exactly the same inside, murder, suicide, rape – with a desire to be raped

D.H. Lawrence, 1928

very strong – same thing really – just like you – only he doesn't face it, and gilds his perverseness. It makes me feel ill. I've had more hemorrhage [*sic*] here and been in bed this week. *Sporca miseria*. If I don't find some spot to climb out of, in this bog, I'm done. I can't stand murder, suicide, rape – especially rape; and especially being raped. Why do men only thrill to a woman who'll rape them?[62]

It is ironic that the very vices Lawrence lists are those that Huxley's novel (the plot of which includes actual murder, suicide and rape) targets, and that the only characters in *Point Counter Point* who are held up for admiration, whose lives are shown to be sane and healthy, are Mark and Mary Rampion, the characters who

– very transparently – stand in for Lawrence and Frieda. What is of interest to us, however, is why Lawrence includes Aldington in this onslaught on the sickness of society. There were certainly aspects of Aldington's behaviour that remind us of characters in *Point Counter Point*. His earlier affair with Capper (about which Yorke may have confided in Lawrence) and his boasting about his relationship with Cunard (which may only have been intended as cover for his affair with Patmore) were both suggestive of sensuality, of a 'cerebral' approach to sex which was anathema to Lawrence, who took sex and the relationship between a man and a woman very seriously.

One of the poems that Lawrence wrote on the island, 'I Know a Noble Englishman' (one of the two removed on the grounds of obscenity from the edition of *Pansies* published in 1929), was about Aldington. ('This moderately young gentleman is very normal,/ as becomes an Englishman, rather proud of being a/ bit of a Don Juan, you know.') The poet has a conversation with the man's partner, 'looking a little peaked towards the end of her little affair with him'. The woman's theory is that 'Ronald' ('like most Englishmen') is either a homosexual or a narcissist, but too frightened to recognise it, so he takes it out on women. She tells the poet:

> You've no idea, when men are in love with themselves,
> how they wreak all their spite on women,
> pretending to love them.

She tells the poet that her partner can be 'so gentle in his delicate lovemaking' and make a woman feel that he is 'serving her as no man ever/ served before'. Then: ' . . . suddenly the ground goes from under her/ feet and she/ clutches in mid-air', while he 'stands aside watching with a/ superior little grin like some indecent malicious little boy.'

The letter and the poem reveal the suffering and resentment felt by both Lawrence and Yorke. This does not in itself mean that their analyses are inaccurate. Jessie Capper, for one, would have agreed with Yorke, but Yorke's partnership with Aldington had been no 'little affair': there had been at least eight years in which there is no sign that he had sought any sexual satisfaction outside their relationship. It is also true that the longer a relationship lasts, the more protracted and bitter its ending is likely to be. Nevertheless, his insensitivity towards her feelings throughout the Capper affair, the infatuation with Dobrée, the vaunted attraction towards Cunard and his conduct of the new relationship with Patmore do appear to have been heartless. Where Lawrence and Yorke were wrong, however, was in their diagnosis of *self-love*; on the contrary, this was a man with low self-esteem, a man who could not afford to recognise the wrong he was doing to others.

We may wonder whether Lawrence had read *A Fool i' the Forest*. There Aldington had revealed the extent to which he knew that he had lost his way and the importance to him of regaining that equilibrium of head and heart that Lawrence himself preached. One had always been a puritan and the other would always be a hedonist, but they had more values in common than either would admit.

∾

As Lawrence's health deteriorated, heavy storms came. The *vigie* became cold and damp; and they ran out of essential supplies because no boats could reach the island. They made plans to leave as soon as conditions improved. Ironically, when the time came for departure, the weather was beautiful, the sky blue and the sea calm. But they had had enough. They left the island on 15 November. At Toulon, Aldington and Lawrence said their farewells. The two would never meet again, and Lawrence would be dead in sixteen months. His final words to Aldington were 'Possess your soul in patience': not advice which Aldington was at the time inclined to follow.[63] He had parted from Yorke and had no intention of returning to England. She travelled first to Paris and thence to her mother's apartment in London. In early December she went down to Padworth, where the Hughes family were still in residence, to start the task of disposing of the contents of the cottage and closing it down.

The memory of setting up their home – also on her own – exactly eight years earlier must have been a painful one. Lawrence, writing to her at her mother's Holland Place apartment in January, attempted to comfort her by telling her that the cottage was 'an unlucky place' and that he was glad that she had got rid of it 'even if it was a wrench'. 'So there we all are', he concludes, 'all at our various loose ends.'[64] By the following spring Yorke and her mother had settled in Paris, where she found work at the bookshop of Edward Titus, owner of the Black Manikin Press, while her mother became Paris fashion correspondent for the New York Herald. Yorke would never recover from the protracted anguish of the break-up of her relationship with Aldington, as her interviews with the Lowenfels and with Selwyn Kittredge in the 1960s showed, and she would never marry. Lawrence's death in 1930 and Frieda's subsequent remarriage and return to New Mexico deprived her of her two most loyal friends at a time when she most needed support.

Aldington and Patmore stayed on in Toulon for two weeks in what appears to have been a romantic idyll. Then she returned to London, her sons, her job and her young lover, while he stayed on in Paris. 'Leaving you at the Gare du Nord was like tearing myself in half', he wrote to her from the hotel in the Place de la Sorbonne near the Jardin du Luxembourg, where Cunard had booked him a room and paid for his first week's stay in advance.[65]

At the Hotel Select he worked on his Boccaccio translation and on a long reflective poem on love and loneliness, and wrote passionate daily love-letters or telegrams to Patmore. If she was to join him again, she had to break her three-year relationship with Haden-Guest and finally distance herself from her husband. She had not told her young lover of the affair ('I knew Stephen would "sense" something', Aldington wrote to her on 4 December), but her attempt to break off the relationship apparently resulted in threats on his side to take his own life if she left him. In her 1929 *roman à clef*, *No Tomorrow*, Guest is Hugh Gaunt, a sadistic lover who has 'wrung' a promise of fidelity from 'Claudine', although he does not practise this himself. And he is filled with 'a stinging, trembling rage' when he discovers that she has taken another lover.[66] Aldington was fearful, both for Patmore herself, and for the future of their relationship, but he did not want to intervene and told her that she must feel free to make her own decisions. 'I don't quite understand about Stephen but I have perfect trust in you', he wrote. 'I believe that nothing in the world can keep lovers separated for long.'[67]

How genuinely Patmore was in fear of Guest and believed in his threats of suicide is hard to tell. There was much to keep her in London, not least her sons, to whom she was devoted. Furthermore, the prospect of losing the independence she had won by leaving her husband may not have been attractive, however much she cared for Aldington. At this stage of their affair, they agreed to maintain secrecy. Patmore was not to tell Guest the identity of her new lover and Aldington had not told Cunard that he was in love with someone else, although she was aware that he had ended his relationship with Yorke. Aldington still imagined that Lawrence did not know, telling Patmore, 'Of course Lorenzo will try to find out. All I fear is that he and/or Frieda came to my bedroom and found me not there!'[68] His initial plan – if Patmore could make the break with Guest – was for them to share the cost of the rental of a small apartment for her, while he continued to live in an hotel: 'If we lived in the same hotel in Paris, people are bound to know.'[69] It is not clear why, given the relaxed outlook of literary Paris, this was important, unless it was to protect Patmore's reputation in London; but Aldington may also have been conscious of his continuing dependence on the conservative worlds of the *TLS*, *The Spectator*, *The Nation* and *The Criterion*. His academic respectability had been achieved with a ten-year struggle and might be undermined if he became a social pariah. It was not that the London literary journals were a source of income he continued to require, since he had severed his links with all but the *TLS*; but their readiness to review the creative work on which he was now engaged mattered to him. Nevertheless, the futile task of attempting to keep the liaison secret would soon have to be abandoned.

Cunard featured prominently in his letters to Patmore. It is not clear whether his intention was to reassure his lover or to stimulate a little jealousy: 'I expect you feel about [Stephen] as I feel about Nancy – a bit remorseful and tender, but quite unable to endure lovemaking. Only it is much easier for me because I was only a small feather in Nancy's smart and exceedingly well-fitted cap, whereas there are the bonds of long association between you and Stephen.' He was critical of Cunard: 'It seems to me that girls like Nancy make a large mistake in being so hard and so promiscuous, and so unemotional.'[70] Yet a few evenings of frequenting Paris night clubs in her company made him realise that the difference between Cunard and most of the other '"quarter" types', who have 'killed all beauty, all poetry, all sensibility, all feelings, all love, with drink, cynicism and unlimited promiscuity', was the 'fineness in her which rebel[led] against this squalid soddenness.' 'Her only hope,' he concluded, 'is her misery.'[71] He saw plenty of that. On his first evening she had taken him out to a café, where they had 'talked for an hour and agreed to be good friends & not lovers' (much, one suspects, to Cunard's relief), and then on to the Plantation Club to hear Crowder perform. Here Aldington had witnessed a spectacular argument between Cunard and Aragon, and then tried to persuade her, without success, into a reconciliation. A few days later he was at her farmhouse at Chapelle-Réanville, being shown her printing press. He was charmed with the house but suspected that Cunard was only just beginning to realise the scale of the job she had taken on and was hoping to employ him; but he told Patmore he would refuse: '[A]fter the Egoist and the Criterion, I have had enough of that sort of thing.'[72]

'Nancy is sweet and charming and kind but I find I do not love her *at all*,' he assured Patmore.[73] On the contrary, he was 'so filled out and, as it were, perfumed' with Patmore's presence, that there was 'not the least touch of desire' in him for anyone else. 'My body is yours and at least now does not feel anything for other women', he told her.[74] We might note here the temporal qualification. Letters flew between them and he also bombarded her with telegrams to declare his love. He wanted her to cut her ties with England and join him on the continent, although he assured her that he understood her need to be able to return to London regularly to see her sons. Patmore was anxious about making herself dependent on him; in London she had a job and a small regular income, and writing could not guarantee her that. Aldington was eager to convince her that her scruples were unfounded. Bruce Richmond, he told her, was delighted with his output in recent weeks; Patmore could share *TLS* reviewing with him. 'If you knew, Brigit, how I long to write and work with you, as well as live and love and laugh with you', he wrote on 15 December. 'If after our common wanderings & errors we have now found the real love, the real life, the real relationship, what a triumphant success our lives will be!' he told her. 'I can for the first time believe in love, complete fulfilled love.'[75]

During those first weeks alone in Paris, he had a lot of explaining to do to other friends. He wrote to tell Crosby Gaige that he and Yorke had agreed to separate 'at least for the time being', that he would be giving up Malthouse Cottage, and that he would be staying in Paris to complete his novel and other books.[76] His first letter to Hughes only informed him: 'We are going to be so much on the continent that I have decided to give up the cottage on 1 March. . . . I expect Dorothy will be down before too long to tell you all about it.' 'Please stay on until we move or sell the furniture, of which we will give you due notice,' the letter continued, '– certainly it won't be until after Christmas at the earliest.'[77] A few days later he felt that he had to come clean about his separation from Yorke but told Hughes: 'Of course I am very anxious that no-one at Padworth shall know anything about it.'[78] If he was thinking of Jessie Capper (and who else's opinion mattered?), he must surely have realised that Yorke would be sharing the story with her.

A letter to Slonimsky would follow in early February 1929, repeating the formula: 'Dorothy and I have agreed to part for a time', but this time adding, 'which will probably be a long time.'[79] He only told Monro that he was going to sell his books and seemed 'likely to be staying away from England for some time.'[80] With Pound he was also slow to tell the whole truth. His first letter, written as soon as he arrived in Paris, is self-consciously jovial:

Darling Ezra (as Nancy would say)

I haven't written to you because of the most obstreperous and unspeakable scenes between everybody and everything at Port Cros. Hell! Well, old son, I've cut the painter; doubtless, Nancy has told you that I've separated definitely from Dorothy & I am living here until matters subside.[81]

Unsurprisingly, Pound got the wrong end of the stick, assuming that Cunard was the cause of the break-up. Aldington had to reassure him that 'there ain't no bloody siren, at least not much. . . . Nancy is what the English call a brick, i.e. a good fellow, one of "us". She made possible, or helped an effort long delayed by regrettable apathy.'[82] He still did not reveal Patmore's role in his separation from Yorke; Pound was a gossip and for the time being Aldington was respecting Patmore's request for discretion. He asked Pound if he could arrange for the first chapter of his war novel to appear in *The Dial* and proceeded to re-work it and prune it, beginning to lose the confidence he had felt in it at Port Cros.

Meanwhile he attempted a more light-hearted task, a satirical thirty-three line poem about the virgin birth entitled 'Hark the Herald'. He asked Cunard to print a hundred and fifty copies so that he could send them as Christmas greetings to his friends and acquaintances. Cunard not only did so in time for Christmas posting, but made a present of them to Aldington. 'Sent out judiciously, it got rid of a lot of rather tiresome acquaintances', he tells us in *Life for Life's Sake*.[83] And indeed, Eliot's tart comment to Pound was: 'I have heard from him and received his carrol, the worst piece he has ever done and you know what that means he's ready for the looney bin.'[84]

On 23 December, he rushed to London to offer Patmore a regular monthly allowance (£12.10) and to transfer to her £200 worth of the shares that he had been given by his mother. (Guest was absent, visiting his new friend H.D. in Switzerland – evidence that H.D. and Patmore continued to be partial to stealing each other's lovers.) He returned to Paris on Christmas Day, feeling in need of Pound's support. The tone of his letter is desperate but abashed. He begins by explaining the problem: 'She loves me right enuff, and wants to come and live in Paris, suitably camouflaged at close quarters, but can't get courage to cut free from last lover, who seems to have hell of power over her.' Then he pleads: 'Help me Unkil Ez, I'm kinder going crazy over it. Can't you send her a letter & tell her to cut free?' It is only at this point that he reveals the identity of the woman: 'Brigit, my dear, yes "our" Brigit, your ole love Vale de Lencour.'[85] He tells his friend: 'Ezry, we are both wildly in love with each other, never anything like it for either of us – been goin on since July – but it will kill us both if she can't get courage to break away from London and Haden-Guest, who is a bloody sadist and torturing her (and me through her) to death. She wants to come, hates him, begs him to let her go, but he tricks her abominably into promises which she keeps with stupid sense of honour.'[86]

Pound, with his usual generosity of spirit, did what he could, and a few more telegrams from her lover brought Patmore to Paris (and a seat at the Plantation

Club cabaret) for New Year's Eve. Aldington had wired Derek Patmore, who was spending Christmas with friends in Monte Carlo, to join them in Paris and offer his approval of his mother's plans. He had also planned further ahead: he had booked train tickets for a leisurely trip to Rapallo via Aix and Genoa. He had in his possession a sealed letter from Pound to Patmore, which he was to give her should she decide that she must instead return to her life in London.

Before Patmore's arrival, Aldington had happened to run into into Robert McAlmon propping up the bar at the Café du Dôme. By late 1926 McAlmon's marriage to Bryher had come to represent, in his own words, 'more things that I did *not* want in life than I could cope with', and they were divorced in 1927.[87] He felt enormously bitter towards Bryher and his judgements must be seen as partial, although he was honest in his perception of himself. He wrote in his memoir that William Carlos Williams had told him that he had 'a genius for life' and commented: 'if absolute despair, a capacity for reckless abandon and drink, long and heavy spells of ennui which require bottles of strong drink to cure, and a gregarious but not altogether loving nature is "a genius for life", then I have it.'[88] Nevertheless, his Contact Press in Paris had published the work of a range of prominent writers of the period which might not otherwise have been published, including H.D.'s *Palimpsest*, Bryher's *Two Selves* and Ernest Hemingway's first book.

Aldington told Patmore: '[McAlmon] strikes me as a bit of a rough-neck, kinder unkulchered, and a bit more uster prairies an' cocktail bars than the West End.' (His tendency to adopt a comic dialect in his letters of this period seems not merely to be a mocking of Pound or McAlmon, but more a manifestation of his awkwardness in his new role of Bohemian artist.) The exciting news, however, was that Bryher and H.D., according to McAlmon, wanted to see H.D. divorced. He confirmed what Patmore had told Aldington: it was fear that he 'would be mean about the child' that had prevented them from taking action. 'Now I am not going to do anything without Darling's advice', wrote Aldington. 'What does she think?'[89] McAlmon would write to H.D.: '[Aldington] was not the fat, repulsive thing Bryher had taught me to suspect. Sentimental and soft, but not unlikeable. And really fond of you, really bowled over by your quality. The man hasn't one fiftieth of the calculation that Bryher has, nor the malice.'[90]

Meanwhile, Aldington had written to ask Glenn Hughes to find the manuscript of *A Dream in the Luxembourg* on a shelf in Malthouse Cottage and send it to him. He told Patmore that he was longing to read it to her: 'In spirit it is a kind of prophecy of our love and of the life and hope I believe we shall live together, although it ends on a note of misery. I think it is the best thing I have written, a sort of agonised cry for a complete life, which you, Darling, my own love, have answered so completely.'[91] It was a skilful elision of his passion for Dobrée, only five months earlier.[92] Now the poem became, not a lament for unrequited love, but a premonition of a fulfilled one that lay in its future.

20. *The Eaten Heart*

Most lives are monologues, and so grow poorer;
But conceive the riches if the response is there,
Question and answer, change and interchange,
Positive life.   (Richard Aldington, *The Eaten Heart*, 1929)

In the spring of 1929 Cunard's Hours Press published the long poem which Aldington had written in Paris in December 1928 after his arrival from Port Cros and Toulon. The two hundred hand-set copies were signed by the author.[1] *The Eaten Heart* was Aldington's reply to Lawrence: while he had seen neither Lawrence's letter to Huxley nor 'I know a noble Englishman', he had a good idea of Lawrence's perception of him and of his sexual conduct – hence the outburst to H.D. Alone at the Hotel Select and in the grip of his passion for Patmore and his uncertainty about whether she would surrender her other lover and return to him, he worked on his long poem about sex, love and loneliness in the post-war world.

Like *A Dream in the Luxembourg*, the poem is organised around two key motifs, but this time they are organising myths, taking the place of the narrative structure employed in both *A Dream in the Luxembourg* and *A Fool i' the Forest*. It is primarily (as, indeed, are they) a philosophical poem.

The story of Philoctetes is introduced in the fourth of the poem's nine sections. Philoctetes, in the play by Sophocles, is left on the island of Lemnos when the Greeks are on their voyage to Troy. He has a snake-bite which has left him incapacitated and in agony, with a wound that smells overpoweringly. He endures ten years of solitary exile which are ended when the Greeks discover that they will not win the war against Troy without the bow of Heracles, which Philoctetes owns. Odysseus and Neoptolemus, the son of Achilles, return to the island and there, while Odysseus hides, Neoptolemus makes false overtures of friendship to Philoctetes in order to trick him into surrendering the bow. Philoctetes becomes Aldington's archetype of the 'dreadful inevitable loneliness of the human soul' and:

> The tragedy of delusive joy
> At the hope of recognition and release,
> The tragedy of real pain and bitterness
> When the hope vanishes before human treachery
> And human incomprehension and indifference.

Since the 'recognition and release' with which the poem concerns itself is sexual love, Aldington was clearly still dealing with the 'incomprehension and indifference' (Dobrée's) and 'treachery' (Yorke's) that he had experienced only a few months earlier.[2] A further passage 'revoices' the myth in these terms:

> But – brief was the joy of Philoctetes –
> All that passionate outpouring of self,
> That sudden release, that immense deliverance,
> Recoil on themselves in blind despair and apathy
> If the response is dull or inadequate,
> If the sister world is not really a sister-world.

Claiming Philoctetes' story as a universal one, he continues, even more revealingly:

> With us the tragedy is more complex and incoherent;
> It is softer and perhaps a little mawkish
> Because it is so complicated with sexual desire
> Which leaves us so exposed to ridicule,
> And we fear ridicule more than we fear the gods.

The other structuring myth does not appear until the sixth section and it is one that had already appeared briefly in *A Dream in the Luxembourg*. It is the mediaeval Provence tale of the eaten heart retold in Boccaccio's *Decameron*, which Aldington was still engaged in translating. Raimon de Castel Rhossilhon, discovering that his wife, Soremonda (or Margarida), is passionately in love with the troubador Guilhem de Cabestanh, kills her lover and serves up his heart for her to eat. When he tells her what she has eaten, she throws herself to her death from the castle walls. For Aldington the tale shows both 'the savage desire which can only grasp or kill' and 'the other love which is the complete exchange of two natures'. While he is not above using the tale to reinforce his intermittent misogyny ('It shows perhaps how a woman devours a man's life,/ But it also shows how the man's gift of himself is total'), the main purpose behind his appropriation of the myth is to show:

> . . . how a woman's vanity and a man's imprudence
> And the brutality of the world of men
> (Who always envy the happiness of others
> And hate nothing so much as the perfect communing of lovers)
> How these things bring a sudden tragic ending
> Leaving no fate for both but death.

The tale also allows him to reinforce another key theme of the poem (and another that links him to Lawrence): that the modern world lacks the power 'to live in this positive tragic intensity'. Both the first and the fifth sections of the poem have already addressed this theme:

Nancy Cunard and Henry Crowder at the Hours Press, 1929

We that are children of despair . . .
Frightened yet moulded by the cold hard patterns
Beaten upon life by the cold machines –
What do we know of love?

In a section which clearly reflects the thinking that was informing Part One of *Death of a Hero*, he concedes that:

> We were right, yes we were right
> To smash the false idealities of the last age,
> The humbug, the soft cruelty, the mawkishness,
> The heavy tyrannical sentimentality,
> The inability to face facts . . .

He claims to like the men and women of his own age, even their hardness:

> For though we are a battered and rather bitter set,
> Still we have faced the facts, we have been pretty honest.

This assessment of his generation may remind us of his comments to Patmore about Cunard.[3] And he goes on to wonder whether too much has been rejected:

> If we have not hardened ourselves too much
> Making it impossible to break out of our self-prisons,
> As if Philoctetes had exiled himself?

and to argue that his generation has been too quick to use the war, along with industrialisation, as an excuse for a spiritual crisis which can be resolved. The war appears elsewhere in the poem too: in lines that prefigure the poem with which he would close his new novel, he writes:

> They who were children when you played a man's part
> Smile at your memories, never knew your dead,
> And lonely, lonely is the spirit within you,
> Lonelier than any Bastille prisoner,
> Lonelier than a barren Aegean islet.

War experience and its incommunicability continue to isolate the veteran soldier. Before we move on to examine the poet's solution to this state of personal imprisonment, it is worth noting that this passage demonstrates the poem's distinctive form of address: whereas *A Fool i' the Forest* and *A Dream in the Luxembourg* are first person narratives, *The Eaten Heart* frequently employs the second person, which, while appearing to constitute an address to the *reader*, actually situates the addressee as *subject* of the poem. In so far as there is a narrative, it is in the second person. This allows the poet to talk of his own spiritual hunger and distress without the note of self-pity that has been a feature of earlier writing. When he speaks in the first person mode in this poem, it is invariably as a commentator or spokesperson for his generation, not as the experiencing subject.

For Aldington, like Lawrence, the route to human fulfilment is sexual love, constituting first, 'recognition' and then, 'release' from isolation:

> With our hands and breasts we speak mysterious things

> Which the filter of speech rejects,
> And only through the known, exterior body
> Do we reach the mysterious unknown within.

Yet, while the poet thinks that Petrarch and Dante were wrong in their visions of idealised love:

> . . . the true tragedy of thwarted sexual desire is nothing,
> The true tragedy is that of inner loneliness.

and in a passage that is reminiscent (unsurprisingly) of Browning's 'By the Fireside' he argues:

> If the response is there, a life is fulfilled,
> For the dialogue life of these two natures
> Grows richer a thousand-fold
> Than the two monologue lives lived separately,
> Dwindling in their own loneliness.[4]

Implicitly defending himself against the (unspoken?) accusations of Lawrence on Port Cros, the poet rejects the merely hedonistic and sensual: '[T]here is more in all this/ Than the delicate friction of two skins.' Furthermore, in experiencing this need for love, he sees himself as one of the 'chosen', an élite. Others may be unhappy in other ways, but not in 'this profound way', and they do not achieve release either; for them, 'The miracle never occurs.' Lastly (and this is where Aldington's vision differs from Browning's), the outcome for lovers is inevitably tragic:

> And even if the release takes place
> And the dialogue of the two natures is perfect,
> Still the end must be tragic. . . .
> None of those chosen can escape the escort of woe
> And the harrying beyond the strength of a man.

Whether the tragic outcome is always brought about by external causes, as this passage implies, or is inherent in the sexual relationship itself, is not entirely clear. We may suspect that Aldington's tragic vision referred to the former, while we may see the latter as having been more characteristic of his own relationships. In seeing tragedy as inevitable, he may have been influenced as much by his current circumstances as his past experiences: he had no doubt that Patmore loved him, but he did fear that she would be unable to break away from Stephen Guest. Nor does the poem address more complex issues such as fidelity. The poet's vision is essentially a romantic one. It is also an exercise in self-justification: if all relationships are doomed, then individuals cannot be held responsible for their failure.

Although *The Eaten Heart* is a much shorter poem than either *A Fool i' the Forest* or *A Dream in the Luxembourg* (a quarter of the length of the former and

less than a third of the length of the latter), the fact that it is written almost
entirely in a discursive mode (apart from one section, which is in the form of an
apostrophe in the Greek manner) makes considerable demands on the reader. Yet
the form succeeds. This is partly because of the texture achieved by the use of the
two structuring myths and a variety of other resonant motifs. It is also because
Aldington seems to have found a personal voice which has gravitas without
being pompous, and a conversational style which does not sacrifice cadence.
If the last two sections, breaking down as they do into fragments with a variety
of unidentified voices, are reminiscent of Eliot's *The Waste Land*, then the opening
of the penultimate section looks forward to the metatext of that poet's *The Four
Quartets:*

> But was it this I meant to say?
> No, for what we mean to say is never said.

The Eaten Heart may not go in for the 'extreme compression and essential
significance of every word', which Aldington had told Read in 1924 were 'the
narrow path that leads to sterility', but the poet does find a means to articulate
his philosophy of life and love which succeeds as poetry. Writing in 1964, only
months before her death, Cunard found that the poem was still as moving as
she had found it when 'letter by letter and line by line' it rose from her fingers
around the type.[5]

21. The Novelist: 1929

By writing 'Death of a Hero' I purged my bosom of perilous stuff which had been poisoning me for a decade. When I had finished, had my say and cussed my cusses, I felt the lightness and tranquillity of a morning after a thunder storm.
(Richard Aldington, *Life for Life's Sake*, 1941)[1]

There is no such thing as ever being through with anything.
(H.D. to George Plank, 3 March 1930)[2]

After the dramas and upheavals of 1928, Aldington was to find 1929 a year of great personal happiness and immense productivity, each fuelling the other. Even before his future with Patmore was settled, Aldington was spending his days at the Select Hotel working hard on both the Boccaccio translation and the war novel, to be called *Death of a Hero*. Pound was impressed enough with his return to creative work to tell Harriet Monroe: 'Aldington seems to have awakened from his slumbers. I may be sending you something of his, before long. Or he may be induced to take direct action.'[3] The tone of Monroe's review of the *Collected Poems* in the April issue of *Poetry* was muted, however. Nostalgic about the early work, so bound up with the beginnings of *Poetry* itself, she concluded that the poet had 'on the whole . . . followed with fair consistency the stern principles under which he and the other imagists began their revolution' nearly seventeen years previously. Of course, the 1929 *Collected Poems* finishes with *A Fool i' the Forest* (which she praises as 'revealing a personality secure in its own inspiration and art') and Aldington's more recent work was very different, but he cannot have found her review particularly encouraging.[4]

On their arrival in Rapallo on 9 January, he and Patmore settled into a healing routine of working in the mornings and meeting up with Pound and Dorothy in the afternoons. The two couples even went dancing; Aldington was becoming, under Patmore's tuition, a competent ballroom dancer, but her account of Pound's efforts is that he danced to no rules she understood, moving with 'extremely odd steps' to 'unearthly beats.'[5] Yeats and his wife were also visiting; drawn to Pound's company, they would settle in Rapallo permanently that autumn. And Glenn Hughes arrived to hear Pound's 'take' on Imagism.

In late February Aldington and Patmore returned to Paris where he had an appointment with Donald Friede, now Pascal Covici's partner.[6] The publisher took away Aldington's carbon copy of the 30,000 completed words of *Death of a*

Hero; within a few days he had cabled his acceptance from London and sent an advance. The novel was completed over the next ten weeks – the whole task, by Aldington's own calculation, taking 52 working days.[7] Paris suited him, for living and for working; he found it stimulating, not simply 'because of the people at the Dôme or even from the intellectual life of the French, but because it [had] the energy and movement of a great city and at the same time an easier way of life that that of London.'[8] It was also a cheaper city – although considerably more expensive than his existence in rural Berkshire had been.

Towards London – which for him meant the *Criterion* circle – he still felt bitter. The fourth volume of Eliot's correspondence, covering 1928-1929 (published in 2013), contains no letters from Eliot to Aldington after the summer of 1928, although Aldington was to tell H.D. in April 1929, when friendly relations had been re-established between them: 'I wrote to Eliot and he replied in the strain of Mr Chadband. I admit I was peevish about it, but I cared quite a lot for Tom.'[9] In his memoir, *The Voyage Home*, Richard Church, one of Aldington's former colleagues in the *Criterion* group, tells a story about Aldington's departure from London in 1928. Towards the end of a *Criterion* dinner at the Ristorante Commercio, Aldington walked in 'with an air almost of hostility'. Church tells us that the group round the table, which included Eliot, Read and Flint, reacted with 'a combination of embarrassment and curiosity'. Aldington announced that he was leaving England: '"I am on my way to Paris," he said. "I've done with this country." ' According to Church, Eliot nodded his head 'with reluctant understanding', and Flint tried to remonstrate, but Aldington 'looked at Flint as though he might be a tree waving in the wind', wished them all good luck and swept out 'as magisterially as he had come in.'[10] The anecdote is persuasive: it accurately conveys Aldington's feelings towards the *Criterion* group by 1928 and his desire to leave England permanently; but it is probably apocryphal. Neither in March that year (when he went to Paris) or in September (when he left for Port Cros via Italy) were his departures intended as final. It was only on Port Cros that he had 'burnt his boats'.

In Paris he had new friends with whom he could enjoy an amity which he had not known since the pre-war days of his friendships with Pound, Cournos, Flint, Plank and the Whitalls. There were Cunard and Crowder, whose hectic lifestyle he did not attempt to share, but he liked them both and enjoyed their company. The Lowenfels were his constant companions and Lilian typed the chapters of his *Death of a Hero* manuscript as he completed them. He did not seek out Pound's friends Joyce and Ford, and Hemingway had left Paris for America in March 1928. It was, however, at Joyce's apartment, 2 Square Robiac, off the Rue de Grenelle, that Aldington met another expatriate Irishman who would become a life-long friend: the poet Thomas MacGreevy.[11]

MacGreevy was a year younger than Aldington and had served as a second lieutenant in the Royal Field Artillery during the war. It is surprising that the two had not met before, since MacGreevy had lived in London between 1925 and 1927, where he had contributed art and literature reviews to *The Nation* and the *TLS*, as well as writing for *The Criterion*. In Paris he was a lecturer in English

Literature at the École Normale Supérieure. In *Life for Life's Sake* Aldington writes of him: 'He is an admirable exponent of the almost lost art of conversation, and therefore I grappled him to my soul with hoops of steel.'[12] MacGreevy would write an affectionate tribute to Aldington after his death: 'I found him one of the most forbearing, most generous, most patient, most devoted and to crown all, most laughter-loving, friends I have ever had. . . . His erudition was immense but it was the erudition of the humanist not of the pedant.'[13] Aldington also met MacGreevy's successor at the École Normale, the twenty-two year-old Samuel Beckett. He would help both young Irishmen find publishers for their work.

News of his separation from Yorke had now reached H.D. She wrote to Cournos: 'I suppose you have heard the rumour that R. and A. have had a violent and final quarrel. I don't myself believe it is final though people say he has sold all his books. . . . He has completely broken up the establishment in the country . . . I heard it reported that he must have more "sex expression" in which case I think he is decidedly a "border-line case" if not actually "certifiable"'.[14] The gossipy tone disguises the extent to which the news had shaken her and revived painful memories. She had a more honest exchange of letters with George Plank. Just how nervous she was is clear from the scattering of ellipses throughout her letter of 18 February: 'It is lovely of you to write about the 'core' of R. being beautiful . . . [*sic*] for that is what so shocked me. When I heard this, I suddenly felt 'why Richard is alive, he is in the world. I might hear about him', just as if he had been dead all this time. The psychic shock to me has been so terrible and so beautiful. Richard is actually in the world among people I might meet and talk to.' She continues: 'It is like my mother dying [in March 1927]. I suddenly felt, O my dear, how lovely you are. You know, like flowers opening in a corner of a garden, a great bush of white lilac that you had forgotten was there. My love for Richard is like that. Richard may be a be-sotted fat sentimentalist . . . [*sic*] nothing can cut across what my 'psychic' self or 'core' feels towards him.'[15]

With Plank's help she made enquiries about the sale of Aldington's library. She knew how much he had treasured his books; if he was selling them because he needed the money, she wanted to buy them and store them for him. She established, however, that the sale had a more symbolic significance; it was part of his abandonment of the old life. Now Pound contacted her on Aldington's behalf, enquiring about the feasibility of a divorce. 'I know about Richard,' she replied. 'He can get a divource [*sic*] any time if he will do it the right way.' The ellipses multiply: 'It wouldn't be feasable [*sic*] to see Richard . . . [*sic*] but I want you to give him my love . . . [*sic*] and perhaps some day if we get divorced [*sic*] I could see him. I don't know . . . [*sic*] what I am writing means nothing, NOTHING. I can't see really Ezra. And my nose needs blowing.'[16]

Pound wrote back a reassuring letter which prompted an immense outpouring of all her past pain and her longing for the old life. In this letter, she returns, again and again, to Aldington's rejection of her and her baby at the Littoral in 1919: '[A]nything in the way of a shock brings that back and I go to pieces.' She felt vulnerable again. 'All of me', she explained to Pound, 'has been growing like an espalier tree, trained and supported and blossoming too, but trained against a wall, supported against a wall. One side of me is rich and creative, the other has not yet had the time to let the sun get to it.' She was nervous of being seen by anyone from her old life: 'I am so old and look so different. I am so ashammed[*sic*] of myself, of my face and even my body sometimes.' And then there was Bryher to consider: 'Bryher looked after Perdita and as that seemed the only thing I was hanging on for . . . [*sic*] I looked after Bryher.' Now, here she was, with 'a very static and "classic" and peaceful relationship with Bryher and MacPherson', although she felt very lonely at times. 'I couldn't bear to see you,' she told Pound, but added, 'not just for the moment', explaining how it had shocked her to find that she still loved Aldington. She continued, 'I love you too Ezra', and concluded: 'Kenneth MacPherson has been very beautiful to me. It would hurt me horribly if you and he didn't get on together.' [17] What she didn't tell Pound was that the 26-year-old MacPherson was her lover and that this is why Bryher had married him in September 1927. [18]

Thomas MacGreevy in his room at the École Normale Supériere, 1928

Contrary to Pound's instructions, Aldington now wrote directly to her. His letter of 14 March was brief but assured her that he had never intended her any harm. 'Try to believe that my feelings are only of regret and tenderness', he urged her, and asked, 'Will you not let me hear from you?' [19] Her reply must have been immediate and encouraging because he wrote at greater length on 20 March. As far as the matter of the divorce was concerned, there was no urgency and he did not intend to marry again, but considered that in view of their long separation, a formalisation would be 'dignified'. He told her that he had stayed too long in Padworth, both for economic reasons and because of 'other things', which included a 'morbid horror of inflicting any more pain'. Only when he felt 'on the verge of spiritual death' had he made 'the decisive step'. He did not mention Patmore, although Pound had told H.D. of this development, but stayed instead on the safer ground of his work. He had become weary of 'the sterility of reviewing, translating and editing' and knew that *The Times* had been destructive of his 'alertness towards modernity'. While he told her that his latest 'break back to life' was an attempt to do something more creative, he was disparaging about the results so far: he had written a great deal of poetry over the past year, but was not very content with it; as for the novel on which he was working, it gave him 'at least the delusion of writing creatively'. This diffidence perhaps arose from his awareness that H.D., Bryher and McAlmon were prominent on the *avant-garde* scene and his fear that his own work might seem dull in comparison, but he promised to send her a copy of his *Collected Poems* and of *The Eaten Heart*.

Only towards the end of the letter is there any reference to the trauma of 1919. 'I was in a very bad state when I came out of the army, my blood poisoned with bad water and my nerves completely shattered', he told her, mentioning his subsequent nervous collapse in February 1925 and adding: 'I have only had any sort of tranquillity of mind in the past four months.' He concludes by promising that their exchange of letters will remain a secret and by advising her: 'Don't live too much alone, Dooley. It is good sometimes to come into the world and be distracted.' It is a coded request to see her and is carefully defused with: 'But, there, I've lived so long in the country that I'm sick of it, and the mere spectacle of people moving in the streets is a constant entertainment.'[20] The whole letter is finely gauged to reassure the timid H.D. and tempt her out of her Swiss retreat.

It worked. She told Plank that Aldington's words had brought her 'such peace and reassurance'. 'Nothing will be any different,' she assured Plank. 'I will never "go back" naturally, nor would he. I imagine it's a matter of something bigger than that.'[21] A regular correspondence ensued. Since each was anxious about how the other would react to their changed physical appearance if and when (and it soon became a question of 'when' rather than 'if') they met, they exchanged photographs. 'I am very happy to see from the snapshot that H.D. is still H.D.', wrote Aldington and told her that he had sent her his (taken at Rapallo in February) so that she could see how 'the reports of [his] corpulence' had been 'somewhat exaggerated'.[22] (He had, in fact, been on a strict diet for the last six months.) They exchanged information about their work, and by early April he felt able to be more intimate: 'I am so very, very glad, dear Astraea, that you feel able to write to me and receive letters from me. It has given me a healthier inner life. I find it hard to speak of this without hurting you. All I will say now is that I do thank you.'[23] Even more riskily, he wrote: 'When I think of us, how little we asked from the world, how unthinkingly we gave what we had to give, how entirely our errors or misfortunes were our own from which we alone suffered, and then think how almost savagely we were both treated – well I am not pleased with humanity. I am so glad that we have endured, beaten out our storms, come to some sort of open sailing. For you it was much harder, but your courage was greater.'[24]

It was H.D. who suggested she might come to Paris and see him. He was delighted, but realised that he had first to address the 'Brigit problem': 'All I can say is that she suffered very much when you ended the friendship, that she does not know why you did it, that I do not think she bears any vindictive feeling to you, & that in any event I should allow neither of you to influence me against the other. . . . I thought it best to speak frankly. I am *not* trying to hurt you, but to clear things up a bit. *Of course*, I don't suggest your meeting Brigit again. Why should you, when you have decided you don't want to?'[25] He was right to be wary; H.D. was upset by his comments and he had to apologise: 'I feel very regretful if I hurt you and stirred up sad feelings by mentioning Brigit. I feel there was a misunderstanding, an error, and thought perhaps I could clear it up. Perhaps that was presumptuous. . . . I won't mention it again. Only don't feel that Brigit feels any resentment against you.'[26]

Meanwhile both Hughes and Pound had come to Paris and both wanted to see H.D. The final arrangements for her meeting with Aldington at the beginning of May were tortuous. She wanted to see Pound first: she knew that she would find her reunion with him less stressful and that she could rely on his affection and understanding to give her confidence for the more difficult meeting. She also intended being accompanied by Eileen MacPherson (Kenneth's sister, although her actual identity would not be made clear to anyone) to defuse the intensity of the occasion. Aldington was clear about one thing: he did not want Pound present at his first meeting with H.D. 'By all means bring your Swedish friend [part of the fiction about Eileen], if you wish, but don't, don't let's meet under the false auspices of Ezra.'[27] He even asked her not to see Pound until *after* she had seen *him*. Given the way he had opened his heart to Pound about his feelings for Patmore, part of his anxiety must have

Brigit Patmore, 1929

been due to embarrassment. And then there was Patmore herself. H.D. had sent her a bouquet of flowers to demonstrate her willingness to be reconciled, but had not really wanted her to be present when she met Aldington; she wrote to Pound on 21 April: 'I am very nervous about going and not very happy. I think it best not to see Bgt this time but do not get me 'wrong' about that. . . . I can't face seeing her until I DO get the thing straight a little with R. first.'[28] Patmore, however, would make sure that H.D. was denied that luxury.

The events of Wednesday 1 May had much of the quality of a farce. Eileen MacPherson's arrival from London was delayed; Pound called on H.D at her hotel (the Auberge du Navigateur on the Quai des Grands Augustins) at the same time as Aldington and Patmore and had to be hidden until they left. He then took her to tea at an attractive spot opposite the hotel on the Île du Cité. She told Bryher, 'He was terribly nice, very big and bulky and fat and very kind.' As Aldington had feared, Pound now proceeded to tell her all the 'dirt': how Aldington had fallen for Cunard, who had 'revitalised him' but was now bored with him and how he had '"winged" Bgt in the hunt for N[ancy].' This may not seem a very fair account on Pound's part, but it may well have been 'doctored' by H.D. for Bryher's consumption. She had to keep up the pretence of despising her husband, who, she told Bryher, seemed 'oddly young and harmless' and 'devitalised'. Pound had apparently also told her that Patmore was still 'carrying on with Stephen [Guest]'.[29]

Pound took H.D. and Eileen MacPherson to dinner that evening and the two women dined with Aldington and Patmore the following night. In a further letter H.D. regaled Bryher with another farcical series of events that took place two days later. Exhausted by her first few days in Paris, H.D. had retired to bed early on the Saturday evening, only to be called to the telephone; it was Aldington inviting her and Eileen to a party. She had refused, gone back to bed, ignored a further telephone call and then been awoken an hour later by a knocking on her door. She had opened it to admit Cunard, 'looking like a goddess, beautiful and all glitter', an embarrassed Aldington and, 'slinking in the background', Patmore. Cunard insisted, 'You must put on your clothes and come', but ended up offering H.D. a cigarette and settling herself down for a chat. H.D. was clearly won over by Cunard's charm but her continuing hostility towards Patmore (perhaps amplified for Bryher's benefit) is clear from her letter.[30]

She was happier once Patmore had departed (for three weeks in London) on the following Monday, and she saw more of both Pound and Aldington, as well as meeting Glenn Hughes, before she herself left for London on the Thursday. After she and Eileen had dined with Aldington on the Tuesday evening, he wrote to Patmore: 'Quite a good séance with H.D. and Egon [Eileen]. After dinner I took them to the Cigogne, and H.D. actually danced, with Egon and with me. . . . then on to the Soufflet. . . . We said goodnight very respectably at midnight.'[31] H.D. would tell Plank: 'He was on his own for a bit, his lady had gone to London, and then it was that we had those marvelous [sic] times together.'[32]

She had clearly enjoyed her week and told Bryher, '[W]e have not met half E.[Pound] and R. [Aldington] wanted, as I was too inhibited and did not like sitting too much at bars just now . . . I do miss you but had no idea I could so enjoy Paris.'[33] To George Plank she could be more honest about the experience and its effect upon her: '[T]hings were very odd, very lovely and most inexplicable. I mean Richard was exactly as he was before the war, it was as if some landslide had taken place in his being, which in fact it has. We saw much of each other though always with others . . . [sic] I was afraid of too much intimacy and he was altogether charming and dear.' In particular, she had been touched by the way in which Aldington remembered all their times together, the memories 'perfectly fresh and untouched, the minutest details startlingly preserved, and fresh and fragrant with none of the intervening dust . . . '[34] Her delight (and perhaps the impossibility of sharing it with Bryher) even led her to write freely to Glenn Hughes, a new acquaintance: 'I was terribly happy in Paris. I have the greatest feeling of joy and tenderness in Richard though any serious renewal of an "alliance" other than delightfully superficial and intellectually very poignant, is out of the question. I want people to know how I do feel about Richard and how happy I was seeing him look so well and happy after the horrible years of the war and the dreadful break-down he had then, and that I, in a different way, shared in.'[35]

There was no further talk of formalising their separation. H.D. seems to have learned from Patmore that the latter was unlikely to be able to obtain a divorce from her husband; more importantly, both the relationship H.D and Aldington had now established with each other and those they enjoyed with their partners were delicate ones that could easily be unsettled by the publicity of the divorce court. The problem of Perdita's paternity had also been side-stepped through her adoption in May 1928 by Bryher and MacPherson. Personally and artistically, both Aldington and H.D. felt particularly fulfilled at this time and their reconciliation had made an important contribution; yet both were still highly sensitive and wary of the public arena.

Instead, their correspondence for some months was concerned with a shared project that was both new and familiar: an Imagist anthology. The suggestion seems to have come either from Hughes or from Walter Lowenfels. It was not to be a new beginning for the movement, simply a tribute to which all those who had appeared in *Des Imagistes* and the later anthologies were to be asked to contribute. In Glenn Hughes's words: 'The Imagists [were] here mustered not for a charge, but for parade', to be considered and enjoyed 'as independent artists, who once upon a time (only fifteen years ago) found it necessary to unite in the assertion of their right to artistic independence.'[36]

Aldington took on the role of editor, but there were poets whom he could not, for personal reasons, approach: Ford, Cournos and Lawrence, with all of whom he had fallen out – the first in 1914, the other two more recently; and Pound, who would be more likely to respond to an appeal from H.D. Not even H.D. could persuade Pound to take part, but she was more successful with Cournos, Ford (who also contributed an introduction for the book) and Lawrence, although the latter's short and unfeeling letter (the first since 1918) must have caused her some pain: '[Now] it's more than ten years since we met and what should we have to say? God knows! Nothing really. It's no use saying anything. That's my last conviction. Least said, soonest mended: which assumes that the breakage has already happened.' He told her that Yorke was in Paris, ' – not in a good way at all, poor Arabella.' Enclosing some of his 'pansies', he commented, 'You won't like any of 'em, but you can't get blood out of a stone.'[37]

As the editorial work drew to a close, Aldington, realising how it had drawn H.D. and himself together on ground on which they could both feel safe, suggested that they might collaborate on another project, but she did not respond to the suggestion. Nevertheless, they both relished their new relationship and met once more in Paris in early June when H.D. was again travelling between Switzerland and London. Aldington wrote her a total of thirty-two letters that year. Those preceding their first meeting commence 'Dear Astraea'; thereafter she became 'Dearest Dooley', an indication of the warmth of his affection. 'Whatever happens, don't let us get separated again', he begged her.[38] She wrote to Cournos: 'Without any intervention, R. wrote me and I have been in close touch with him ever since. We saw one another much in Paris and write constantly. We are very, very close to one another intellectually and spiritually. . . . There is no question of R. and self ever becoming in any way "intimate" again and that is why this other relationship is so exquisite and sustaining.'[39]

Her relationship with Patmore remained one of mutual distrust, perhaps complicated by her own growing friendship with Stephen Haden-Guest. That

Richard Aldington in a Chatto and Windus publicity photograph, 1929

summer Patmore would write to her: 'I was so happy and excited at the thought of seeing you once more and your flowers – but somehow there was great pain and I don't know if it was yours or mine.'[40] She accused H.D. (probably correctly) of only seeing her because she was with Aldington. The letter reveals the extent to which Patmore was finding the revitalised intellectual and artistic connection between Aldington and H.D. threatening and excluding. She craved the kind of relationship between the three of them that had existed in the early days of their friendship – and which H.D. had eventually come to experience as a threat to her marriage. H.D. was also experiencing complications in her domestic relationships, as she revealed to Plank in July: 'There have been alarrums [*sic*] and excursions from this end. I impishly enjoy it all.'[41] And she wrote a month later: 'He [Aldington] is beginning to write rather affectionate letters (your prediction!!!) And that seems just funny – and just incredible. But it did help seeing him and you helped so, dear George. But you "SEE" – *Kenneth* – Gawd!'

In the circumstances, it is not surprising that, despite the renewed affection and trust between them, she and Aldington were content to maintain a primarily epistolary friendship. Her unconventional triangular relationship with Bryher and MacPherson brought her tranquillity and security but their marriage also gave her a space in which to be independent and solitary when she wished. As for Aldington, despite the growing warmth of his affection for H.D., his passion for Patmore was unabated, as his letters and telegrams to her throughout her three-week absence in London that May reveal. Guessing her anxieties about his relationship with H.D., he wrote: 'My life is filled with happiness because of you. It is Brigit and Brigit only who is the perfect lover, the perfect companion and the perfect woman. I am completely happy with you, dear, and want only you. There is nothing as lovely as you in the world. You mean all happy things to me now. So long as you are you I shall be happy. Our love delights me – I like the idea of us.'[42] You mustn't ever worry about my being unfaithful to you! I want *you*', he reassured her.[43]

During her absence a bizarre incident occurred. On the night of 18 May he was involved in a taxi-cab collision. The following day, Walter Lowenfels wrote to H.D. at Aldington's request to pass on information concerning the Imagist Anthology for which she was waiting, telling her about the accident and reassuring her that Aldington was unhurt but rather shocked and needed a few days' rest.[44] The next day Aldington himself wrote, detailing the circumstances of the accident and telling H.D.: 'Everyone else is in hospital and pretty dicky. I escaped with miraculous luck. I got a few cuts on the head, feel a bit sore and stiff all over, and have a tendency to faint away if I walk, but I'm perfectly O.K., eating well, and sleeping not too badly. The woman who was with me is pregnant (NOT by me!) and was telling me all about it and asking my advice when the smash happened. She was too ill to see anyone today, poor darling, but she's being looked after.'[45]

A further letter on 25 May assured H.D. that the woman was recovering and her baby unharmed, but H.D. was still curious and eventually he revealed the identity of the girl who 'got a nasty bang in the tummy as well as a very bad bruise with black eyes'.[46] It was Valentine Dobrée and we might wonder why Aldington was alone in a cab with her in Paris on an evening when Patmore was in London. Her pregnancy (and her child was not harmed by the accident, being born in January the following year) is perhaps our guarantee that no more than a flirtatious rendezvous was involved.[47] He told H.D.: 'She's a nice girl, but a little frightening to me. Rather terrifyingly highbrow – you know the sort of thing, the English upper class disdain put into intellectual and spiritual things.' He adds: 'That's where Nancy's so wonderful; she is completely free of any snobbery of any sort.' And hypocrisy, we might find ourselves wanting to add, particularly since the 1928 *Collected Poems* volume is dedicated to the Dobrées – a public acknowledgment of his admiration for her.

His letter to the injured Dobrée provides a rather different picture of his feelings: 'I want most awfully to keep in touch with you, & I do want you to get free of the intertwinings which worry you. Why on earth should I quarrel with you? I'm only happy that you want me as a friend. One can't define the limits of friendship, & honestly I don't want to force you where you don't want to go. But don't let's get utterly estranged.' He does take the opportunity to express his regrets for his behaviour of the previous year: 'I owe a great deal to you. It was the shock of last summer which turned my eyes in upon myself, & showed me how I was allowing myself to be degenerate.'[48] He concludes by asking her to 'try to like' Patmore.

Despite the developments in his personal life, the novel was Aldington's chief preoccupation during these weeks, although one not unconnected break from his work was to see a performance of *Journey's End* on the evening of 14 May. '[I] wept & wrung my hands through all the last act', he told Patmore. 'Bad art, perhaps, but the stuff of life & deep emotion.'[49]

He wrote the last three chapters on 10 May and took them straight round to the Lowenfels' apartment for Lilian to type. After the strains of meeting with H.D., Patmore's departure and completing the novel, he was in a state of emotional collapse for a few days. He had been sending the manuscript piece by piece to Chatto and Windus, whom Friede had recommended as his British publishers. On 14 May he was able to wire Patmore: 'Chatto accept novel. £100 advance.'

Thus it was that he came to know Charles Prentice, senior partner at Chatto and Windus.[50] Aldington's portrayal of him in *Pinorman*, his 1954 group memoir of Prentice, Pino Orioli and Norman Douglas, is warm and affectionate: 'Charles was a shy and reserved man, gentle and almost hesitant in manner, often silent, with a very clear complexion and benevolent expression. With his gold-rimmed glasses and bald head and kindliness he had some resemblance to Mr Pickwick. . . . [I]f I was asked to name a really 'good' man I have known I should at once say "Charles".' Aldington respected him for his scholarship and genuine love of literature. Prentice was the right man to see this potentially prickly writer and his controversial novel through to publication. In *Pinorman* Aldington gives us some idea of his working methods: 'He liked to have a novel sent to him chapter by chapter, to watch it develop, and to collaborate with encouragement, suggestions and gentle but shrewd criticisms.'[51] Prentice would have to insist on many cuts in Aldington's outspoken text and it is remarkable that he retained the writer's trust and good will throughout the painful process.

Aldington outlined some of the details in a letter to Patmore on 16 May: 'Among the words objected to are "penis", "orgasm", "hymen", "impregnate a virgin bride", "balls", "application" (cold water to genitals). Among passages objected to are mention of physical relations between children, George touching Priscilla's breasts (!), Maisie's legs, invocation to Aphrodite, whole long passage on sexual intercourse & the British journalist, long passages on free love and sexual problems

(4 pages!), passage on contraception, 4 more pages on sex, both passages of love-scene with Fanny.'[52] It is a measure of his trust in Prentice (whom he had not yet met in person) and perhaps also of his long familiarity (mostly through the experiences of Lawrence) with the British censorship laws and the attitudes of the middle-class public and popular press, that he blamed the publisher not at all.[53] However, he would not delete or replace the expurgated words and passages. (The exception to this was his use of the word 'mucking' to replace – in thirty-six instances – the more common word with which it rhymes.) He had already come up with his preferred tactic for combating the problem, the method already employed by Djuna Barnes in her recently published novel, _Ryder_: the publishers were to replace the deleted words with asterisks – one for every letter of each deleted word, so that readers would be in little doubt about the omissions. Of course, this would not address the problem of longer expurgated passages, which, for aesthetic reasons, could only be indicated by one or two rows of asterisks. There was to be a total of nearly a thousand expurgated words in the British edition of the novel; Friede, both because American censorship was not so strict and because his experience with _The Well of Loneliness_ had made him bolder, made less than a quarter of that number.[54]

Apart from supervising the expurgations and soothing his author, Prentice would monitor and manage public reaction to the novel's outspokenness. The lending libraries – Mudies, Smiths and Boots – were particularly sensitive to any expression of moral outrage in the press. ('[T]hese people are afraid of their subscribers coming in and waving walking sticks and umbrellas at them,' Prentice explained to Aldington.)[55] While permitting him to print a hundred copies of the expurgated passages for distribution through Titus's and Beach's bookshops, Prentice refused to allow an unexpurgated limited edition of the novel until they could be sure that all the reviews had appeared. (An unexpurgated edition was published by Jack Kahane and Henry Babou in Paris in the autumn of 1930.)[56]

His novel completed, Aldington was soon back at work. Far from 'writing out' his war experience, _Death of a Hero_ had prompted some 'war sketches' and he sought Prentice's advice on where he could place these. By August 1929 he had written four of these stories.[57] There was also translation still to be done: he had the Boccaccio to finish before moving on to Gérard de Nerval's _Aurélia_ and then to Euripides.[58] Friede had shown an interest in translations of classic Greek drama and Aldington had decided to begin with _Alcestis_. Meanwhile, he offered both Friede and Prentice his _A Dream in the Luxembourg_; Friede accepted it and Prentice told Aldington that he thought it 'a charming and unforced poem' but that Chatto would defer a decision until they saw how sales of the novel went.[59] (Prentice's further comment that he could not quite believe in any poem 'just now' being a best-seller unless it was by Kipling or Masefield 'or one of those worthy people' shows us that Aldington's cynicism about the English reading public was not unjustified.) By the end of the year Cunard's Hours Press would produce a limited edition of two hundred signed copies of his other long poem, _The Eaten Heart_.

He did not forget, however, that his new life must not repeat the mistakes of the old; there must be time for relaxation and pleasure. As soon as H.D.'s June visit to

Paris was over, he and Patmore headed for the Mediterranean coast. Toulon now had romantic associations for them and they settled for the rest of the summer at Fabregas, ten miles to the south-west. They had rooms in the Hotel Rivage overlooking the sea; far in the distance they could see the island of Port Cros. Aldington's routine was relaxed but disciplined. He worked on Greek translation from six-thirty to eight in the morning; after breakfast he took a walk before settling to creative work – poetry or the war sketches; he would go for a swim before lunch and in the afternoon there would be a siesta, another swim and then translation or writing articles until seven, when he would go for an hour's walk by the sea before dinner. He told H.D., 'I feel better down here than I've felt since 1916.'[60]

It was from Fabregas that he wrote what seems to have been his last ever letter to Monro.[61] The two men had grown apart and this may have been due as much to Monro's increasing depression and distressing eyesight problems, and the fact that he was losing his battle with alcohol, as to Aldington's loss of interest in London and its intellectual world. In *Life for Life's Sake* he tells us that he was to have been Monro's literary executor but that Monro replaced him with Flint in the early 1930s after a sharp exchange of views in a journal.[62] Monro would die in March 1932, at the age of fifty-three, not from his alcoholism, as might have been expected, but from tubercolosis.

Aldington was back in Paris – this time at the Hotel Corneille, overlooking the Jardin du Luxembourg – for the publication of *Death of a Hero*. The American edition appeared first, on 6 September, the British edition two weeks later. Prentice had sent copies to Wells, Shaw, George Moore, Wyndham Lewis, Woolf and Bennett. Wells wrote to Aldington: 'I wasn't merely interested, I was deeply moved by it. I don't think the state of mind in London among intellectual people has ever been done so well or nearly as well.'[63] Lewis wired, 'Death of Hero Splendid Congratulate You War Chapters Superb Writing'. Arnold Bennett's review appeared in *The Evening Standard* on the day of publication; it was a mixed response, but concluded that the novel had 'genuine quality' and was 'imposssible to ignore.'

The recognition of these literary 'giants' was gratifying and went a long way towards repairing Aldington's confidence and self-esteem. He had earlier been disheartened by Herbert Read's response. Since *In Retreat* had been his original inspiration, he had sent Read the proofs in July, keen to hear his friend's reaction. 'The novel is great fun, Herbert, and once you get started it's amazing how the thing buzzes along', he had told him, adding more seriously, 'What you have done in criticism is great and valuable, but you have much to say about life as well as about thought and literature, and the satisfaction of creative work is very, very great.'[64] Read's lukewarm response to the novel, however, prompted his rather tart comment: 'It was very good of you to spend so much time in writing about my hero – quite a junior Clark lecture! I confess that precepts and theorising about writing arouse a very languid interest in me . . . '[65] It had been more of a blow than Read probably realised; Aldington had been seeking the reactions of a friend and former soldier, not those of a literary critic.

Richard Aldington at Fabregas, 1929

He was more fortunate with Flint, who wrote him an affectionate and enthusiastic letter. Unsurprisingly, it was the satirical portraits of Eliot, Ford and, especially, Pound ('I simply revelled in Upjohn's conversation') that most engaged Flint but, more seriously, he told Aldington that the novel was 'a big performance' and that it held together firmly, was 'well-knit, organic': 'You talk about despising form in the novel; but dammit, your novel has distinct form, clear-cut.'[66] An even more surprising correspondent was Cournos, who wrote: 'Whatever has passed between us, I will not deny myself the privilege of saluting you for your Death of a Hero.' He called it 'an honest and courageous piece of work' which 'moves the reader . . . to the fierce indignation the author himself must have felt.'[67] It is worth noting that Aldington, who generally destroyed his correspondence, kept these two letters.

Another letter that he kept came from William Carlos Williams. Given the sharpness of his criticism of Aldington's war poems exactly ten years earlier, his warm response to the novel must have been gratifying.[68] However, unlike almost every critic, at the time and subsequently, Williams preferred the pre-war sections of the novel to its account of the hero's war experiences: 'The parts of the book leading up to the war are *superb*, the war part is less well told than it is in either *All Quiet on the Western Front* and *The Case of Sergeant Grischa*. I think the reason is that you felt the horror and welter of the war so, that there is a subconscious mental stiffening as you approach it, just as you had to stiffen yourself when you actually endured the crucifixion of it.' He concluded: 'To me the great thesis and the great message of your book is to be found in your statement that the post-war minds of men are poisoned. We can't shove millions of young chaps under the sod and not be poisoned.'[69]

Weasel words came from another old friend: Whitham, with whom Aldington had finally re-established contact in May. This dilatoriness may well have been due to consideration for Yorke, of whom the Whithams were very fond, but the correspondence had become a regular and affectionate one by the time the novel was published. Unfortunately, Aldington had promised Whitham a copy and had failed to send one by the time the most damning review of the novel appeared: that of St John Ervine in the *Daily Express* on 3 October.[70] Whitham wrote to Aldington: 'I saw Ervine's notice. He may have reasoned grounds for a reasoned criticism; but his criticism, as a rule, over-reaches itself and he drowns whatever sense is in him by torrents of rudeness', and he told Aldington that the book must be touched with genius, 'since half the readers seem to hate it viciously and t'other half to admire it hysterically.'[71]

It is fortunate that Aldington was unaware of the letter Whitham had sent Ervine only two days earlier: 'You were marvellous on Aldington's book. He promised me a copy, has not sent it; so I have not read it. Probably you were justified in swingeing him for his rancour and hatreds and perpetuated chicken's pip; but, by Jove! you must have made him smart; and let us hope you have given him a medicine he will take. But surely his book was touched with greatness somewhere, was it not? He has never quite freed himself from the rage and tatters of the 'Egoist' and the

Pound-Eliot-Joyce-Lewis school have much to answer for in the way of nonsense, impudence; and one or perhaps two redemptive virtues.'[72] We may feel more forgiving of Whitham's disloyalty here if we remind ourselves that he had been a serious and hard-working novelist for almost twenty years without achieving any popular success.

And a success Aldington's novel was. The British sales outstripped the American ones by the end of November and had almost reached ten thousand by the end of the year. Rights had been sold to France, Germany, Sweden and the Soviet Union. Chatto and Windus were happy to go ahead with the publication of *A Dream in the Luxembourg*, the *Imagist Anthology* and the war stories; they would go on to publish Aldington's translations of *Alcestis* and Gourmont's *Lettres á l'Amazone* and a revised edition of his Lawrence chapbook. He had also landed a profitable contract (£400 a year) as literary critic for *The Sunday Referee*.[73] His earnings for 1929 were in the region of £1,000; by the end of the following year they would be £2,500. 'In the autumn of 1929 it seemed to me,' he wrote in *Life for Life's* Sake, 'that I could accept the remainder of life with a certain amount of confidence and cheerfulness.'[74]

He could certainly subsidise the lifestyle he wanted: the life of the traveller recommended to him by Lawrence in 1926. In November he and Patmore set off south to Florence and Rome, where they visited the Randalls. From there they followed in his 1913 footsteps to Naples, Amalfi, Sorrento and on to Capri before continuing to Palermo and Agrigentum. ('[W]henever I stopped for more than a few days a miserable tendency to start working asserted itself, so I decided to push on', he tells us in *Life for Life's Sake*.)[75]

He wrote to H.D.: 'I went up to Anacapri, and drank some wine at the Pensione del Lauro. . . . I thought very tenderly over old times.'[76] 'Youth, spring in a Mediterranean island, Greek poetry, idleness – these were the simple factors of an enchantment whose memory will only end with life', he had written in 1924.[77] Now aged thirty-seven and with a new lover, who had also been his first lover, a successful novelist with two more novels already taking shape in his mind and with a long poem recently completed, he had returned for the first time to the Italy he had shared with H.D. in 1913. The young man who had walked south down Gower Street one day in the spring of 1911 could not have foreseen how troubled his journey to success, maturity and happiness would be. Now, however poignantly, he could face recalling one of its happiest moments.

22. Death of a Hero

We hear so much of the bravery and horrors at the front. Brave the men were, all honour to them. It was at home the world was lost. We hear too little of the collapse of the proud human spirit at home, the triumph of sordid, rampant, raging meanness. 'The bite of a jackal is blood-poisoning and mortification.' And at home stayed all the jackals, middle-aged male and female jackals. And they bit us all. And blood-poisoning and mortification set in. D.H. Lawrence, *Kangaroo*, 1923)[1]

[This] book is really a threnody, a memorial in its ineffective way to a generation which hoped much, strove honestly and suffered deeply.
(Richard Aldington, dedicatory letter to Halcott Glover,
Death of a Hero, 1929)[2]

In late May 1928 H.D. sent Aldington a copy of the recent translation of Erich Remarque's *Im Westen Nichts Neues*. Writing to her on 6 June, he told her that he thought it a great book and 'a great thing to have done', but he had been struck by its 'delight in brutality for brutality's sake'. He continued: 'Admitted that the whole business was so brutal that its brutality can't be exaggerated, still the work of art demands a sort of restraint, and the choosing of typical rather than exceptional horrors. Moreover, I also think that he concentrates too much on battles and too little on the dreary spaces between battles.' These comments are an indication of how seriously he took the task of rendering the experience of warfare authentically and without melodrama; it was the achievement for which he had admired Read's *In Retreat* back in 1925.

The letter continues: 'My book is a bigger and different sort of affair, covering three generations – you know my weakness for the historical method! More than half the book is pre-war. The style abruptly changes with the war, and becomes impersonal instead of occasionally humorous and occasionally prose-poetic. The war part is quite calm and impersonal. . . . I think that playing the fool a bit in the opening part makes the subsequent tragedy more poignant.'[3]

Coming fresh to the novel after twenty years as a professional writer, Aldington was determined to find a form that served his purposes. He was disingenuous (we might compare Wilfred Owen's claim not to be interested in poetry) in his claim to Halcott Glover that he had ignored conventions of form and method and thought that 'the excuse for the novel [was] that one can do any damned thing one pleases.'[4] (No less a professional novelist than Arnold Bennett took exception to this remark, writing in his *Evening Standard* review of *Death of a Hero* that 'one can't with impunity do any damn thing one pleases in a novel' and that Aldington's novel suffered throughout from lack of form.)[5] In his essay 'Notes on the War Novel' Aldington further claimed that the war novel as a genre was closer to reporting than to the traditional novel, but when he suggests Dickens as a model for the kind of 'observation of life' he hoped to achieve, we see that he is not advocating either detachment or naturalism.[6]

In a 1934 letter to the American critic Gorham Munson, he explained: 'So far as the form of the Hero went I determined it should be organic, not pre-conceived, i.e. the shape had to grow out of the matter and emotions. But I gave myself a couple of guides. I kept a rough concept of the Euripidean tragedy in mind, which is why I give the whole plot of the story in the Prologue – the intention there being to avoid false surprise.'[7] The Prologue therefore concerns the reception of the news of the death in battle of the hero, George Winterbourne, by his parents, wife and mistress, and ends with the diegetic narrator's explanation of his need to tell George's story:

> The death of a hero! What mockery, what bloody cant! What sickening putrid cant! George's death is a symbol to me of the whole sickening bloody waste of it, the damnable stupid waste and torture of it. . . . That is why I am writing the life of George Winterbourne, a unit, one human body murdered, but to me a symbol. It is an atonement, a desperate effort to wipe off the blood-guiltiness.[8]

Like a Greek tragedy, the novel then proceeds to three major episodes in the drama of George Winterbourne's life: Part One covers his family life and upbringing and Part Two his pre-war and early wartime life as a young painter (rather than poet) in London and, in particular, his relationships with two young women, and the intellectual and artistic circle within which he moves. Part Three covers George's wartime service until his death on 4 November 1918, but actually ends with Field Marshall Foche's Armistice letter to the troops of the Allied Armies. True to the Greek model, the novel concludes with an epilogue, an elegiac poem which begins:

> Eleven years after the fall of Troy,
> We, the old men – some of us nearly forty –
> Met and talked on the sunny rampart
> Over our wine. . . .[9]

Thus, if we take the Trojan War as a metaphor for the Great War, the poem is set at the time of the writing of *Death of a Hero* by the thirty-six year old veteran.

The constant commentary on the action by the unnamed narrator (an army officer acquaintance of the protagonist) resembles that of the chorus in a Greek tragedy. Aldington moves his narrator in and out of the diegesis as he relates matters to which as a character he would not have had access. Critics like Blunden, who remarked of the narrator that, 'at times his sharply defined pictures of incident and reports of conversation are seen to be those of actual contact, at others he is the phantasm who sees through walls and hears all secrets', are using as a reference point a realist mode that was not intended.[10] Like a Greek chorus, the narrator is both within and outside of the narrative. He is, unapologetically, the authorial voice.

Aldington told Munson that his other guide was 'a rough concept of a symphony' and he gave the four narrative sections headings that suggest sonata form: the Prologue is headed *allegretto* and the three main sections *vivace*, *andante cantabile* and *adagio*. Andrew Frayn in a recent (unpublished) study of the novel suggests that 'these musical directions descend in pace and also correspond to the pace of George's life', the Prologue 'showing how rapidly George's friends have adapted to life without him, the "rapidity with which he was forgotten"', and the subsequent sections demonstrating 'the slowing down of his life towards his eventual death.' As Frayn points out, the novel has other musical features: 'In contrast to the slowing pace . . . the volume builds to a barely tolerable cacophony':

> CRASH! Like an orchestra at the signal of a baton the thousands of guns north and south opened up. The night sprang to flickering daylight with the gun-flashes, the earth trembled with the shock, the air roared and screamed with shells.[11]

In a prefatory letter to Hal Glover, Aldington also refers to the work as a 'jazz novel' – in the same sense, he suggests, as *A Fool i' the Forest* was 'jazz poetry' – and he comments, 'You will see how appropriate that is to the theme.' In recalling *A Fool i' the Forest* he seems to be referring to that poem's variety of forms, voices and languages, suggestive of the improvisation characteristic of jazz. *Death of a Hero* flits between George's viewpoint and that of the narrator, and it incorporates a poem (the epilogue), a document (Foche's proclamation), trench signposts, snatches of soldiers' and music-hall songs, onomatopoeic (and capitalised) representations of the sounds of artillery, and a range of prose styles from the satirical and the didactic (even declamatory) to evocative descriptions of the sounds, sights and smells of the battlefield. It retains throughout a sequential narrative that never becomes fragmented. Aldington was, of course, frequenting Henry Crowder's Plantation Club at the time he was writing the novel and it is feasible that he saw his eclectic approach as reflecting the style of music to which he was listening. However, in his comment that the term 'jazz' seemed appropriate to the theme, he was perhaps evoking the surface brilliance and gaiety and the deeper disillusionment characteristic of the post-war 'jazz age', summed up for him in the personalities and life-styles of Cunard and her contemporaries.[12]

Nevertheless, both contemporary and later critics have been disconcerted by the difference in tone and style between, the Prologue and Parts One and Two, with their satirical portraits and angry commentary and Part Three, in which the novelist achieves, with moving effect, the restraint which he so admired in Read, and the absence of which he deplored in Remarque. Although many of these critics describe the novel as 'formless', what they seem to be objecting to is the tone of the Prologue and Parts One and Two. The extreme example was Ervine with his comment that Aldington was 'a peevish person in sad need of being turned over someone's knee and severely spanked'.[13] Bennett found the writer 'extremely and convincingly destructive', but remarked that he could have achieved finer effects with less violence, and that 'naive preachment' ruined many pages of the novel. In contrast, he found the 'war sections' 'superb' and commented that the opening of Part Three ranked 'with any chapter in any war-novel, English, French, Russian or German', while the close of the book was 'very powerful indeed.'

Of course, many contemporary criticisms of the pre-war parts of the novel were based on a conservative objection to their analysis of Victorian and Edwardian Britain. It is interesting to note that Edmund Blunden, who would suffer from the effects of his war-service for the rest of his life, had no objection to the virulent tone of the novel: 'The quality of Mr Aldington's book is its indignation and study of revenge. . . . We do not wish him in this *Death of a Hero* other than he is – a man appalled by the inhumanities suddenly come upon those who were in their hopeful youth at the outbreak of the war, and assailing with inspired intensity those who seem responsible for and apathetic towards the sacrifice.'[14] The objections of more recent critics have tended to be on aesthetic grounds, the hectoring tone of the earlier sections being seen as artistically excessive (perhaps an echo of Bennett's comment that 'first-rate novelists rarely indulge themselves with anger').[15]

Hugh Cecil is one of the few commentators to suggest that the novel is, in some ways, 'a work of comedy': 'Aldington enjoyed expressing himself extravagantly, shocking his readers with impermissible sentiments, accusing women of finding the death of their loved ones erotically stimulating, accusing artists of treating war not as a tragedy but as an opportunity for art. In truth he did not think this of all artists or all women.'[16] This assessment reminds us of Aldington's own comments to H.D. that he had 'play[ed] the fool a bit in the opening part' and that, in his opinion, this '[made] the subsequent tragedy more poignant.'

The caricatures of George's parents and of his artistic acquaintances in London are extremely entertaining. Knowing how close some of these portraits are to their originals, we may feel that on a personal level, Aldington was – like Lawrence on many occasions – betraying certain relationships, and that whether this was in pursuit of artistic expression, for satirical effect, or out of a genuine feeling that he had himself been betrayed by those originals, may be unimportant. George's childhood experiences so closely mirror Aldington's, as related in his memoir and in his sister's recollections and *roman à clef*, that we can have little doubt that George's parents resemble Jessie May and Albert Edward. In Part One of the novel, which covers their meeting and courtship, their marriage and their parenting, they are portrayed, not entirely unsympathetically, as products, even victims, of their Victorian upbringing; but in the Prologue, which is the reader's introduction to them, they are grotesques (the word the narrator uses). George's mother is 'as sordid, avaricious, conventional and spiteful a middle-class woman as you could dread to meet', while his father possesses 'a genius for messing up other people's lives' and takes refuge in 'a drivelling religiosity'.[17] While she finds the news of her son's death erotically stimulating, he resorts to 'a pleasantly emotional evening' with his confessor.[18]

In Chapter Two we explored the connection between the writer's upbringing and that of George Winterbourne, but it is important to note that in the Prologue and Part One of the novel the contempt he expresses through his narrator for George's father and the anger with which he portrays his mother are breathtakingly personal and violent. Aldington also presents us with an analysis of the materialism, philistinism and hypocrisy of middle-class society at the turn of the century ('An England morally buried in great foggy wrappings of hypocrisy and prosperity and cheapness') and a rational judgement that '[i]t was the regime of Cant before the war which made the Cant during the War so damnably possible and easy'.[19] George's personal problems are clearly laid at the door of 'his singular home life and appalling mother'.[20] (Nevertheless Aldington told H.D. cheerfully: '[T]here is a satirical onslaught on my family which ought to amuse you.')[21]

The portraits of Pound, Ford and Eliot are of a different order.[22] First of all, they are not completely uncharitable: Shobbe (Ford), Tubbe (Eliot) and Bobbe (Lawrence) are all 'more or less honest cranks' or 'at least' possess 'so much vanity and obstinacy that they seemed honest'; Upjohn (Pound) may be 'a bit of a charlatan' and 'odiously conceited', but '[t]here was something very kind-hearted and generous' in him. The portraits are also both apt and very funny, realised as much through beautifully observed comic dialogue as through commentary. It is unsurprising that both Wells and Flint thought them masterly. Nevertheless, there were certainly scores being settled here, and, more importantly, there is a relevant message: the artists and intellectuals, who claimed to be rejecting the humbug and hypocrisy of the Victorians, were themselves guilty of the same vices: 'Self-interest, though universal, is less tolerable in those who are supposed to be above it' and '[v]anity is none the less odious even when there is some reason for it.'[23] The most damning episode of the novel, in this regard, is the one in Part Three when George returns home on leave from the front and is patronised by Upjohn and Tubbe, who have little interest in his experiences or in what is happening on the other side of the Channel. (*Death of a Hero* would not be Aldington's final satirical portrait of either Pound or Eliot.)[24]

Aldington brought to his vignette of Upjohn all the scepticism, irritation, amusement and affection that Pound had always excited in him. Ford and Eliot, on the other hand, are coldly drawn. Shobbe is 'a plump and talented snob of German origin . . . an excellent example of the artist's amazing selfishness and vanity, who, after the comfort of his own person, really cared for nothing but his prose style and literary reputation'. Tubbe is portrayed as 'an exceedingly ardent and patriotic British Tory, standing for Royalism in Art, Authority in Politics and Classicism in religion', who found that 'an interrogative silence on his part forced other people to talk, and made them slightly ill at ease, so that they betrayed what they did not always wish to express'.[25]

The portrait of Lawrence is another matter. There is a savagery that is absent from the merely malicious renderings of Ford and Eliot. Bobbe is 'a sandy-haired, narrow-chested little man with spiteful blue eyes and a malevolent class-hatred', who 'exercised his malevolence with comparative impunity by trading upon his working-class origins and his indigestion, of which he had been dying for twenty years'. From a man who had so recently witnessed Lawrence's losing battle with tuberculosis, this seems lacking in compassion. 'Nobody of decent breeding could hit Mr Bobbe as he deserved,' we are told, 'because his looks were a perpetual reminder of his disease, and his behaviour and habits gave continual evidence of his origin.' Entering the battleground of sex and sexuality, Aldington tells us that '[Bobbe's] vanity and class consciousness made him yearn for affairs with upper-class women, although he was obviously a homosexual type.' The portrait is not entirely damning: Bobbe has '[a]dmirable energy, a swift and sometimes remarkable intuition into character, a good memory and excellent faculty of imitation.'[26] There is also an extremely entertaining parody of one of Lawrence's diatribes against women. Nevertheless, it would be hard to guess from this portrait that Aldington admired Lawrence more than any other man or writer of his age and would write twenty years later that his personality was 'on a different, a higher level from that of other people' and that '[t] he sensitiveness, the range, the acuity, the profundity of perception and intuition put him quite apart from if not above all the other writers of his time.'[27] Lawrence's judgemental attitude at Port Cros had cut him to the quick. In *The Eaten Heart* he had attempted to address seriously the sexual issues that had caused the rift between them. In *Death of a Hero*, as in the letter to H.D. written at around the time that he was composing this portrait, he gave way instead to rancour.[28]

The novel's most detailed portraits are those of Elizabeth and Fanny, George's wife and mistress. Given the 'real-life' basis of the other portrayals, commentators have often been puzzled by the fact that there does not seem to be a simple equation between Elizabeth and H.D. and between Fanny and Yorke (as the wife and mistress of Aldington's wartime life). Aldington himself told H.D. that Elizabeth and Fanny were based on Cunard and Dobrée, and although this has been dismissed as an attempt to prevent H.D. from feeling hurt, it is actually a significant remark.[29] First of all, it was his coded way of telling H. D. about his relationships with these two women. The fact that both had rejected him was something that this broad hint need not reveal; he wanted H.D. to understand that he continued to attract beautiful women. Then the advocacy of free love by both his female characters is based on Cunard's lifestyle: 'They knew all about the sexual problem and how to settle it. There was the physical relationship and the emotional relationship and the intellectual relationship; and they knew how to manage all three, as easily as a pilot with twenty years' experience brings a handy ship to anchor in the Pool of London. They knew that freedom, complete freedom, was the only solution.'[30] (Like Pound and Eliot, Cunard would be subjected to a more sustained and savage satirical portrait in 1932.)[31] On the other hand, Fanny, gay, pretty, charming and confident, and capable of greater empathy and tenderness than Elizabeth, reminds us of the Dobrée of *A Dream in the Luxembourg*.

Yet there are striking resemblances between Elizabeth and H.D. and between Fanny and Yorke, not the least of these being the nature of their relationships with George Winterbourne and the parallels with Aldington's own pre-war and wartime love affairs. Physically, Elizabeth has Yorke's 'black glossy hair' and dark eyes (H.D.'s hair was soft-brown, her eyes grey), but the 'lovely line of her throat and jaw', her 'high intellectual forehead' and, most of all, her 'nervous manner' are H.D.'s.[32] (Derek Patmore speaks of H.D.'s 'finely-chiselled head' and his mother of her 'magnificent line of jaw and cheek' and the 'wild and wincing look' in her 'large, distracted eyes'.)[33] Fanny, on the other hand, although fair and blue-eyed, has many of the attributes of the Yorke with whom Aldington fell in love in 1917: 'Where Elizabeth hesitated, mused, suffered, Fanny acted, came a cropper, picked herself up gaily and started off again with just the same zest for experience. She was more smartly dressed than Elizabeth. Of course, Elizabeth was always quite charming and attractive, but you guessed that she had other things to think about beside clothes. Fanny loved clothes, and with no more money than Elizabeth, contrived to look stunningly fashionable, where Elizabeth merely looked O.K.'[34]

Even more revealingly, Fanny is the experienced and 'marvellous' lover that Aldington found Yorke to be, and we are reminded of the poems of *Images of Desire*: 'It was not only that she was golden and supple and lithe, where Elizabeth was dark and rather stiff and virginal, but she really cared about love-making. It was her art. It was for her neither a painful duty nor a degrading necessity nor a series of disappointing experiments, but a delightful art which gave full expression to her vitality, energy and efficiency.'[35] 'She was,' the narrator tells us, 'emotionally and mentally far less complicated than Elizabeth, less profound'. Therefore, 'to her the new sexual regime, where perfect freedom has happily taken the place of service, presented fewer possible snags.'[36]

The reason why Elizabeth and Fanny bear close resemblances to H.D. and Yorke, as well as more superficial ones to Cunard and Dobrée, is that the two characters exist as vehicles for Aldington's views on women and sexual relationships. The result is very different from his portrayals of the Winterbourne parents. Whereas his exposition on Victorian parenting and bourgeois values is overwhelmed by the bitterness of his feelings towards his own parents, the two young female characters are not handled with malice or resentment; as the narrator points out, they are not 'grotesques'. Aldington was sceptical about women and their attitudes to sex; he had had his fingers burned. But he continued to believe in the primacy of heterosexual relationships (as *The Eaten Heart* demonstrates) and to love women. He still admired and cared for H.D., liked Cunard, had a continuing 'tendresse' for Dobrée, and was passionately in love with Patmore. (Patmore has a cameo appearance in the novel as Mrs Lamberton, 'something very lovely and precious').[37]

George kills himself (if, indeed, he does) because he is 'a bit off his head', 'done for, used up'.[38] The narrator tells us that 'the situation he had got into with Elizabeth and Fanny Welford was not inextricable, but it would have needed a certain amount of patience and energy and determination and common sense to put right.'[39] Unlike his protagonist, Aldington did return, but he, too, as he subsequently realised, was too war-damaged to sort out the 'tragical mess' of his personal life.[40] Fanny and Elizabeth are not responsible for George's death. Indeed, his own naivety and inexperience are seen to be the main cause of the failure of his relationships – even if the women are portrayed as wilier and harder.

On the issue of sexual relationships, *Death of a Hero* is as confused as was its author. While the Victorian sexual code and the hypocrisy to which it led are strongly condemned, Aldington's approval of the more liberated sexual attitudes of George, Elizabeth and Fanny often carries a hint of irony. This is partly because he sees women as having double standards: approving of sexual freedom, even perhaps desiring it for themselves, but not accepting such conduct from their male partners. Aldington is speaking here from bitter experience, of both Yorke and H.D. Nevertheless, there is a dishonesty about his portrayal of the naïve, trusting George and his affair with Fanny; when embarking on his own 'extra-marital' affairs at various times – with Fallas, Yorke, Capper, Dobrée and Patmore – he can have been in little doubt of the pain he was causing his 'marital' partner. He knew, as he implies, that 'the separation of the physical relationship and the emotional relationship and the intellectual relationship' was not that simple. As in *The Eaten Heart*, it is an issue he does not confront.

Issues that are more completely addressed, but also, the reader may feel, unsatisfactorily, concern male relationships and masculinity. We are led to understand that George's upbringing has made him shy and diffident in the company of others, and he only finds fully satisfactory male relationships twice in the novel. First with Donald Conington, the young barrister who takes him walking as a boy, from whom he learns that companionship with men is about 'the frank, unsuspicious exchange of goodwill and talk, the spontaneous collaboration of two natures';[41] and secondly, with the narrator at Officers' Training Camp. George and the narrator are drawn to each other not by the war (in fact it is their difference from most of the other officer cadets that brings them together) but by the fact that they are both artists. However, the narrator tells us that, 'Friendships between soldiers during the war were a real and beautiful and unique relationship . . . an undemonstrative exchange of sympathies between ordinary men racked to extremity under a great common strain in a great common danger.'[42] These relationships are seen to contrast, first with relationships among civilians – like the self-serving relationships of George's pre-war London life, and secondly, with homosexual relationships, for which both the narrator and George Winterborne express distaste.

While comradeship was essential for survival on the battlefield, such relationships were invariably transitory, both because they all too soon ended in the death of one or other of the companions, and because they were based on shared experience rather than shared interests. In *Life for Life's Sake* Aldington recalls the disappointment of attending a regimental reunion after the war: 'We were no longer one hundred per cent soldiers, but subtly and inevitably turning back into civilians, with different aims, hopes and antipathies.'[43]

In this regard, George Winterbourne's respect for his junior officer is of interest. Evans, a typical public school product, is everything that Aldington, his narrator and his protagonist should despise: 'He accepted and obeyed every English middle-class prejudice and taboo' and, of course, 'had no doubts whatever about the War'. And yet, 'Winterbourne could not help liking the man. He was exasperatingly stupid, but he was honest, he was kindly, he was conscientious, he could obey orders and command obedience in others, he took pains to look after his men.'[44]

Equally surprising is the paeon of praise – through George's point of view – for the veteran infantrymen he sees on the ship as he crosses to France for the first time: 'There was something intensely masculine about them. . . . They looked barbaric, but not brutal; determined but not cruel. Under their grotesque wrappings, their bodies looked lean and hard and tireless. They were Men. . . . They had saved something from a gigantic wreck, and what they had saved was immensely important – manhood and comradeship, their essential integrity as men, their essential brotherhood as men.'[45]

These portraits of both the fighting man and the middle-class junior officer are idealised and nostalgic. We have to set alongside them our knowledge that for much of his war service Aldington had found ordinary soldiers coarse and ignorant, and that, once commissioned, he had made no firm friendships amongst his fellow officers. Had George Winterbourne survived the war, he would not have been able to make a connection with either category of man. Aldington seems to be searching here for something in which to put his faith. His post-war male relationships had disappointed him. He had felt distanced, not only from an older generation, but also from those of his own generation who had not served in the front line (even Flint). He had attempted to bridge that gap with some, like Monro and Eliot; but his relationships with those who shared both his literary interests and his combat experience, like Read and Dobrée, had also failed. Glover was perhaps an exception – but he was older and the two men had not lived in sufficient proximity to develop the relationship. Now perhaps there was Tom MacGreevy – and men of a younger generation, like Walter Lowenfels. In the prefatory letter to Glover, Aldington writes: 'I believe in men, I believe in a certain fundamental integrity and comradeship without which society could not endure.'[46] He undercuts this statement, however, by adding, 'How often that integrity is perverted, how often that comradeship betrayed, there is no need to tell you'. The compassion of the narrator in *Death of a Hero* for his friend George Winterbourne and his commitment to write the story of his life stand as examples of that integrity and comradeship.

The novel's condemnation of homosexuality is even more problematic. 'I never saw any signs of sodomy, and never heard anything to make me suppose it existed', insists the narrator of *Death of a Hero*. Aldington has him add, acidly: 'However, I was with the fighting troops. I can't answer for what went on behind the lines.'[47] On leave in London, George sits alone in a café, and, 'Opposite him at a couple of tables was a brilliant bevy of elegant young homosexuals, two of them in Staff Officer's uniform.'[48] The equation of a lack of courage and manliness with homosexuality is clear and the contempt seems out of keeping with an otherwise liberal outlook on sexual matters. Aldington has Elizabeth point this out to George, but his response is: '[I]t's no good my mind trying to defend what my instincts and feelings reject. Frankly, I don't like homosexuals. I respect their freedom, of course, but I don't like them.'[49]

The inconsistency seems to be that of George's creator, who was struggling in this period to accept the sexual orientation of Patmore's sons. Derek Patmore knew of his difficulty, writing in his preface to his mother's memoirs: 'Richard . . . was always aggressively anti-homosexual and, like so many Englishmen of his type, gloried in his supposed manhood.'[50] While Patmore was in London in May 1929, Aldington wrote to H.D. – in response to a (well-meant?) warning about Patmore's social life in London – concerning the problem he had in accepting Derek's circle of friends. He told her: 'It's so absolutely different in women, something quite normal and natural. But these little vindictive half-men are intolerable, especially to me, since I have lived and suffered with real men, and know how magnificent they are.'[51]

To understand his intolerance and inconsistency and his insistence on the 'masculinity' of the fighting man, in short, his homophobia, we need to return to his childhood and adolescence and particularly to his upbringing as an only son by an incompetent and ineffective father and a domineering mother.[52] The public school training he received is briefly outlined in *Life for Life's Sake* (the 'stress upon mere games and a narrow-minded bourgeois outlook' and the 'quasi-military discipline') and more extensively parodied in *Death of a Hero*, where George Winterbourne's sensitivity is perceived as abnormal and he is forced to hide his artistic interests, while resisting the attempts to make him join the Officers' Training Corps.[53] It can only have served to complicate further Aldington's anxieties about masculinity. The fact that he was removed from this environment – possibly from *any* school environment – before his fourteenth birthday allowed him the freedom to develop his artistic interests, but must have intensified his sense of 'difference' from other middle-class boys of his age. At university he at last found a male group with shared interests – from which he was again exiled with his enforced departure from University College in 1911.

We have observed the self-consciously 'masculine' ethos of the pre-war avant-garde literary circles in which Aldington moved – and their extreme manifestation in the aggressive sexism of Hulme and Lewis, whose attitudes to women he despised.[54] It was deemed necessary to demonstrate that a sensitive and artistic temperament was not incompatible with heterosexual masculinity, and Aldington did so through such activities as the Blunt 'Peacock Dinner' and the mock-battles against Futurism. However, his enlistment in 1916 faced him with yet another kind of masculine regime, which at first he resisted, as his letters to Flint and Cournos during his training indicate. In the end he was forced to measure himself against its standards and to prove to himself and others that he was capable of achieving them. His consequent pride in his membership of the fighting forces is apparent in his letters of the time to Flint, particularly in such remarks as: '[There] are things you do not know & cannot know & may never know', and '[H]onestly I think that a week in the trenches teaches a man more than six months in England'.[55] H.D. became very conscious of his new soldier persona, as did Lawrence, who summed it up as Aldington's '"Now we are all men together" stance'.[56]

As Part Three of *Death of a Hero* vividly shows, the pride in soldierly virtues is driven by several impulses: a genuine admiration for male comradeship, courage and endurance; a sense of alienation from the civilian world; and a determination not to give in to the overwhelming threat of neurasthenia. In *Death of a Hero* we are told that George's state of mind by the autumn of 1918, 'what with sleeplessness and worry and shock and ague – which came back as soon as he was in the front line again – and physical exhaustion and inhibited fear, almost fringed dementia, and he would have collapsed but for his strength of will and pride.'[57] It was in this state of physical and emotional ill-health that Aldington returned to England – to personal difficulties with which he could not cope and a world from which he felt alienated – in February 1919. We may not find it easy to understand or sympathise with the tenacity with which he clung to intolerance and prejudice, but the fears in which they were rooted were strong. It was necessary for him to write *Death of a Hero* and the speed with which it was written is an indication of that need. In writing it he found an outlet for the personal bitterness which had been consuming him for years. However, the novel is not predominately invective or satire. It is the tragedy of George Winterbourne. One of the reasons the third part of the novel is so powerful is that Aldington lets George tell his own story; we get only one brief appearance by the narrator. George is even given the opportunity for the kind of exposition that has formerly been the province of the narrator, when, at rest camp at Boulogne, having observed – and admired – the fighting men, he asks himself, '[W]ho were their real enemies?' and he sees the answer 'with a flood of bitterness and clarity': 'Their enemies – the enemies of German and English alike – were the fools that had sent them to kill each other instead of help each other. Their enemies were the sneaks and the unscrupulous; the false ideals, the unintelligent ideas imposed on them, the humbug, the hypocrisy, the stupidity. If those men were typical, then there was nothing essentially wrong with common humanity, at least as far as the men were concerned. It was the leadership that was wrong – not the war leadership but the peace leadership. The nations were governed by bunk and sacrificed to false ideals and stupid ideas.'[58]

This is the continuation of the thoughts that have begun to consume George from the moment the draft set off on the journey to France, and this extended passage of exposition is the last one in the novel. And so George becomes not the earnest and naive dupe and victim that he has been for much of the earlier part of the novel, but the thinker and observer, through whose artistic, sensitive and increasingly mature vision, we are introduced to the actualities of the battlefield. One of the most moving passages in Part Three is his account of watching the shattered remnants of a battalion – fifty men and one officer – coming away from a devastating local attack. That George is a witness, not a member of this group, objectifies the scene and sharpens its poignancy as he describes it with his artist's eye. It is because we have been brought close to his character and no longer perceive him – through the eyes of the narrator – as merely a victim, that we experience his death as a tragedy.

Part Three ends with George's death (as a line of machine gun bullets 'smash across his chest like a savage steel whip') followed by the ironic insertion of Foche's Armistice tribute, but this is not the end of the novel.[59] There is an epilogue – and, set eleven years later, it concerns, not the dead, although they are remembered:

> And I thought of the graves by desolate Troy
> And the beauty of many young men now dust

but the survivors, who are ignored and unregarded by the young. ('Why should they bore us for ever / With an old quarrel and the names of dead men / We never knew, and dull forgotten battles?'):

> And I looked at the hollow cheeks
> And the weary eyes and the grey-streaked heads
> Of the old men – nearly forty – about me;
> And I . . . walked away
> In an agony of grief and pity.[60]

The narrator expresses the agony of survival in an outburst towards the end of Part Two of the novel: 'You, the war dead, I think you died in vain. I think you died for nothing, a blather, a humbug, a newspaper stunt, a politician's ramp. But at least you died. You did not reject the sharp sweet shock of bullets, the sudden smash of the shell-burst, the insinuating agony of poison gas. You got rid of it all. You chose the better part.'[61]

Aldington's *threnody* is not only for the dead but also for the living. George Winterbourne's pre-war life and his war experience are his creator's in almost every detail; but the unnamed narrator and the survivors in the epilogue stand in for the post-war Aldington. Adrian Barlow argues that the 'split perspective' of *Death of a Hero* reflects the notion explored in *Eumenides* and in *A Fool i' the Forest* of 'the murdered self', Aldington's belief that his unique and creative personality ('A self which had its passion for beauty / Some moment's touch with immortality –') did not survive the war.[62] Like the allegory of *A Fool i' the Forest*, the fictional form and narrative devices of *Death of a Hero* enabled him to avoid the note of self-pity which often marked his more confessional poetry. But the novel was also his 'atonement', his opportunity to commemorate that dead self and to move on. He had not finished with the war but it had finished with him. He had indeed 'purged his bosom of perilous stuff'.

Afterword

In the beginning
But we do not know the beginning,
In the end
But we do not know the end.

(Richard Aldington, *Life Quest*, 1935)[1]

A child, grubbing about in the garden, finds the chrysalis of a tiger moth. An old boot
box is begged from the kitchen . . . the box is forgotten, and then one day carelessly
opened. The bright-winged creature may be lying dead, with the cream and black and
scarlet all tarnished and scattered in dust; or it may still be alive and, seeing its one
chance of freedom, make a sudden dart and flutter blindly round and round the larger
prison of the room until it finds the open window and is gone.

(Richard Aldington, *Rejected Guest*, 1939)[2]

There would be more novels – seven of them. There would be two more long
poems. There would be short stories and satires. More controversially, there
would be memoirs and biographies: of Wellington; of D.H. Lawrence; of Charles
Prentice, Pino Orioli and Norman Douglas; of Robert Louis Stevenson; and, most
controversially of all, of T.E. Lawrence, the man Aldington began by admiring but
for whom he came to feel contempt.

And, of course, there would be other lovers. And other struggles. Other fraught
relationships – and some fulfilling ones. The moth had burst out of the box, but
whether the damage to its wings was irreparable remains to be seen.

Notes

Editorial note
The short-title reference system has been used for all references except those referring to collections of letters. In these cases, author/editor name and letter number are provided.

Academic institutions holding unpublished material are referenced in parentheses.

Preface

1. (*Exile and Other Poems*, 1923; *A Fool i' the Forest*, 1925) There are such poems by Blunden, Graves, Gurney, Sassoon and Read, but they do not represent a substantial body of work, as in Aldington's case.

1. Orwell, George, 'Reviews', *New English Weekly*, 24 September 1936.

Introduction

1. Morgan, Louise, 'Writing a Best Seller in Seven Weeks', *Everyman,* 21 August 1930.

2. Preface to Aldington, Richard, *All Men Are Enemies: A Romance* (London, Chatto and Windus, 1933).

3. Aldington married Netta McCullough in 1938. Their daughter was born in the same year.

4. Paper given at the First International Richard Aldington Conference, 2000 (published as 'Meetings with H.D. and Bryher in Switzerland' in *Writers in Provence*, ed. Kempton, D. and Stoneback, H.R. (Les Saintes-Maries-de-la-Mare, Gregau Press, 2003), p. 6

5. H.D., *Bid Me To Live* (New York, The Dial Press, 1960), p. 12.

6. Guest, Barbara, *Herself Defined: The Poet H.D. and Her World* (London, Macmillan, 1985), pp. 85-86.

7. Doyle, Charles, *Richard Aldington: A Biography* (Basingstoke, Macmillan, 1989), p. 60.

1. Bohemia: London 1911-12

1. McEwan, Ian, *Enduring Love* (London, Vintage, 1998), p. 1.

2. Aldington, Richard, *Life for Life's Sake: a Book of Reminiscences* (New York, Viking, 1941), p. 77.

3. See, for example, Richard Aldington to Winifred Ellerman (Bryher), 5 October 1918 (Yale).

4. Aldington, Richard, *Very Heaven* (London, William Heinemann, 1937), pp. 3-6.

5. The flat was no. 4, Russell Chambers in Bury Street (now Bury Place) just south of Russell Square.

6. Aldington, *Life for Life's Sake*, p. 71. Aldington probably came across Gerald Gould (1885-1936) again in 1914, when the latter was an official in Masterman's Wellington House Propaganda Department; after the war, like Aldington, he pursued a career as a reviewer (of fiction) and critic; on Gould's career as a reviewer Aldington is scathing, however (see *Life for Life's Sake,* p.71).

7. Aldington, *Life for Life's Sake*, p. 69.

8. Aldington contributed a poem in memory of Chapman to the University College Union Magazine, and there are two affectionate letters to him from Chapman – written only weeks before he died – in the memorial volume of Chapman's writings published by his parents in 1912.

9. Kershaw, Alister and Temple, F.J. (eds), *Richard Aldington: An Intimate Portrait* (Carbondale and Edwardsville, Southern Illinois University Press, 1965), p. 112.

10. Aldington, *Life for Life's Sake*, p. 86.

11. Carr, Helen, *The Verse Revolutionaries* (London, Jonathan Cape, 2009), p. 99.

12. Yeats and Rhys had formed the Rhymers' Club in 1890. The group met at Ye Olde Cheshire Cheese in Fleet Street until around 1904 and had published two anthologies, in 1894 and 1896.

13. Thomas Ernest Hulme (1883-1917) would become more interested in philosophy, aesthetic theory and art than in poetry and, despite his early death, was a major influence on the development of English modernism.

14. Edward Marsh 1872-1953) was Private Secretary to Winston Churchill between 1905 and 1929. He was an important patron of young artists and writers.

15. Patmore, Brigit, *My Friends When Young* (London, William Heinemann, 1968), p. 60. Maude had four brothers and the family was a close one, having lost their parents when still quite young. Aldington knew them from his teen years in Kent, when Malcolm and William had befriended him. Three of the brothers were lawyers and Malcolm Hilbery would go on to become a high court judge.

16. Brigit Patmore (1882-1965) was born in Dublin and christened Ethel Elizabeth Morrison Scott. She married John Deighton Patmore in 1907.

17. *ibid*. Introduction, pp. 2-3.

18. Lawrence, D.H., *Aaron's Rod* (New York, Thomas Seltzer, 1922; Harmondsworth, Penguin Books, 1950), p. 73.

19. Hunt, Violet, *The Flurried Years* (London, Hurst and Blackett, 1926), p. 217. Hunt had reason to feel jealousy towards Patmore, for whom Hunt's lover, Ford Madox Hueffer, was to develop a passion.

20. Patmore, *My Friends When Young*, p. 60

21. Hunt, *The Flurried Years*, p. 217.

22. Patmore, *My Friends When Young*, p. 58.

23. In a letter to F.S. Flint on 30 January 1921 Pound described his early London poetic identity as 'Browning'd, Yeats'd, stuffed with undigested middle ages, barbarian zeal, Xtianity etc.' (Yale)

24. Patmore, *My Friends When Young*, p. 61.

25. Richard Aldington to Amy Lowell, 20 November 1917 (Harvard)

26. Aldington, *Life for Life's Sake*, p. 111.

27. H.D., *End to Torment* ((New York, New Directions, 1979), p. 8.

28. Although the convention is to refer to biographical subjects by their surnames, Hilda Doolittle was always averse to her own and therefore eagerly adopted the name 'H.D.', which Pound appended to her first published poems in January 1913. The current writer has therefore chosen to use the latter name, as being the one by which she is now universally known, even though it was not employed until that date.

29. H.D., *End to Torment*, p. 8.

30. Patmore, *My Friends When Young*, p. 65.

31. HD to Bryher 14 February 1919 (Yale).

32. Patmore, *My Friends When Young*, p. 48.

33. H.D., *Bid Me to Live*, p. 68.

34. Zilboorg, Caroline (ed.), *Richard Aldington and HD: their lives in letters 1918-1961* (Manchester and New York, Manchester University Press, 2003), p.7.

35. Patmore, *My Friends When Young*, p.66.

36. H.D., *Asphodel* (Durham and London, Duke University Press, 1992), pp. 49, 62. Pound had placed some of Gregg's poems in a New York magazine, where they appeared in December 1911.

37. H.D., *Paint It Today*, p. 7.

38. Writing to Pound in September 1912 to inform him that he must give up his hopes of marrying Dorothy, Olivia Shakespear tells him that her daughter can't go about with him 'American fashion' – 'not till she is thirty-five and has lost her looks'. *Ezra Pound and Dorothy Shakespear: Their Letters, 1909-1914*, edited by Pound, Omar and Litz, A. Walton (London, Faber and Faber, 1985), no.116.

39. He wrote to Amy Lowell on 20 November 1917: 'H.D.'s poetry is the only modern English poetry I really care for. Its austerity, aloofness, its profound passion for that beauty which only Platonists know, make it precisely the kind of work I would like to do myself, had I the talent.' (Harvard).

40. *The Poetry Review* was actually owned by the Poetry Society, from whom Monro had purchased editorial and financial responsibility for a year, after which the situation would come under review. The membership of the Poetry Society (initially the 'Poetry Recital Society') consisted chiefly of middle-class suburban readers of poetry, many of whom were also amateur poets.

41. Hibberd, Dominic, *Harold Monro: Poet of the New Age* (Basingstoke, Palgrave, 2001), p. 86.

42. Aldington's reviews appeared in vol. 1 nos. 3, 4, 6, 7 and 9 of *The Poetry Review* (March, April, June, July and September 1912).

43. Richard Aldington to Harold Monro [Spring 1912] (UCLA).

44. H.D., *End to Torment*, p. 8.

45. By this stage of events, this is precisely what Aldington was, his mother having taken over the tenancy of The Mermaid Inn at Rye, when his father lost all his money.

46. H.D., *Paint It Today*, p. 28.

47. H.D., *Asphodel*, p. 86.

48. H.D., *Paint It Today*, pp. 8-9.

2. Family Secrets

1.　Aldington, *Death of a Hero*, p. 43.

2.　H.D., *Paint It Today*, p. 51; *Asphodel,* p. 84.

3.　H.D., *Asphodel*, pp. 68, 63.

4.　H.D. to Isabel Pound, 26 February 1912 (Yale).

5.　Aldington, *Very Heaven*, p. 34.

6.　Lyon Gilbert, Margery, *Pavane to an Unborn Child* (unpublished), p. 30.

7.　Aldington, *Death of a Hero*, pp. 37.

8.　*ibid*. p. 57.

9.　Richard Aldington to P.A.G. Aldington 20 December 1958 (S.I.U.).

10.　Aldington, *Death of a Hero*, p. 50.

11.　Aldington, *Life for Life's Sake*, p. 11.

12.　*ibid*. p. 18.

13.　Aldington, 'Childhood', lines 25-27.

14.　Aldington, *Life for Life's Sake*, p.17.

15.　*ibid*. pp. 62.

16.　Richard Aldington to Amy Lowell 20 November 1917 (Harvard).

17.　Lyon Gilbert, Margery, 'Early Memories of Richard Aldington', undated and unpublished typescript.

18.　The college magazine, *The Dovorian*, records Aldington's arrival at the school in issue no.157 vol.XVI (November 1904) and his departure in issue no.168, vol XVIII (June 1906).

19.　Aldington, *Death of a Hero*, p.58.

20.　Bloom, Ursula, *Holiday Mood* (London, Hutchinson, 1934), p. 21.

21.　Aldington, *Life for Life's Sake*, pp. 42, 59 and 162.

22.　*ibid*. p. 38. However, later in the memoir, when writing that he tried to enlist in 1914, he tells us that he was rejected when, under question, he mentioned that he 'had undergone an operation in 1910' (p. 162). There is a marked confusion over dates here.

23.　Aldington, *Death of a Hero*, p. 60.

24.　Aldington, *Life for Life's Sake*, p. 42.

25.　*ibid*. p.49.

26.　It was Maude Hilbery who would introduce Aldington to Brigit Patmore in 1911.

27.　Aldington, *Death of a Hero*, p. 80.

28.　Aldington, *Life for Life's Sake*, p. 21.

29.　Aldington, *Death of a Hero*, pp. 63.

30.　Bloom, *Holiday Mood*, p. 21. The early date of the events recalled by Bloom – the summer of 1905 – may be explained by Aldington's comment in *Life for Life's Sake* that the family purchased the house in St-Margaret's-at-Cliffe and spent summers there 'for a couple of years' before they moved there entirely.

31.　Lyon Gilbert, 'Early Memories of Richard Aldington'.

32.　Lyon Gilbert, *Pavane to an Unborn Child*, p. 28. It is important to note that Gilbert's manuscript predates *Life for Life's Sake* by at least five years and so cannot have been influenced by it.

33.　Aldington, *Death of a Hero*, pp. 83.

34.　Aldington et al., *Some imagist poets: an anthology* (Boston, Houghton Mifflin, 1915).

35. Aldington *All Men are Enemies: a Romance* (London, Chatto and Windus, 1933), pp. 12-14, 31-37.

36. Aldington, *Death of a Hero*, p.71.

37. Bloom, *Holiday Mood*, p. 18.

38. *ibid*. p. 20.

39. Thorne's *Wait Until Dark*, described in *Death of a Hero* (p.64) as 'a crude-Christian moral novel', had topped all the best-selling lists in 1903.

40. Aldington, *Life for Life's Sake*, p. 46-47.

41. Aldington, *Death of a Hero*, p.73.

42. *ibid*. p. 2.

43. *ibid*. p. 6.

44. *ibid*. p. 44.

45. Dorothy Yorke to Walter and Lilian Lowefels, New Jersey, 25 October 1964.

46. Aldington, *Very Heaven*, p. 35.

47. Aldington, *Death of a Hero*, pp. 86-87.

48. Lyon Gilbert, *Pavane to an Unborn Child*, pp. 31-32.

49. Aldington, *Death of a Hero*, pp. 87, 88-89.

50. Lyon Gilbert, *Pavane to an Unborn Child*, p. 34.

51. Aldington, *Life for Life's Sake*, pp. 63-64.

52. A.E. Aldington to J.S.L. Strachey 7 June 1910 (British Library). John St Loe Strachey was the extremely successful editor of *The Spectator* from 1867 to 1925.

53. In 1924 Aldington would become a literary reviewer on *The Spectator* (a year before Strachey retired from the editorship) but the post-war Aldington was a very different man.

54. Aldington, *Life for Life's Sake*, p. 65.

55. *ibid*. p. 78.

56. *ibid*. p. 78

57. Rupert Brooke to Katherine Cox, undated letter headed 'Saturday night' [March 1912]. *The Letters of Rupert Brooke*, edited by Keynes, Geoffrey (London, Faber and Faber, 1968), pp. 365-367.

58. Read, Mike, *Forever England: the Life of Rupert Brooke* (Edinburgh, Mainstream, 1997), pp. 143-145.

3. The Perfect Year: France and Italy, 1912-1913

1. Aldington, 'Theocritus in Capri', *Literary Studies and Reviews* (London, Allen and Unwin, 1924; New York, Dial Press, 1924), p. 241.

2. H.D., *Asphodel*, p. 111.

3. *ibid*. pp. 27-28.

4. The portrait was by the American painter Eugene Paul Ullman: Cravens had commissioned it in 1911 and Ullman had painted a companion portrait of Cravens herself.

5. H.D., *Asphodel*, p. 93.

6. Rachewiltz, Mary de, Moody, A. David and Moody, Joanna (eds.), *Ezra Pound to His Parents, Letters 1895-1929* (Oxford University Press, 2010), no. 392.

7. Rummel and Chaigneau married in 1912 and went on to have two sons, but she was committed to a mental asylum in 1918.

8. H.D., *Asphodel*, p. 94.

9. *ibid*. p. 95.

10. H.D.'s unpublished diary (Yale).

11. H.D., *Asphodel*, p. 96.

12. Aldington, *Life for Life's Sake,* p. 111.

13. Carr, *The Verse Revolutionaries*, p. 447.

14. Rachewiltz, Moody and Moody, no. 396.

15. See H.D.'s *Autobiographical Notes* (Yale).

16. Pound and Litz no. 87.

17. H.D., *Asphodel*, p.105.

18. On Cravens' recommendation she had moved to the Rue des Ciseaux.

19. The Garton Peace Foundation was founded by an industrialist, Sir Richard Garton, to develop the principles which Norman Angell had outlined in his book, *The Grand Illusion* (1910). Angell argued that international prosperity depended on commercial co-operation between nations and that military conflict would lead to economic ruin.

20. Aldington, *Life for Life's Sake*, p. 120.

21. Olivia Shakespear to Ezra Pound 13 September 1912, Pound and Litz, no. 116.

22. *ibid*. nos.109, 113, 114 and 119.

23. 2 Samuel 13.

24. Patmore, *My Friends When Young*, pp. 69-70.

25. Pound and Litz, no. 113.

26. Ezra Pound to Harriet Monroe, 18 August 2012. Paige, D.D. (ed.), *Ezra Pound: Selected Letters, 1907-1941* (London, Faber and Faber, 1950), no. 5.

27. 'Dynamism' was an aspect of the Futurist manifesto: the requirement that works of art capture the speed and movement of contemporary life; the 'Unanimistes' were a school of French poets which included Jules Romains, Charles Vildrac, René Arcos and Georges Duhamel, their work being characterised by a simplicity and concreteness of style, the use of free verse and urban subject matter.

28. Ezra Pound to Harriet Monroe [18] August 1912 (Paige, no. 5). It was April 1913 before Pound would make the effort to meet some of the contemporary French poets (Romains, Vildrac, Duhamel and Arcos), as he passed through Paris on his way to Italy.

29. Aldington, *Life for Life's Sake*, p. 135.

30. Ezra Pound to Alice Corbin Henderson. Nadel, Ira B. (ed.), *Letters of Ezra Pound to Alice Corbin Henderson* (Austin, University of Texas Press, 1993), p. 4. (Henderson, also a poet, was Monroe's assistant editor.)

31. It is possible to date this meeting only approximately: it had not taken place when Pound wrote to Monroe on 24 September, but he sent her the H.D. poems in early October ('Hermes of the Ways', 'Priapus, Keeper of Orchards' and 'Epigram').

32. The Vienna Café at the corner of New Oxford Street and Bloomsbury Street (destroyed in the Blitz), the most popular teashop for those frequenting the British Museum, may have been the location; if the meeting was in Kensington, it may have been at Miss Ella Abbott's teashop at no. 6, Holland Street, another popular venue for the group.

33. H.D., *End to Torment*, p. 18.

34. Ezra Pound to Harriet Monroe, October 1912 (Paige, no. 7).

35. *Poetry: a magazine of verse*, vol. 1, no. 4, January 1913, p. 135.

36. *ibid*. pp. 126 and 135

37. Ezra Pound to Dorothy Shakespear [23 September 1912]. Pound and Litz, no. 121.

38. Aldington's prose-poem translations of Renaissance Latin poems appeared in *The New Age* on 28 November 1912 and 9 January 1913. Orage had accepted this work on Pound's recommendation and it was unpaid, but he had agreed to pay for a series of articles if Aldington could come up with a suitable subject.

39. *The New Age*, vol.12, nos 20 and 21, 20 March (p. 481) and 27 March (p. 498) 1913.

40. See Carr, *The Verse Revolutionaries*, p. 522.

41. *The New Age*, vol. 12, no. 24, 17 April 1913, p.580.

42. *ibid*. vol. 12, no. 19, 13 March 1913, p. 454.

43. The image of the lizards would surface again in his 1924 poem *A Fool i' the Forest* (section IV), one of the many small indications of how Aldington's time in Italy in 1913 would remain fresh in his mind for the rest of his life.

44. *The New Age* 24, vol. 12, no. 25, April 1913, p. 610.

45. H.D., *Paint It Today*, pp. 58-59.

46. Zilboorg, *Richard Aldington and HD: their lives in letters 1918*, p. 10.

47. Bottome, Phyllis, *The Challenge* (London, Faber and Faber, 1962), p. 184.

48. *The New Age*, vol. 13, no. 8, 19 June 1913, p. 206.

49. *The New Age*, vol. 12, nos 23 and 25, 10 April 1913 (p. 559) and 24 April 1913 (p. 610); and vol. 13, no. 1, 1 May 1913 (p. 14).

50. *ibid*. vol. 13, no. 2, 8 May 2013, p. 35.

51. See *The New Age*, vol. 13, no. 2, 8 May 1913, p. 35 and Aldington, 'Theocritus in Capri', *Literary Studies and Reviews*, p. 243.

52. *The New Age*, vol. 13, no. 8, 19 June 1913, p. 205.

53. Aldington, 'Theocritus in Capri', *Literary Studies and Reviews*, pp. 241-242.

54. *The New Age*, vol. 13, no. 1, 1 May 1913; see also vol. 13, no. 2, 8 May 1913, p. 35. Symonds (1840-1893) was a poet and art historian, whose seven-volume *The Renaissance in Italy* appeared between 1875 and 1886. Aldington would have been introduced to Symonds's writings by Dudley Grey.

55. H.D., *End to Torment*, p. 5. See Aldington, Richard, *Pinorman* (London, Heinemann, 1954), p. 150 for Aldington's comment that the spring of 1913 'was the happiest of [his] life'.

56. Aldington, *Life for Life's Sake*, pp. 128-129.

57. H.D., *Asphodel*, pp. 110-111.

58. *The New Age*, vol. 13, no. 4, 22 May 1913, p. 87.

59. Georgie Hyde-Lees would become Yeats's wife in 1917.

60. Rachewiltz, Moody and Moody no. 314, April 1910.

61. Pound and Litz no. 146, 21 April 1913.

62. A revised version of 'The Faun' was published in *Poetry and Drama* no. 2, March 1914. 'Capriped' is a play on 'capripes', the Latin for 'goat-footed', and 'Capri'. The Latin 'ut flosculus hyacinthus' translates as 'like a little hyacinth flower'. 'Auster' and 'Apeliota' are the south and east winds.

63. Pound and Litz no. 150, 29 April 1913.

64. *ibid*. no. 152.

65. *ibid*. no. 153.

66. H.D., *Autobiographical Notes* (Yale).

67. Pound and Litz no. 155.

68.   *ibid.* no. 156.

69.   (Yale).

70.   30 September 1939 (S.I.U). Henry Slonimsky (1884-1970) went on to teach philosophy at various universities in the United States, eventually becoming Professor of Ethics and Philosophy of Religion (and Dean) of the Jewish Institute of Religion in New York.

71.   Aldington, *Life for Life's Sake*, p.119.

72.   Hunt, *The Flurried Years*, p. 245.

73.   Rachewiltz, Moody and Moody, no. 438.

4. 'Les Jeunes': Creativity and Carnival, 1913-1914

1.   Bottome, *The Challenge,* p. 391.

2.   H.D. to Isabel Pound [October 1913], (Yale).

3.   Manning and Pound had been friendly since Pound's arrival in England in 1909. Born and brought up in Sydney, Frederic Manning (1882-1935) spent his adult life up to the First World War as a scholar, writer and virtual recluse, in the Lincolnshire rectory of his former tutor, Arthur Galton, but had become a regular guest at the literary salons of Eva Fowler and Olivia Shakespear (who was a friend of Galton).

4.   Rachewiltz, Moody and Moody, no. 429.

5.   *ibid.* no. 434.

6.   Even Flint's article had originally been written by Pound as an 'interview' between Flint and himself, which Flint was merely to sign. Flint, however, had insisted on a rewrite.

7.   *Poetry* vol. 1, no. 6, March 1913, p. 201.

8.   *ibid.* p. 204.

9.   *ibid.* p. 199.

10.   *ibid.* pp. 200-201.

11.   Pound had already sent poems by Flint to Monroe and they appeared in *Poetry* in July 1913.

12.   Pound and Williams had met at the University of Pennsylvania in 1902. Williams (1883-1963) was a practising doctor as well as a poet. He would become an important figure in American literary modernism.

13.   Skipwith Cannell (1887-1957) was another Philadelphian and a friend of William Carlos Williams. John Gould Fletcher (1886-1950) had in fact been resident in London for much of the last four years, but had led a reclusive life.

14.   Joyce (1882-1941) and his family had lived on the continent since 1904, mostly in Trieste.

15.   John Cournos (1881-1966). The interview with Pound appeared in the *Philadelphia Record* on 5 January 1913. Cournos himself places his first meeting with Aldington and H.D. in the autumn of 1913 when they returned from Italy and Paris (Cournos, *Autobiography*, p. 260).

16.   Carr, *The Verse Revolutionaries*, p. 573. Amy Lowell (1874-1925) had started to write poetry at the age of twenty-eight but published nothing until she was thirty-six. The title of this collection (taken from Shelley's 'Adonais') hints at her admiration for Keats, a biography of whom she would publish in 1925, the year of her death.

17.   Pound and Litz no. 170,n 3 August 1913.

18.   Ezra Pound to Isabel Pound [late July 1913], Rachewiltz, Moody and Moody no. 431.

19. Rudolph, L., Carpenter, L., and Simpson, E.C. (eds.), Fletcher, John Gould, *Selected Letters of John Gould Fletcher* (Fayetteville, University Of Arkansas Press, 1996), pp. 2-5,

20. Fletcher, John Gould, *Life is My Song* (New York, Farrar and Reinehart, 1937), pp. 78-79.

21. Ezra Pound to Harriet Monroe, 23 September 1913 (Paige no. 23).

22. Ezra Pound to Harriet Monroe, 13 August 1913 (Paige no. 21).

23. Dora Marsden (1882-1960) would increasingly withdraw from public life to concentrate on her writing. Her work was eventually published by The Egoist Press as *The Definition of the Godhead* (1928) and *Mysteries of Christianity* (1930). She would spend the last twenty-five years of her life in hospital, suffering from mental illness.

24. Harriet Weaver (1876-1961) was a doctor's daughter but her family inherited a large fortune from her maternal grandfather. She would devote her life (and resources) to the causes she believed in, including *The New Freewoman* and its successor, *The Egoist*, and to supporting until their deaths two writers whose work she admired: Dora Marsden and James Joyce.

25. Stirner's book had been published in Germany in 1845 but an English translation was not available in England until 1911, which is when Marsden read it.

26. Rebecca West (1892-1983) was born Cicely Fairfield. She adopted the name Rebecca West (after Ibsen's heroine in the play *Rosmersholm*) shortly after beginning her journalistic career on *The Freewoman*.

27. Letter from Ezra Pound to his father, mid-November 1913. Rachewiltz, Moody and Moody, no. 439.

28. *The New Freewoman*, no. 8, 1 October 1913 p. 155 and no. 9, 15 October 1913 p. 168.

29. Remy de Gourmont (1858-1915) was a French poet, philosopher and critic, and one of the founders of the journal, *Mercure de France*. A disfiguring and painful skin disease had made him a semi-recluse by this period.

30. 'Remy de Gourmont After the Interim', *Little Review* vol. 5, nos. 10/11, February/ March 1919 pp. 32-34. 'Sophrosyne' has no exact translation; it suggests moderation, harmony and serenity.

31. *The Egoist* vol. 1, no. 2, 15 January 1914 pp. 35-36. Gino Severini (1883-1966) was an Italian Futurist painter; Henri-Martin Barzun (1881-1974) was a French poet and founder of the journal *Poème et Drame*.

32. Rachewiltz, Moody and Moody, no. 449.

33. Harmer J.B., *Victory in Limbo: Imagism 1908 – 1917* (London, Secker and Warburg 1975), p. 1.

34. The print run of *The Egoist* was around 750 copies and the number of subscribers hovered at around ninety to a hundred, even before the war affected its circulation. Morrisson, Mark, *The Public Face of Modernism: Little Magazines, Audiences and Reception 1905-1920* (Madison, The University of Wisconsin Press, 2000), pp. 104 and 108.

35. 'Wyndham Lewis', *The Egoist* vol. 1, no. 12, 15 June 1914, p. 233.

36. Victor Plarr (1863-1929), librarian of the Royal College of Surgeons, had published a collection entitled *In the Dorian Mood* in 1896 and *The Tragedy of Asgard* in 1905, but nothing since. Thomas Sturge Moore (1870-1944) was a poet, playwright, critic and wood engraver, and brother of the philosopher G.E. Moore. John Masefield (1878-1967) would succeed Robert Bridges as Poet Laureate in 1930.

37. 'Homage to Wilfrid Blunt', *Poetry* vol. 3, no. 6, March 1914, p. 221.

38. Unfortunately, Pound's poem, reproduced in his report for *Poetry*, confuses the Italian liberationist Mazzini with the Egyptian Ahmed Urabi, for whose cause Blunt had shown support.

39. *Poetry* vol. 3, no. 6, March 1914, p. 220.

40. Henri Gaudier-Brzeska (1891-1915) was a primitivist sculptor working in London. Despite his early death, his work had a considerable influence on British modernist sculpture.

41. Diary of Wilfrid Scawen Blunt, 18 January 1914, quoted in Longford, Elizabeth, *A Pilgrimage of Passion: the Life of Wilfrid Scawen Blunt* (London, Weidenfeld and Nicolson, 1979), p. 394.

42. Quoted in Aldington's report of the occasion in *The Egoist* vol. 1, no. 3, 2 February 1914, p. 57.

43. 'Presentation to Mr W.S. Blunt', *The Egoist* vol. 1, no. 3, pp. 56-57.

44. Carr, *The Verse Revolutionaries*, p. 627.

45. Blunt's comment about the box was made in a letter written to Sidney Cockrell on 28 January 1914 (quoted in Longford, *A Pilgrimage of Passion*, p. 396).

46. Carr, *The Verse Revolutionaries*, pp. 639-40. Percy Wyndham Lewis (1882-1957) had trained at the Slade and in Paris, and was a novelist as well as a painter.

47. The title demonstrated Pound's imperfect grasp of the French language.

48. *The Glebe*, vol. 1, no. 5, February 1914. *The Glebe* was short-lived, consisting of ten issues between September 1913 and November 1914. Kreymborg, along with Man Ray, went on to found another journal, *Others*, which ran for four years from July 1915 and was a much more radical showcase for contemporary American poetry than Monroe's *Poetry*.

49. 'Modern Poetry and the Imagists', *The Egoist*, vol. 1, no. 11, 1 June 1914, pp. 201-203.

50. 'Wyndham Lewis', *The Egoist*, vol. 1 no. 12, 15 June 1914 p. 234.

51. Filippo Tommaso Marinetti (1876-1944) was a poet and critic; his first Futurist manifesto had been published in 1909.

52. The Centre's associates included Malcolm Arbuthnot (the photographer), the painters Lawrence Atkinson, Jessica Dismorr, Frederick Etchells, Cuthbert Hamilton, Richard Nevinson, William Roberts, Helen Saunders, and Edward Wadsworth, and the sculptor, Gaudier-Brzeska. Jacob Epstein and David Bomberg were also sympathetic to the group and its principles but valued their independence. The rift between Lechmere and Lewis was caused by Hulme's forming a relationship with Lechmere which resulted in the two men coming to blows.

53. John Collings Squire (1884-1958) was the literary editor of the *New Statesman*; in later years he would be editor of *The London Mercury* and acquire a reputation as an extreme conservative.

54. Aldington, *Life For Life's Sake*, p. 108.

55. C.W.R. Nevinson (1889-1946) had trained at the Slade School of Art, like many of the Rebel Art Centre group. He would become one of the British war artists, in the process abandoning Futurism.

56. The artists featured were Lewis, Gaudier-Brzeska, Wadsworth, Roberts and Hamilton, as well as Frederick Etchells and Jacob Epstein, who did not appear as signatories to the manifesto, and Spencer Gore, who had died of pneumonia in March, aged only thirty-six.

57. *The Fortnightly Review* was actually a *monthly* and prestigious long-running London-based periodical. (Its first editor was George Henry Lewes, George Eliot's partner.) Its interests were politics, philosophy, literature and science and its editor at this period was W.I. Courtney.

58. 'Vorticism', *The Fortnightly Review*, no. 96, 1 September 1914, pp. 461-471.

59. *The Egoist*, vol. 1, no. 13, p. 248.

60. *The Egoist*, vol.1, no. 14, 15 July 1914, p. 273.

61. H.D., *End to Torment*, p. 5.

62. Aldington, *Life for Life's Sake,* p. 168.

63. Plank (1883-1965) would continue to design *Vogue* covers until 1936. He lived with the Whitalls until taking his own studio apartment at Thurloe Square in the autumn of 1915.

64. H.D., *Palimpsest* (Carbondale, Southern Illinois University Press, 1968), p. 102.

65. Whitall, James, *English Years* (New York, Harcourt, Brace and Company, 1936), pp. 54-58.

66. James Whitall (1888-1954) returned to America permanently in 1926.

67. Richard Aldington to F.S. Flint, [Spring 1915]. Copp, Michael (ed.), *Imagist Dialogues: Letters Between Aldington, Flint and Others* (Cambridge, The Lutterworth Press, 2009), no. 34. This letter was actually written in the spring of 1915, so Aldington was not being entirely truthful to Flint about his relationship with Whitall, which dated from the early summer of 1914.

68. See letter from Ezra Pound to F.S. Flint, [January/February] 1914 (Texas).

69. F.S. Flint to Robert Frost, [26 July 1913] (Copp, no. 9). For an account of Robert Frost's dealings with Ezra Pound see *The Verse Revolutionaries* pp. 595-598 and 734. Flint's observation is not dissimilar from one made around the same time by Dorothy Shakespear (on an occasion when Pound had tried to tell her whom the Shakespears should or should not invite to a recital in their drawing room by Walter Rummel): 'I think you fortify yourself too much against other people, & so do not realize how much you hurt them by doing that kind of thing.' (Pound and Litz, no. 162).

70. Cournos, *Autobiography*, p. 330.

71. Richard Aldington to F.S. Flint, 4 July 1914 (Copp, no. 25. See also no. 24.)

72. Ford, F.M., *It Was the Nightingale* (London, William Heinemann, 1934), p. 220-221.

73. Aldington, *Life for Life's Sake*, pp. 156.

74. See Paige nos. 37-41.

75. *Sword Blades and Poppy Seed* was published in the U.S. in September 1914, and in England the following month.

76. Since this constituted a group of thirteen people, two (according to Fletcher) had to sit at a separate table, a manifestation of superstition we may find surprising.

77. Fletcher, *Life is My Song*, p. 149.

78. *ibid*. p. 151.

79. Paige no. 47

80. 'Affirmations IV: As for Imagisme', *The New Age*, vol. 16, no. 13, 28 January 1915.

81. Ezra Pound to Amy Lowell, 12 August 1914 (Paige, no. 48).

82. Ezra Pound to Harriet Monroe, January 1915 (Paige, no. 59).

83. Amy Lowell to Richard Aldington, 19 January 1915 (Harvard).

84. F.S. Flint to Amy Lowell, 24 January 1915 (Harvard).

85. This advert appeared in the October 1914 issue of *Poetry* (vol. 5, no. 1).

86. Aldington, *Life for Life's Sake*, p. 140.

5. The Imagist Poet: 1912-1916

1.   Ezra Pound to Harriet Monroe (Paige no. 60).

2.   'The Poems of Richard Aldington', *The English Review*, 32, May 1921, pp. 400-401.

3.   *viz.* the ten poems published in *Des Imagistes*, the fourteen in either the1915 or the 1916 *Some Imagist Poets*, as well as a further twenty-two published in either *Images (1910-1915)* or the American edition, *Images Old and New*(1915). Most of these poems appeared in print for the first time in journals, such as *The New Freewoman, The Egoist, Poetry and Drama, Poetry* and *The Little Review*.

4.   'Refuge from War', *Poetry* vol. 12 no. 1, April 1918.

5.   Richard Aldington to H.D., 21 June 1918 (Zilboorg, no. 17).

6.   Monroe, Harriet, *A Poet's Life: Seventy Years in a Changing World* (New York, Macmillan, 1938), p. 352.

7.   Gates, N.T., *The Poetry of Richard Aldington: a critical evaluation and an anthology of uncollected poems* (Pennsylvania, Penn State University Press, 1975), p. 36.

8.   Doyle, *Richard Aldington: A Biography*, p. 48.

9.   Harmer, *Victory in Limbo*, p. 69.

10. MacGreevy, Thomas, *Richard Aldington, An Englishman* (London, Chatto and Windus, 1931), p. 15.

11. So Aldington informed Amy Lowell in a letter of 20 November 1917 (Harvard).

12. Gates, *The Poetry of Richard Aldington*, p. 36.

13. *Poetry* vol.8, no.1, April 1916, p. 51.

14. *ibid.*

15. In a letter to Amy Lowell, 21 December 1914, he expresses his irritability over the ongoing conflict with Pound over proprietary rights to Imagism and also his exasperation with Ford, whom he is finding 'incurably vain and self-satisfied'.

16. *The New Republic*, 20 November 1915.

17. Chapter Two referred to the fictionalisation of Daisy's story in *Death of a Hero* (p. 83); here, too the treatment of the experience could be said to lack sensitivity. (See p. 37 above.)

18. Quoted by Read in Kershaw and Temple, *Richard Aldington: an intimate portrait*, pp. 125-126.

19. 'Richard Aldington's Poetry', *The Little Review*, vol. 2, no. 6, September 1915, p. 15.

20. Gates, *The Poetry of Richard Aldington*, pp. 28-29.

6. War: 1914-1916

1.   H.D., *Paint It Today*, pp. 45-46.

2.   Cournos, *Autobiography*, p.274.

3.   The Prisoners (Temporary Discharge for Ill Health) Act 1913 allowed the authorities to release imprisoned suffragettes who were on hunger strike for short periods to recover their health, so that they would not be seen as martyrs.

4.   One of the most recent casualties had been John Singer Sargent's portrait of Henry James, slashed by Mary Wood at the Royal Academy's Summer Exhibition in May.

5.   The Curragh Mutiny of 20 March occurred when fifty-seven British army officers (of General Hubert Gough's Third Cavalry Brigade) resigned rather than have to obey orders to enforce the Home Rule Bill in Ulster.

6. FitzGerald would take part in the 1916 Easter Rising. Aldington enthusiastically reviewed Campbell's poetry collection, *Irishry*, in *The Egoist* of 1 August 1914.

7. Hanscombe, G. and Smyers, V., *Writing for their Lives: The Modernist Women 1910 to 1940* (London, The Women's Press, 1987) pp. xiv, 3.

8. Aldington, *All Men Are Enemies*, pp. 279, 45-46.

9. 'Notes on the Present Situation', *The Egoist* vol. 1, no. 17, 1 September 1914, pp. 326-327.

10. Richard Aldington to Amy Lowell, 21 October 1914 (Harvard).

11. Aldington, *Life for Life's Sake*, p. 162. The Honourable Artillery Company raised three infantry battalions and several artillery batteries in the First World War. Hulme enlisted (as a private soldier) in the 1st battalion, which, as a unit of 8th and then 7th Brigade, joined the (Regular) Third Division on the Western Front. Hulme and the other new recruits joined their battalion in the trenches in December. He was invalided home in April 1915 and subsequently commissioned into the Royal Marine Artillery. He was killed by a shell on 28 September 1917.

12. Richard Aldington to Harriet Monroe, 16 August 1914 (Chicago).

13. See Aldington, *Life for Life's Sake*, p. 154.

14. In a letter to Samuel Hynes in 1954 Aldington gave the very early date of 5 August 1914 for his visit to the H.A.C. Headquarters, and remarked that Hulme was pleased to hear that the H.A.C. had rejected him, on the grounds that in his (Hulme's) opinion, 'war was not for sensitive men.' 30 April 1954, (Texas).

15. John Gould Fletcher to Amy Lowell, 24 September 1914 (Harvard).

16. The American poet and novelist Conrad Aiken (1889-1973) remained a life-long friend of Eliot.

17. Charles Masterman (1873-1927) had been financial secretary to the Treasury in the Liberal government. Those who attended the Wellington House meeting included J.M. Barrie, Arthur Conan Doyle, Arnold Bennett, John Masefield, G.K. Chesterton, Henry Newbolt, John Galsworthy, Thomas Hardy and H.G. Wells. One of the most influential publications to be produced by the Bureau was the Report on Alleged German Outrages in early 1915, detailing alleged German atrocities in Belgium and France.

18. Hueffer, F.M., *Between St Dennis and St George* (London, Hodder and Stoughton, 1915), pp. 9, 204, 60. The books appeared in March and September 1915 respectively.

19. Richard Aldington to Amy Lowell 7 December 1914 (Harvard).

20. Aldington, *Life for Life's Sake*, p. 161.

21. Hynes, Samuel, *A War Imagined: The First World War and English Culture* (London, Bodley Head, 1990), p. 72.

22. Richard Aldington to Amy Lowell 21 November 1914 (Harvard). By the time he came to write *Life for Life's Sake*, Aldington had become much more charitable towards Hueffer, asserting that while he had known many men in his time, he had known few 'so fundamentally innocent of real harm as Ford.' (p. 142)

23. Hueffer's article was entitled 'Literary Portraits - XVI: Germania' and had appeared in *Outlook* on 3 October 1914. Copp, nos. 26-28.

24. Richard Aldington to Amy Lowell, 1 February 1915 (Harvard); Pound's letter to his mother is no. 469 in Rachewiltz, Moody and Moody.

25. In England the series was published by Constable.

26. Marianne Moore (1887-1992) had been a contemporary of H.D.'s at Bryn Mawr College. Lowell's contribution to the journal was actually five short pieces in her new 'polyphonic prose', rather than a poem.

27. *The Egoist* vol. 2, no. 5, May 1915, pp. 78-80.

28. *ibid.* vol. 2, no. 7, July 1915, p. 88.

29. H.D. to F.S. Flint, [5] July 1915 (Copp, no. 42).

30. Eliot's friend Conrad Aiken, now back in Boston and fast becoming a friend of Fletcher, nevertheless attacked it in *The New Republic* (22 May 1915) as did Padraic Colum (20 November 1915). A highly critical survey of Imagism also came from William Ellery Leonard in *The Chicago Evening Post* between 18 September and 9 October 1915.

31. Richard Aldington to Amy Lowell 21 May 1915 (Harvard).

32. H.D., *Tribute to Freud* (Manchester: Carcanet Press, 1985), p. 40.

33. This writer was prompted to examine p. 8 of the typescript of *Magic Mirror* (Yale) after reading of this fact in Susan Stanford Friedman, *Psyche Reborn: The Emergence of HD* (Bloomington, Indiana University Press, 1981), p. 301, n. 20. H.D. corrected the draft in 1956.

34. *Asphodel* was written in 1921-1922.

35. Guest, *Herself Defined: The Poet H.D. and Her World*, p. 73.

36. H.D., *Asphodel*, p. 113.

37. Rachewiltz, Moody and Moody no. 484.

38. The five poems that appeared in *Poetry* were: 'Windsleepers', 'Garden', 'Storm', 'The Pool' and 'Moonrise'.

39. Carr, *The Verse revolutionaries*, p. 727.

40. Richard Aldington to F.S. Flint 16 June 1915 (Copp no. 39). It is interesting to note that those crimson foxgloves become 'Tall bloody pikes' in the poem 'Summer', an indication of Aldington's darkening mood.

41. The six were: *The Poems of Anyte of Tegea* (Aldington); *Poems and Fragments of Sappho* (Storer); *Choruses from Euripides Iphigeneia in Aulis* (H.D.); *Latin Poems of the Renaissance* (Aldington); *Poems of Leonidas of Tarentum* (Whitall); and *The Mosella of Ausonius* (Flint).

42. Richard Aldington to Amy Lowell, 8 September 1915 (Harvard).

43. H.D., *Bid Me To Live*, pp. 12-13.

44. Richard Aldington to Amy Lowell, 8 July 1915 (Harvard).

45. Richard Aldington to Amy Lowell, 12 November 1915 (Harvard).

46. H.D., *Paint it Today*, p. 45.

47. *ibid.* p. 170.

48. H.D., *Bid Me To Live*, pp. 24-25.

49. H.D. to Amy Lowell 29 November 1915 (Harvard).

50. H.D. to Amy Lowell 22 January 1916 (Harvard).

51. H.D., *Bid Me To Live*, p. 65.

52. Richard Aldington to Marjorie Pollard, 12 May 1933 (SIU).

53. Richard Aldington to Amy Lowell, 29 October 1915 (Harvard).

54. Amy Lowell to Richard Aldington, 15 December 1915 (Harvard).

55. Aldington, *Life for Life's Sake*, p. 176; Cournos, *Autobiography*, p. 249. In 1955 Fallas

(1885-1962) would receive the Prime Minister's Literary Award for his fictionalised account of his war experience, *St Mary's Village*; his other novels were: *The Wooden Pillow* (1935), *Down the Proud Stream* (1937) and *Eve with Her Basket* (1951). *The Gate is Open* (1938) is a memoir.

56. Cournos, *Autobiography*, p. 249.

57. Aldington, *Life for Life's Sake*, p. 161.

58. *Broom* 1912; *Starveacre* 1915. Whitham (1883-1956) would go on to publish eight more novels and a two-volume biographical account of the French Revolution. He never achieved popular success.

59. John Mills Whitham to Carl Fallas, 18 April 1934 (Exeter).

60. Fallas, Carl, *The Gate is Open* (London, Heinemann, 1938), pp. 6-10. Whitham's letter of 18 April 1934 (Exeter) also recalls the event.

61. Letter from Florence Fallas to Bryher, 3 March 1963 (Yale).

62. Undated letter from H.D. to F.S. Flint, headed 'Wednesday' [22 March 1916] (Texas).

63. The phrase is from a letter from Aldington to Flint 27 March 1916 (Texas).

64. F.S. Flint to H.D., 6 May 1916 (Copp, no. 77).

65. Richard Aldington to F.S. Flint, 27 March 1916 (Texas).

66. The poem was never published in Aldington's lifetime, appearing only in Gates, *The Poetry of Richard Aldington* (p. 177) in 1974. Consideration for H.D. must have played a part in Aldington's decision not to publish.

67. Richard Aldington to F.S. Flint, 26 May 1916 (Texas) (Copp's translation: Aldington frequently wrote to Flint in French, particularly when the content of his letter was sensitive.)

68. See Gates, *The Poetry of Richard Aldington*, pp. 183, 194.

69. Richard Aldington to F.S. Flint, 12 June 1916 (Texas) (Copp's translation).

70. Richard Aldington to Marjorie Pollard, 12 May 1933 (S.I.U).

71. Amy Lowell to H.D., 12 January 1916 (Harvard).

72. Amy Lowell to Richard Aldington, 5 February 1916 (Harvard).

73. *The Little* Review, vol. 3, no. 4, June/July 1916, pp. 26-31; *Poetry* vol. 8, no. 5, August 1916, pp. 255-259.

74. *Times Literary Supplement*, 11 January 1917, p. 19.

75. *Poetry*, vol. 8, no. 1, April 1916, pp. 49-51.

76. *The Little Review* vol. 3, no. 3 (May 1916), pp. 30-35; the other two Imagists were H.D. and Flint, discussed in *The Little Review*, vol. 3, no. 4, June/July 1916.

77. *Times Literary Supplement*, 4 May 1916. The reviewer was believed to be Professor J.W. Mackail, the translator of *Select Epigrams from the Greek Anthology*. *Ion* would not be published until 1937.

78. *Poetry*, vol. 9, no. 2, November 1916, pp. 101-104.

79. Bubb would publish: *The Choruses from Iphigenia in Aulis* in August 1916; *Latin Poems of the Renaissance* in October 1916; *The Tribute and Circe: Two Poems* and *The Poems of Anyte of Tegea* in February 1917; *The Garland of Months* in May 1917; *The Love Poems of Myrrhine and Konallis* in June 1917; and *Reverie: A Little Book of Poems for H.D.* in August 1917. He also published Storer's *The Poems and Fragments of Sappho* in November 1917.

80. Richard Aldington to Charles Bubb, 19 June 1916. Keller, Dean H., *Bubb Booklets: Letters of Richard Aldington to Charles Clinton Bubb* (Francestown: Typographeum, 1988), p. 20 (UCLA).

81. He was released in September, but was set to work on the land for the rest of the war.

82. Cournos, *Autobiography*, p. 288.

83. H.D. to F.S. Flint, 25 May 1916 (Texas).

84. Florence Fallas mentions this in a letter written to H.D.'s friend Bryher some two years after H.D.'s death. 3 March 1963 (Yale).

85. Aldington, *Life for Life's Sake*, p. 177.

86. The Derby Scheme was the voluntary recruitment policy which had been created in 1915: those who registered under this scheme would be called upon for service only when necessary. Men were classified in groups according to their year of birth and marital status and were to be called up with their group when it was required.

7. The Soldier: 1916

1.   Cournos, *Autobiography*, p. 289.

2.   Cournos, John, *Miranda Masters* (New York, Alfred Knopf, 1926), p. 124.

3.   Richard Aldington to F.S. Flint, 28 June 1916, Copp, no. 84 (Copp's translation of Aldington's French).

4.   Richard Aldington to F.S. Flint, 10 July 1916, Copp no. 85.

5.   Richard Aldington to F.S. Flint, 13 July 1916, Copp no. 86 (Copp's translation from French).

6.   Richard Aldington to John Cournos, undated letter (Harvard) (around the same date as the letter to Flint, i.e. 13 July 1916).

7.   H.D. to John Cournos, undated letter (probably Sunday evening 23 July 1916) (Harvard).

8.   H.D. to F.S. Flint 24 July 1916, Copp, no. 88.

9.   Amy Lowell to Richard Aldington 28 June 1916 (Harvard).

10. Richard Aldington to F.S. Flint, 24 July 1916, Copp, no. 89 (Copp's translation).

11. Bell, John (ed.), *Wilfred Owen, Selected Letters* (Oxford University Press, 1998), nos. 476 and 481 (4 and 19 January 1917).

12. Richard Aldington to F.S. Flint 16 July 1916 (Texas) (Copp's translation).

13. Aldington, *Death of a Hero*, p. 217.

14. 'Culture in the Army', *The Sphere*, 3 May 1919.

15. Graham, Stephen, *A Private in the Guards* (London, Macmillan, 1919), p. 20.

16. *ibid*. p. 159.

17. Aldington, *Death of a Hero*, p. 217.

18. *ibid*. p. 216.

19. H.D. to F.S. Flint, 24 July 1916, Copp no. 88.

20. D.H. Lawrence to Amy Lowell, 23 August 1916 (Healey, Claire and Cushman, Keith (eds.), *The Letters of D.H. Lawrence and Amy Lowell 1914-1925* (Santa Barbara, Black Sparrow Press, 1985, no. 20).

21. The poem appeared in *Some Imagist Poets, 1917*.

22. Richard Aldington to F.S. Flint, letters of 13 July and 9 August, Copp nos. 86 and 90 (Copp's translation of Aldington's French).

23. H.D. to John Cournos, undated letter headed Thursday [probably 14 September 1916] (Harvard).

24. Richard Aldington to John Cournos, 14 August 1916 (Harvard).

25. Richard Aldington to Charles Bubb, 9 August 1917 (Keller, p. 33).

26. See Chapter One, n. 14. The most vivid account of that boyhood walking holiday is the fictionalised one in *Death of a Hero* (pp.79-81), where William Hilbery is 'Tom Conington'.

27. Vol. l, no. 4 (August 1916). Both poems would be included in Aldington's contribution to the 1917 edition of the Imagists anthology. In the form in which he sent it to Flint in his letter of 26 May 1916, 'Images', then untitled, had been twice as long and an even more intense expression of 'the violence of [his] desire'. The original poem can be found in Gates, *The Poetry of Richard Aldington*, pp. 178-179.

28. H.D. to John Cournos, 5 September 1916 (Harvard).

29. Carr, *The Verse Revolutionaries*, p. 837.

30. H.D. to John Cournos, undated letter headed 'Friday' (probably 8 September 1916) (Harvard).

31. H.D. to John Cournos, undated letters, headed 'Wednesday' and 'Thursday' (probably 13 and 14 September 1916) (Harvard).

32. Respectively: 'Fragment 41' (missing the original poem's last two sections); Fragment 40 (missing the original poem's first two sections); Fragment 68 (missing the original poem's third section).

33. H.D. to John Cournos, undated letter headed 'Wednesday' [probably 4 October 1916] (Harvard).

34. H.D. to John Cournos, undated letter [probably 6 September 1916] (Harvard).

35. 'Adonis' and 'The God' appeared in the January *Egoist*, 'Pygmalion' in February and 'Eurydice' in May; these four poems were H.D.'s contribution to *Some Imagist Poets 1917*.

36. H.D. to John Cournos, undated letter headed 'Wednesday' [probably 13 September 1916] (Harvard).

37. F.S. Flint to Amy Lowell, 8 October 1916 (Harvard).

38. John Gould Fletcher to Amy Lowell, 25 September 1916 (Harvard).

39. H.D. to John Cournos, undated letter headed 'Tuesday' [probably 31 October 1916] (Harvard)

40. H.D., *Bid Me To Live*, p. 52.

41. At this stage, H.D.'s intended contribution to the anthology was her long poem 'The Tribute'.

42. D.H. Lawrence to Edward Marsh, 29 January 1917, Boulton, J. and Robertson, A. (eds.), *Letters of D.H. Lawrence vol. 3, October 1916-June 1921* (Cambridge University Press, 2002), no. 1366.

43. H.D., *Bid Me To Live*, p. 80.

44. Delany, Paul, *D H Lawrence's Nightmare: The Writer and His Circle in the Years of the Great War* (Hassocks: Harvester Press, 1978), p. 191.

45. H.D., *Bid Me To Live*, pp. 138-139.

46. D.H. Lawrence to Cecil Gray, 7 November 1917 (Boulton, no. 1482).

47. H.D., *Bid Me To Live*, p. 136.

48. H.D. to John Cournos, undated letter headed 'Wednesday' [probably 13 September 1916] (Harvard).

49. H.D. to Charles Bubb 9 September 1916 (UCLA).

50. Richard Aldington to Charles Bubb, 29 June 1917 (Keller, p. 27).

51. Verne Citadel was built on the highest point of Portland Island in the nineteenth century as a barracks for prisoners building the harbour breakwaters. Today it is a prison once again, but from the First World War until the 1960s it was a military training camp.

52. Richard Aldington to F.S. Flint, undated letter headed 'Saturday' [19 November 1916] (Copp. No. 104).

53. Richard Aldington to F.S. Flint, 15 November 1916, Copp no. 107 (Copp's translation).

54. Aldington, *Death of a Hero*, p. 229.

55. Aldington, *Life for Life's Sake*, p. 184.

8. To the Front and Back: 1917

1. Mitchinson, K.W., *Pioneer Battalions in the Great War* (London, Leo Cooper, 1997), p. 142.

2. For example, on 13 April 1917 such an incident claimed the lives of one officer and 2 men from the battalion, wounding 2 more officers and 5 men (WO95 1601 45E).

3. The 11th Leicestershires had 10 officer and 258 other ranks fatalities during the course of the war.

4. Aldington, *Death of a Hero*, pp. 252-253.

5. *ibid.* pp. 263-264; the 11th Leicestershire Battalion War Diary records that 10 men were admitted to the Field Ambulance as a result of gas-shelling on 3 March 1917; further such incidents (and more casualties) occurred on 21, 23, 24, 25 and 28 April (WO95 1601 45E); the 6th Divisional History records that 7,000 enemy gas shells were dropped on Maroc, Philosophe and Vermelles on 29 April. Marden, T.O. (ed.), *A Short History of the 6th Division, August 1914-March 1919* (London: Hugh Rees, 1920).

6. Aldington, *Death of a Hero*, pp. 279.

7. *ibid.* p. 269.

8. *ibid.* p. 241.

9. *ibid.* pp. 291-292.

10. *ibid.* pp. 260-261.

11. See Lawrence's letter to Lowell, 23 August 1916, quoted in chapter 7, and numerous references in *Bid Me To Live* and *Asphodel*.

12. *The Egoist*, vol. 4, no. 8, September 1917, p. 118.

13. Richard Aldington to F.S. Flint, 2 February 1917 (Copp, no.118).

14. *ibid.*

15. Aldington, *Death of a Hero*, p. 242.

16. Richard Aldington to F.S. Flint, 3 March 1917 (Copp, no. 126).

17. Richard Aldington to F.S. Flint, 22 January 1917 (Copp, no. 115).

18. Richard Aldington to F.S. Flint, 29 January 1917 (Copp, no. 116).

19. 'Notes from France', *The Egoist* vol. 4, no.3, April 1917, p. 38.

20. Aldington, *Death of a Hero*, p. 261.

21. Richard Aldington to F.S. Flint, 29 January 1917 (Copp, no. 116).

22. F.S. Flint to Harriet Shaw Weaver, 21 February 1917 (Copp, no. 122).

23. John Cournos to F.S. Flint ,22 February 1917 (Copp, no. 123).

24. Richard Aldington to F.S. Flint, 22 February 1917 (Copp, no. 124).

25. Richard Aldington to F.S. Flint, 22 January 1917 (Copp, no. 115).

26. Richard Aldington to Amy Lowell, 20 November 1917 (Harvard).
27. *Poetry* vol. 9 no. 2, November 1916, p. 101.
28. Richard Aldington to F.S. Flint, 2 February 1917 (Copp, no 118).
29. *New Statesman* 3 March ('Reflections on Vers Libre') and 19 May ('The Borderline of Prose') 1917.
30. H.D. to Amy Lowell, 4 March 1917 (Harvard).
31. Richard Aldington to F.S. Flint, 22 January 1917 (Copp, no. 115).
32. H.D. to Charles Bubb, [early 1917] (UCLA).
33. Richard Aldington to F.S. Flint, 20 April 1917 (Copp, no. 131).
34. Aldington, *Death of a Hero*, p. 259.
35. *ibid*. p. 260.

9. Interlude: 1917

1. Aldington, *Death of a Hero*, pp. 311-313.
2. Richard Aldington to Charles Bubb, 4 September 1917 (Keller, p. 35).
3. Ezra Pound to Margaret Anderson, January 1917 (Paige, no. 120).
4. EzraPound to Margaret Anderson, August 1917 (Paige, no. 127).
5. Carpenter, Humphrey, *A Serious Character: The Life of Ezra Pound* (London: Faber and Faber, 1988), p. 255.
6. Ezra Pound to Homer Pound, 23 August 1917 (Rachewiltz, Moody and Moody, no. 539).
7. Richard Aldington to H.D., 7 July 1918 (Zilboorg, no. 24).
8. Richard Aldington to Charles Bubb, 12 July 1917 (Keller, p. 21).
9. Richard Aldington to Martyn Johnson, 29 July 1917 (Texas).
10. Richard Aldington to Charles Bubb, 22 June 1917 (Keller, pp. 25-26). The phrase 'napoo' (British soldiers' corruption of the French 'il n'y en a plus') means 'finished', 'washed up', 'of no use'.
11. Richard Aldington to Charles Bubb, 29 June 1917 (Keller, p. 29).
12. Richard Aldington to Charles Bubb, 6 August 1917 (Keller, p. 31).
13. Richard Aldington to Charles Bubb, 9 August 1917 (Keller, p. 34).
14. Richard Aldington to Charles Bubb, 29 June 1917 (Keller, p. 27).
15. Eliot had already been critical of the poems in his article in the *New Statesman* on 19 May 1917.
16. Richard Aldington to Charles Bubb, 29 June 1917 (Keller, p. 27).
17. H.D. to F.S. Flint, 30 August 1917 (Yale).
18. *ibid*.
19. Richard Aldington to F.S. Flint, 5 September 1917 (Copp, no.135).
20. The appointment appeared in the *London Gazette* on 19 December 1917.

10. Betrayals: 1917-1918

1. H.D., *Bid Me To Live*, p. 57.
2. See pp. 156-157 above.
3. The others were The Scottish journalist and novelist Catherine Carswell and Lady Cynthia Asquith.
4. D.H. Lawrence to Catherine Carswell, 9 March 1917, Boulton, vol. 3, no. 1386.

5.   H.D. to Marianne Moor,e 29 August 1917 (Rosenbach Foundation).

6.   Both men were classified as 'C grade', i.e. 'suitable for home service only'; Gray was 'C2' ('able to walk 5 miles, see and hear for ordinary purposes'), while Lawrence was 'C3' ('only suitable for sedentary work').

7.   The incident is recounted in Gray's autobiography, *Musical Chairs* (London, Home and van Thal, 1948) and in a fictionalised version in Lawrence's *Kangaroo* ((London, Martin Secker, 1923).

8.   Delany, *D.H. Lawrence's Nightmare*, p. 320.

9.   Dollie was married to Ernest Radford, one of the 'Rhymers Club' group of poets. The couple were in their sixties and in poor health.

10. D.H. Lawrence to Cynthia Asquith 20 November 1918, Boulton, vol. 3, no. 1487.

11. H.D., *Bid Me To Live*, pp. 77-89.

12. *ibid*. p. 167.

13. *ibid*. p. 175.

14. *ibid*. p. 88.

15. H.D. to Bryher, 15 May 1933 (Yale). H.D. is not here referring to her own letters from Lawrence, which had been destroyed by Aldington in 1920; she has probably been reading either Catherine Carswell's *The Savage Pilgrimage* (London, Martin Secker, 1932) or Middleton Murry's *Son of Woman* (London, Jonathan Cape, 1931).

16. H.D., *Notes on Recent Writing* (Yale). This was H.D.'s post-war attempt, at Norman Pearson's instigation, to put in order her unpublished writing.

17. H.D. to Richard Aldington, 14 January 1953 (Zilboorg, no. 180).

18. *ibid*.

19. H.D. to Bryher, 16 January 1935 (Yale).

20. Martz, Louis (ed.) *Collected Poems of H.D. 1912-1944* (New York, New Directions, 1983), p. xx.

21. H.D., *Bid Me To Live*, p. 13.

22. *ibid*. p. 140.

23. *ibid*. p. 87.

24. D.H. Lawrence to Amy Lowell, 23 August 1916 (Healey and Cushman, no. 20).

25. H.D., *Asphodel*, p. 128.

26. H.D., *Bid Me To Live*, pp. 47, 75.

27. D.H. Lawrence to Cecil Gray, 7 November 1917 (Boulton, vol. 3, no. 1482).

28. H.D., *Bid Me To Live*, p. 88.

29. In *Aaron's Rod* (New York, Thomas Seltzer, 1922).

30. *ibid*. p. 60.

31. H.D., *Bid Me To Live*, p. 95.

32. Cournos, *Autobiography*, p. 187.

33. Richard Aldington to H.D. 17 and 20 May (Zilboorg, nos. 5 and 6).

34. Richard Aldington to Marjorie Pollard 12 May 1933 (SIU).

35. H.D., *Bid Me To Live*, p. 117.

36. *ibid*. p. 148.

37. Richard Aldington to Amy Lowell 2 January 1918 (Harvard).

38. H.D., *Bid Me To Live*, p. 148.

39. *ibid*. p. 23.

40. Patmore's current lover – whom she had probably met through Yeats – was James

White, co-founder of the Irish Citizen Army, who had just spent three months in Pentonville for inciting the Welsh miners to go out on strike to protest against the execution of James Connolly in May 1916.

41. Richard Aldington to Amy Lowell, 21 October 1914 (Harvard).
42. Patmore, Brigit, *This Impassioned Onlooker* (London, Robert Holden and Co., 1926), pp. 143-144.
43. H.D., *Bid Me To Live*, pp. 67-68.
44. Patmore, *My Friends When Young*, p. 80.
45. H.D., *Bid Me To Live*, pp. 111-112.
46. *ibid*. p. 140.
47. *ibid*. p. 48. (The actual air-raid took place on 18 December; it brought down the ceiling of the room of one lodger at 44: Alida Klemantaski, Harold Monro's assistant (and, later, wife), who had been running the Poetry Bookshop since Monro had been called up the previous year.)
48. *ibid*. p. 140.
49. Richard Aldington to F.S. Flint, 28 December 1917 (Copp, no. 139).
50. D.H. Lawrence to Amy Lowell 13 December 1917 (Harvard).
51. H.D., *Bid Me To Live*, p. 103.
52. Published by Elkin Mathews June 1919.
53. Richard Aldington to Charles Bubb 8 February 1918 (Keller, pp. 44-45).
54. Foreword to *War and Love* (Four Seas Press, 1919). This American edition of the war and love poems was the first one planned, in January 1918. However, it was not published until September 1919, thus appearing after both Beaumont's limited edition of *Images of War* (April 1919) and Elkin Matthews's edition of *Images of Desire* (June 1919).
55. Amy Lowell to Richard Aldington, 11 April [1918] (Harvard).
56. H.D. to Amy Lowell, (undated) (Harvard).
57. Amy Lowell to H.D., 15 June 1918 (Harvard).
58. Lawrence, *Aaron's Rod*, p. 38.
59. H.D., *Palimpsest*, pp. 51, 53.
60. H.D., *Asphodel*, p. 149.
61. H.D., *Palimpsest*, pp. 51, 53.
62. H.D. to John Cournos, undated letters [postmarked 25 January 1918 and 2 February 1918] (Harvard).
63. H.D. to John Cournos, 2 February 1918 (Harvard).
64. Richard Aldington to Amy Lowell, 3 March 1918 (Harvard).
65. Richard Aldington to F.S. Flint, 28 December 1917 (Copp no. 139).
66. James Campbell defines combat gnosticism as 'the belief that combat represents a qualitatively separate order of experience that is difficult if not impossible to communicate to any who have not undergone an identical experience'. 'Combat Gnosticism: The Ideology of First World War Poetry Criticism', *New Literary History*, vol. 30, no. 1, Winter, 1999, pp. 203-215.
67. Richard Aldington to Charles Bubb, 30 December 1917 (Keller, p. 40).
68. Richard Aldington to Amy Lowell 2 January 1918 (Harvard).
69. H.D., *Bid Me To Live*, p. 71.
70. 'Art and Ardor in World War One: Selected Letters from H.D. to John Cournos' in *The Iowa Review*, vol. 16, no. 3, p. 128.

71. Cecil Gray to H.D., undated letter headed Monday evening (Yale).

72. Cecil Gray to H.D., undated letter headed 'Monday' [postmarked 12 March 1918] (Yale).

73. Richard Aldington to John Cournos, 6 April 1918 (Harvard).

74. H.D. to John Cournos, undated letter headed 'Monday' [early April 1918] (Harvard).

75. 'Advent', *Tribute to Freud*, p. 134.

76. H.D., *Bid Me To Live*, pp. 134-142.

77. The 9th Royal Sussex Regiment (C.O. Lt. Col. M.V.B. Hill) was in 73 Brigade of 24th Division (C.O. Major General C.A. Daly). In the Spring Offensive, 24th Division was in XIX Corps (C.O. Lieutenant-General Sir Herbert Watts) in General Sir Hubert Gough's Fifth Army. Gough was replaced on 28 March by General Sir Henry Rawlinson.

11. Back to the Front

1. Aldington, Richard, *Roads to Glory* (London, Chatto and Windus, 1930), p. 271.

2.   Hill 70 had been captured by the British – or, rather, by the Canadian Corps – after Aldington left the area in 1917, but the city of Lens remained in German hands. Throughout the German offensive, this sector had been quiet, the thrust having taken place south of Arras initially, while the Battle of the Lys was still taking place north of La Bassée, and only wound down at the end of April.

3. Aldington, *Death of a Hero*, p. 335.

4. *ibid*. p. 329.

5. *ibid* p. 331.

6. *ibid*. p. 328.

7. *ibid*. p. 332.

8. The incident is also fictionalised in the short story 'Farewell to Memories' (*Roads to Glory*), which includes this prose poem.

9. Aldington, *Death of A Hero*, pp. 335.

10. Richard Aldington to H.D., 17 May 1918 (Zilboorg, no. 5).

11. Richard Aldington to H.D., 20 May 1918 (Zilboorg, no. 6).

12. Richard Aldington to Alec Randall, 2 May 1918 (Huntington).

13. Richard Aldington to H.D., 20 May 1918 (Zilboorg, no. 6).

14. Richard Aldington to H.D., 28 May 1918 (Zilboorg, no. 7).

15. Richard Aldington to H.D., 31 May 1918 (Zilboorg, no. 8).

16. viz. 'Sorcery of Words' and 'Our Hands'; see also 'Fatigues' and 'The Road' (in Beaumont and *War and Love*). The prose poems written in the trenches at Loos in 1918 were: 'Stand-To; 'In An Old Battlefield'; 'Escape'; 'Landscape' and 'Dawns'. Four of them appeared in *Poetry* vol. 13 no. 11 (November 1918), while 'Dawns' was printed in *The Egoist*, vol. 5, no. 9 (October 1918)

17. Richard Aldington to H.D., 1 and 2 June 1918 (Zilboorg, nos. 9, 10 and 11).

18. 'The Lost Leader', Robert Browning.

19. See also his letter of 24 July, quoted at the end of this chapter.

20. Richard Aldington to F.S. Flint, 2 June 1918 (Copp, no. 139).

21.   *ibid*. (Copp's translation: this part of the letter is written in French.)

22. Richard Aldington to H.D., 2 June 1918 (Zilboorg, no. 11).

23. H.D., *Bid Me To Live*, p. 146.

24. *ibid*. p.155

25. Richard Aldington to H.D., 26 June 1918 (Zilboorg, no. 20).

26. In a letter dated 7 July he wrote: 'Prose? No! You have so precise, so wonderful an instrument — why abandon it to fashion another perhaps less perfect?' (Zilboorg, no. 24).

27. 'The Chateau de Fressin', *The Sphere*, 13 September 1919.

28. 'Discouragement', 'Fantasy', 'Reaction' and 'Prayer'; along with four of the Loos pieces, they appeared as 'Prayers and Fantasies' in *Poetry*, vol. 13, no. 11, November 1918.

29. Richard Aldington to F.S. Flint, 16 June 1918 (Copp, no. 142: Copp's translation of Aldington's French).

30. Richard Aldington to H.D., 20 June 1918 (Zilboorg, no. 16).

31. See Richard Aldington to F.S. Flint, 7 July 1918 (Copp, no. 143).

32. Richard Aldington to H.D., 12 June 1918 (Zilboorg, no. 13). Zilboorg's translation: Zilboorg suggests that, although Aldington regularly corresponded in French with Flint, both as an academic exercise and as a way of 'privileging intimate information', his choice of that language for this letter to H.D. probably stemmed from a desire to soften the impact of the irritation he was feeling towards her – as well as occupying him in a period of 'boredom and dislocation'. (*ibid*. p. 57) It is significant that his next letter (18 June 1918) is also in French and similarly bluff in tone.

33. Richard Aldington to H.D., 12 June 1918 (Zilboorg, no. 13) (again, Zilboorg's translation).

34. Richard Aldington to H.D., 21 June 1918 (Zilboorg, no. 17).

35. Richard Aldington to H.D., 9 July 1918 (Zilboorg, no. 26).

36. Richard Aldington to H.D., 12 July 1918 (Zilboorg, no. 28).

37. Richard Aldington to H.D., 16 July 1918 (Zilboorg, no. 30).

38. Presumably: the Somme (when he was first in training); Messines and Third Ypres (after his departure from the 11th Leicesters); Cambrai in November 1917; and the German offensive of March 1918 (in which the 9th Royal Sussex had suffered badly).

39. It would be some weeks before the 9th Royal Sussex were engaged in the Allied counter-offensive. Meanwhile the French and the Americans had begun, and Gilbert, H.D.'s much loved brother, thirty-three years old and a captain in 303rd Engineer Regiment, 78th Division, was caught up in the fighting. He would be killed in action on 25 September and is buried in St Mihiel American Cemetery at Thiaucourt.

40. 9th Royal Sussex, 7th Northamptonshire Regiment and 13th Middlesex.

41. An allusion to Deighton Patmore, Brigit's wayward husband.

42. Richard Aldington to H.D., 24 July 1918 (Zilboorg, no. 34). Aldington again turns to Browning to express his love for H.D. – the quotation is from 'Life in a Love'.

12. Complications

1. Richard Aldington to Ezra Pound, 14 September 1918 (Yale).

2. Bryher had already published a pamphlet, 'Amy Lowell: A Critical Appreciation' (Eyre and Spottiswode, 1918).

3. The two women were to celebrate the anniversary of that day for the rest of their lives.

4.   Bryher, *Two Selves,* (Paris, Contact Press, 1923) p. 289.

5.   H.D., *Palimpsest,* pp. 88-89.

6.   This is clear from H.D.'s letters to Bryher of 13 and 18 July 1918 (before and after the visit). (Yale).

7.   Richard Aldington to H.D., 28 July 1918 (Zilboorg, no. 35).

8.   Richard Aldington to H.D., 3 August 1918 (Zilboorg, no. 36).

9.   Richard Aldington to H.D., 4 August 1918 (Zilboorg, no. 37).

10. Richard Aldington to H.D., (Zilboorg, no. 45).

11. Richard Aldington to H.D., 21 August 1918 (Zilboorg, no. 46).

12. Richard Aldington to H.D., 14 August 1918 (Zilboorg, no. 43).

13. The private papers of Canon H.R. Bate MC, document no. 10782, Imperial War Museum.

14. Richard Aldington to F.S. Flint, (Copp, no. 145).

15. Richard Aldington to H.D., 31 August 1918 (Zilboorg, no. 48).

16. *ibid.*

17. H.D., *Palimpsest,* p. 51.

18. Richard Aldington to H.D., 1 September 1918 (Zilboorg, no. 49).

19. The new tenant was Margaret Postgate, the young feminist, pacifist, and socialist, shortly to become the wife of the socialist economist, G.D.H. Cole. In her autobiography, *Growing Up Into Revolution*, Cole describes the last place where she had lived before her marriage as: 'a lovely first-floor room in Mecklenburgh Square belonging to the poet H.D., with three tall windows, a balcony looking out on the plane-trees of the Square, very inadequate heating and a large population of mice.' (p. 80.)

20. It was Daphne Bax who, a few months later, would introduce H.D. to Havelock Ellis, the psychologist and early sexologist, thus starting H.D. and Bryher on their life-long involvement with psychoanalysis.

21. It is clear from a letter written by Margaret Snively Pratt to Bryher on 8 August 1962 (after Aldington's death) that she never realised that H.D.'s child was not Aldington's daughter (Yale).

22. He had married the Irish poet, Dora Sigerson in 1895. In 1920 he would remarry – Bryher's school-friend, Doris Banfield.

23. H.D. always had difficulty in understanding army organisation and routines; Aldington was 'back of the lines' – but because he was in training.

24. H.D. to Amy Lowell, undated letter [September 1918] (Harvard).

25. Richard Aldington to H.D., 27 September 1918 (Zilboorg, no.54).

26. Published by Constable in 1920 as *Development*.   ·

27. Richard Aldington to F.S. Flint, 6 October 1918 (Copp, no. 149).

28. Aldington, *Death of a Hero*, p. 336-337.

29. Richard Aldington to Eric Warman, 10 November 1958 (S.I.U.). See also the short story 'Meditation on a German Grave' in *Roads to Glory.*

30. Richard Aldington to H.D., 14 October 1918 (Zilboorg, no. 58)..

31. Richard Aldington to H.D., 23 October 1918 (Zilboorg, no. 60).

32. Richard Aldington to H.D., 23 October 1918 (Zilboorg, no. 60).

33. Aldington, 'Meditation on a German Grave', *Roads to Glory*.

34. Richard Aldington to H.D., 8 November 1918 (Zilboorg, no. 64).

35. Aldington, 'Victory', *Roads to Glory*.

36. Aldington, 'Farewell to Mermories', *Roads to Glory*, p. 277.

37. H.D. to Bryher, undated letter headed 'Monday' [probably written from Speen on Armistice Day] (Yale).

38. Richard Aldington to Amy Lowell (Harvard).

39. H.D. to Clement Shorter (Leeds).

40. Richard Aldington to H.D., 1 December 1918 (Zilboorg, no. 67).

41. D.H. Lawrence to Amy Lowell, 28 December 1918 (Harvard).

42. D.H. Lawrence to Selina Yorke, 16 December 1918 (Boulton, vol. 3, no. 1672).

43. 'Tantignies', *Images of War*, (Allan and Unwin, 1919).

44. Aldington, *Life for Life's Sake*, pp. 196.

45. 'Culture in the Army', *The Sphere*, 3 May 1919.

46. Richard Aldington to H.D., 1 January 1919 (Zilboorg,, no. 76).

47. Richard Aldington to H.D., 6 January 1919 (Zilboorg, no. 79).

48. Richard Aldington to H.D., 21 January 1919 (Zilboorg, no. 83).

49. Richard Aldington to H.D., 9 January 1919 (Zilboorg, no. 81).

50. Aldington, *Life for Life's Sake*, p. 195.

51. Richard Aldington to H.D., 29 January 1919 (Zilboorg, no. 84).

13. The Poet of War and Desire

1. This chapter will survey only the war poetry written up until the Armistice. Work written between that date and Aldington's demobilisation appeared in either *The Love of Myrrhine and Konallis and Other Prose Poems* in 1926 or in *Exile* in 1923.

2. Richard Aldington to Amy Lowell, 2 January 1918 (Harvard).

3. Richard Aldington to Charles Bubb, 8 February 1918 (UCLA).

4. A letter to Charles Bubb dated 14 October 1917 acknowledges Aldington's receipt of his complimentary copies (UCLA).

5. *To-Day* vol. 6, no. 32, October 1919, p. 64.

6. Kershaw and Temple, *Richard Aldington: An Intimate Portrait*, p. 162.

7. See Wilfred Owen's 'Strange Meeting' and 'Spring Offensive' and Robert Graves's 'Escape'.

8. *Poetry* vol. 12, no. 1, April 1918, p. 45.

9. Richard Aldington to Amy Lowell, 2 January 1918 (Harvard).

10. This figure excludes the ten poems written in 1916 when he was in uniform but had not yet been sent to the front ('Vicarious Atonement', 'Bondage', 'A Moment's Interlude', 'Field Manoeuvres', 'Prayer', 'Captive', 'Leave-Taking', 'The Lover', 'On the March', 'Dawn'). It also excludes the poems 'Apathy' and 'The Blood of the Young Men', written in England, in the summer of 1917 and January 1918 respectively, both of which were included in *War and Love* and the Allen and Unwin edition of *Images of War*. ('Apathy' also appeared in the Beaumont edition.)

11. Richard Aldington to F.S. Flint, 2 June 1918 (Copp, no. 141).

12. Cyril Beaumont (1891-1976) ran an antiquarian bookshop in Charing Cross Road and specialised in publishing attractive limited editions. He later achieved fame as a dance historian and critic.

13. Bubb had meanwhile, of course, printed privately 50 copies of *Reverie: a little book of verse for H.D.* and a handful of poems had appeared in *Poetry* and *The Egoist*. There were also two poems in the limited edition anthology *New Paths*, published by Beaumont in May 1918.

14. The next two chapters will reveal the change in circumstances which allowed him to contemplate their inclusion.

15. Richard Aldington to Amy Lowell, 2 January 1918 (Harvard); Richard Aldington to Charles Bubb, 8 February 1918 (UCLA); Richard Aldington to F.S. Flint, 7 July 1918 (Copp, no. 143).

16. Richard Aldington to Amy Lowell, 8 February 1918 (Harvard).

17. Hueffer (Ford) is here excluded as he was not, strictly speaking, a combatant.

18. See, for further examples, 'Living Sepulchres', 'April Lieder'.

19. *Poetry* vol. 1, no.6, March 1913 and the Preface to *Some Imagist Poets 1915*.

20. MacGreevy, p.30.

21. See Sassoon's 'The Fathers', 'Does It Matter?', 'To the Warmongers' and 'The Glory of Women'.

22. Rather mysteriously, he omitted the poem from his *Collected Poems* in 1928 (Covici Friede) and 1929 (Allen and Unwin) but restored it for his *Complete Poems* (Wingate) in 1948.

23. 'The Faun Captive' appeared as 'The Captive Faun' in *The Nation*, 31 May 1919 and was subsequently included in the second Egoist Press edition of *Images* in September 1919 and in the *Collected Poems* in 1928 and 1929. For a discussion of the two unpublished poems sent to H.D. in letters of 8 and 20 July 1918, see Zilboorg: 'Two Poems for H.D.', *Journal of Modern Literature*, vol. 16, no. 1, Winter 1989.

24. Gates, *The Poetry of Richard Aldington*, p. 76.

25. The poem did appear in *The Egoist* in November/December 1918.

26. 'The Borderline of Prose': 19 May 1917. (See p. 168 above.)

27. Published by Covici (Chicago) in *The Love of Myrrhine and Konallis and Other Prose Poems*. 'Fatigues', 'Sorcery of Words' and 'Our Hands' had meanwhile appeared in the Beaumont edition of *Images of War* and in the American *War and Love*, and 'Sorcery of Words' and 'Our Hands' in *Reverie: a little book of verse for H.D.* 'The Road' was printed in *The Egoist*, vol. 5, no. 7, August 1918.

28. 'Discouragement', 'Fantasy', 'Stand-To', 'In an Old Battlefield', 'Reaction', 'Escape', 'Prayer' and 'Landscape' appeared (untitled) in *Poetry*, vol. 13, no. 11, November 1918, as 'Prayers and Fantasies' nos. I to VIII, while 'Dawns' appeared in *The Egoist*, vol. 5, no. 9, October 1918.

29. Richard Aldington to H.D. 20 June 1918 (Zilboorg, no. 16). (Quoted on p. 210, above.)

30. The prose poems included are: 'Fatigues', 'Sorcery of Words' and 'The Road' from 1917; 'Stand-To', 'In an Old Battlefield', 'Landscape', 'Dawns', 'Escape', 'Discouragement' and 'Prayer' (one line only) from 1918; and two post-war prose poems, 'Lethe' and 'The Last Salute'.

31. Gates, *The Poetry of Richard Aldington*, pp. 70-71.

32. *ibid*. p. 69.

33. This poem is entitled 'Postlude' in *War and Love*, in which a different poem appears as 'Epilogue'.

34. Gates, *The Poetry of Richard Aldington*, p. 63.

35. H.D., *Bid Me To Live*, p. 95.

36. Richard Aldington to F.S. Flint, 17 May 1919 (Copp, no. 159: Copp's translation of Aldington's French).

37. After the Armistice, Aldington told Lowell: '*Images of Desire* is down to four poems since my drastic revision. I may rewrite some of the others.' (8 December 1918: Harvard). However, there are few discrepancies between the versions in *War and Love* and those in *Images of Desire*, with only four poems not carried forward. Furthermore, all the *Images of Desire* poems would be included in the *Collected Poems* and the *Complete Poems*.

14. The Aftermath: 1919

1. Bryher, *The Heart to Artemis* (Ashfield: Paris Press, 2006), p. 232.

2. Richard Aldington to Charles Bubb, 21 February 1919 (Keller, p. 55). Bubb had printed 32 copies of Aldington's *Latin Poems of the Renaissance* in 1916 and four titles in 1917: *The Poems of Anyte of Tegea* (40 copies); *The Garland of Months* by Folgore da San Gemignano (40 copies); *The Love Poems of Myrrhine and Konallis* (40 copies); and *Reverie, A Little Book of Poems for H.D.* (50 copies). Aldington had subsequently sent him his only copies of a second series of the Latin Poems of the Renaissance and of a revised version of *The Love Poems of Myrrhine and Konallis*. Bubb also had other manuscripts in his possession, including Aldington's translation of Remy du Gourmont's *Les Saintes du Paradis*, but the Clerk's Press published nothing after 1917; why this fruitful partnership and warm correspondence between the two men came to an end remains a mystery.

3. Richard Aldington to Martyn Johnson, 17 February 1919 (Texas); Richard Aldington to Amy Lowell 21 February 1919 (Harvard); Richard Aldington to Harriet Monroe 17 February 1919 (Chicago).

4. These appeared as: 12 April: 'Books in the Line'; 19 April: 'The Bookshop at Grenay'; 26 April: 'Crosses'; 3 May: 'Culture in the Army'; 10 May: 'War Poetry'; 17 May: 'Preferences in French Literature'. A further four appeared later in the year: 16 August: 'The Russian Ballet'; 3 September: 'The Chateau de Fressin'; 20 September: 'The Poetry Bookshop'; 27 September: 'The Present Discontent'.

5. H.D. to Bryher, several undated letters from Speen [late December 1918 and January 1919] (Yale). In the earlier of these letters H.D. addresses Bryher as 'Dear W.B.'; by mid-January she has become 'Dear Girl'.

6. H.D. to Clement Shorter, undated letter [January 1919] (Leeds).

7. Bryher, *The Heart to Artemis,* p. 223.

8. Richard Aldington to H.D. 24 February 1919 (Zilboorg, no. 85). H.W. Massingham (1860-1924) edited *The Nation* from 1909 to 1923.

9. Richard Aldington to H.D., 1 March 1919 (Zilboorg, no.86).

10. Richard Aldington to Clement Shorter, 17 March 1919 (Leeds).

11. Richard Aldington to Ezra Pound, 9 February 1919 (Yale).

12. Ezra Pound to William Carlos Williams, 3 February 1909 (Paige, no. 3).

13. Aldington, *Life for Life's Sake*, p. 217.

14. Sinclair, May, *Mary Olivier: A Life* (London, Virago, 1980), p. 374.

15. Shorter's wife, the Irish poet Dora Sigerson, had died the previous year and her portrait had been painted posthumously by Sir John Lavery. Sinclair, now in her mid-fifties, was already developing the early signs of the Parkinson's Disease which would increasingly afflict her. However, she would never forget her affection for Aldington,

H.D. and Pound, although they would lose touch with her when she retired to the Cotswolds in the mid 1920s; when she died in 1946, she left each of them fifty pounds and their own choice of books from her library.

16. Aldington, *Life for Life's Sake,* p. 215-216.

17. *ibid*. p. 216.

18. Aldington suggests that this was during this early post-war period; Read dates it earlier, to Aldington's return from the front in 1917. See: *Life for Life's Sake,* p. 221; *Richard Aldington: An Intimate Portrait,* p. 122.

19. *The Sphere*, 10 May 1919.

20. Kershaw and Temple, *Richard Aldington: An Intimate Portrait*, p. 123.

21. *ibid*. p.163.

22. Aldington, *Life for Life's Sake*, p. 222.

23. Vivian Arthur Watkins (1887-1961) was not, in fact, Canadian by birth or upbringing, having, like many of the Canadian servicemen of the First World War, emigrated from the U.K. just before the war (April 1914). He had served as a pilot in the war, and he was only five years older than Aldington.

24. Hibberd, *Harold Monro: Poet of the New Age*, p. 204.

25. Apart from the poets listed in this paragraph, the other contributors were: John Alford, Walter de la Mare, Siegfried Sassoon, D.H. Lawrence, Edith Sitwell, Charlotte Mew, Robert Nichols, Rose Macaulay, W.H. Davies, Frederic Manning, W.P. Ker, Frank Flint and Monro himself.

26. 'Belgium To-Day', A Scene of Desolation' and 'Revive the Terriers: Training for Demobilised Men' appeared anonymously in the *Pall Mall Gazette* on 26 February and 26 March, signed 'an infantryman'; 'The Professor's Class' and 'Liaison Officers' appeared in the *Daily Express* on 28 March and 11 April, signed 'frontiersman'. Aldington referred to these articles as 'rank journalism' in his letter to Amy Lowell of 17 June 1920 (Harvard).

27. Shorter paid him more handsomely: Aldington received 6 guineas each for his first six articles. Payments of 16 guineas in August and 12 guineas in October suggest a higher rate of 7 guineas for the August and September articles.

28. Richard Aldington to Amy Lowell, 31 March 1919 (Harvard). The Egoist Press would publish a second series of the P.T.S. in 1919-20, a much more modest scheme than Aldington had envisaged, consisting of re-issues from the first series, with the addition of H.D.'s choruses from Euripides' 'Hippolytus', Aldington's translations of Anacreon and Meleager, and Edward Storer's translations of Asclepiades and and Poseidippos.

29. The 'Letters to Unknown Women' appeared in *The Dial* as follows: 14 March 1918: 'To the Slave in "Cleon"; 9 May 1918: 'To Sappho'; 6 June 1918: 'To Helen'; 28 December 1918: 'Heliodora'; 22 February 1919: 'To the Amaryllis of Theocritus; 17 May 1919: 'To La Grosse Margot'.

30. The essay on Duhamel appeared in vol. 3, no. 1, February 1920, of the *Anglo-French Review*. Apart from poems and prose poems, Davray also accepted an essay on Gourmont (vol. 2, no. 3, October 1919) and one entitled 'Francis Gribble, Humours of Dramatic Censorship' (vol. 4, no. 4, November 1920).

31. Bruce Richmond (1871-1964) edited the *TLS* from 1902, shortly after it was founded, until 1936.

32. The poems were: 'Proem', 'Disdain', 'Doubt' and 'Bombardment' from *Images of War*

and 'Possession', 'Epigrams' and 'Reserve' from *Images of Desire*. In 1918, 'Apathy' had appeared in the February issue of *The Egoist*, 'Soldier's Song' in April, 'The Road' in August, 'Dawns' in October and 'Deaths of Common Men' in November/December.

33.   *Times Literary Supplement*, 905, 22 May 1919, p. 274. *Wheels* was an annual 'modernist' anthology (from 1916-1921) produced by the Sitwells to publish their work and that of others in their circle, such as Aldous Huxley, Sherard Vines and Iris Tree.

34.   Aldous Huxley (1894-1963) was a member of a distinguished family of intellectuals. A conscientious objector during the war, he had worked as labourer on the Morrells' farm at Garsington Manor. He was already a published novelist and poet.

35.   The other members were: Eliot, T.W. Earp, Huxley, Wyndham Lewis, Nina Hamnett and Russell Green. *Coterie* only lasted for six quarterly issues, however.

36.   *Times Literary Supplement*, 924, 2 October 1919, p. 527.

37.   *Poetry* vol. 52, no. 3, June 1938, pp. 160-164.

38.   *To-Day* no.32, October 1919, pp. 61-64.

39.   'Remy de Gourmont, after the Interim', *The Little Review* vol.5, no. 10-11, February/March 1919, p. 34; we might notice the characteristic echo of Browning's 'The Lost Leader' ('Never bright confident morning again').

40.   'Insouciance' and 'Loss'. (The others were: 'Two Impressions', 'Compensation' and 'Beauty Unpraised'.)

41.   *The Little Review* vol. 6, no. 5, September 1919, pp. 36-39.

42.   Richard Aldington to Harriet Monroe 15 October 1919 (Chicago).

43.   *Poetry* vol. 14 no. 6, September 1919, pp. 338-341.

44.   *The Dial* vol. 66, no. 791, 31 May 1919, p. 576.

15. Separation

1.   MacGreevy, Thomas, *Proust* (New York. Grove Press 1931), p. 3. MacGreevy uses this quotation from his friend Beckett's book as an epigraph for his study of Aldington, *Richard Aldington, An Englishman*.

2.   Richard Aldington to H.D., 6 October 1918 (Zilboorg, no. 56).

3.   Richard Aldington to H.D., 31 August 1918 (Zilboorg, no. 48).

4.   Richard Aldington to H.D., undated letter (Zilboorg, no. 87).

5.   It was headed 52, Doughty Street: at the end of March, Aldington had to vacate this studio and return to the Littoral.

6.   H.D., *Asphodel*, p. 191-192. That moment in the Protestant cemetery in Rome in 1913 was for H.D. a vividly romantic symbol of her relationship with Aldington which she also used in *Paint it Today* (p. 88).

7.   References to Aldington's lovers: Yorke, Flo Fallas and Patmore

8.   H.D., *End to Torment*, pp. 7-8.

9.   Perdita's speech in Act Four, Scene Four of *A Winter's Tale*. Both H.D. (in *Asphodel* and *Tribute to Freud*) and Bryher (in *The Heart to Artemis*) associate this particular quotation from the play with Perdita's birth; but only H.D. further links it to Aldington's visits, bringing her daffodils.

10.   H.D., *Tribute to Freud*, p. 135.

11.   See H.D., *Asphodel*, p. 196.

12.   Richard Aldington to H.D., undated letter headed Wednesday (Zilboorg, no. 88).

13. 1, 10, 13, 19 April (see H.D.'s letters to Bryher of 13 and 19 April: Yale).

14. Richard Aldington to H.D., 5 April 1919 (Zilboorg, no. 89).

15. McAlmon, Robert and Boyle, Kay, *Being Geniuses Together* (London, Hogarth Press, 1984), p. 59.

16. *ibid.* p. 2.

17. H.D., *Tribute to Freud*, p. 170.

18. It was 19 December 1918 before H.D. revealed to Bryher that she was even pregnant.

19. H.D. to Bryher, 21 April 1919 (Yale).

20. Bryher to H.D., 22 April 1919 (Yale).

21. H.D. did in fact breast-feed her daughter for the first week, although she was then advised to stop in order to improve her own health and strength. Letter to Bryher 10 April 1919 (Yale).

22. Richard Aldington to H.D., 31 August 1918 (Zilboorg, no. 48).

23. Richard Aldington to H.D., undated letter headed Thursday [17 April 1919] (Zilboorg, no. 90).

24. H.D. to Bryher, 18 April 1919 (Yale).

25. H.D. to Bryher, 19 April 1919 Yale).

26. Richard Aldington to Amy Lowell, 19 April 1919 (Harvard).

27. H.D. to Bryher, 13 April 1919 (Yale).

28. Bryher to H.D., 21 April 1919 (Yale).

29. Bryher to H.D., 22 April 1919 (Yale).

30. H.D. to Ezra Pound, undated letter [April 1929] (Yale).

31. H.D., *Asphodel*, pp. 196-197.

32. *ibid.* p. 199.

33. *ibid.* p.198.

34. *ibid.* pp. 196-197.

35. Zilboorg, p.171.

36. H.D. to George Plank, 4 February 1929 (Yale).

37. H.D. to John Cournos, 4 February [1925] (Harvard).

38. H.D. to Ezra Pound, undated letter [April 1919] (Yale).

39. Richard Aldington to H.D., 26 April 1919 (Zilboorg, no. 91).

40. See chapter 14, note 40.

41. Richard Aldington to F.S. Flint 17 May 1919 (Copp no. 159: Copp's translation).

42. That poem would be 'In the Palace Garden' (*Exile and Other Poems*, 1923).

43. Richard Aldington to Amy Lowell, 31 March 1919 (Harvard).

44. Richard Aldington to F.S. Flint, [1 September 1919] (Copp no. 172).

45. Richard Aldington to Amy Lowell, 11 October 1919 (Harvard).

46. Richard Aldington to Harriet Monroe, 15 October 1919 (Chicago).

16. Retreat: 1920-1925

1. Aldington, *Life for Life's Sake*, p. 235.

2. David Wilkinson's unpublished record of his investigations into Aldington's Hermitage and Padworth years includes an interview with Mrs Hilda Cotterell, who was the daughter of the tenants of no. 2 Chapel Farm Cottages. As a young girl, Hilda Brown had been befriended by the Lawrences, while they were living next door from 1917

to 1918 and continued to correspond with them for some years afterwards. Her recall of Aldington's subsequent tenancy of the cottage was that he lived on his own much of the time and she assumed, knowing Aldington to be a writer, that 'Miss Yorke', who was a regular visitor, was his secretary.

3. Richard Aldington to H.D., 28 January 1920 (Zilboorg, no. 92).

4. He came to regret this offer, writing to Flint that he wished he had never had anything to do with the 'accursed manuscript' (*Hymen*) and failing to persuade Monro to take it on; it was eventually published by the Egoist Press in 1921. However, he admired it, telling Flint, when the title poem appeared in *Poetry* in December 1919, that it was 'quite stunning . . . assured and well-handled'. (Copp, no. 174: Copp's translation)

5. *Life for Life's Sake*, p. 239

6. *ibid*. p. 236.

7. Mr Judd in *The Colonel's Daughter*, Mr Brown and Mr Crowder in *Women Must Work* and Mr Brown again in *Seven Against Reeves*.

8. *Exile and Other Poems*, also published in the U.S. by The Dial Press. Both editions were limited to 750 copies.

9. *Poetry*, vol. 18, no. 2, May 1921, pp. 99-100.

10. Richard Aldington to Harold Monro, 28 September 1920.

11. Aldington, *Life for Life's Sake*, p. 241.

12. Richard Aldington to F.S. Flint [undated, 1924] (Copp, no. 246).

13. This practice was not phased out until 1974.

14. *Medallions in Clay* consisted of Aldington's translations of *Anyte of Tegea*; *Meleager of Gadara*; *The Anacreontia* and *Latin Poems of the Renaissance*.

15. 'Letter from London', *Poetry*, vol. 15, no. 4, January 1920, pp. 226-227.

16. 'The Poet and Modern Life', *Poetry*, vol. 18, no. 2, May 1921, pp. 98-100.

17. 'The Poet and His Age', *The Monthly Chapbook*, no. 17, September 1922, pp. 4-12.

18. Richard Aldington to Amy Lowell, 12 October 1920 (Harvard).

19. 'The Influence of Mr James Joyce', *The English Review* vol. 32, no. 4, April 1921, pp. 333-341.

20. Richard Aldington to T.S. Eliot, 14 September 1920 (Harvard).

21. Richard Aldington to T.S. Eliot, 18 July 1919 (Harvard). It is worth noting that, at least before the publication of *The Waste Land* in 1922, his views of Eliot's poetry fluctuated: in an article published in January 1922, he expressed admiration for the way in which the poet combined originality with the traditions of English Renaissance poetry and 'the ironic French poets', concluding that 'Mr Eliot is to be honoured as a poet who has brought new vigour to the intellectual tradition of English poetry.' 'The Poetry of T.S. Eliot', *Outlook*, vol. 49, no. 7, pp. 12-13.

22. *Poetry*, vol. 17, no. 6, March 1921, pp. 345-348, *To-Day*, vol. 8, no. 47, September 1921, pp. 191-193.

23. *Poetry*, vol. 17. No. 6 p. 346.

24. 'Poetry in Prose: Three Essays, by T.S. Eliot, Frederic Manning [and] Richard Aldington', *The Monthly Chapbook*, no. 22. Aldington's essay, 'A Note on Poetry in Prose' appears on pages 16-24.

25. Richard Aldington to Amy Lowell, 17 June 1920 (Harvard).

26. Richard Aldington to Amy Lowell, 7 April 1921 (Harvard).

27. Richard Aldington to Amy Lowell, 27 September 1921 (Harvard).

28. Kittredge, Selwyn, *The Literary Career of Richard Aldington* (dissertation, 2 volumes) (Ann Arbour, Michigan, New York University Press, 1976), p. 222.

29. Richard Aldington to Amy Lowell, 27 September 1921(Harvard).

30. Aldington never published the poem. It appears in Gates, *The Poetry of Richard Aldington*, p. 278. Flint's poem for Aldington, 'Soldiers', appeared in *Some Imagist Poets, 1917* and is reproduced on page 147 above.

31. *Poetry* vol. 17, no. 1, October 1920, p. 44.

32. Richard Aldington to Harold Monro, 24 October 1920 (UCLA).

33. The other poets were: Julian Grenfell, Rupert Brooke, R.E. Vernede, Francis Ledwidge, Edward Thomas, F.W. Harvey and Alan Seeger.

34. Moore, T. Sturge, *Some Soldier Poets* (London, Grant Richards, 1919), pp. 97-98.

35. Richard Aldington to Harold Monro, 9 March 1921 (UCLA).

36. Richard Aldington to Sturge Moore, 14 November 1920 (London).

37. This is another detail gleaned by David Wilkinson from his conversations with Hilda Cotterell.

38. Undated letter from Richard Aldington to F.S. Flint, probably early 1921(Copp, no. 205: Copp's translation).

39. Richard Aldington to Amy Lowell, 7 April 1921 (Harvard).

40. Aldington, *Life for Life's Sake*, pp. 253-259.

41. Richard Aldington to Amy Lowell, 26 August 1921 (Harvard).

42. Church, Richard, *The Voyage Home* (London: Heinemann, 1964), p. 58.

43. Richard Aldington to Herbert Read, 2 September 1925 (Victoria).

44. Richard Aldington to F.S. Flint (Copp, no. 211).

45. He would obtain a legal separation from her in 1933. She was committed to a mental asylum in 1938, where she died in 1947.

46. Richard Aldington to F.S. Flint, 3 May 1921(Copp, no. 209: Copp's translation).

47. From David Wilkinson's unpublished interview with Margery Lyon Gilbert, 30 January 1982.

48. *The Art of Lydia Lopokova*, C.W. Beaumont, 1920.

49. Sylvia Mills Whitham (née Milman) (1878-1957) had been a founder member of Vanessa Bell's 'Friday Group' in 1905.

50. Richard Aldington to Amy Lowell, 26 August 1921(Harvard).

51. Ezra Pound to Richard Aldington, 9 July 1922 (Texas).

52. Amy Lowell to Richard Aldington, 24 June and 12 September 1922 (Harvard).

53. *The New Age*, vol. 30, no. 22, 30 March 1922, pp. 284-285.

54. Richard Aldington to Harold Monro, 13 March 1921 (UCLA).

55. Richard Aldington to Harold Monro, 28 March 1921 (UCLA).

56. Aldington, *Life for Life's Sake*, pp. 261-264; Copp, no. 245.

57. Letters from Richard Aldington to Herbert Read, headed Friday [26 June 1925] and 15 November 1925 (Victoria).

58. *Times Educational Supplement*, 1067, 29 June 1922, p. 417.

59. The translations were: the Cyrano *Voyages to the Moon and Sun* (1923); *French Comedies of the Eighteenth Century* (1923); *Les Liaisons Dangereuses* (1924); *A Book of Character from Theophrastus* (1924); *Les Quinze Joyes de Mariage* (1926); *Candide* (1927); a selection of the letters of Madame de Sevigné (1927); the letters of Voltaire and Frederick the Great (1927); the letters of Voltaire and Madame du Deffand (1927); Julian Benda's *La Trahison des Clercs* (1928). The term 'Republic of Letters' which Routledge adopted

for their series refers to the group of scholars and literary figures across Europe and America that existed in the 'Age of Enlightenment of the 17th and 18th centuries.

60. It was simultaneously printed in the USA in *The Dial*, owned and run by Eliot's friend Schofield Thayer.

61. T.S. Eliot to Charles Whibley, 27 May 1923. *Collected Letters of T.S. Eliot, vol. 2, 1923-1925*, edited by Eliot, Valerie and Haughton, Hugh (London, Faber and Faber, 2009), p. 148. Charles Whibley (1859-1930) was a Cambridge don, conservative journalist and literary critic.

62. T.S. Eliot to his mother [mid-October 1923]. (Eliot, vol. 2, p. 255)

63. George Dunning Gribble (1882-1956).

64. Aldington, *Life for Life's Sake*, p. 285.

65. Richard Aldington to F.S. Flint, 9 February 1924 (Copp, no. 238).

66. Richard Aldington to Harold Monro, 1 January 1924 (UCLA).

67. *A Fool i' the Forest* was published by Allen and Unwin in Britain and by The Dial Press in the U.S.

68. Aldington, Richard, *Voltaire* (London, Routledge, 1925), pp. 204, 174, 140, 173.

69. Richard Aldington to Harold Monro, 8 May 1924 (UCLA).

70. *The Nation* had been founded in 1907, with H.W. Massingham as its editor. H.M. Tomlinson was its literary editor from 1917 to 1923. The journal had merged with *The Athenaeum* in 1921 and Massingham remained at the helm. However, in 1923, John Maynard Keynes took over control of the journal, returning it from a left wing stance to its Liberal roots, and Massingham and Tomlinson resigned. The new editor was Hubert Henderson and Leonard Woolf became the literary editor, although the post was first offered to Eliot. *The Spectator*, under the editorship of John St Loe Strachey from 1887 to 1925, had become politically conservative. During Aldington's period of reviewing its literary editors were, first, Strachey's daughter, Amabel Williams-Ellis, and then the young Oxford poet Alan Porter.

71. Aldington, *Life for Life's Sake*, p. 295.

72. *ibid*.

73. Robert McAlmon (1895-1956) was just six months younger than Bryher and had been brought up in the mid-West, the youngest of the ten children of an itinerant Presbyterian minister. In New York in 1920 he and Williams had founded *Contact*, a journal to promote modern American writing. In Paris in the 1920s, with Bryher's money, McAlmon would start the Contact Press.

74. H.D. to George Plank, 7 November 1922 (Yale).

75. H.D. to George Plank, 1 May 1935 (Yale).

76. Doris Oppenheimer (1901-1982) married twice, her second husband being Sir Walter Hannay, but she achieved fame from the late 1920s as a novelist and historical biographer under the name of Doris Leslie; Dorothy Cole (1889-1961), who married Gerald Henderson, the librarian at St Paul's Cathedral, in 1933, also published novels, under the name of Maude Cole.

77. Brigit Patmore to Bryher, 22 February 1922 (Yale).

78. Brigit Patmore to H.D., 2 November 1924 (Yale).

79. H.D. to George Plank, 26 November 1925 (Yale).

80. H.D. to George Plank, 14 September 1924 (Yale).

81. H.D. to George Plank, 31 March 1925 (Yale).

82. Bryher to Brigit Patmore, 4 March 1925 (Yale).

83. Amy Lowell to Richard Aldington, 4 April 1923 (Harvard).

84. The poet and critic Richard Church (1893-1972) was, like Flint a civil servant; John Trend (1887-1958) was an authority on Spanish music and culture; Orlo Williams (1883-1967) was Clerk to the House of Commons and an authority on Italian literature and culture; Humbert Wolfe (1885-1940) was a poet and critic and a senior civil servant at the Ministry of Labour; Frank Morley (1899-1985) was an American mathematician and essayist; the university lecturer and critic Bonamy Dobrée (1891-1974) had contributed poems to *The Egoist* in 1916 and had been an officer in the Royal Field Artillery both before and during the war.

85. In the early days the weekly lunches were held at The Cock in Fleet Street; they were subsequently moved to The Grove Tavern in Beauchamp Place for the convenience of Read and other members of his staff at the Victoria and Albert Museum. The monthly dinners were held at the Ristorante Commercio in Soho.

86. 'Francois Villon' was a review of a new three-volume edition of Villon's complete works. (*The Criterion* vol. 3, no. 11, April 1925, pp. 376-388).

87. Richard Aldington to Harold Monro 29 March 1922 (Victoria).

88. Aldington, *Life for Life's Sake*, p. 222. Aldington reviewed *In Retreat* in *The New Criterion*, vol. 4, no. 2, April 1926, pp. 363-367.

89. Richard Aldington to Herbert Read, 2 October 1925 (Victoria).

90. Richard Aldington to Herbert Read, [undated], letter headed 'Wednesday' [written shortly after 11 November 1925] (Victoria).

91. The story of the cat is delightfully recounted in Aldington's essay 'Mrs Todgers' in *Artifex: Sketches and Ideas* (London, Chatto and Windus, 1935).

92. Richard Aldington to Herbert Read, 16 October 1925 (Victoria).

93. Richard Aldington to Herbert Read, 17 August and 2 October 1925 (Victoria).

94. Richard Aldington to Ezra Pound, 12 August 1925 (Yale).

95. Glenn Hughes (1894-1964) would publish *Imagism and the Imagists* in 1931.

96. George Saintsbury (1845-1933) had been Professor of English Literature at Edinburgh University and the author of many books on French literature as well as a translator; Edmund Gosse (1849-1928) was an influential literary and art critic, a poet and Librarian to the House of Lords, although he is best known today for his memoir, *Father and Son*.

97. Richard Aldington to Glenn Hughes, 26 November 1925 (Texas).

98. Richard Aldington to Herbert Read, undated letter headed 'Wednesday' [early November 1925] (Victoria).

99. Richard Aldington to Herbert Read, 9 and 13 December 1925 (Victoria).

100. Richard Aldington to Herbert Read, 15 December 1925 (Victoria).

101. Richard Aldington to T.S. Eliot, 3 January 1925 (Eliot, vol. 2).

102. Richard Aldington to F.S. Flint, 19 January 1925 (Copp, no. 250).

17. *Exile* and *A Fool i'the Forest*

1. Richard Aldington to Herbert Read, 23 December 1924 (Victoria).

2. For the figure of the sentry, see, for example, Sassoon's 'War Experience', Blunden's 'The Watchers' and Graves's 'Retrospect: The Jests of the Clocks'.

3. The Blunden phrase occurs in a poem entitled '1916 seen from 1921'.

4. Aldington, *Life for Life's Sake*, p. 239.
5. Richard Aldington to Harriet Monroe, 22 September 1924 (Chicago).
6. Richard Aldington to Herbert Read, 23 December 1924 (Victoria).
7. Richard Aldington to T.S. Eliot, 18 July 1919 (Harvard).
8. 'A Mind's Mirror', *Times Literary Supplement,* 22 January 1925, p. 51. (The anonymous reviewer was Hugh l'Anson Fausset.)
9. 'The Poet and Modern Life', *Poetry* vol. 18, no. 2, May 1921, pp. 99-100.

18. The Cracks Appear: 1926-1927

1. D.H. Lawrence to Richard Aldington, 24 May 1927 (S.I.U.).
2. Aldington, Richard, *The Colonel's Daughter* (London, Chatto and Windus, 1986), p. 31
3. See Aldington, *Life for Life's Sake*, p. 252-253.
4. Born in 1858, Major Darby-Griffith committed suicide in 1932 and the Padworth estate was sold.
5. See Aldington, *Life for Life's Sake*, pp. 249-251.
6. Like Sir Douglas Haig, Brigadier Mills was a product of Clifton College.
7. *The Curious Reader*, David Wilkinson's unpublished account of his Padworth investigations; Aldington, *Life for Life's Sake*, p. 252.
8. The first of the ten names on the memorial is that of Walter Clinton, a regular officer in the King's Royal Rifle Corps, who was the son of the Rector of Padworth. The Rector, who had been the incumbent since 1888, did not live to see his son's name commemorated, as he died at Padworth less than a year after Aldington's arrival in the village. However, there is a memorial plate in the church, which records that Walter Clinton died in the Military Hospital in Belgrade eleven days after the Armistice, having escaped from prisoner-of-war camp in West Prussia on 4th October 1918. That Aldington approved attempts to honour the dead of the war can be ascertained from his comments to Herbert Read on the Two Minutes Silence on Armistice Day 1925: 'I was on a bus-top at Marble Arch at 11 and I must say I was impressed by the very genuine emotion of the crowd and the real effort to show reverence. . . . I think the nation hasn't forgotten, does in a dumb way feel the need for a collective expiation, an homage to the unappeased manes.' Richard Aldington to Herbert Read, 15 November 1925 (Victoria).
9. Aldington, *Roads to Glory*, pp. 189-203.
10. Aldington, *The Colonel's Daughter*, p. 84.
11. Aldington, *Life for Life's Sake*, p. 296-297.
12. *ibid.* pp. 299-301.
13. Aldington, *All Men Are Enemies*, pp. 316-344.
14. Humbert Wolfe had provided a workmanlike review for *The Criterion*, vol. 4, no. 2, April 1925.
15. *Candide*; a selection of the letters of Madame de Sevigné; the letters of Voltaire and Frederick the Great; the letters of Voltaire and Madame du Deffand. All were published by Routledge in 1927.
16. the *Daily Telegraph,* 26 January 1926. Arthur Waugh (1866-1943), father of Alec and Evelyn, was a conservative figure, the literary critic on the *Daily Telegraph* from 1906-1931 and director of the publishing firm, Chapman and Hall. Favourable reviews also

appeared in *New Statesman*, vol. 26, no. 667, 6 February 1926, *The Nation*, 6 March 1926, and in *The Dial*, vol. 81, 1926. Since *The Nation*'s review was written by William Rose, series editor of the Routledge Republic of Letters imprint, it would not have been written from a disinterested standpoint!

17. Gaige's interest clearly reminded Squire of Aldington's existence; he would use him as a reviewer for *The London Mercury* on several occasions between October 1926 and October 1927.

18. Roscoe Conkling Gaige (1882-1949) started his private press in 1927. Siegfried Sassoon, Joyce, Conrad, Hardy, Virginia Woolf, Lytton Strachey and Yeats would be amongst the authors he published. He had produced 22 titles altogether when he lost his fortune in the Wall Street Crash in 1929.

19. Richard Aldington to Herbert Read, 28 January 1926 (Victoria).

20. Richard Aldington to Bonamy Dobrée, 27 July 1926 (Leeds).

21. Richard Aldington to James Hanley, 23 October 1929 (S.I.U.).

22. Lady Rothermere had become increasingly unhappy with the journal and insisted in June 1925 that Eliot find additional sponsors; Charles Whibley had put Eliot in touch with Faber and Gwyer, who already published the successful *The Nursing Mirror*, and the journal was published under their auspices from January 1926. Although it became a monthly in May 1927, Lady Rothermere's complete withdrawal of her patronage in 1928 forced Faber back to quarterly publication in June of that year.

23. Richard Aldington to Bonamy Dobrée, 25 April 1926 (Leeds).

24. T.S. Eliot: 'The Idea of a Literary Review', *The Criterion,* 4 April 1926; King, James, *The Last Modern: a Life of Herbert Read* (London, Weidenfeld and Nicolson, 1990), pp. 84-85.

25. Richard Aldington to Herbert Read, 29 November 1926 (Victoria).

26. Aldington had written 12 reviews for *The Nation* in 1924 and a similar number in 1925. By 1926 the journal was giving him less work: his total number for the year was 7 reviews, with none in May or July and nothing in the last three months of the year, owing to the Walpole fiasco.

27. Richard Aldington to Herbert Read, 4 August 1926 (Victoria). This letter was written on the day the Padworth war memorial was unveiled, which may suggest that Aldington was too dispirited to face attending the occasion.

28. Aldington, *Life for Life's Sake*, pp. 305-306 and 259-260.

29. Aldington, *D.H. Lawrence: An Indiscretion* (University of Washington Chapbooks no. 6) was published in 1927.

30. Aldington and Yorke arrived at the Villa Mirenda on 6 October 1926.

31. Richard Aldington to Herbert Read, 29 November 1926 (Victoria).

32. Aldington, Richard, *Portrait of a Genius, But . . .* (London, Heinemann, 1951), p. 317.

33. Aldington, *Life For Life's Sake,* pp. 306-308.

34. Gates, *The Poetry of Richard Aldington,* pp. 216-219.

35. Richard Aldington to Herbert Read, 29 November 1926 (Victoria).

36. Aldington's *Fifty Romance Lyric Poems* appeared in 1928, in an edition of 900 copies, designed by the American typographer Bruce Rogers. The third private printer with whom he would be associated was Nancy Cunard and her Hours Press in 1929.

37. *Remy de Gourmont: A Modern Man of Letters* was no. 13 in the University of Washington

Chapbooks series and appeared in 1928. *The Treason of the Intellectuals* was published by Gaige and (as *The Great Betrayal*) by Routledge in 1928; this essay by Julien Benda (1857-1956) had only recently appeared in the original.

38. D.H. Lawrence to Richard Aldington, 24 May 1927 (S.I.U.).

39. 'Her psychic shock with R.A. was not so unlike my own', H.D. told Ellis on 5 May 1933, while Capper, in her letters to Ellis, frequently acknowledges the autobiographical nature of her novel. (Yale). Walter and Lilian Lowenfels were friends of Aldington's in Paris in the 1920s.

40. Courtenay, Jennifer, *Several Faces* (London, Victor Gollancz, 1930), p. 223.

41. Capper's chronology is detailed and corresponds to the one we can construct for the real life events, except that she places the fictional events two years earlier.

42. Courtenay, *Several Faces*, p. 265.

43. *ibid*. p. 256.

44. Aldington, *Life for Life's Sake*, p. 314-315.

45. Richard Aldington to Samuel Putnam, 21 June 1928 (S.I.U.).

46. Doran would have been a 'catch' for Aldington. That year, his company merged with Doubleday, Page & Company, forming the largest publishing business in the English-speaking world. By 1930 Doubleday, Doran and Co. would consider Aldington a safer investment.

47. Richard Aldington to Alec Randall, 10 August 1927 (Huntington).

48. Richard Aldington to Bonamy Dobrée, 3 September 1927 (Leeds). Dobrée's predecessor at the University of Cairo had been Robert Graves, who, still shell-shocked, and now struggling to resolve the conflict between his marriage and his relationship with the American poet Laura Riding, had lasted only three months in the post. Dobrée would stay in Cairo until 1929.

49. Richard Aldington to Ezra Pound, 2 August 1927 (Yale).

50. In his autobiography of these years, *Downhill All the Way: an autobiography of the years 1919 to 1939* (New York, Harcourt, Brace and World, 1967), Leonard Woolf tells us that Aldington withdrew from *The Nation* on the same pretext, extending a 'formal ultimatum'. Aldington's review (of Eliot's edition of Newton's *Seneca, his Tenne Tragedies*) of 29 October 1927 was his last for *The Nation*.

51. Ezra Pound to Richard Aldington, 26 August 1927 (Texas).

52. Herbert Read to T.S. Eliot, 18 August 1927. *Collected Letters of T.S. Eliot vol. 3, 1926-1927*, edited by Eliot, Valerie and Heffenden, Hugh (London, Faber and Faber, 2012), p. 639.

53. T.S. Eliot to Herbert Read, letter headed Wednesday [probably 24 August 1927] (Eliot, vol. 3 pp. 654-655)

54. T.S. Eliot to Herbert Read, 30 August 1927 (Eliot, vol. 3 p. 668)

55. T.S. Eliot to Richard Aldington, 25 August 1927 (Eliot, vol. 3, pp. 657-659).

56. T.S. Eliot to Herbert Read, Wednesday [24 August 1927] (Eliot, vol. 3, pp. 654-655).

57. H.D., *Bid Me To Live*, pp. 100, 133.

58. See the 1933 correspondence between the two men at the time of Read's abandonment of both his academic career and his first wife (Victoria).

59. Since 1924 Slonimsky had been teaching at the Jewish Institute of Religion in New York, where he would eventually become Dean.

19. The Walls Fall Down: 1928

1. Aldington, *Life for Life's Sake*, p. 320.
2. *ibid*. p. 319.
3. Richard Aldington to Glenn Hughes, 10 March 1928 (Texas).
4. Richard Aldington to Ezra Pound, 5 January 1928 (Yale).
5. See Richard Aldington to Alec Randall, 23 April 1928 (Huntington).
6. Aldington, *Life for Life's Sake*, p. 319.
7. Ezra Pound to Richard Aldington, 14 January 1928 (Texas).
8. Ezra Pound to Richard Aldington, 23 January 1928 (Texas).
9. Richard Aldington to Samuel Putnam, 21 June 1928 (S.I.U.).
10. Ezra Pound to Richard Aldington, 20 March 1928 (Texas).
11. His income for 1928 was £818. 11.3 (S.I.U.).
12. John Mills Whitham to Richard Aldington, 19 March 1928 (Exeter).
13. Walter Lowenfels (1897-1976) published his first book of poems in 1925. The following year he left his father's business to move to Europe and devote himself to writing.
14. Courtenay, *Several Faces*, p. 307.
15. *ibid*. p. 314.
16. *ibid*. p. 320.
17. See Richard Aldington to Samuel Putnam, 21 June 1928 (S.I.U.). Valentine Dobrée's first novel, *Your Cuckoo Sings By Kind*, appeared in 1927. *The Emperor's Tigers* was published by Faber in 1929.
18. Dora Carrington to Gerald Brennan, 21 September 1921 (quoted in McDougall p. 187).
19. Charles Prentice to Richard Aldington, 23 July 1929 (S.I.U.).
20. *Times Literary Supplement*, 22 May 1930, p. 428 (The anonymous reviewer was Hugh l'Anson Fausset.)
21. Hughes, Glenn, *Imagism and the Imagists: a study in modern poetry* (California, Stanford University Press, 1931), p. 108.
22. See chapter 20, below.
23. Richard Aldington to Valentine Dobrée, two undated letters, headed 'Saturday' and 'Monday' [probably 14 and 16 July 1928] (Leeds).
24. Courtenay, *Several Faces*, p. 323.
25. Giuseppe Orioli (1884-1942) was a long-time friend of the British writer Norman Douglas and one of the subjects of Aldington's group biography *Pinorman* in 1954.
26. Samuel Koteliansky (1880-1955) was a close friend of Lawrence and of Mark Gertler. He was Ukrainian and had fled Russia in 1911. He became a prominent translator of Russian literature.
27. Ezra Pound to Richard Aldington, 12 August 1928 (Texas).
28. Richard Aldington to Ezra Pound, 7 August 1928 (Yale). The source for this recent piece of information about H.D. was probably Brigit Patmore.
29. Richard Aldington to Ezra Pound, 14 August 1928 (Yale).
30. Courtenay, *Several Faces*, pp. 317-318.
31. *This Impassioned Onlooker* is actually three linked short stories and has elements of a roman à clef.
32. *ibid*. p. 320-321.

33. Brigit Patmore to H.D., 16 February 1925 (Yale).

34. Stephen Haden-Guest (1902-1974) was the son of Leslie Haden-Guest, a doctor and a Labour M.P. Leslie Haden-Guest was knighted in 1950 and Stephen succeeded to the title on his father's death in 1960.

35. H.D. to Ezra Pound, undated letter headed Friday [late February or early March 1929].

36. T.S. Eliot to Richard Aldington, 12 and 18 February 1926 (Eliot vol. 3 pp. 70 and 80).

37. Patmore, *My Friends When Young*, p. 102.

38. Earl Brewster (1878-1957) and his wife were American painters and writers who had lived outside America since their marriage in 1910. After Lawrence's death they would publish their reminiscences of him and their correspondence with him.

39. D.H. Lawrence to Dorothy Yorke, 4 August 1928. *Letters of D.H. Lawrence vol. 6, March 1927-November 1928*, edited by Boulton, James, Boulton, Margaret and Lacy, Gerald (Cambridge University Press, 2002), no. 4572, pp. 491-492.

40. Kershaw and Temple, *Richard Aldington: An Intimate Portrait*, p. 119; see also Alec Randall to Richard Aldington, 13 November 1955 (S.I.U.).

41. Richard Aldington to Ezra Pound, 15 September 1928 (Yale).

42. Ezra Pound to Richard Aldington, 10 November 1927 (Texas).

43. Cunard, Nancy, *These Were The Hours* (Carbondale: Southern Illinois University Press, 1969), p. 52.

44. Richard Aldington to Ezra Pound, 1 October 1928 (Yale).

45. D.H. Lawrence to Aldous Huxley, 2 September 1928 (Boulton vol. 6, no. 4636, p. 584).

46. D.H. Lawrence to Earl Brewster, 3 October 1928 (Boulton vol. 6, no. 4693, pp. 491-492).

47. Aldington, *Life for Life's Sake*, p. 329.

48. See, for example his letters to Orioli, Harry Crosby, Emily King and the Brewsters, 20 October 1928 (Boulton vol. 6, nos. 4711, 4712, 4713 and 4714, pp. 590-593).

49. Worthen, John, *D H Lawrence, The Life of an Outsider* (London, Penguin Books, 2006), p. 376.

50. Aldington, *Life for Life's Sake*, p. 330; Patmore, *My Friends When Young*, p. 133-134.

51. Aldington, *Life for Life's Sake*, p. 331.

52. Richard Aldington to Herbert Read, 2 October 1925 and undated letter headed 'Wednesday' [mid November 1925] (Victoria).

53. Aldington, *Life for Life's Sake*, p. 333.

54. Worthen, *D H Lawrence, The Life of an Outsider*, p. 384.

55. Yorke's unpublished interview with Walter and Lilian Lowenfels, 25 October 1964.

56. Courtenay, *Several Faces*, p. 331.

57. Richard Aldington to H.D., 20 March 1929 (Zilboorg, no. 94).

58. Aldington, *Life for Life's Sake*, p. 291.

59. Aldington, *Portrait of a Genius, But . . .* , p. 337.

60. See note 45, above.

61. D.H. Lawrence to Lawrence Pollinger, 26 October 1928 (Boulton, vol. 6, nos. 4720, p. 597).

62. D.H. Lawrence to Aldous Huxley, 28 October 1928 (Boulton, vol. 6, no. 4724, pp. 600-601).

63. Aldington, *Life for Life's Sake*, p. 339.

64. D.H. Lawrence to Dorothy Yorke, 24 January 1929. *Letters of D.H. Lawrence vol. 7, November 1928-February 1930*, edited by Boulton, James and Sagar, Keith (Cambridge

University Press, 2002), no. 4905.

65. Richard Aldington to Brigit Patmore, 4 December 1928 (Texas).

66. Patmore, Brigit, *No Tomorrow* (London, Century Company, 1929), p. 245.

67. Richard Aldington to Brigit Patmore, undated letter headed 'Saturday' (Texas).

68. Richard Aldington to Brigit Patmore, undated letter headed 'Thursday evening' [6 December 1928] (Texas).

69. Richard Aldington to Brigit Patmore, 4 December 1928 (Texas).

70. *ibid.*

71. Richard Aldington to Brigit Patmore, undated letter headed 'Wednesday evening' [19 December] (Texas).

72. Richard Aldington to Brigit Patmore, undated letter headed 'Thursday evening' [6 December 1928] (Texas).

73. *ibid.*

74. Richard Aldington to Brigit Patmore, 4 December 1928 (Texas).

75. Richard Aldington to Brigit Patmore, 15 December 1928 (Texas).

76. Richard Aldington to Crosby Gaige, 1 December 1928 (Texas).

77. Richard Aldington to Glenn Hughes, 30 November 1928 (Texas).

78. Richard Aldington to Glenn Hughes, 4 December 1928 (Texas).

79. Richard Aldington to Henry Slonimsky, 20 February 1929 (S.I.U.).

80. Richard Aldington to Harold Monro, 28 December 1928 (UCLA).

81. Richard Aldington to Ezra Pound, 4 December 1928 (Yale).

82. Richard Aldington to Ezra Pound, 9 December 1928 (Yale).

83. Aldington, *Life for Life's Sake*, p. 335.

84. T.S. Eliot to Ezra Pound, 31 December 1928 (*Collected Letters of T.S. Eliot, vol. 4, 1928-1929*, edited by Eliot, Valerie and Heffenden, Hugh (London, Faber and Faber, 2013), p. 370).

85. Pound had dedicated *Lustra* (1916) to Patmore under the troubadour name of 'Vail de Lencour'.

86. Richard Aldington to Ezra Pound, 26 December 1928 (Yale).

87. McAlmon, *Being Geniuses Together*, p. 256.

88. *ibid.* p. 169.

89. Richard Aldington to Brigit Patmore, letter headed 'Wednesday evening' [19 December 1928] (Texas).

90. Robert McAlmon to H.D., 16 October [1929] (Yale).

91. Richard Aldington to Brigit Patmore, 15 December 1928 (Texas).

92. The only public evidence of his passion for Dobrée would be the 1928 *Collected Poems*, which is dedicated to her and her husband.

20. *The Eaten Heart*

1. Chatto and Windus would publish the poem in both limited and popular editions in 1933.

2. In a letter to Dobrée, he had used the story of Philoctetes grasping the hand of Neoptolemus to describe her impact upon him. (See p. 351 above).

3. See p. 304, above.

4. See for example:

You might have turned and tried a man,
Set him a space to weary and wear,
And prove, which suited more your plan,
His best of hope or his worst despair,
Yet end as he began.

But you spared me this, like the heart you are,
And filled my empty heart at a word.
If two lives join there is oft a scar,
They are one and one, with a shadowy third;
One near one is too far.

A moment after, and hands unseen
Were hanging the night around us fast;
But we knew that a bar was broken between
Life and life; we were mixed at last
In spite of the mortal screen.

5. Cunard, *These Were the Hours,* pp. 51-52.

21. The Novelist: 1929

1. Aldington, *Life for Life's Sake*, p. 308.
2. H.D. to George Plank, 3 March 1930 (Yale).
3. Ezra Pound to Harriet Monroe, 30 December 1928 (Paige, no. 233).
4. *Poetry,* April 1929, pp. 42-46.
5. Patmore, *My Friends When Young*, p. 110.
6. Donald Friede (1901-1965) had previously worked for Alfred Knopf and Boni and Liveright. He was a 'larger than life' character, currently on the third of his six marriages. Covici Friede had recently published Radclyffe Hall's *The Well of Loneliness*, so were experienced in the matter of censorship battles.
7. Interview with Louise Morgan, 'Writing a Best Seller in Seven Weeks', *Everyman*, 21 August 1930.
8. Richard Aldington to H.D., 3 April 1929 (Yale).
9. Richard Aldington to H.D., 22 April 1929 (Zilboorg, no. 97).
10. Church, *The Voyage Home*, pp. 72-73.
11. Thomas MacGreevy (1893-1967) would become Director of the National Gallery of Ireland in 1950. In 1931 Chatto and Windus published two MacGreevy monographs, one on Eliot, the other (*Richard Aldington: An Englishman*) on Aldington.
12. Aldington, *Life for Life's Sake*, p. 312.
13. Kershaw and Temple, *Richard Aldington: An Intimate Portrait*, p. 55.
14. H.D. to John Cournos, 5 February [1929] (Yale).
15. H.D. to George Plank, 18 February 1929 (Yale).
16. H.D. to Ezra Pound, 20 February [1929] (Yale).
17. H.D. to Ezra Pound, undated letter headed 'Friday' [early March 1929] (Yale).
18. Kenneth MacPherson (1902-1971) had been introduced to H.D. by Frances Gregg

in September 1926 and become her lover early the following year. He, Bryher and H.D. founded the film company 'The Pool Group' and the film journal *Close-Up*, going on to make the experimental 1930 film *Borderline*, starring H.D. and Paul Robeson.

19. Richard Aldington to H.D., 14 March 1929 (Zilboorg, no. 93).
20. Richard Aldington to H.D., 20 March 1929 (Zilboorg, no. 94).
21. H.D. to George Plank, 1 April [1929] (Yale).
22. Richard Aldington to H.D., 30 March and 3 April 1929 (Yale).
23. Richard Aldington to H.D., 3 April 1929 (Yale).
24. Richard Aldington to H.D., 8 April 1929 (Zilboorg, no. 95).
25. Richard Aldington to H.D., 14 April 1929 (Zilboorg, no. 96).
26. Richard Aldington to H.D., 22 April 1929 (Zilboorg, no. 97).
27. Richard Aldington to H.D., 26 April 1929 (Zilboorg, no. 98).
28. H.D. to Ezra Pound, 21 April 1929 (Yale).
29. H.D. to Bryher, undated letter headed 'Wednesday' [1 May 1929] (Yale).
30. H.D. to Bryher, 5 May 1929 (Yale).
31. Richard Aldington to Brigit Patmore, 8 May 1929 (Texas).
32. H.D to George Plank, undated letter headed 'Thursday' [probably late May or early June 1929] (Yale).
33. H.D. to Bryher, 5 May 1929 (Yale).
34. H.D. to George Plank, 30 May 1929 (Yale).
35. H.D. to Glenn Hughes, undated letter [early May 1929] (Yale).
36. *Imagist Anthology 1930*, p. xviii. The anthology was published by Covici Friede in America and by Chatto and Windus in Britain. Those who did contribute were: Aldington, H.D., Flint, Fletcher, Joyce, Lawrence, Ford, Cournos and Williams.
37. D.H. Lawrence to H.D., 10 August 1929 (Boulton, vol. 7, no. 5254).
38. Richard Aldington to H.D., 20 May 1929 (Yale).
39. H.D. to John Cournos, 3 July 1929 (Yale).
40. Brigit Patmore to H.D., 19 August 1929 (Yale).
41. H.D. to George Plank, 18 July 1929 (Yale).
42. Richard Aldington to Brigit Patmore, undated letter headed 'Monday' [13 May 1929] (Texas).
43. Richard Aldington to Brigit Patmore, 14 May 1929 (Texas).
44. Walter Lowenfels to H.D., 19 May 1929 (Yale).
45. Richard Aldington to H.D., 20 May 1929 (Zilboorg, no. 100).
46. Richard Aldington to H.D., 6 June 1929 (Zilboorg, no. 101).
47. Georgina Dobrée (1930-2008) would become a celebrated clarinettist.
48. Richard Aldington to Valentine Dobrée, undated letter headed 'Friday' (Leeds).
49. Richard Aldington to Brigit Patmore, 15 May 1929 (Texas).
50. Charles Prentice (1892-1949) retired from publishing in 1934 to concentrate on Greek studies, at which point Aldington left Chatto and Windus for Heinemann.
51. Aldington, *Pinorman*, pp. 87-88.
52. Richard Aldington to Brigit Patmore, 16 May 1929 (Texas).
53. Aldington and Prentice did not meet until 12 October, when Prentice came to Paris.
54. In part this discrepancy can be explained by the fact that while both publishers felt

obliged to handle any sexual vocabulary and subject matter carefully, Friede did not have to concern himself with likely public reaction to Aldington's criticisms of the prosecution of the war.

55. Charles Prentice to Richard Aldington, 22 September 1929 (S.I.U.)

56. Even this edition was not entirely unexpurgated, as the word 'muck' and its derivatives still appear, as in the Chatto and Covici Friede editions. It would be 1965 before a completely unexpurgated edition was published. Jack Kahane (1887-1939) went on to found the Obelisk Press in Paris, dedicated to publishing books that fell foul of censorship laws in Britain and America.

57. 'Deserter', 'Killed in Action', 'Booby Trap' and 'Victory'. *Nash's Pall Mall Magazine* published three of the stories early in 1930 ('Meditations on a German Grave', 'Victory' and 'Killed in Action') There would eventually be thirteen, published by Chatto and Windus in 1930 as *Roads to Glory*.

58. *The Decameron* was published by Covici Friede, and by Putnam in Britain, in 1930. *Aurélia* had been commissioned by the Aquila Press, but they went bankrupt and Chatto and Windus published this translation in 1932. Covici Friede would also run into financial difficulties – the Wall Street Crash came a month after the publication of *Death of a Hero* – and the Greek drama project would be abandoned; it was left to Chatto and Windus to publish Aldington's translation of *Alcestis* in 1930.

59. Covici Friede would publish the poem as *Love in the Luxembourg* and Chatto and Windus would use the original title; in both cases it appeared in 1930.

60. Richard Aldington to H.D., 26 August 1929 (Yale).

61. Richard Aldington to Harold Monro, 4 August 1929 (SUNY).

62. Aldington, *Life for Life's Sake*, p. 240.

63. H.G. Wells to Richard Aldington, 29 September 1929 (S.I.U.).

64. Richard Aldington to Hebert Read, 15 July 1929 (Victoria).

65. Richard Aldington to Herbert Read, 25 July 1929 (Victoria). Following in the footsteps of Eliot, who had given them in 1926, Read was due to deliver the Clark lectures at Cambridge in 1930.

66. F.S. Flint to Richard Aldington, 29 September 1929 (S.I.U.).

67. John Cournos to Richard Aldington, 18 August 1929 (S.I.U.)

68. *Little Review* vol. 6, no. 5, September 1919, pp. 36-39 (see pages 267-268 above).

69. William Carlos Williams to Richard Aldington, 9 October 1929 (S.I.U.).

70. St John Ervine (1883-1971) was an Irish dramatist and critic. He fought in the Royal Dublin Fusiliers in the First World War and lost a leg. In the post-war years he became increasingly conservative and a hostile critic of the Irish Republic.

71. John Mills Whitham to Richard Aldington, 17 October 1929 (Exeter).

72. John Mills Whitham to St John Ervine, 15 October 1929 (Exeter).

73. Formerly a sporting newspaper, *The Sunday Referee* had rebranded itself as 'the national newspaper for all thinking men and women' and was now in serious competition with the leading Sunday papers.

74. Aldington, *Life for Life's Sake*, p. 360.

75. *ibid*.

76. Richard Aldington to H.D., 10 January 1930 (Yale).

77. Aldington, 'Theocritus in Capri', *Literary Studies and Reviews,* p. 124.

22. Death of a Hero

1.   Lawrence, *Kangaroo,* p. 241 (Harmondsworth, Penguin Books, 1950)
2.   Aldington, *Death of a Hero*, p. 202.
3.   Richard Aldington to H.D. 6 June 1929 (Zilboorg, no. 101).
4.   Aldington, *Death of a Hero*, prefatory letter to Halcott Glover, p. xxi. Owen's draft preface for his intended volume of war poems, written at Ripon in 1918, claimed: 'This book is not about heroes. English poetry is not yet fit to speak of them. Nor is it about deeds, or lands, nor anything about glory, honour, might, majesty, dominion, or power, except War. *Above all I am not concerned with Poetry*. My subject is War, and the pity of War.' We might notice that there are other respects in which the thinking here resembles Aldington's: its problematising of the notion of heroism and its focus on the pity of war.
5.   *The Evening Standard,* 19 September, 1929, p. 7.
6.   Aldington, 'Notes on the war novel', *This Quarter* no. 2, Spring 1930, pp. 542-543.
7.   Richard Aldington to Gorham Munson, 23 January 1936 (S.I.U.).
8.   *Death of a Hero,* pp. 23-24.
9.   *ibid*. p. 343
10. *Times Literary Supplement,* 19 September 1929, p. 713.
11. Aldington, *Death of a Hero*, pp. 339-340.
12. For his views on Cunard and her contemporaries, see pp. 369-370 above.
13. the *Daily Express*, 3 October 1929, p. 8.
14. *Times Literary Supplement,* 19 September 1929, p. 713.
15. See for example: Bergonzi (1965, 1996), pp. 173-178; Morris (ed. Klein) (1976) pp. 183-196; Rutherford (1978), pp. 88-91; Parfitt (1988), pp. 42-65; Onions (1990), pp. 70-76. (This is not to say that *none* of these writers finds qualities to admire in the novel.)
16. Cecil, Hugh, *The Flower of Battle* (London, Secker and Warburg, 1995), p. 36.
17. Aldington, *Death of a Hero*, pp. 7, 2.
18. *ibid*. p. 6.
19. *ibid*. p. 27 and p. 198.
20. *ibid*. p. 21.
21. Richard Aldington to H.D., 14 May 1929 (Zilboorg, no. 99).
22. Eliot, of course, was not part of the pre-war London scene; Aldington uses artistic licence to include him here, although his appearance is Part Three is authentic.
23. Aldington, *Death of a Hero*, pp. 122-123.
24. See Aldington, Richard, 'Stepping Heavenward' and 'Nobody's Baby' in *Soft Answers* (London, Chatto and Windus, 1932).
25. Aldington, *Death of a Hero*, pp. 113, 94, 111.
26. *ibid*. p. 108.
27. Aldington, Richard, *D.H. Lawrence: An Appreciation* (Harmondsworth, Penguin Books, 1950), p. 5
28. Richard Aldington to H.D. 20 March 1929 (see p. 363 above).
29. See Richard Aldington to H.D. 14 May 1929 (Zilboorg, no. 99): 'My "heroines" are drawn from Nancy and Valentine Dobrée, who said I might . . . '
30. Aldington, *Death of a Hero*, p. 13.
31. Aldington, 'Now Lies She There', *Soft Answers.*

32. Aldington, *Death of a Hero*, p. 115.
33. Patmore, *My Friends When Young*, pp. 7, 65.
34. Aldington, *Death of a Hero*, p. 158.
35. *ibid*. p. 185.
36. *ibid*. p. 159.
37. *ibid*. p. 115.
38. *ibid*. p. 13.
39. *ibid*. p. 12.
40. Aldington, *Life for Life's Sake*, pp. 206-207.
41. Aldington, *Death of a Hero*, p. 80.
42. *ibid*. p. 19.
43. Aldington, *Life for Life's Sake*, p. 216.
44. Aldington, *Death of a Hero*, pp. 258-259.
45. *ibid*. pp. 228-233.
46. *ibid*. p. xxii.
47. *ibid*. p. 19.
48. *ibid*. p. 318.
49. *ibid*. pp. 175-176.
50. Patmore, *My Friends When Young*, p. 30.
51. Richard Aldington to H.D. 20 May 1929 (Zilboorg, no. 100).
52. He was eighteen years old before his only brother was born.
53. Aldington, *Life for Life's Sake*, p. 62).
54. See p. 82 above.
55. Richard Aldington to F.S. Flint 22 February and 20 April 1917 (Copp, nos. 124 and 131).
56. D.H. Lawrence to Amy Lowell 23 August 1916 (Healey and Cushman, no. 20).
57. Aldington, *Death of a Hero*, p. 334.
58. *ibid*. p. 233.
59. *ibid*. p. 340.
60. *ibid*. pp. 343-344.
61. *ibid*. p. 179.
62. 'Answers to My Murdered Self' in Kelly, Lionel (ed.), *Papers from the Reading Symposium* (University of Reading, 1987), pp. 22-33; Aldington, 'Eumenides'.

Afterword

1. Aldington, Richard, *Life Quest* (London, Chatto and Windus, 1935), section 6.
2. Aldington, Richard, Rejected Guest (New York, The Viking Press, 1939), p. 21.

Bibliography

Works by Richard Aldington: 1914-1930

Poetry

Images: 1910-1915 (London, Poetry Bookshop, 1915); *Images Old and New* (Boston, Four Seas, 1916)

The Love of Myrrhine and Konallis, and Other Prose Poems (Cleveland, Clerk's Press, 1917; Chicago, Pascal Covici, 1926)

Reverie: a Little Book of Poems for H.D (Cleveland, Clerk's Press, 1917)

Images of War: a Book of Poems (Westminster, C.W. Beaumont, April 1919); expanded edition (London, Allen and Unwin December 1919)

Images of Desire (London, Elkin Mathews, June 1919)

War and Love (Boston, Four Seas, September 1919)

Images (London, Egoist Pyaleress, September 1919)

The Berkshire Kennet (London, Curwen Press, 1923)

Exile and Other Poems (London, Allen and Unwin, 1923)

A Fool i' the Forest: a Phantasmagoria (London, Allen and Unwin, 1924)

Hark the Herald (Paris, Hours Press, 1928)

The Eaten Heart (Chapelle-Reanville, Eure, France: Hours Press, 1929)

Collected Poems (New York, Covici Friede, 1928; London, Allen and Unwin, 1929)

A Dream in the Luxembourg (London, Chatto and Windus, 1930); *Love and the Luxembourg* (New York, Covici, Friede, 1930)

Anthologies

Des Imagistes (New York, Boni and Liveright; London, The Poetry Bookshop)

Some imagist poets: an anthology (Boston: Houghton Mifflin, 1915, 1916 and 1917)

New paths: verse, prose, pictures, 1917-1918, edited by C.W. Beaumont and M.T.H. Sadler (London, C.W. Beaumont, 1918)

Imagist Anthology 1930 (London, Chatto and Windus, 1930)

Prose Works

Death of a Hero: a novel (New York, Covici, Friede, 1929; London, Chatto and Windus, 1929; Paris, Babou & Kahane, 1930; London, Hogarth Press, 1984; New York, Penguin Books, 2013)

Biographies and Essays

Literary Studies and Reviews (London, Allen and Unwin, 1924; New York, Dial Press, 1924)

Voltaire (London, Routledge, 1925; New York, E.P. Dutton, 1925)

French Studies and Reviews (London, Allen and Unwin, 1926; New York, Dial Press, 1926)

D.H. Lawrence: an Indiscretion (Washington, University of Washington Chapbooks, no. 6; Seattle, University of Washington Book Store, 1927)

D.H. Lawrence (London, Chatto and Windus, 1930)

Remy de Gourmont: a Modern Man of Letters (University of Washington) Chapbooks, no. 13) (Seattle, University of Washington Book Store, 1928)

Translations

The poems of Anyte of Tegea (Poets' Translation Series, no. 1) (London, The Egoist Press, 1915; Cleveland, The Clerk's Press, 1917)

Latin Poems of the Renaissance (Poets' Translation Series, no. 4) (London, The Egoist Press, 1916)

The garland of months, by Folgore da San Gemignano (Poets' Translation Series, no. 5) (London, The Egoist Press, 1915; Cleveland: Clerk's Press, 1917)

Greek songs in the manner of Anacreon, Poets' Translation Series Second set, no. 1 (London, The Egoist Press, 1920)

The poems of Meleager of Gadara, Poets' Translation Series, Second set, no. 6 (London, Egoist Press, 1920)

Medallions in clay (Contents: *The poems of Anyte of Tegea; The poems of Meleager of Gadara; Greek songs in the manner of* Anacreon; *Latin poems of the Renaissance*) (New York, A. A. Knopf, 1921); *Medallions from Anyte of Tegea, Meleager of Gadara, the Anacreontea, Latin poets of the renaissance* (London, Chatto and Windus, 1930)

The Good Humoured Ladies, A Comedy by Carlo Goldoni (London, C.W. Beaumont, 1922)

French Comedies of the XVIII Century (London, Routledge, 1923; New York, Dutton, 1923)

Voyages to the moon and the sun, by Cyrano de Bergerac (London, Routledge & Sons, 1923; New York, E.P. Dutton, 1923)

Dangerous Acquaintances, by Choderlos de Laclos (London, Routledge, 1924; New York, Dutton, 1924)

Sturly, by Pierre Custot (London, Jonathan Cape, 1924; Boston: Houghton Mifflin, 1925)

A Book of Characters from Theophrastus (London, Routledge and Sons, 1924; New York, Dutton, 1924)

The Fifteen Joys of Marriage, ascribed to Antoine de la Sale (London, Routledge and Sons, 1926; New York, Dutton, 1926)

Letters of Madame de Sevigné to Her Daughter and Her Friends (London, Routledge and Sons, 1927)

Letters of Voltaire and Frederick the Great (London, Routledge, 1927; New York, Brentano's, 1927)

Letters of Voltaire and Madame du Deffand (London, Routledge and Sons, 1927; New York, Brentano's, 1927)

Candide and other romances, by Voltaire (London, Routledge & Sons, 1928; New York, Dutton, 1928)

The Great Betrayal, by Julian Benda (London, Routledge and Sons, 1928); *The Treason of the Intellectuals* (New York, Crosby Gaige, 1928; London, Chatto and Windus, 1931)

Fifty Romance Lyric Poems (New York, Crosby Gaige, 1928; London, Allan Wingate, 1928; Chatto and Windus, 1931)

Remy de Gourmont, selections from all his works (Chicago, Covici, Friede, 1928)

The Decameron of Giovanni Boccaccio (New York, Covici, Friede, 1930; London, G.P. Putnams Sons, 1930)

Alcestis, by Euripides (London, Chatto and Windus, 1930)

Letters to the Amazon by Remy de Gourmont (London, Chatto & Windus, 1931)

Editions of Letters

Bubb Booklets: Letters of Richard Aldington to Charles Clinch Bubb, edited by Keller, Dean H. (Francestown, N.H., Typographeum, 1988)

Imagist Dialogues: Letters between Aldington, Flint and Others, edited by Copp, Michael (Cambridge, The Lutterworth Press, 2009)

Richard Aldington and HD: their lives in letters 1918-1961, edited with an introduction and commentary by Zilboorg, Caroline (Manchester; New York, Manchester University Press, 2003)

Editions of others' Letters

Brooke, Rupert, *The Letters of Rupert Brooke,* edited by Keynes, Geoffrey (London, Faber and Faber, 1968)

Eliot, T.S., *Collected Letters vol. 1, 1898-1922,* edited by Eliot, Valerie and Haughton, Hugh (London, Faber and Faber, 2009)

Eliot, T.S., *Collected Letters vol. 2, 1923-1925,* edited by Eliot, Valerie and Haughton, Hugh (London, Faber and Faber, 2009)

Eliot, T.S., *Collected Letters vol. 3, 1926-1927,* edited by Eliot, Valerie and Heffenden, Hugh (London, Faber and Faber, 2012)

Eliot, T.S., *Collected Letters vol. 4, 1928-1929,* edited by Eliot, Valerie and Heffenden, Hugh (London, Faber and Faber, 2013)

Fletcher, John Gould, *Selected Letters,* edited by Rudolph, Carpenter and Simpson (Fayetteville, University Of Arkansas Press, 1996)

Lawrence, D.H., *Letters of D.H. Lawrence vol. 3, October 1916-June 1921,* edited by Boulton, James and Robertson, Andrew (Cambridge, Cambridge University Press, 2002)

Lawrence, D.H., *Letters of D.H. Lawrence vol. 4, June 1921-March 1924,* edited by Boulton, James and Mansfield, Elizabeth (Cambridge, Cambridge University Press, 2002)

Lawrence, D.H., *Letters of D.H. Lawrence vol. 5, March 1924-March 1927,* edited by Boulton, James and Vasey, Lindeth (Cambridge, Cambridge University Press, 2003)

Lawrence, D.H., *Letters of D.H. Lawrence vol. 6, March 1927-November 1928,* edited by Boulton, James, Boulton, Margaret and Lacy, Gerald (Cambridge: Cambridge University Press, 2002)

Lawrence, D.H., *Letters of D.H. Lawrence vol. 7, November 1928-February 1930,* edited by Boulton, James and Sagar, Keith (Cambridge, Cambridge University Press, 2002)

Lawrence, D.H. and Lowell, Amy, *The Letters of D.H. Lawrence and Amy Lowell 1914-1925*, edited by Healey, Claire and Cushman, Keith (Santa Barbara, Black Sparrow Press, 1985)

Owen, Wilfred, *Wilfred Owen, Selected Letters*, edited by Bell, John (Oxford, O.U.P., 1998)

Pound, Ezra and Shakespear, Dorothy, *Ezra Pound and Dorothy Shakespear: Their Letters, 1909-1914*, edited by Pound, Omar and Litz, A. Walton (London, Faber and Faber, 1985)

Pound, Ezra, *Ezra Pound: Selected Letters, 1907-1941*, edited by Paige, D.D. (London, Faber and Faber, 1950)

Pound, Ezra, *Ezra Pound to His Parents, Letters 1895-1929*, edited by Rachewiltz, Mary de, Moody, A. David and Moody, Joanna (Oxford, O.U.P., 2010)

Pound, Ezra, *Letters of Ezra Pound to Alice Corbin Henderson*, edited by Nadel, Ira B. (Austin, University of Texas Press, 1993)

Primary Sources

Aldington, A.E., *The Queen's Preferment* (London, Digby, Long and Co.,1896)

Aldington, May:

Love Letters that caused a Divorce (London, Sisley's Ltd., 1906)

Songs of Life and Love (London, David Nutt, 1907)

Meg of the Salt Pans (London, Everett and Co., 1909)

God's Toys, (London, Collier, 1909)

A Man of Kent (London, A.M. Gardiner and Co., 1911)

The King Called Love (London, Heath, Cranton and Ouseley, 1913)

Love Letters to a Soldier (London, T. Werner Laurie, 1915)

Roll of Honour and other poems (Rye, Adams and Sons, 1917)

Beaumont, Cyril, *The Art of Lydia Lopokova* (drawings by Dorothy Yorke)

Bloom, Ursula, *Holiday Mood* (London, Hutchinson, 1934)

Bottome, Phyllis, *The Challenge* (London, Faber and Faber, 1962)

Bryher:

Development (London, Constable and Co., 1920)

Two Selves (Paris, Contact Press, 1923)

Two Novels (Wisconsin, University of Wisconsin Press, 2000)

The Heart to Artemis: A Writer's Memoirs (New York, Harcourt, Brace and World, 1962; London, Collins, 1963; Ashfield, Paris Press, 2006)

Church, Richard, *The Voyage Home* (London, Heinemann, 1964)

Cole, Margaret Postgate, *Growing Up into Revolution* (London, Longmans, 1949)

Cournos, John:

Miranda Masters (New York, Alfred Knopf, 1926)

Autobiography (New York, Van Rees Press, 1935)

Courtenay, Jennifer, *Several Faces* (London, Victor Gollancz, 1930)

Cunard, Nancy, *These Were The Hours* (Carbondale, Southern Illinois University Press, 1969)

Fallas, Carl, *The Gate is Open* (London, Heinemann, 1938)

Fletcher, John Gould, *Life is My Song* (New York, Farrar and Reinehart, 1937)

Ford, Ford Madox (see also under Hueffer)

Return to Yesterday (London, Gollancz, 1931)

It was the Nightingale, (London, William Heinemann, 1934)

Goldring, Douglas, *South Lodge* (London, Constable, 1943)

Graham, Stephen, *A Private in the Guards* (London, Macmillan, 1919)

Gray, Cecil, *Musical Chairs* (London, Home and van Thal, 1948)

Gregg, Frances, *The Mystic Leeway*, edited by Jones, Ben (Ottawa: Carleton Univ. Press 1995)

H.D.:

Paint it Today (New York and London, New York University Press, 1992)

Asphodel (Durham and London, Duke University Press, 1992)

Palimpsest (Paris: Contact Editions, 1926; Carbondale: Southern Illinois University Press, 1968)

Bid Me To Live (New York, The Dial Press, 1960)

Tribute to Freud (New York, Pantheon, 1956; Manchester: Carcanet Press, 1985)

End to Torment (New York, New Directions, 1979)

Collected Poems 1912-1944, edited by Martz, Louis (New York, New Directions, 1983)

Hueffer, Ford Madox:

Between St. Dennis and St. George: A Sketch of Three Civilisations (London, Hodder and Stoughton, 1915)

When Blood is Their Argument: An Analysis of Prussian Culture (London, Hodder and Stoughton, 1915)

Hunt, Violet, *The Flurried Years* (London, Hurst & Blackett, 1926)

Lawrence, D.H.: *Aaron's Rod* (New York, Thomas Seltzer, 1922; Harmondsworth, Penguin Books, 1950)

Kangaroo (London, Martin Secker, 1923; Harmondsworth: Penguin Books, 1950)

McAlmon, Robert, and Boyle, Kay, *Being Geniuses Together* (London, Hogarth Press, 1984)

Lawrence, Frieda, *Not I But the Wind* (London, William Heinemann, 1935)

Monroe, Harriet, *A Poet's Life: Seventy Years in a Changing World* (New York, Macmillan, 1938)

Patmore, Brigit:

This Impassioned Onlooker (London, Robert Holden and Co., 1926)

No Tomorrow (New York and London, Century Company, 1929)

My Friends when Young (London, William Heinemann, 1968)

Patmore, Derek, *Private History: An Autobiography of the Years 1919-1939* (London, Hogarth Press, 1967)

Sinclair, May, *Mary Olivier: A Life* (London, Macmillan, 1919; London, Virago, 1980)

Whitall, James, *English Years* (New York, Harcourt, Brace and Company, 1936; London, Jonathan Cape, 1936)

Wilkinson, Louis, *Buffoon* (New York, Alfred Knopff, 1916)

Woolf, Leonard, *Downhill all the way: an autobiography of the years 1919 to 1939* (New York, Harcourt, Brace and World: 1967)

Secondary Sources

Barlow, Adrian, 'Answers to My Murdered Self: Aldington's Post-War Poetry' in Kelly, Lionel, *Papers from the Reading Symposium* (Reading: University of Reading, 1987), pp. 22-33

Bergonzi, B, *Heroes' Twilight, A Study of Literature of the Great War* (London, Constable, 1965)

Blayac and Zilboorg (eds), *Richard Aldington: essays in honour of his birth: papers from the Montpellier Conference* (Montpellier, Université Paul Valery, 1992)

Boll, Theophilus, E.M., *Miss May Sinclair: Novelist* (Rutherford, Fairleigh Dickinson University Press, 1973)

Brooker, Peter, *Bohemia in London, The Social Scene of Early Modernism* (Basingstoke, Palgrave Macmillan, 2007)

Carpenter, Humphrey, *A Serious Character: The Life of Ezra Pound* (London, Faber and Faber, 1988)

Carr, Helen: *The Verse Revolutionaries* (London, Jonathan Cape, 2009)

Cecil, Hugh, *The Flower of Battle* (London, Secker and Warburg, 1995)

Cobley, Evelyn, *Representing War: Form and Ideology in First World War Narratives* (Toronto, University of Toronto Press, 1994)

Coffman, S.K., *Imagism: a chapter for the history of modern poetry* (Oklahoma: University of Oklahoma Press, 1951)

Coleman, Vera, *The Last Exquisite: a portrait of Frederick Manning* (Carlton, Victoria, Melbourne University Press, 1990)

Collecott, Diana, *HD and Sapphic Modernism: 1910-1950* (Cambridge, Cambridge University Press, 1999)

Delany, Paul, *D H Lawrence's Nightmare: The Writer and His Circle in the Years of the Great War* (Hassocks, Harvester Press, 1978)

Doyle, Charles, *Richard Aldington: A Biography* (Basingstoke, Macmillan, 1989)

Doyle, Charles (ed.), *Richard Aldington: Reappraisals* (Victoria, University of Victoria Press, 1990)

DuPlessis, Rachel Blau, *HD, The Career of that Struggle* (Brighton, Harvester, 1986)

Ellis, David, *D H Lawrence: Dying Game 1922-30* (Cambridge, Cambridge University Press, 1998)

Ferguson, Robert, *The Short Sharp Life of T E Hulme* (London, Faber and Faber, 2012)

Friedman, Susan Stanford:

Psyche Reborn: The Emergence of HD (Bloomington, Indiana Univ. Press, 1981)

Penelope's Web: Gender, Modernity and H.D.'s Fiction (Cambridge, Cambridge University Press, 1990)

Gates, Norman T. (ed.):

A checklist of the letters of Richard Aldington (Carbondale: Southern Illinois University Press, 1977)

The poetry of Richard Aldington: a critical evaluation and an anthology of uncollected poems (Pennsylvania: Penn State University Press, 1975)

Gould, Jean, *Amy: The World of Amy Lowell and the Imagist Movement* (New York, Dodd, Mead and Co., 1975)

Guest, Barbara, *Herself Defined: The Poet H.D. and Her World* (London, Macmillan, 1985)

Hanscombe, Gillian and Smyers, Virginia, *Writing for their Lives: The Modernist Women 1910 to 1940* (London, The Women's Press, 1987)

Hardwick, Joan, *An Immodest Violet: The Life of Violet Hunt* (London, Andre Deutsch, 1990)

Harmer, J.B., *Victory in Limbo: Imagism 1908-1917* (London, Secker and Warburg 1975)

Hibberd, Dominic, *Harold Monro: Poet of the New Age* (Basingstoke, Palgrave, 2001)

Howarth, P, *British Poetry in the Age of Modernism* (Cambridge, Cambridge University Press, 2005)

Hughes, Glenn, *Imagism and the Imagists: a study in modern poetry* (California, Stanford University Press, 1931)

Hutchins, Patricia, *Ezra Pound's Kensington: An Exploration 1885 -1913* (London, Faber and Faber, 1965)

Hynes, Samuel, *A War Imagined: The First World War and English Culture* (London, Bodley Head, 1990)

Jones, P (ed.), *Imagist Poetry* (London, Penguin 1972)

Kelly, Lionel (ed.), *Richard Aldington: Papers from the Reading Symposium* (Reading, University of Reading, 1987)

Kempton, Daniel and Stoneback, H.R. (eds.):

Writers in Provence: Proceedings of the First and Second International Richard Aldington Conferences (2003)

New Places: Proceedings of the Third International Richard Aldington Conference (2005)

Locations and Dislocations: Proceedings of the Fourth International Richard Aldington Conference (2008)

Aldington, Pound and the Imagists at Brunnenburg: Selected Essays from the Sixth International Richard Aldington / Second International Imagism Conference (2012)

(All published at Stes-Maries-de-la-Mer and New Paltz: Gregau Press and International Richard Aldington Society)

Kershaw, Alister, and Temple, F.J. (eds.), *Richard Aldington, An Intimate Portrait* (Carbondale and Edwardsville, Southern Illinois University Press, 1965)

King, James, *The Last Modern: a Life of Herbert Read* (London, Weidenfeld and Nicolson, 1990)

Kittredge, Selwyn, *The Literary Career of Richard Aldington* (dissertation, 2 volumes) (Ann Arbour, Michigan, New York University Press, 1976)

Klein, Holgar, *The First World War in Fiction* (London, Macmillan, 1978)

Laity, Cassandra, *H.D. and the Victorian Fin du Siècle: Gender, Modernism, Decadence* (Cambridge, Cambridge University Press, 1996)

Lidderdale, Jane and Nicholson, Mary, *Dear Miss Weaver: Harriet Shaw Weaver 1876-1961* (London, Faber and Faber, 1970)

Longford, Elizabeth, *A Pilgrimage of Passion: the Life of Wilfrid Scawen Blunt* (London, Weidenfeld and Nicolson, 1979)

MacDougall, Sarah, *Mark Gertler* (London, John Murray, 2002)

Bottom of Form

McDowell, Lesley, *Between the Sheets* (New York, Overlook Press, 2010) MacGreevy, *Richard Aldington, An Englishman* (London, Chatto and Windus, 1931)

Marden, T.O. (ed.), *A Short History of the 6th Division, August 1914-March 1919* (London, Hugh Rees, 1920)

Martin, Wallace, 'The Forgotten School of 1909 and the Origins of Imagism' in Woolmer, J Howard, *A Catalogue of the Imagist Poets* (New York, J. Howard Woolmer, 1966)

Mitchinson, K.W., *Pioneer Battalions in the Great War* (London, Leo Cooper, 1997)

Monro, H, *Some Contemporary Poets* (London, Leonard Parsons, 1920)

Moody, A David, *Ezra Pound Poet, A Portrait of the Man and His Work, vol.1: The Young Genius 1885-1920* (Oxford, Oxford University Press, 2007)

Moore, T. Sturge, *Some Soldier Poets* (London, Grant Richards, 1919)

Morgan, Louise, *Writers at Work*, (London, Chatto and Windus, 1931)

Morrisson, Mark, *The Public Face of Modernism: Little Magazines, Audiences and Reception 1905-1920* (Madison, The University of Wisconsin Press, 2000)

Onions, J, *English Fiction and Drama of the Great War 1918-39* (Basingstoke, Macmillan, 1990)

Parfitt, George, *Fiction of the First World War, A Study* (London, Faber and Faber, 1988)

Pearson, Neil, *A History of Jack Kahane and the Obelisk Press* (Liverpool: Liverpool University Press, 2007)

Pettipiece, Deidre, *Sex Theories and the Shaping of Two Moderns: Hemingway and HD* (London, Routledge, 2002)

Pondrom, Cyrena, The *Road from Paris: French Influence on English Poetry 1900-1920* (Cambridge, Cambridge University Press, 1974)

Pratt, William (ed.), *The Imagist Poem: Modern Poetry in Miniature*, (New York, Dutton, 1963)

Pratt, William and Richardson, Robert (eds.), *Homage to Imagism* (New York, AMS Press, 1992)

Raitt, Suzanne, *May Sinclair, A Modern Victorian*, (Oxford, Oxford University Press, 2000)

Read, Mike, *Forever England: the Life of Rupert Brooke* (Edinburgh: Mainstream, 1997)

Robinson, Janice, *HD: The Life and Work of an American Poet* (New York, Houghton Mifflin, 1982)

Rutherford, Andrew, *The Literature of War: Five Studies in Heroic Virtue* (London, Macmillan, 1978)

Saunders, Max, *Ford Madox Ford: a dual life* (Oxford, Oxford University Press, 1996)

Selver, Paul, *Orage and the New Age Circle: Reminiscences and Reflections* (London, Allen and Unwin, 1959)

Sherry, Vincent (ed.) *The Cambridge Companion to the Literature of the First World War* (Cambridge: Cambridge University Press, 2005)

Smith, R, *Richard Aldington* (London, Twayne 1977)

Stead, C K, *The New Poetic* (London, Hutchinson 1964)

Swinnerton, Frank, *The Georgian Literary Scene 1910-1935* (London, Radius/Hutchinson, 1935)

Symons, Julian, *Makers of the New: the revolution in literature 1912-1939* (London, Andre Deutsch, 1987)

Tate, Trudi, *Modernism, History and the First World War* (Manchester, Manchester University Press, 1998)

Worthen, John, *D H Lawrence, The Life of an Outsider* (London, Penguin Books, 2006)

Zilboorg, Caroline, 'Gender and Warfare in the Twentieth Century', in Smith, Angela, K, *The Second Battlefield: Women, Modernism and the First World* War (Manchester: Manchester University Press, 2000)

Journal Articles

Crawford, Fred D., 'Misleading Accounts of Aldington and H.D.', *English Literature in Transition, 1880-1920* vol. 30, no. 1 (1987), pp. 49-67

Du Plessis, Rachel Blau, 'Romantic Thralldom in H. D.', *Contemporary Literature* vol. 20, no. 2 (Spring 1979), pp. 178-203

Firchow, Peter E., 'Rico and Julia: the HD-DHL affair reconsidered', *Journal of Modern Literature* vol. 8, no. 1 (1980), pp. 51-76

Getsy, David, 'Give and Take: Henri Gaudier Brzeska's Coffer for Wilfrid Scawen Blunt and Ezra Pound's Homosocial Modernism in 1914', *Sculpture Journal* vol. 16, no. 2. (2007), pp. 39-51

Hollenberg, Donna, 'Art and Ardor in World War One: selected letters from HD to John Cournos', *Iowa Review* vol.16, no. 3 (Autumn 1986), pp. 126-155

Morrisson, Mark, 'Marketing British Modernism: The Egoist and Counter-Public Spheres', *Twentieth Century Literature* vol. 43, no. 4 (Winter 1997), pp. 439-469

Pondrom, Cyrena, 'Selected Letters from HD to F S Flint: a commentary on the Imagist period', *Contemporary Literature* vol. 10, no. 4 (Autumn 1969), pp. 557-586

Satterthwaite, Alfred, 'John Cournos and H.D.', *Twentieth Century Literature* vol. 22, no. 4 (December 1976), pp. 394-410

Sword, Helen, 'Orpheus and Eurydice in the Twentieth Century: Lawrence, H. D., and the Poetics of the Turn', *Twentieth Century Literature* vol. 35, no. 4 (Winter, 1989), pp. 407-428

Willis, J.H. Jr., 'The Censored Language of War: Richard Aldington's Death of a Hero and Three Other War Novels of 1929', *Twentieth Century Literature* vol. 45, no. 4 (Winter, 1999), pp. 467-487

Zilboorg, Caroline, 'Richard Aldington in transition: his pieces for The Sphere in 1919', *Twentieth Century Literature* vol. 34 (1988) pp. 489-506

Zilboorg, Caroline, 'A New Chapter in the lives of HD and Richard Aldington: their relationship with Clement Shorter, *Philological Quarterly* vol. 68, no.2 (Summer 1989), pp. 241-262.

War Diaries

11th Battalion Leicestershire Regiment (Pioneers), 31 March 1916-31 August 1919 (WO95 1601/1)

9th Battalion, The Royal Sussex Regiment, in France and Belgium, 21 August 1915-30 June 1919 (WO95 2219)

Unpublished Manuscripts

Beinecke Rare Book and Manuscript Library, Yale University: Bryher Papers, General Collection (GEN MSS 97)

Yale Collection of American Literature:

George Plank Papers (YCAL MSS 28)

Ezra Pound Papers (YCAL MSS 43)

Richard Aldington Papers, General Collection (GEN MSS 321); and H.D. Papers, (YCAL MSS 24)

Houghton Library, Harvard University: Amy Lowell Collection (MS Lowell 19- letters from H.D. (8), Richard Aldington (9), John Gould Fletcher (431), F.S. Flint (432), D.H. Lawrence (709) and Ezra Pound (982); and MS Lowell 19.1 – letters from Lowell to Richard Aldington (16) and H.D. (15)); the John Cournos Collection (I bMS Eng 998 and IIb MS Eng 998.1); and the T.S. Eliot editorial correspondence 1904-1930 (bMS Am 1432 (4-15)

Special Collections Research Center, the Morris Library, Southern Illinois University, Carbondale: Richard Aldington Collection (1/1/MSS 068)

Harry Ransom Humanities Research Center at the University of Texas at Austin: Richard Aldington Collection, Ezra Pound Collection, Glenn Hughes Collection, Frank Stuart Flint Collection

Special Collections, Charles E. Young Research Library, University of California, Los Angeles: letters from Richard Aldington to Harold Monro and from Richard Aldington to Charles Bubb, in the Harold Monro Papers (Collection 745).

Special Collections Department at the University of Victoria: letters from Richard Aldington to Herbert Read and letters from Richard Aldington to Harold Monro (Sir Herbert Edward Read Fonds (SC100))

The Huntington Library, San Marino, California: letters from Richard Aldington to Alec Randall (HM 40701 – 40708)

Special Collections at the Brotherton Library, University of Leeds: Clement Shorter Collection (BC MS 20c Shorter); Bonamy Dobrée Collection (BC MS 20c Dobrée)

Senate House Library, University of London, letters from Richard Aldington to Thomas Sturge Moore in the Thomas Sturge Moore Papers (MS978/1/2/1)

Special Collections at the University of Exeter: Jan Mills Whitham Literary Papers (EUL MS 38)

Poetry Collection, State University of New York at Buffalo: letters from Richard Aldington to Harold Monro

Special Collections Research Center at the University of Chicago Library: records of *Poetry: A Magazine of Verse* (Box 30, Folders 8-11)

Index